T0366846

THE KENNEDY WITHDRAWAL

THE
KENNEDY
WITHDRAWAL

Camelot *and the* American Commitment *to* Vietnam

Marc J. Selverstone

HARVARD UNIVERSITY PRESS

Cambridge, Massachusetts
London, England

2022

FIRST PRINTING

Publication of this book has been supported through the generous
provisions of the Maurice and Lula Bradley Smith Memorial Fund.

Library of Congress Cataloging-in-Publication Data

Names: Selverstone, Marc J., author.
Title: The Kennedy withdrawal : Camelot and the American commitment to
Vietnam / Marc J. Selverstone.
Description: Cambridge, Massachusetts : Harvard University Press, 2022. |
Includes bibliographical references and index.
Identifiers: LCCN 2022009251 | ISBN 9780674048812 (cloth)
Subjects: LCSH: Kennedy, John F. (John Fitzgerald), 1917–1963. | Vietnam War,
1961–1975. | United States—History, Military—20th century. |
United States—Military policy. | United States—Foreign
relations—Vietnam. | Vietnam—Foreign relations—United States.
Classification: LCC DS557.6 .S45 2022 | DDC 959.704/3373—dc23/eng/20220420
LC record available at https://lccn.loc.gov/2022009251

For Mom and Dad

Contents

THE KENNEDY WITHDRAWAL

INTRODUCTION

The Great "What If?"

The question of what John F. Kennedy might have done in Vietnam had he lived into 1964 and won a second term as president has long animated debate about America's calamitous war in Southeast Asia. Almost from the moment in March 1965 when U.S. combat troops came ashore at Danang, countless observers have weighed in and reached wildly different conclusions about Kennedy's intentions and the contours of that virtual history. From a belief that JFK would have gone to war much as his successor did to a conviction that he would have withdrawn American forces after his presumed reelection, these positions frame the conversation about Kennedy and his commitment to Vietnam. The matter therefore carries enormous implications for how we understand Kennedy, the Kennedy presidency, the presidency of Lyndon B. Johnson, the fate of the war—even the course of American history itself.

While it is impossible to answer "the great what if" with any certainty, it is beyond dispute that planning for the withdrawal of U.S. troops began at the midpoint of Kennedy's thousand days in office. Evidentiary support for that planning is overwhelming and appears in numerous archives and documentary collections. These sources, as well as supplementary accounts in memoirs and oral histories, provide indisputable proof that the Kennedy administration undertook a sustained and systematic effort to schedule the removal of American servicemen from South Vietnam and turn the war over to the government in Saigon.

They are less helpful, however, in answering key questions about the Kennedy withdrawal, several of which are vital to the broader "what if" of Kennedy and Vietnam: When did that planning begin? Who were its major proponents? Why was it undertaken? Why did it end? Was it contingent on the course of the war? And what did it mean to those at the time?

This book seeks to answer these questions and others suggested by that planning. It is, therefore, not a comprehensive history of JFK and Vietnam, though it covers much the same ground.[1] Rather, it offers a more targeted history of the Kennedy withdrawal, a subject of enduring interest, but one without extensive scholarly treatment. Initial chapters explore Kennedy's deepening involvement in South Vietnam and the commitment he made to its preservation. Succeeding chapters, which become increasingly granular in scope, trace withdrawal planning from its origins in mid-1962 to its formulation, revision, and halting implementation in 1963, and on to its cancellation under President Johnson in the spring of 1964. An Epilogue considers its half-life in books and films, in retrospectives and commemorations of the Kennedy presidency, and in contemporary debates about America and its use of military force. In all, it is a study of Kennedy's commitment to Vietnam as viewed through the lens of his planning to withdraw from it.

Although few works have explored the withdrawal in any depth, writing on its generalities has produced a historiography nonetheless. Gary Hess has identified two primary schools of thought: a "Cold Warrior" camp, which highlights the continuities between Kennedy and Johnson, and a variant he describes as "Kennedy exceptionalism," which holds that JFK would have pulled the United States out of the looming tragedy. Fredrik Logevall weaves a survey of this writing into an exploration of "What Might Have Been" and finds that Kennedy likely would have taken the United States down a less belligerent path in Vietnam, perhaps removing U.S. troops altogether. Marc Trachtenberg's analytic treatment of the literature examines the "audience costs" involved in Kennedy's approach, finding that JFK was souring on the war but seeking to stay in the fight. Andrew Preston categorizes these works still further.[2] Mainstream studies, he finds, either question Kennedy's commitment to withdrawal or assert that JFK would not have Americanized the war.[3] More presumptuous accounts have claimed knowledge of Kennedy's true intentions and hidden agendas—replete with a commitment to withdraw—while a radical strand has argued that JFK's withdrawal planning led a host of shadowy figures in the defense, intelligence, and organized crime communities to conspire in his assassination.[4] Each of these works—the overviews as well as the monographs—inform *The Kennedy Withdrawal*, which incorporates a range of sources, from oral histories to textual records to, crucially, JFK's secret White House tapes, to highlight the ways and means of serious and extensive planning to remove U.S. troops from Vietnam.[5]

As such, this book straddles the Cold Warrior and exceptionalist camps and finds that Kennedy, who had grown deeply uncomfortable with the U.S. assistance program, was nevertheless looking to sustain it at the time he went to Dallas. The October 1963 announcement of a scheduled withdrawal granted him the latitude to do so in a domestic environment that had grown impatient with Saigon, if not with the commitment itself. This book, therefore, challenges the "Camelot" view of the Kennedy withdrawal, an interpretation partial to the exceptionalist position on JFK.

Over the last twenty years, that narrative has refocused attention on the Kennedy period and alternative paths in Vietnam—hypothetical histories which, for several observers, offered models for more circumspect policies in the period since 9/11. These accounts largely embraced the idea that the Kennedy approach, as expressed through JFK's planning for a Vietnam withdrawal, warranted emulation as a template for more chastened and wiser courses of action in South Asia and the Middle East. While Vietnam was not the sole element of that model—Kennedy's handling of the Cuban Missile Crisis was at least as salient—JFK's skepticism about Vietnam and his presumed inclination to withdraw from it has been a touchstone for those who sought to celebrate his presidency, chide his successors, or both. But, as this book argues, the planning to withdraw from Vietnam, while charting the course of a potential force reduction, was conceived and implemented in the service of more complicated ends.

That planning, moreover, bore few of Kennedy's fingerprints. Instead, it was chiefly the brainchild of Secretary of Defense Robert S. McNamara, who developed its contours with seemingly little to no engagement from Kennedy himself. It also came to combine two distinct threads: a comprehensive scheme to remove virtually all of the almost 17,000 U.S. military advisers then in Vietnam by the close of 1965, and a more limited plan to remove the first thousand of them by the end of 1963. Those schedules emerged at different times for different reasons but intersected during the summer and fall of 1963, as the administration sought to reap political advantage, at home and abroad, from publicizing the plan's existence. Its viability, however, rested on key assumptions: that the war would progress satisfactorily, that the South Vietnamese would prove capable of managing their own defense, and that the Vietnamese Communists would not escalate their insurgency. When those assumptions collapsed amid the transition to a new president in Washington—a president less enamored of withdrawal yet similarly desirous of political and policy flexibility—withdrawal itself collapsed. By March 1964, the Johnson administration was more inclined to deepen its commitment to Vietnam and deploy additional troops than to bring them home.

The New Frontier of National Security

The planning to withdraw U.S. military advisers from South Vietnam, like the decision to send them there in the first place, stemmed from strategic assumptions, policy priorities, and political calculations that became increasingly intertwined throughout the course of Kennedy's thousand days in office. Collectively, they emerged out of the global conflicts that marked JFK's coming of age in the American Century.[6] Kennedy was hardly alone in embracing them. Tacking close to the center of national politics, JFK reflected public sentiment on the need for a strong defense, the necessity of U.S. leadership, and the virtues of the American way.

Kennedy thus entered the Oval Office as a Cold Warrior. He could hardly have done otherwise, given the imperatives of elective office in the years following the Second World War. Allied victory over Nazism, fascism, and militarism had left Americans acutely aware of threats and opportunities that came with their newfound role—a position they consciously assumed and then expanded the world over. They and other democratic peoples soon mobilized against the challenge of international communism they deemed even more dangerous. Kennedy embraced the precepts of that struggle—an existential one, as he saw it—as well as the premises and goals of containment, the national security strategy that aimed to counter the Soviet Union and its ideological brethren.[7]

The ensuing Cold War took shape in Europe, but its geography quickly expanded to Asia. The victory of Chinese Communists in their civil war against the Nationalist government was a seminal moment in the struggle, providing Moscow with a fraternal force to look after revolution in the East.[8] With perceptions of socialist solidarity hardening into dread of a global Communist "monolith," the zero-sum character of the struggle, in which a loss for one side represented a gain for the other, became more ominous. Virtually any setback, whether it took place in the industrial heartland of Europe or the peripheral rimland of Asia, could be equally catastrophic and destabilize the international system. According to this calculus, American policymakers came to fear that a "defeat for free institutions anywhere" constituted "a defeat for free institutions everywhere."[9]

Setbacks in Europe became less likely during the 1950s as the continent settled into an uneasy political equilibrium. But developments elsewhere were more fluid and potentially more dangerous. By June 1950, widespread fighting on the Korean Peninsula had transformed the Cold War from a nervy standoff into a red-hot conflict. Less than a year after the Soviets had broken Washington's atomic monopoly and welcomed Beijing as an ideological ally, the Korean War pitted principals and proxies in a militarized conflict that assumed a more menacing cast. For American observers, it raised the specter of Communist challenge the world over. Against that backdrop, the struggle for Southeast Asia, in which Communist-led nationalists battled both French imperial revanchists and non-Communist Vietnamese, became a new front in the global confrontation. Although Washington had previously viewed the Indochinese tangle through anticolonial as well as anticommunist lenses, the Korean War transformed it into a more nakedly Cold War contest, prompting a more fulsome commitment to Paris and to victory over Vietnamese Communism. Those developments were emblematic of the lethal contests that marked the postwar era, as armed conflict took shape as proxy wars within and between nations on either side of the ideological divide. The horrifying alternative of direct superpower violence made those guerrilla and unconventional clashes all the more brutal and frequent.[10]

What made them additionally frightening were the presumed dynamics that linked them together. Not only was the Cold War a struggle in which defeats anywhere amounted to defeats everywhere; global politics were such that a single setback was likely to spark a chain of events that might cascade out of control. In the vernacular of the day, the fall of a single domino—a nation either in the Western camp or not yet in the Eastern one—was likely to topple succeeding dominoes, be they territorially contiguous or psychologically vulnerable. Although its precepts were operative long before the Cold War, this "domino theory" of international relations, which President Dwight D. Eisenhower articulated in 1954, influenced a generation of Americans who found it persuasive and alarming. Indeed, political scientist Jack Snyder regards the domino theory as "the central organizing concept behind American containment strategy."[11]

That construction of national security acknowledged the dangers of a more interconnected world and the likelihood of violence coming to America's shores. The December 1941 attack on Pearl Harbor locked in that understanding of threat and the need for a more forward defense, with security purchased through the projection of power abroad. For a people accustomed to enlarging rather than contracting their sphere of responsibilities, it seemed a logical approach.[12] It was also self-perpetuating, as the perception of global interdependence encouraged a sprawling view of national security that collapsed the distinction between vital and peripheral interests. Postwar developments magnified those dynamics, engendering what historian Andrew Preston has labeled "globalized national security." John F. Kennedy internalized its precepts through his wartime experience and then political career as a liberal internationalist Democrat. Embracing the era's technocratic, problem-solving ethos, which inclined Americans toward managing the global order, Kennedy recognized that some of its more deep-seated challenges—poverty, hunger, disease, the environment—could significantly affect international relations and the diffusion of power.[13]

The linchpin of that new understanding was the slippery yet salient concept of credibility. Although open to interpretation, credibility communicates a nation's willingness to act in defense of its fundamental interests. According to historian Robert McMahon, the term comprises "a blend of resolve, reliability, believability, and decisiveness," qualities that are reflective of a country's "image and reputation." For American policymakers during the Cold War, credibility presumed "an interdependence among commitments, interests, and threats" that rendered all regions of the globe "potentially vital to U.S. interests."[14] Concerns about credibility certainly predated the Cold War, but the nature of the postwar conflict, as a bipolar and an ideological competition, heightened its importance to geopolitical stability. The maintenance of that balance thus became all-important. According to political scientist Christopher Fettweis, "the smallest demonstration of irresolution" could lead to disaster, reinforcing the dynamics of a tightly linked global system "in which there are no inconsequential events." The Cold War thus magnified the credibility imperative, McMahon writes, as it "pushed issues of reputation and image to the fore."[15] Policymakers, in turn, and particularly in the United States, came to regard perceptions of national power as fragile, malleable, and critical determinants of actual power.[16]

Central to that framework was the nuclear revolution, which, because of its capacity to inflict widespread destruction, heightened the relevance of credibility in the postwar world. With enhancements to weapons and delivery systems reducing the benefit of great-power war, the need to convey resolve at lower levels of conflict became increasingly paramount. Policymakers thus sought to communicate that determination without having to risk superpower confrontation, the trajectory of which could spiral out of control. The audience for those demonstrations included allies as well as adversaries, both of whom needed to believe that Washington would defend its interests and honor its commitments, whether close to home or farther away.[17]

Though its dynamics were hardly unique to the Kennedy administration, the credibility imperative took hold among the New Frontiersmen, who were acutely conscious of the need for its display. Perhaps their concerns stemmed from an awareness of their relative youth. The torch of leadership had passed to a new generation, born in the twentieth century and serving in junior capacities during the Second World War, and their inexperience may have strengthened an impulse toward boldness and activism. Indeed, JFK rode into office on a pledge to get the country "moving again" after the perceived torpor of the Eisenhower years. In all likelihood, those reputational concerns also reflected Kennedy's understanding of public relations and the power of images, developed through a lifetime of being in the public eye. Perhaps, too, they stemmed from a desire to exhibit toughness and counter perceived weakness, embodied in what historian Robert Dean describes as an "ideology of masculinity" shared widely by senior officials.[18] As historian John Lewis Gaddis suggests, the drivers of Kennedy foreign policy may well have been the threats of embarrassment and humiliation, of appearing to be weak and irresolute. Those fears likely sustained Kennedy's engagement in certain theaters long after the wisdom for being there had vanished. While JFK might have believed the nation was overextended abroad, and particularly in Southeast Asia, he could not abandon its commitments, Gaddis writes, "without appearing to call into question more vital obligations elsewhere."[19]

The U.S. commitment to South Vietnam therefore involved increasingly dramatic displays of firmness so that the messages sent were also the ones received. But those dynamics also meant that any talk of an American withdrawal would likely create tricky optics for the United States; as much as Washington sought to energize Saigon and enhance its capacity to prevail against the Communists, signs of withdrawal carried with them the appearance of a flagging American effort. Intimations of a waning commitment, therefore, let alone a full withdrawal, might not only undermine the first commandment of the Kennedy program—the stiffening of South Vietnamese morale—but raise troubling questions about Washington's policy writ large.

Those concerns informed not just Kennedy's involvement in Vietnam but his strategic posture worldwide. The need to challenge Moscow and its allies wherever they threatened Western interests mandated a new approach to war. With nuclear weapons unsuited to combat in the developing world (and, as Kennedy thought, to the rest of the world as well), the administration explored a more nimble approach to armed conflict. "Flexible response," as it came to be known, offered a range of choices of graduating intensity along a spectrum of martial options, from the "small wars" of counterinsurgency, to the big unit wars of conventional conflict, to the nuclear option itself. The ability to mount those responses required the means for doing so, and once in power, the administration enhanced its conventional and unconventional capabilities. It also developed a doctrine for using them that was grounded in the notion of "graduated response"—actions that signaled a willingness to move up the escalatory ladder and confront all manner of enemy hostility, especially on the global periphery. It was there, as Kennedy was fond of saying, that the "free world" was getting "nibbled away" and where the most significant battles of the 1960s would likely be fought.[20]

Each of those dynamics—the impulse toward symmetrical response, the fixation on credibility, the fear of falling dominoes, and the belief in a zero-sum environment—informed the calculations of most elected officials at the time. But they were particularly operative for Kennedy, who burnished a national reputation during his climb from six years in the U.S. House of Representatives, to a first term in the U.S. Senate, to a failed but stirring run at the vice-presidential slot on the 1956 Democratic ticket, and on to a second term in the upper chamber.[21] His seat on the Senate Foreign Relations Committee served as a platform for his evolving thoughts on America in the world, which included a subtle understanding of the interplay between nationalism and communism, as well as more alarmist descriptions of the nation's strategic deficit. Thereafter, major speeches and writings, along with his exploits at the 1956 Democratic National Convention, launched Kennedy into contention for the 1960 presidential nod. His adroit and energetic courting of party insiders facilitated his capture of the Democratic nomination that July, a contest replete with dramatic moments during the primaries and at the convention, and one Kennedy earned with dogged campaigning, inspiring rhetoric, ample funding, and a powerful organization.

Transitioning to the Presidency

Thereafter, Kennedy campaigned with an eye toward governing. A "Committee on National Security Policy," established in late August, reached out to Republicans as well as Democrats to identify and prioritize foreign policy challenges the country would face in a Kennedy administration.[22] The group addressed several concerns and hot spots such as Berlin, NATO, and disarmament, but paid little attention to Southeast Asia. Its only guidance on the region held that "the situation in Laos may have collapsed before the new Administration takes over," and that recent measures "to reorganize and train the Vietnamese anti-guerrilla forces should be vigorously supported."[23]

That focus on counterguerrilla warfare captured Kennedy's imagination, and the president's interest in it grew markedly during his time in office. According to Arthur Schlesinger, JFK made its enhancement "a personal project" following the Bay of Pigs debacle in April 1961. Singling out the Army's Special Forces for the role they would play in those military campaigns, Kennedy elevated their profile by allowing them to don green berets.[24] In turn, the Army instituted courses on special warfare and expanded its training in counterguerrilla tactics, instruction which became essential for officers seeking promotion. Those methods and principles fit under the strategic umbrella of counterinsurgency, which acquired a panache that aligned with the activist, can-do, problem-solving spirit of the New Frontier. Institutional arrangements emerged in kind, with the administration establishing a special interagency group to tackle the problem. Vietnam would be the proving ground for this new mode of warfare, and Kennedy officials, including the president and Secretary of Defense McNamara, frequently referred to it as a "laboratory" for their efforts. They also universalized its application, developing internal security plans for nations currently or potentially under siege. To the extent possible, those states were to look after their own needs, using local police and paramilitary forces to shield themselves from Communist subversion.[25]

But it was better to stop those wars before they began, so the administration looked to aid societies transitioning from colonialism to independence. According to a coterie of social scientists, the passage from preindustrial to modern conditions—what came to be called "modernization"—made countries dangerously susceptible to the lure of Communism, which offered a quick fix to peoples emerging from imperial rule. Foremost among those theorists was economist Walt W. Rostow, who regarded Communists as "scavengers of the modernization process" and sought to aid societies navigating those perilous transformations.[26] As deputy national security adviser during Kennedy's first year in office, Rostow embodied the administration's activist bent. That stance, expressed through the modernizing impulse itself, captured the optimism and idealism of the era. According to historian Michael Latham, modernization tapped into an existing set of assumptions, held by the nation's elite, which called on America to realize its historical mission to uplift the world. So profound was that impulse, Latham observes, that its goal was to move beyond the Cold War verities of containment and transform the structure of the international environment itself.[27]

To facilitate that forward-looking approach to national security, Rostow recommended a far-reaching program of foreign aid to undeveloped areas. It would be "the most important single initiative required of the Kennedy Administration," he argued.[28] The Kennedy team would launch that effort as part of its determination to pursue long-term solutions to political problems. Rostow and the New Frontiersmen called for doubling or tripling the amount of economic assistance for what they termed "nation-building," establishing in host countries the institutions they deemed necessary to guide the process of modernization on an extended basis.[29] Kennedy laid out that program in his inaugural address and in subsequent statements on foreign aid. He was not the first president in the postwar era to do so, but he was the first to prioritize it so highly. In time, the administration would codify and organize that effort through several bodies, including the Peace Corps, the Alliance for Progress, and the Agency for International Development. Along with innovations such as the Special Group for Counterinsurgency (CI), those departures reflected the need for new structures and bureaucracies to manage an increasingly interconnected and dynamic world.

Southeast Asia and Vietnam

Those considerations—modernization, foreign aid, counterinsurgency, and flexible response—shaped JFK's approach to Vietnam, as did more general concerns about credibility and falling dominoes. But so did Kennedy's early encounters with Asia and the global East, which were memorable and formative ones for his life and career. As commander of a PT boat in the South Pacific, Kennedy helped rescue crew members who had survived a nighttime ramming by a Japanese destroyer; two of his charges died in the attack. The experience brought home the chaos of combat, as well as its mismanagement by the military brass. Kennedy's public positions on Asia, which came during his six-year stint as a Democratic member of Congress from Massachusetts, were sharply critical of the Truman administration—for its handling of the Chinese civil war (insufficient support of the anticommunist Nationalists) and for its handling of the Korean War (a diversion from Europe). He also criticized its accommodation of the French and their soft-pedaling of Vietnamese independence during the Franco-Vietnamese War—complaints he continued to lodge during the Eisenhower administration.[30]

That struggle between France and Vietnam stretched back to the early postwar period when Paris sought to reassert colonial control over Indochina. The French had first imposed their *mission civilisatrice* in the 1860s and then governed with an iron first through the early decades of the twentieth century. They retained considerable sovereignty even following the fall of France in 1940, after which Japan extended its regional expansion into Southeast Asia. That arrangement collapsed, however, with the Japanese coup of March 1945. Five months later, with Japan itself crumbling in the waning days of the Pacific war, Communist Vietnamese, acting under the banner of the unified Viet Minh independence organization, founded the Democratic Republic of Vietnam (DRV).[31]

But a liberated France sought to reimpose its authority and reclaim its stature after the humiliations of defeat, occupation, and collaboration. Its reassertion of power owed much to Great Britain, motivated by its own concerns about imperial arrangements in the postwar era. Their collusion thwarted the aims of DRV president Ho Chi Minh, who had been challenging French colonialism since before the First World War; Ho's fame in both nationalist and Communist circles, and his guile as a political opportunist, had thrust him into a position of unparalleled leadership he would hold for the better part of two decades. Despite Ho's efforts to broker a peaceful resolution to Franco-Vietnamese skirmishing, more serious fighting between Paris and Hanoi broke out in December 1946. It would last for over seven years and, in one form or another, embroil each of the world's major powers.[32]

During its early phases, the Franco-Vietminh War took shape as an anticolonial struggle. But with the hardening of divisions in Europe and ideological warfare in Asia, it came to look like an anti-Communist one—an image the French were eager to magnify. Americans drew that conclusion on their own, however, particularly in light of efforts to secure markets in Asia for a reconstructed, pro-Western Japan. With Moscow and Beijing recognizing the DRV in early 1950, and with all-out war on the Korean Peninsula breaking out that June, President Harry S. Truman ramped up economic and military aid to Paris, dispatching a U.S. Military Assistance Advisory Group to Vietnam in December. But French complaints about fighting in Southeast Asia while defending Western Europe led Washington to expand its support, financing roughly 80 percent of the French war effort by the time peace talks began in May 1954. Those negotiations, which brought the belligerents and their respective allies together in Geneva, dismembered French Indochina, transforming Cambodia, Laos, and Vietnam into independent states. The conferees also created a political process for reconciling the Communist and anti-Communist Vietnamese, temporarily dividing them into regroupment zones north and south of the 17th parallel. All-country elections to unify Vietnam were slated for July 1956. Until then, the two polities would build their societies and position their cadres for the coming plebiscite.

Those tasks fell to Ho and the Vietnamese Workers Party in the north, and to Prime Minister Ngo Dinh Diem in the south.[33] Diem had been as ardently nationalist as Ho during the prewar period, having assumed and then resigned a position in the French administrative bureaucracy. But as a devout Catholic, Diem had no truck with Communist efforts to gain independence and ran afoul of the Viet Minh in the postwar period. Fearing for his life, he left Vietnam, traveling to Japan and to the United States, where he befriended influential political and religious figures, establishing his credentials as a potential leader of a non-Communist Vietnam. Those attributes made him attractive to Vietnamese emperor Bao Dai, a placeholder monarch from the prewar period of French rule and a pliable figure for French purposes during the war against the DRV. Diem, for his part, had been angling for the premiership and was therefore well positioned to accept Bao Dai's May 1954 invitation to serve as prime minister. Having agreed to form a cabinet in June, Diem formally took office the following month.[34]

But the all-country elections mandated by Geneva never took place, as Diem refused to participate in preliminary negotiations on the vote. Although France, Britain, and the United States encouraged him to engage in the electoral process, each recognized that a truly free election would result in victory for Ho and the Communists. With Diem's hostility to Paris limiting French influence in Vietnamese affairs, and with the Geneva powers focusing on other priorities, the elections to unite southern and northern Vietnam fell by the wayside. By the time they were supposed to take place in the summer of 1956, Diem had consolidated his power and was reshaping southern Vietnam's society and government. Thenceforth, he would build an avowedly anti-Communist state, and Ho a decidedly Communist one, each with the dream of unifying the country under his own flag.

They did so with massive amounts of funds from their respective patrons. While Moscow and Beijing kept Hanoi afloat, Washington did likewise with Saigon. American economic, military, and administrative assistance flowed freely, with the United States providing over two billion dollars of aid during the Eisenhower administration. Support for the policy came from several sources, including Senator John F. Kennedy, who repeatedly stumped for Diem and his nation-building efforts. A charter member of the American Friends of Vietnam (AFV), the lobbying group established in the mid-1950s, Kennedy designated Diem's Republic of Vietnam (RVN) as a vital player in the Cold War struggle. It was "the cornerstone of the Free World in Southeast Asia," he proclaimed, "the keystone to the arch, the finger in the dike."[35] With Saigon's importance acknowledged by Democrats and Republicans alike, Washington bankrolled Diem as he ascended from prime minister to president, crushing his political foes and rigging a referendum on Bao Dai's rule. His consolidation of power complete by the fall of 1955, Diem turned on the Communists who had stayed in the south following Geneva. Those campaigns were brutal and insufficiently discriminate. Along with his other missteps—a failure to address peasant grievances, an austere approach to achieving a "personalist" revolution, and a penchant for privileging fellow Catholics (a minority group in a religiously heterodox country)—Diem's "Denounce the Communists" campaign alienated increasing numbers of his own people.[36]

Those energies led Communists north and south to take more targeted action against Saigon. Pleas for the defense of southern cadres had been mounting since 1956, with Ho and the Politburo acceding to requests for greater political agitation. But with no countrywide elections in the offing, and with Communist ranks being decimated below the 17th parallel, the time had come for a more martial response, a position ascendant in the north and championed by southern regroupee and Politburo member Le Duan. Along with several equally militant members of the Communist hierarchy, Le Duan prevailed upon more moderate elements in Hanoi, including Ho Chi Minh, to support their comrades and establish political and military structures for revolution in the South. The National Liberation Front (NLF), a coalition dominated by Communists and directed by Hanoi, came into being in December 1960 to manage the movement. Its military arm—the People's Liberation Armed Forces (PLAF), derisively labeled the "Viet Cong" or "VC"—soon launched sustained and deadly attacks throughout South Vietnam.[37] It was this new reality that Kennedy confronted as president: a growing brushfire war against a celebrated American ally—*Life* had dubbed Diem the "The Tough Miracle Man of Vietnam"—in a geopolitical environment JFK warned was turning toward the Communists' advantage.[38]

But Kennedy also approached Vietnam with a subtle eye. Undoubtedly, he viewed the challenges of Southeast Asia through the lens of the Cold War; his anticommunism was politically savvy but also sincerely held, a long-standing feature of his public persona. Still, a 1951 visit to the region stimulated deeper thinking about the struggle and its implications for U.S. policy. JFK had embarked on the seven-week journey to Asia and the Middle East to burnish his foreign policy credentials in advance of a 1952 bid to unseat Senator Henry Cabot Lodge Jr. [R-MA]. Upon his arrival in Indochina, interviews with U.S. diplomat Ed Gullion and journalist Seymour Topping confirmed Kennedy's pessimism about the war. The Americans were coming to resemble colonialists, he realized, and French policy had become overly militarized. Moreover, the real danger in Indochina was not communism but the scourges of poverty, disease, injustice, and inequality. Kennedy emphasized those themes in speeches he delivered upon returning home, criticizing the Truman administration for allying with Paris against the popular and nationalist efforts of the Viet Minh. Those stands marked a philosophical and political break with his earlier support of more hawkish Cold War policies. His exposure to Indochina, as well as his conversations with Asian leaders, convinced him that "the United States must align herself with the emerging nations," as Logevall writes, "and that Communism could never be defeated by relying solely or principally on force of arms."[39]

Having won his 1952 contest against Lodge, Kennedy continued to urge that Washington support the nationalist impulses of formerly colonized peoples. Aid to France, he argued, should be conditioned on its handling of Indochinese independence, and he rejected calls for U.S. intervention in the war. "No amount of American military assistance," he told his Senate colleagues in 1954, "can conquer an enemy which is everywhere and at the same time nowhere," and which has the "sympathy and covert support of the people."[40] His realism about Southeast Asia also informed his critique of fighting in Algeria, where Paris was again seeking to thwart an independence movement. Addressing the Senate in July 1957, he lashed out at the French but also at the Eisenhower administration for its shortsighted policy of blocking nationalist aspirations. Subsequent remarks on the need to nurture independence movements behind and beyond the Iron Curtain added further luster to his foreign policy credentials as he considered a run at the White House.[41]

Indices of Commitment

Once inaugurated as president, Kennedy looked to assist Saigon through increasing levels of support. The aid took several forms: administrative, economic, and military assistance; high-level missions of civilian and defense officials; public and private assurances about Vietnam's role in the broader anti-Communist struggle; and verbal pledges about American determination. Central to all were the signals they sent about Washington's firmness, as Kennedy officials were acutely aware of and responsive to the need for advertising the U.S. commitment. While audiences included allies and adversaries, the most important targets were the South Vietnamese themselves.

Yet no demonstration of resolve matched the value of sending U.S. troops to South Vietnam. Both Washington and Saigon regarded those forces as the ultimate symbols of national purpose, and discussions about their numbers and role—within each government as well as between them—were ever present during the Kennedy years. Those talks were often a barometer of bilateral relations and reflected mutual concerns about the depth and impact of the U.S. commitment. So, too, did the command structure under which they served. The elevation of a Military Assistance Advisory Group to a Military Assistance Command, which flowed from the 1961 "limited partnership" between the two countries, testified to the heightened seriousness of the effort. The installation of a four-star general as its new commanding officer, who replaced the three-star general previously in charge, elevated it still further. In time, a willingness to take casualties, which climbed from less than 10 American deaths to roughly 200 during the Kennedy years, sent additional messages about Washington's devotion to the cause.[42]

But the use of U.S. troops to convey that commitment threatened to undermine their very purpose. Over the course of 1962 and 1963, the expanding American footprint led Diem and his brother, political counselor Ngo Dinh Nhu, to worry about the effect of U.S. servicemen on South Vietnamese politics. More advisers meant more contact between the two peoples, the wider transmission of U.S. views on the counterinsurgency, and, as Diem feared, his weakened grip on the populace. The influx of troops also implied increasing alarm about Saigon's stability and its capacity to cope with the insurgency. Ironically, then, the flow of American men and matériel into Vietnam, designed to bolster South

Vietnamese morale and stiffen its fighting spirit, was having the opposite effect—generating suspicion about U.S. intentions, compromising the partnership, and creating an even more volatile polity. Americans, too, were wary of the elevated profile. The dispatch of U.S. troops raised the stakes of the conflict, generating fears of a wider war and mounting unease about the American commitment. Yet even as deployments multiplied, Saigon continued to seek Washington's assurance of lasting support.

This was especially true in light of U.S. policy toward neighboring Laos. Carved out of French Indochina and accorded neutral status by the Geneva agreements of 1954, Laos had been consumed by violence during the First Indochina War. An uneasy truce between political factions broke down in the late 1950s as royalist, Communist, and neutralist forces vied for power. A series of coups left the nation lurching between pro- and anti-Western alignments until December 1960, when a combined neutralist and Communist force requested a Soviet airlift of war matériel to counter CIA-backed elements seeking to consolidate control. With the prospect of a more violent proxy conflict emerging in a land Eisenhower regarded as key to regional security, the outgoing president advised the incoming one to intervene unilaterally if necessary. But Laos was a poor locale for U.S. military action. Kennedy thus sought a neutral solution to its troubles—one that Moscow ultimately supported, and the international community codified, in July 1962.[43]

Its spillover effects on Vietnam, however, were of enormous consequence. Neutralization not only failed to stabilize Laos, but it facilitated North Vietnamese infiltration into South Vietnam. Moreover, it had lasting implications for South Vietnamese morale; even as Washington maintained that Laos and Vietnam were entirely separate cases, and repeatedly dismissed talk about neutralizing South Vietnam, the Government of the Republic of Vietnam (GVN) remained dubious. More than almost any other development during the Kennedy years, the diplomacy surrounding Laos, and the possibility of replicating it elsewhere in the region, generated persistent fears about the durability of America's commitment to Saigon and Southeast Asia.[44]

But Kennedy officials were never likely to neutralize South Vietnam. Its people were made of sterner stuff, they thought, and its geography more hospitable to the intake of American aid. Indeed, the optics of neutralizing Saigon after doing so with Vientiane were fraught with political danger. In the wake of the Bay of Pigs and the Berlin Wall, shrinking from yet another Cold War challenge was too much for Kennedy to consider; there were "just so many concessions that one can make to the communists in one year and survive politically," he reportedly said.[45] His general approach to neutralism, moreover, further militated against its application in South Vietnam. As historian Robert Rakove notes, the administration acceded to neutralism only for those states outside the Western camp and rejected neutralism for nations already within it. Should a regime allied with the United States turn toward neutrality, additional defections might ensue, leading yet another row of dominoes to fall.[46] As a result, officials in both the Kennedy and Johnson administrations intensified their rhetorical and material commitments to Saigon. In time, and in conjunction with a series of political and military setbacks in South Vietnam, those rhetorical commitments became operational. Thereafter, questions about the disposition of U.S. troops no longer centered around how and when to take them out, but whether and when to put more of them in.

Nevertheless, the planning to withdraw American troops from Vietnam was real. The following account seeks to trace its history, focusing more on its meaning at the time than on whether Kennedy would have carried it out. As indicated, others have pronounced on the latter with creativity and rigor. The increasing prevalence of counterfactual history has sustained those efforts, acclimatizing the reading public, if not large swaths of the academy, to the practice.[47] The matter is ultimately unknowable, a reality Kennedy aides have repeatedly acknowledged, even when expressing strong suspicions about the president's leanings. Still, the observations of those closest to Kennedy, both personally and professionally, are likely closest to the mark. Longtime counselor Ted Sorensen, as well as chief Vietnam aide Michael Forrestal, conceded that JFK, at the time he went to Dallas, probably did not know what he would do if faced with Saigon's ultimate collapse.[48] The president's brother, Robert Kennedy, said much the same, telling interviewers in the spring of 1964 that the matter would simply await their judgment. "We'd face that when we came to it," he said.[49]

They never had to, of course—at least not on JFK's watch—which is why judgments about the Kennedy withdrawal have remained so contested. This book explores why its planning began, why it ended, and what it meant.

1

Assumption

January 1961–December 1961

Vietnam was not a front-burner issue for John F. Kennedy when he became president in January 1961, but it would assume much greater importance by the end of his first week in office. Just days after vowing that Americans would "bear any burden" in the Cold War struggle against international communism, JFK learned about the price they might have to pay to assure "the survival and success of liberty," at least in Southeast Asia.[1] Kennedy's engagement with the region would be lengthy and difficult, and he would spend much of 1961 groping toward a response. By its close, he would commit the United States to supporting the Republic of [South] Vietnam (RVN) in its struggle against a growing and effective Communist insurgency.

Kennedy's tutelage came by way of the Pentagon's "guerrilla guru," Air Force colonel Edward G. Lansdale. A brash and independent figure inside the national security establishment, Lansdale helped the Philippines stanch its own insurgency in the late 1940s and came to Saigon in the mid-1950s to help Prime Minister Ngo Dinh Diem solidify his government. Returning on an inspection tour in January 1961, Lansdale found South Vietnam—a "combat area of the cold war," as he described it—in need of "emergency treatment." His trip report made its way to Walt W. Rostow, the new deputy national security adviser, who sent it on to Kennedy. The president read it and was deeply distressed.[2] Complaining that outgoing president Dwight D. Eisenhower had said nothing about

Vietnam during their two transition meetings, JFK now sensed the country's "high importance." He promptly called a meeting to discuss the Lansdale report with its author and senior national security officials. Although the session would also focus on the Caribbean—plans for a covert operation to topple Cuban strongman Fidel Castro, developed during the Eisenhower administration, were rapidly coalescing—Kennedy was now equally concerned about Southeast Asia. According to National Security Adviser McGeorge Bundy, Lansdale's memo had awakened JFK to "a sense of the danger and urgency of the problem in Viet-Nam."[3]

That perception owed much to developments in Moscow just prior to Kennedy's inauguration. Addressing a closed session of Kremlin officials on January 6, Soviet premier Nikita S. Khrushchev summarized the fruits of a recent meeting of Communist parties from around the world. Although he acknowledged ideological differences with Mao Zedong and the Chinese Communists—the Sino-Soviet split was by then evident and a topic of growing international interest—Khrushchev also voiced his support for "wars of national liberation." Those conflicts, like the one ongoing between the Algerian people and the French colonialists, were both "inevitable" and "sacred," and very much the wave of the future. Kennedy found Khrushchev's speech deeply troubling. Rejecting advice that he treat it as standard Soviet rhetoric, he appraised those remarks as reflective of Soviet intentions and implored his aides to treat them as gospel.[4] His overreaction to the speech, which was intended largely for internal consumption, contributed to the alarmist atmosphere settling over Washington.

Kennedy thus turned to Vietnam with a marked sense of impatience. Signaling his desire for immediate action, the president asked, "how do we change morale; how do we get operations in the north; how do we get moving?" He called for a task force to address the problem, just as he had for Cuba, citing those two hot spots, along with Laos and the Congo, as the "four main crisis areas" his administration would likely confront. "We must change our course in these areas," Kennedy pronounced, "and we must be better off in three months than we are now." Regarding Indochina, he wanted the Republic of Vietnam Armed Forces (RVNAF) to shift its focus from defense to offense, and for South Vietnamese guerrillas to operate north of the 17th parallel.[5] Acting swiftly following the Lansdale meeting, Kennedy authorized $28.4 million to boost

RVNAF numbers from 150,000 to 170,000, and another $12.7 million for the paramilitary forces serving South Vietnam's forty-four provinces.[6] He then issued the second National Security Action Memorandum (NSAM) of his administration, directing the Defense Department and other relevant agencies to channel their energies into enhancing America's counterguerrilla capabilities.[7] It was an early illustration of his approach to unconventional wars—a central challenge of the New Frontier.

It also reflected Kennedy's general posture during those first days in office. As he warned Congress in a January 30 address, the need for active engagement and steely resolve extended to all areas of national life. Depicting developments in the most lurid of terms, he confessed to being "staggered upon learning" just how difficult those trials would be over the next four years. The crises multiplied and grew more vexing with each passing day, drawing the country nearer to "the hour of maximum danger." The nation's economy was "in trouble," with its budget and international payments "out of balance." But those problems paled beside the ones confronting the United States in its struggle against international communism, requiring a reappraisal of its entire defense strategy. While there was reason for hope, the moment was critical, the tide "unfavorable." "The news will be worse before it is better," he warned, and while all Americans should work "for the best, we should prepare ourselves now for the worst." Indeed, in their "hour of national peril," he wondered whether "a nation organized such as ours can endure." It was a sobering message, bracing in its alarm.[8]

The numerous and varied threats seemed almost overwhelming. Kennedy's greatest concern was the outbreak of nuclear war, and efforts to lessen it would absorb much of his time in office. Although he expanded the American arsenal of nuclear (and conventional) weapons, he persisted in efforts to scale back the danger through arms control and limitations on testing.[9] He was equally gripped by numerous hot spots around the globe. Berlin remained the most sensitive flashpoint, a city occupied by the allied powers after the Second World War, divided between East and West since the late 1940s, and situated ninety miles inside the confines of the German Democratic Republic (GDR). Beginning in 1958, Soviet threats to end Western access rights and transfer sovereignty to East Germany had sparked a series of crises between Moscow and Washington, any one of which carried the seeds of armed conflict. So, too, did developments in the Caribbean, Central Africa, and Southeast Asia. Revolutions in each had produced charismatic leaders whose anti-Western and anti-American rhetoric offered potential footholds for the expansion of Soviet power. While the "Communist monolith" seemed to be crumbling, Kennedy officials presumed that Leftist inroads into Cuba, the Congo, and Indochina posed grave dangers to American security.

Anxieties over Southeast Asia were particularly acute, though initial concern centered not on Vietnam but on neighboring Laos. Wracked by instability and fighting since the recent collapse of a power-sharing agreement between Communist and non-Communist factions, Laos presented Kennedy with few good options. Within days of his inauguration, Kennedy created a task force to explore the prospect of securing the country's pro-Western orientation. Unfavorable assessments of the warring groups, as well as the logistics of the supply chain, led JFK to reject calls for military action and to embrace plans for neutralizing the kingdom. In so doing, he repeatedly overrode Pentagon officials who called for a more belligerent response. Kennedy preserved the military option as a last resort and pre-positioned U.S. forces on land and sea to signal American resolve. But he wanted to settle his "first grave cold war challenge," as *Time* magazine was describing it, through diplomacy.[10]

All the while, Kennedy made clear his opposition to a Communist triumph in Laos. According to Llewllyn "Tommy" Thompson, the U.S. ambassador to the Soviet Union, Kennedy thought Southeast Asia was "absolutely vital" to American interests, and that under no circumstances would Washington countenance Communist subversion; the United States, moreover, would "take any measures necessary" to combat Communist treachery.[11] Commentary in the *New York Times* echoed that position, maintaining that Washington would "face all the risks of a test of wills with the Soviet Union rather than let Laos fall under Communist control."[12] Kennedy himself warned that "the security of all Southeast Asia will be endangered if Laos loses its neutral independence."[13] Should it fall to the Communists or remain mired in its multisided factional war, neighboring Thailand would seek an accommodation and South Vietnam would also suffer. Indeed, if Saigon succumbed to the Communists or even moved toward a neutralist position, "the impact upon the countries of Southeast Asia," according to U.S. intelligence, "would be similar in kind but considerably more severe than that resulting from the loss or division of Laos." What mattered most was the perception that Washington was committed to stopping the spread of Communism throughout the region.[14]

Indeed, credibility concerns eclipsed more tangible interests as the primary reason for the American commitment, especially to South Vietnam. Previous rationales for Saigon's preservation—as a market for Japanese goods, as a major exporter of rice, as a firewall against further economic losses should Malaya and Indonesia succumb to the Communists—none of these carried as much weight in the early 1960s as they had ten years earlier. Instead, the psychological and political ramifications of a Communist victory—equally salient for policymakers in the late 1940s and 1950s, but now dominant for the Kennedy administration—would govern much of its thinking about the importance of American resolve.[15]

Given the importance of perceptions, recent developments in another region—the Caribbean—seemed virtually catastrophic. Months of planning to oust Castro culminated in mid-April when the Kennedy administration launched its ill-fated effort at Cuba's Bay of Pigs. The amphibious assault, which relied on anti-Castro refugees and an array of U.S. military assets, began with an abbreviated bombing campaign on April 15; it ended four days later with the capture of roughly 1,200 partisans and the death of over 100 comrades. It was a failure of the first order, even more so as it brought Havana and Moscow closer together and weakened Kennedy's support among nationalists, neutrals, and the developing world. Publicly, Kennedy took the blame, telling journalists on April 21 that he was the responsible officer of government. Privately, he fumed—at himself for being "so stupid"—and at the Pentagon, the CIA, the State Department, White House aides, and a host of officials who misled him, failed to provide their best counsel, or told the press of their pre-invasion doubts. The experience was shattering. For a president so cognizant of the power of images, the perception of him as a paper tiger posed great dangers.[16]

In fact, an air of crisis soon permeated the White House. With the emergency in Laos still cresting, and with Castro seemingly more emboldened, Kennedy empaneled a task force to address the deteriorating situation in South Vietnam. It was a long time in coming—roughly three months after the Lansdale report—but Kennedy had remained fixated on the need for "rapid and energetic action" in Vietnam.[17] The task force would now provide that energy, as well as a more systematic approach to addressing the problem. Chaired by Deputy Secretary of Defense Roswell L. Gilpatric, the interagency group held a series of contentious sessions in late April. At issue were military and civil concerns, political and economic reforms, the expansion of GVN security forces, worries about border protection, and the propriety of deploying U.S. troops.[18] Gilpatric sent his final report to Kennedy on May 11, but only after refinements at several meetings and repeated interjections from the president. Its findings became codified as NSAM 52, which established policy toward Saigon and a program of action. It pledged the administration "to prevent Communist domination of South Vietnam; to create in that country a viable and increasingly democratic society; and to initiate, on an accelerated basis, a series of mutually supporting actions of a military, political, economic, psychological and covert character designed to achieve this objective." Having completed its work, the Task Force would remain operative, monitoring progress and directing the Pentagon to study "the size and composition of forces which would be desirable in the case of a possible commitment of U.S. forces to Vietnam."[19]

But American servicemen were already streaming into South Vietnam. Following a National Security Council (NSC) meeting on April 29 to review Gilpatric's draft recommendations, Kennedy authorized several deployments: 78 Army security staffers to handle communications intelligence; roughly 40 CIA personnel on top of the 70 already in place; and 100 Military Assistance Advisory Group (MAAG) troops to join the 685 presently in South Vietnam. More would be on the way, as officials were angling to provide roughly 3,200 instructors for training the Army of the Republic of Vietnam (ARVN), 400 U.S. Special Forces troops to train their South Vietnamese counterparts, and 6,000 members of a Marine brigade.[20] In addition to this front-line support, Kennedy also sanctioned the expansion of radar surveillance capabilities and further training for South Vietnam's Civil Guard and Self Defense Corps—units providing security on the province and local levels, respectively.[21] The "Presidential Program," as it came to be known, was thus up and running even before it received official sanction.

The deployment of those servicemen created inconvenient optics, as their presence flouted the 1954 Geneva Accords on Indochina. Those agreements, in addition to creating northern and southern regroupment zones in Vietnam and providing for elections to unify them, established the number of foreign troops permissible in the two zones and a process for their replacement. At the time of the Franco-Vietminh cease-fire, 342 American soldiers were serving in Vietnam under the U.S. MAAG, establishing the ceiling for U.S. advisers providing logistical support to French and Vietnamese state forces. Following the withdrawal of French combat units, U.S. troops joined with French military advisers to train the Vietnamese Army; for the moment, Paris remained solely responsible for training the Vietnamese Air Force and Navy. Coordinating those efforts was a Training Relations Instruction Mission (TRIM), which directed the activities of the combined 888 French and American personnel attached to it. TRIM disbanded in 1956 as France further reduced its presence in southern Vietnam, leaving the United States to conduct all training activities for the Vietnamese Army. To compensate for the shortfall in French forces, Washington created a Temporary Equipment Recovery Mission (TERM)—a "subterfuge," admitted U.S. officials, which allowed Washington to increase its forces while nominally observing the Geneva limit on American troops. The arrival of 350 additional military advisers brought the American contingent in South Vietnam to 692, a figure that expanded to 736 when MAAG assumed training duties for the Vietnamese Navy and Air Force. But the Pentagon's own discomfort with the ruse, compounded by pressure from the International Commission of Supervision and Control (ICC)—the body established at Geneva to administer the agreements—led to the dissolution of TERM in 1960. The transfer of TERM's forces back to the MAAG that April resulted in a final tally of 685 U.S. military advisers— the number of U.S. troops serving in South Vietnam at the time of Kennedy's inauguration.[22]

The onset of the Laos crisis put upward pressure on those figures and led the administration to consider blowing straight through the Geneva ceiling. Beginning in February 1961, the State Department suggested raising the MAAG contingent in South Vietnam to 888 and then to over 1,800 to facilitate the delivery of matériel to the GVN.[23] By April, the White House was pushing much the same line, as Walt Rostow wanted the administration to distance itself from Geneva altogether. Neither Washington nor South Vietnam had signed the accords, he maintained, and those who did were violating them.[24] Rostow's NSC colleague Robert Komer thought likewise. He urged that Diem disavow and "abrogate" the agreements prior to the upcoming Geneva conference on

Laos, making it easier for the United States to introduce troops to South Vietnam and for the Southeast Asia Treaty Organization (SEATO)—the anti-Communist security alliance created in the wake of Geneva—to do the same. The value of inserting American soldiers—not to fight the PLAF but "to establish a US 'presence'"—would be substantial.[25] Secretary of State Dean Rusk worried about deploying military advisers prior to the start of negotiations on Laos, but he, too, thought the United States should "augment the MAAG" by adding 100 military personnel.[26] Indeed, the numbers U.S. officials were considering—currently upwards of 4,000 additional troops—were likely just the tip of the spear, as more significant deployments might be required to forestall Communist domination of South Vietnam.[27]

Kennedy himself seemed supportive of those measures. According to MAAG chief Lt. Gen. Lionel C. McGarr, the president was willing to "work outside" the Geneva agreements. Gen. Lyman L. Lemnitzer, chair of the Joint Chiefs of Staff (JCS), likewise maintained that JFK "was ready to do anything within reason to save Southeast Asia."[28] Yet both officials framed Kennedy's position more expansively than his remarks warranted, a dynamic that would hold throughout JFK's term in office. Enlarging Kennedy's stance on the U.S. commitment, Lemnitzer claimed that the administration would "take whatever action is required to save Vietnam." With American prestige "literally at stake," Lemnitzer thought the administration should go all out to provide the requisite support in men, money, and matériel "to definitely assure that we do not lose Vietnam."[29] McGarr, too, divined a commitment deeper than the one Kennedy expressed. Both Lemnitzer and the president, McGarr said, had "repeatedly stated Vietnam is not to go behind Bamboo Curtain under any circumstances, and we must do all that is necessary to prevent this from happening."[30] While McGarr and Lemnitzer were more accurate than not in describing the administration's depth of concern, their inclination to stretch those understandings highlighted a central truth. The United States would escalate its commitment to Vietnam through its most tangible expression—the blood, and the treasure that came with it, of American troops.

McGarr's reference to the "Bamboo Curtain" reflected the fear among U.S. officials that Communist China represented the most direct threat to the region. As much as Kennedy focused on Moscow's support for "wars of national liberation," Beijing's support of them was even more problematic. Not only had Kennedy read Mao and encouraged aides to do likewise, the founding of the People's Republic—through a peasant revolution—made it even more likely that Beijing would back similar anti-imperialist and anti-Western struggles, especially in its own backyard. Kennedy's appointment of two China hawks to senior positions— Dean Rusk in the State Department and John McCone at the CIA— further inclined Washington toward viewing Chinese designs as expansionist and malevolent. That perception came to be a self-fulfilling prophecy, as the introduction of U.S. forces intensified the escalatory spiral that shaped Beijing's increasing support of Hanoi.[31]

But the dangers of that spiral seemed less immediate than the demands of stiffening Saigon's spine. That was precisely what Bob Komer concluded after asking the question, "How do we demonstrate our determination in unmistakable terms?" The answer was troops; Washington should publicly commit to armed intervention in the event of overt warfare and to the introduction of "token" U.S. forces in cases short of combat.[32] Indeed, the need to communicate Washington's resolve was among the most important objectives to come out of the task-force process, equal to the material measures designed to bolster Saigon's military capabilities. To send those signals persuasively, policymakers needed to dramatize the stakes involved, particularly since talk about neutralizing Laos suggested an erosion of American will. To that end, Rusk indicated in early May that Washington would provide Saigon with "every possible help across the entire spectrum in which help is needed." While he declined to say whether that included direct U.S. intervention, he parried concerns about American troops getting bogged down in a so-called "peripheral" theater. If the United States ignored the periphery, Rusk cautioned, "the periphery changes. And the first thing you know the periphery is the center."[33] That reluctance to distinguish between peripheral and vital interests, to treat them as one and the same, elevated the importance of virtually any conflict affecting American interests, especially the one quickening in Southeast Asia.

The insertion of American troops soon became a matter of presidential concern as journalists questioned Kennedy in early May about his intentions in Vietnam. It was indeed a subject under consideration, he conceded, though it was hardly a foregone conclusion. The United States could offer economic and military assistance, as well as guarantees against outright military invasion. "But in the final analysis," he said, the South

Vietnamese "have to—and we cannot do it for them—they have to organize the political and social life of the country in such a way that they maintain the support of their people."[34] To assist in that effort, Vice President Lyndon B. Johnson would soon travel to Saigon to discuss how best to aid the GVN. Johnson's trip, in addition to the troops and matériel already en route, further elevated the struggle's importance for audiences in the United States, in South Vietnam, and around the world.

In fact, the use of high-profile visits such as Johnson's was vital to the overall effort and central to enhancing South Vietnamese morale.[35] Arriving on May 11 and staying for two days, LBJ played his part, toasting Diem as the "Winston Churchill of Asia" and conveying U.S. support in Saigon's fight for survival. He also floated the possibility of introducing U.S. combat troops to South Vietnam, a matter the Joint Chiefs asked him to raise with the South Vietnamese president. Diem expressed no interest in those units, except in the case of overt Communist aggression. But he was eager to host "as many U.S. military personnel as needed for training and advising Vietnamese forces." In all, he greatly appreciated the offer of tangible and rhetorical support.[36]

Johnson came away from his visit believing that Washington had reached a fork in the road. "We must decide whether to help these countries," he wrote Kennedy, "or throw in the towel in the area and pull back our defenses to San Francisco and a 'Fortress America' concept." With Washington's credibility at stake, LBJ called for a "clear-cut and strong program of action" that would "meet the challenge of Communist expansion" in Southeast Asia. That commitment was likely to be long and costly, but it was in the interest of "all free nations that the effort be made." The central task involved raising South Vietnamese morale. As he relayed to Kennedy, the Laotian talks had "created doubt and concern about the intentions of the United States throughout Southeast Asia." Rebuilding that sense of confidence, Johnson maintained, was the key variable in enabling the region to defend itself against a Communist takeover.[37]

But the delivery of military and economic aid, and the training of South Vietnam's armed forces, were also vital to the task. Johnson suggested a three-year plan to provide that support and recommended the use of U.S. military units only in the event of a "massive invasion" from outside the country's borders. Combat troops were therefore neither required nor desirable; indeed, if the three-year plan was insufficient, "then we had better remember the experience of the French who wound up with several hundred thousand men in Vietnam and were still unable to do it." But let there be no mistake: the proposed program "plunges us very deeply into the Vietnamese internal situation." There was "a chance for success," he noted, but "not a moment to lose."[38] The commitment simply had to be made. Whether an American president could do so and still apply the lessons Johnson cited—essentially, committing to a positive effort and then reversing it if deemed necessary—would be the fundamental question at work in the Kennedy withdrawal.

Implementing the Presidential Program

In the weeks following the Johnson trip and the issuance of NSAM 52, the administration organized its Vietnam program at some remove from the crisis atmosphere engulfing it that spring. The Cuban debacle had shaken its confidence, though a postmortem study and Kennedy's rising approval numbers suggested it not only would weather the storm but learn from its mistakes. Tensions over Laos had raised the possibility of U.S. military action, but initial fears of intervention were now giving way to multilateral talks on the country's neutrality. Closer to home, the Freedom Rides revealed, yet again, the deep-seated prejudice and hostility confronting Black Americans and their allies; negotiations between the Justice Department and southern officials, spearheaded by Attorney General Robert F. Kennedy, allowed the administration to dampen the attendant violence and publicity, though it exposed the president's reluctance to embrace civil rights as a moral cause. Even the shock of Yuri Gagarin's successful orbital flight, which symbolized Russian preeminence in missile technologies—and its implications for Soviet military might—was receding as the United States braced itself for the demands of the space age.

Each of those events were on the president's mind as he reset his administration and restated the challenges of the New Frontier. Speaking to a joint session of Congress on May 25, Kennedy reflected on the previous four months with a message that aimed to warn, prepare, and inspire. This updated State of the Union address on "Urgent National Needs" laid out Kennedy's "freedom doctrine," a set of commitments far-reaching in their scope: economic support for underemployed citizens at home and emerging nations abroad; security partnerships with like-minded peoples around the world; provisions for civil defense and the pursuit of disarmament; and the modernization of America's armed forces. Memorably, it also included the goal of landing a man on the moon and returning him safely to earth—a prospect more tenable following Alan Shepard's suborbital flight earlier that month.

The speech also launched Kennedy on his own voyage—first to Paris to speak with French president Charles de Gaulle, then to Vienna to meet with Khrushchev. Those discussions would allow Kennedy to promote his agenda, a slate of measures that demanded further sacrifice on the part of all Americans. The burdens would be especially heavy in the Third World—"the great battleground for the defense and expansion of freedom," Kennedy intoned, "the lands of the rising peoples." In Vietnam, where guerrillas and saboteurs had assassinated thousands of civil servants, the struggle was over "minds and souls as well as lives and territory." It was a contest, Kennedy declared, in which "we cannot stand aside."[39]

Developments in Central Europe soon made it more difficult to focus on Southeast Asia. The Kennedy-Khrushchev summit of early June devolved into a rancorous affair, foreshadowing a chilly summer between the superpowers. Discussions about Cuba, China, the fate of the two Germanys, "wars of national liberation," and the orientations of the rival camps were contentious and unproductive. While the protagonists shared a common desire to ensure Laotian neutrality—the only bright spot in their two-day meeting—the conference foundered over the status of Berlin. Repeating a pledge he had made since 1958, Khrushchev threatened to withdraw from the postwar occupation agreements and turn the sovereignty of East Berlin over to East Germany—a development with major implications for German unification and Cold War symbolism. Having taken his measure of Kennedy following the Bay of Pigs, Khrushchev was threatening to end western occupation rights by the end of the year. If he did so, Kennedy assured him, it would mean war.[40]

That high-stakes showdown provided the backdrop for continuing discussions about Vietnam. Precisely because the consequences of miscalculation seemed so great, Cold War tussles in locales such as Southeast Asia, where the impact of armed conflict was less immediately catastrophic, seemed more likely—and given the optics of disengaging from those battles—more necessary. Vietnam, therefore, became a touchstone of American will, a dynamic that governed much of Washington's misadventure in Vietnam. As Kennedy disclosed to columnist James Reston after the difficult talks in Vienna, the United States now had "a problem in making our power credible, and Vietnam is the place."[41] White House aides were equally convinced of the need to display resolve. "Few things would be better calculated to show Moscow and Peiping that we mean business," Komer argued, "than an obvious (if not yet definitive) turnaround in Vietnam." Such progress would go a long way toward reassuring America's allies in the Far East, "most of whom have been led by Laos to wonder whether we have the moxie to protect them any longer." Komer suggested a total effort, with the president "directing that all wraps are off" in supporting the GVN against the Communists. "After Laos, and with Berlin on the horizon," he believed, "we cannot afford to go less than all-out in cleaning up South Vietnam."[42] Rostow agreed, acknowledging a fear that the Vietnam and Berlin crises might peak together and that the war in Vietnam might get nastier.[43]

Berlin was the first to go. In an effort to stanch a brain drain that had brought the crisis to a head—tens of thousands were fleeing the German Democratic Republic through West Berlin every month—the Soviet Union and the GDR, beginning on August 13, stopped all traffic through the center of the city, ultimately formalizing its division in concrete. The Berlin Wall traumatized the Germans and darkened the prospects for East-West relations, but it alleviated a major concern of Communist officials who feared the implosion of their westernmost outpost. It also quieted Kennedy's nerves; as the president remarked, "a wall is a hell of a lot better than a war." Still, the symbolism was unmistakable. While a tacit admission of Communist defeat, the Wall represented the hardening of positions between East and West, and JFK's inability to do much about it. Kennedy responded by sending Vice President Johnson and an armed column of troops into West Berlin. That show of force, he hoped, would deliver the right message to the right audiences about American resolve.[44]

Similar concerns were animating U.S. policy in Southeast Asia, where symbolic actions joined with concrete ones as demonstrations of American firmness. Those gestures were increasingly necessary as Washington balked on funding an increase in ARVN strength without more clarity on how those troops were to be used. The financing ultimately came through, based on Ambassador Frederick E. Nolting's desire for a "political demonstration of full U.S. support at time when Lao situation poses most grave military and psychological threat to GVN."[45] By mid-July, Nolting would report that the Presidential Program, owing to its rhetorical and material contributions, was providing the necessary boost in morale. "First commandment of the task force report," he relayed, "to build confidence—was, in my judgment, soundly conceived, is being carried out, and is being reciprocated." While he found the "net security situation" no better than it was in May, the ambassador remained "optimistic."[46]

To bolster the psychological and security needs of the South Vietnamese, the administration augmented the program it established in May. Embracing the report of a subsequent fact-finding mission, the administration adopted its conclusions in mid-August and converted them into a "Joint Action Program" for South Vietnam. Henceforth, the United States would prioritize physical security over economic, political, and social reforms, though officials recognized that victory over the Communists depended upon success in each. Kennedy, in turn, sanctioned a further expansion of ARVN, agreeing to enlarge its numbers from 170,000 to 200,000 by the end of 1962. But he also called for benchmarks to guide its progress, including guidelines on how Diem would use those additional troops, joint agreement on a "geographically phased strategic plan" to end Communist subversion, a thorough evaluation and reformation of GVN planning for the war, and long-range planning in South Vietnam's civil, economic, and military sectors. Still, bolstering South Vietnamese morale remained a vital dimension of the effort. As had been the case with the earlier Presidential Program, the Joint Action Program was designed to achieve "an effective projection to the nation, its friends and its enemies, of our confidence in a long-range future for an independent Viet-Nam."[47]

Along with developing the material and psychological bases for defeating the NLF, the administration sought to wrap them in a more theoretical approach to unconventional conflict. Its efforts captured the fascination with this new mode of warfare and the need to align it with the demands of the era. Following the issuance of NSAM 2 on counterguerrilla capabilities, officials repeatedly emphasized the need to develop them with alacrity.[48] The administration's public statements spoke to those concerns as well. Walt Rostow delivered a pointed address on the subject at Ft. Bragg, North Carolina, home to the Special Forces and

Special Warfare School. Khrushchev's commitment to aiding "wars of liberation," Rostow charged, made it necessary to confront guerrilla warfare, the military arm of Soviet doctrine. The State Department's Roger Hilsman, who headed its Bureau of Intelligence and Research, also sounded the alarm. In an address at West Point, Hilsman called for transforming U.S. military training and capabilities, and for deeper U.S. involvement in "internal wars" and greater levels of military, police, and economic support for beleaguered governments.[49] Vietnam would come to serve as a "laboratory" for learning how to fight unconventional wars. Saigon became home to a "Combat Development and Test Center" that would develop new weapons and tactics, including novel uses for boats, planes, chemicals, and dogs, as well as new rifles, grenades, and bullets. Established by the Pentagon's Project AGILE, the center aimed to localize those conflicts as much as possible. Indeed, AGILE's director, William Godel, hoped those innovations would allow indigenous forces to fight their own wars and keep U.S. troops off the battlefield.[50]

Kennedy himself shifted resources to meet those emerging threats. He requested greater sums for military assistance and an expansion of funds for "nonnuclear war, para-military operations and sub-limited or unconventional wars."[51] Even when highlighting the increasingly parlous situation in Berlin, as he did in a special message that July, Kennedy drew attention to the troubles in Southeast Asia, "where the borders are less guarded, the enemy harder to find, and the dangers of communism less apparent to those who have so little." He thus called for accelerating the defense upgrades he requested in March and May, and for the ability "to meet all levels of aggressor pressure with whatever levels of force are required"—options necessary to provide "a wider choice than humiliation or all-out nuclear action." Over three billion dollars in additional appropriations would augment nonnuclear capabilities, increase troop strength, double and even triple the draft calls, activate reserve units and extend tours of duty, and boost spending for civil defense. Those burdens and others had to be borne "if freedom is to be defended," a freedom that ran through developing nations as much as it did through Berlin.[52]

In the wake of that dire warning, officials responsible for Southeast Asia were imploring Kennedy to commit to Vietnam more decisively. John Steeves, the deputy assistant secretary of state for Far Eastern Affairs and director of a new Southeast Asia Task Force, urged the president to "make the basic decision now to resist [Communist] encroachment by appropriate military means, if necessary, with or without unanimous SEATO support." NSC staffer Robert H. Johnson likewise told Kennedy that planning for Vietnam could move forward more effectively if the president "would at some future time have a willingness to decide to intervene if the situation seemed to him to require it." Kennedy would neither decide to decide, nor was he inclined to intervene militarily in Laos, as many had recommended.[53] Aides recognized his preference for diplomacy over troops and for local forces to carry the brunt of the fighting should overt war break out.[54] But American servicemen were already finding their way into combat, even if U.S. officials were frustrated by Saigon's reluctance to introduce them formally.[55] Within weeks, U.S. military advisers were engaging in hostilities and regularly accompanying the ARVN on operations at the battalion and company levels, a departure from previous guidance that proscribed them from doing so.[56]

Those dynamics changed as summer turned to fall. On September 18, over 1,000 Vietnamese Communists stormed Phuoc Vinh, the capital of Phuoc Thanh province, sixty miles north of Saigon. It was the second major PLAF attack in a month and the largest such assault to date, marking the first time a provincial capital in South Vietnam had fallen to the NLF. Its demise sent shock waves through Saigon that reverberated in Washington. *Time* magazine, the nation's premier newsweekly, reported on the assault in ominous tones. With over forty members of the Civil Guard killed in their sleep and another thirty-five wounded, U.S. officials feared the operation "may well be the signal for a new Red drive against South Viet Nam, part of an over-all, constant movement to infiltrate and encircle the whole area." The implications were dire: should Diem's pro-Western government fall, "Cambodia, Thailand, Burma and Malaya will have little chance of staying free."[57] The dominoes were thus ripe for toppling.

From Assistance to Partnership

The assault on Phuoc Vinh changed the relationship between the United States and South Vietnam. Sparking weeks of fevered deliberations about Saigon and its significance to U.S. national security, the attack ultimately led Washington to alter its advisory role and greatly expand its assistance. That shift stemmed from geostrategic and regional considerations about dominoes, credibility, morale, and the strength of the U.S. commitment. Central to those concerns were the signals Washington sent to South Vietnam and the peoples of Southeast Asia. At root, they rested on America's ability to embolden the GVN and its people to win their war against the Communists.

Pervading those discussions was a sense of crisis shared by U.S. and South Vietnamese officials. Ambassador Nolting and MAAG chief McGarr thought Saigon ill-prepared to deal with the uptick in Communist violence likely to come after the rainy season and that the American position in Southeast Asia was now at stake. With Diem fearing the imminence of a massive invasion by North Vietnam, the U.S. Country Team, encompassing the entirety of Washington's presence in South Vietnam, recommended immediate implementation of plans to preposition military forces in the region.[58] Saigon and Washington were so concerned about what lay ahead that both reached for measures that had long been off the table. Owing to his "deep fear" that a neutralized Laos would be incapable of halting infiltration from North Vietnam, Diem asked for a bilateral treaty with the United States.[59] Kennedy officials, for their part, reconsidered the merits of deploying U.S. troops to South Vietnam, seizing the opportunity to promote measures many had long wanted to carry out.[60]

By the first week of October, the crisis atmosphere enveloping South Vietnam had breached the Oval Office. The situation in Southeast Asia was "genuinely coming to a head," observed McGeorge Bundy, "and I myself am now persuaded that we must promptly find a way of acting much more vigorously in South Viet-nam." So, too, was Bundy's deputy, Walt Rostow, who was prone to even more panicky views and recommendations. The situation was "actively deteriorating," Rostow said, but "if we go in now, the costs—human and otherwise—are likely to be less than if we wait."[61] The Pentagon was also sounding the tocsin. William P. Bundy, McGeorge's brother and the deputy assistant secretary of defense for International Security Affairs, thought it was "really now or never" if Diem was to be saved, and recommended "an early and hard-hitting operation" to arrest Communist gains.[62] Indeed, developments in Vietnam were so serious that the Joint Chiefs warned against subordinating them to the manifest dangers of Berlin. They advocated strenuously for the use of military force—even with the situation in Laos entangled in delicate diplomacy—and called for U.S. and SEATO troops to move into South Vietnam, a recommendation supported by Secretary of Defense Robert S. McNamara.[63]

The sense of crisis was so acute that Kennedy began an October 11 press conference by noting that Gen. Maxwell D. Taylor, the president's military representative, would soon visit Vietnam to consider how the United States could assist Saigon in "meeting this threat to its independence." Responding to a reporter's question about the conditions under which he might deploy U.S. troops to Southeast Asia, Kennedy said he would await Taylor's return before adopting a specific course of action.[64] But public speculation about a troop deployment was rampant. Journalists quoted U.S. and Vietnamese officials describing the conflict as "a real war," a situation "so menacing," according to the *New York Times,* that Kennedy was considering "the dispatch of American combat units" to Vietnam. Columnist Joseph Alsop, an influential voice on foreign affairs, was himself lobbying for a troop deployment, claiming that "nearly as much is at stake in Southeast Asia as at Berlin."[65] In fact, reports of a possible troop deployment had become so frequent that Nolting requested immediate guidance on whether Washington was actually considering the dispatch of American forces to South Vietnam.[66]

Diem had made such guidance essential. Although he previously called for a bilateral defense treaty, he had remained firm in dismissing the need for U.S. combat forces. Now, in the aftermath of the Taylor trip announcement, Diem welcomed their use in Vietnam. His hope was that their presence would allow the RVNAF to occupy positions in provincial capitals and provide "symbolic" strength at the 17th parallel. Delivering the news to Washington, Nolting wrote that officials should give "serious and prompt consideration" to Diem's request.[67]

Such talk startled President Kennedy, who sought to counteract speculation about a troop announcement. He complained to NSC officials about the public focus on troops and worried about "a tremendous letdown in Vietnamese morale if they expected such action and we decided otherwise." In fact, his opposition to sending troops was well-known and appeared prominently in the press—including through his own unattributed leaks to journalists.[68] Kennedy therefore sought to reshape the purpose of Taylor's trip to diminish enthusiasm for a troop deployment. While his initial guidance referenced "the introduction of SEATO or United States forces into South Vietnam," his final instructions omitted that clause. Instead, Kennedy asked Taylor for his views "on the courses of action" the United States might take "to avoid a further deterioration in the situation in South Viet-Nam and eventually to contain and eliminate the threat to its independence." Primary responsibility for eliminating that threat, Kennedy stressed, lay with "the people and government of that country," and both U.S. efforts and Taylor's recommendations needed to be formulated "with this fact in mind."[69]

Support for Kennedy's more circumspect position came from military as well as civilian officials. Adm. Harry D. Felt, the commander of U.S. forces in the Pacific and the nominal authority for operations in Vietnam, opposed the introduction of American troops. The longer they stayed in South Vietnam, the more likely they would become engaged in combat; it was unwise, therefore, to introduce them "until we have exhausted other means for helping Diem."[70] Detractors also included Under Secretary of State Chester Bowles, who regarded Southeast Asia as an area inhospitable to the use of military force.[71] U.S. Ambassador to India John Kenneth Galbraith likewise frowned on the emerging policy, admitting to Kennedy that he found the situation in Southeast Asia more troubling than that of Berlin.[72] Journalist Theodore White, a longtime student of Asian affairs who had chronicled the 1960 presidential race, was also discouraged by the looming American commitment. Diem was a "political incompetent," White wrote Kennedy, and "any investment of our troops in the paddies of the delta will, I believe, be useless—or worse."[73]

But voices opposing a troop deployment were, for the most part, less well positioned to shape policy than those supporting it. Official comment, moreover—from the Pentagon, the State Department, and NSC officials at the White House—leaned heavily toward the use of American military units. The symbolism of U.S. forces entering the fray, even in noncombat capacities, was especially potent. Their sheer presence, many believed, would help reverse the decline in South Vietnamese morale that tracked with deteriorating conditions. Several troubling developments, Nolting relayed, had alarmed the GVN and argued for that commitment, including Washington's failure to consult with Saigon in advance of Taylor's mission; its inability to come up with a specific aid figure for economic assistance; fear that a neutral Laos would facilitate further North Vietnamese infiltration; and the State Department's outright dismissal of talk about dispatching U.S. forces. A decision to make good on that deployment, therefore, would give Saigon a badly needed shot of confidence.[74]

Taylor and Diem considered the merits of that approach during the envoy's trip to Vietnam, which began on October 18. The situation in Laos was the root of the problem, Diem maintained, but the presence of SEATO or U.S. troops could reverse the collapse in morale.[75] Diem also conveyed that sentiment to Senator Stuart Symington [D-MO], who happened to be in Saigon at the time of Taylor's visit. Troops were vital, Symington relayed, but the South Vietnamese were equally "worried" about the absence of a formal U.S. commitment to Saigon; without it, Diem feared that Washington might abandon the GVN and withdraw its forces if the situation deteriorated. No need for concern, Symington countered: once troops were deployed and the commitment made, "no responsible member of Congress would rise to ask that to back down."[76] Left unsaid was whether a sitting president might do so.

Yet even as Kennedy stressed both publicly and privately that South Vietnam needed to win its own fight, officials in the White House, the State Department, and the Pentagon continued to advocate and plan for U.S. military action. Walt Rostow leaned toward "limited but systematic harassment" of North Vietnam by U.S. air and naval forces.[77] Defense officials considered deploying a combat unit or engineer battalion to train the RVNAF.[78] Nolting floated the stationing of U.S. troops near the 17th parallel, as well as in the high plateau near the Laotian border, to free up South Vietnamese forces. Even Ambassador-at-Large Averell Harriman, who had dismissed the value of positioning troops in Laos, supported their use in Vietnam, believing the logistics more favorable and the country "of enormous political, strategic and economic importance."[79] Officials closest to the center of policymaking were thus the most supportive of deploying U.S. forces to Vietnam.

For those still on the fence, the recent flooding of the Mekong River allowed them to side with the hawks. The deluge, which the *New York Times* described as "one of the most grievous natural catastrophes" in the country's history, destroyed over 200,000 homes, left 500,000 people hungry, and consigned another million people to "rock-bottom poverty," killing the pigs and poultry in three local provinces and wiping out surplus rice stocks for the coming year.[80] To U.S. officials, the prospect of American troops aiding the displaced and disadvantaged seemed too good to be true. Nolting urgently sought to explore the "feasibility" of a flood relief operation to introduce U.S. military units for humanitarian purposes "which might be kept if necessary."[81] McGarr thought likewise and indicated that those forces could remain "if desirable" and could be withdrawn later if it made sense to do so.[82] Even Felt came around to the idea, as he believed that flood relief mitigated his earlier concerns about a troop deployment.[83]

Although arguments for a military presence now seemed more compelling, several aides—including those supportive of it—thought it inadvisable to deploy forces without a clear-eyed understanding of the implications. Chalmers B. "Ben" Wood, the Vietnam desk officer in the State Department's Bureau of Far Eastern Affairs, stressed the need for advance decisions to "send in enough troops to finish the job" if necessary, or to "fix a ceiling (say 100,000) on the number of U.S. troops which we would commit to Southeast Asia no matter what circumstances might arise."[84] The NSC's Robert Johnson also urged the administration to weigh the consequences of a troop commitment "and decide in principle the question of whether we are prepared, if necessary, to step up very considerably our military commitment in Viet Nam." If Washington deployed that first contingent of troops only to pull them out "when the going got rough," the United States would "be finished in Viet Nam and probably in all of Southeast Asia."[85] It was a point he returned to frequently and one shared by senior officials at the State and Defense Departments, including Robert McNamara.[86]

None of those worries were lost on Taylor. Having completed his Vietnam tour on October 24, he warned Kennedy about the significance of the deployment he would soon recommend. "If the first contingent is not enough to accomplish the necessary results," he cautioned, "it will be difficult to resist the pressure to reinforce." There would be "no limit to our possible commitment" if the ultimate objective were to seal the country's borders and eliminate the Communist insurgents, save for attacking their "source" in Hanoi. The presence of U.S. troops might even heighten tensions and spark a wider regional war.[87] But those forces could be withdrawn after providing flood relief or phased "into other activities if we wish to remain longer."[88] The bottom line was that the situation in South Vietnam was critical, a condition exacerbated by PLAF success and Western policy toward Laos. Along with the flood, those conditions "combined to create a deep and pervasive crisis of confidence and a serious loss in national morale."[89]

Taylor therefore concluded, as did senior U.S. officials, Vietnamese observers, and Diem himself, that nothing would convince South Vietnam of Washington's "seriousness of purpose," and therefore be sufficiently reassuring to its government and people, as much as the introduction of American troops.[90] Their arrival would counter the "double crisis in confidence" that plagued not only the South Vietnamese but all peoples in the region: doubt that the United States was "determined to save Southeast Asia," and doubt that Diem was capable of defeating the Communists. American measures, Taylor told Kennedy, "will be decisive to the end result." He therefore recommended the deployment of a military task force to raise South Vietnamese morale and convey the gravity of U.S. intentions.[91]

News of Taylor's impending recommendation created a stir in Washington, prompting the White House to keep it under wraps. The president was "most concerned," as McGeorge Bundy put it, that Kennedy and Taylor be on "firm common ground" in arriving at a decision, as rumors of Taylor's conclusions "could obviously be damaging."[92] Speculation about the use of American troops had disturbed several officials, including Senate Majority Leader Mike Mansfield [D-MT], who feared a deployment "could become quicksand for us." Mansfield was supportive of providing additional military and economic aid to the GVN, but only so Saigon could handle the fighting itself. He advised taking every precaution "to avoid another Korean-type involvement on the Asian mainland."[93] Rusk, too, worried that a deployment would tie Washington's fate to Ngo Dinh Diem. "While attaching greatest possible importance to security in Southeast Asia, I would be reluctant [to] see US make major additional commitment [of] American prestige to a losing horse."[94] Sterling J. Cottrell, who directed the interdepartmental Vietnam Task Force, voiced similar concerns, believing it was far from clear that Saigon could defeat the insurgency even with U.S. military support. He thought "it would be a mistake for the U.S. to commit itself irrevocably to the defeat of the Communists in SVN." And since division-sized units could not be deployed effectively in South Vietnam, "they should not be introduced at this stage, despite the short range favorable psychological lift it would give the GVN."[95]

The biggest skeptic, and the one with the greatest personal access to JFK, was Ken Galbraith. He and Kennedy had maintained a running dialogue about Vietnam since early that spring, with the ambassador writing the president no less than six memos on the subject and engaging him in direct conversation during return visits to the United States. Galbraith happened to be in Washington upon Taylor's arrival home in early November and finagled his way into seeing a copy of the trip report, which confirmed his fears about the direction of U.S. policy. Kennedy was unaware Galbraith had purloined a copy of the study, but he asked for the ambassador's thoughts nonetheless. Galbraith subsequently encouraged the president to internationalize the conflict, seek the aid of neutral India, and reorganize American representation in Saigon, arguments Kennedy also heard from Under Secretary Bowles.[96]

By the time that Galbraith had shared his counsel on November 3, Taylor had formally submitted his report to the president, along with a cover letter conveying guarded optimism about U.S. objectives. There was no need for "fatalism," Taylor maintained, nor resignation that Southeast Asia would "inevitably fall into Communist hands." But the time for action was now, as Moscow's "wars of liberation" were well on their way to success.[97] To counter Saigon's "double crisis of confidence," Taylor recommended a "U.S. military presence capable of raising national morale" and demonstrating Washington's seriousness in resisting a Communist takeover. It should take the form of a military task force, comprising roughly 8,000 troops to conduct logistical operations in support of flood relief, as well as combat operations necessary for self-defense and area security.[98] Beyond the tactical deployment of those forces, Taylor urged that the United States change its strategic relationship with South Vietnam, transforming it from an assistance and advisory mission into a "limited partnership." That commitment, while essential, would nevertheless demand national resolve. He advocated against undertaking it "unless we are prepared to deal with any escalation the communists might choose to impose," up to the nuclear threshold. Once again, Kennedy's advisers were asking the president to confront the prospect of military escalation with his eyes wide open.[99]

Taylor did more than call for the insertion of U.S. forces, as his proposal covered a wide range of administrative, economic, intelligence, and military matters. But his troop recommendation highlighted grave concerns about South Vietnamese morale and the credibility of the U.S. commitment. Civilian and military officials lobbied for those forces, even on a massive scale. The Joint Chiefs doubted that 8,000 troops could effectively preserve South Vietnam's independence, and wanted to treat those forces as the first installment of successively larger increments.[100] Secretaries McNamara and Rusk speculated that their numbers could rise exponentially; if the U.S. deployment provoked a corresponding intervention by Hanoi and Beijing, then Washington needed to face the prospect of committing roughly six divisions, or 205,000 troops, to battle.[101] Figures such as those terrified Under Secretary of State for Economic Affairs George W. Ball, who worried that an initial deployment might ultimately result in 300,000 Americans descending upon the jungles of Southeast Asia. Not to worry, the president assured him, "that just isn't going to happen."[102] Whether Kennedy thought a troop deployment of that magnitude would not take place on his watch or whether it was simply inconceivable in any event is unclear.

More evident was the president's instinctive aversion to sending U.S. soldiers to South Vietnam. Kennedy was firmly opposed to a troop deployment, writes Arthur Schlesinger, as he feared it would become a bottomless pit. It would be "just like Berlin," Kennedy said. "The troops will march in; the bands will play; the crowd will cheer; and in four days everyone will have forgotten. Then we will be told we have to send in more troops. It's like taking a drink. The effect wears off, and you have to take another." The only recourse, Kennedy believed, was for South Vietnam to fight its own battles.[103]

But to many top U.S. officials, Saigon's battles *were* Washington's battles, and winning them depended upon communicating the depth of America's commitment to audiences at home and abroad. McNamara, Rusk, and the Joint Chiefs were categorical about the need to signal that resolve and indicated as such in a series of memos to the president. Given that the deployment of 8,000 troops would likely elicit a Communist response and mire greater numbers of American forces "in an inconclusive struggle," Washington needed to convey the sanctity of its word to forestall any potential quagmire. It was the promise itself that mattered, wrote McNamara, and only by accompanying the troop deployments with "a clear commitment to the full objective" of securing Saigon's independence was the administration likely to convince the Communists that "we mean business." Although the approach risked incurring domestic political blowback, McNamara thought the nation would respond "better to a firm initial position than to courses of action that lead us in only gradually, and that in the meantime are sure to involve casualties."[104]

A genuine intention to intervene, and more than just a promise to do so, was therefore crucial. The loss of South Vietnam, senior officials believed, would activate domino dynamics and force Southeast Asia and Indonesia into accommodation with the Communists, even perhaps their formal integration into the bloc itself; moreover, it would undermine U.S. credibility worldwide and fuel a bitter and divisive domestic controversy. The United States, therefore, "should commit itself to the clear objective of preventing the fall of South Viet-Nam to Communism." Saigon should bear the primary burden of managing its own defense, but Washington should be prepared to introduce combat troops if "necessary for success," recognizing that the current rationale for inserting forces should be to improve the morale of the South Vietnamese.[105]

President Kennedy finally addressed those proposals in a November 11 meeting that dramatized his reservations about the Taylor Report and the papers it prompted. He would neither deploy forces to South Vietnam nor make a categorical commitment to save it from Communist rule. "Troops are a last resort," he said, making clear his worry about congressional blowback were he to commit armed units to the struggle. If any outside troops should be introduced, they should come from SEATO. Attorney General Robert F. Kennedy was even more adamant about rejecting the use of American soldiers. "We are not sending combat troops," he stated flatly, nor "committing ourselves to combat troops." McNamara and JCS chair Lemnitzer pushed back on the no troops pledge, maintaining that the Taylor recommendations "will not by themselves solve this problem and that further action will be required."[106]

The president would have none of it. After first indicating his reluctance even to decide whether to make a firm commitment to Saigon, he later came down more firmly on the matter: he would "not accept" the commitment clause McNamara and Rusk had proposed, which tied the United States to "preventing the fall of South Viet-Nam to Communism," and which recognized that doing so might necessitate the use of U.S. and SEATO forces. Although he was prepared to approve Taylor's other recommendations, including the provision of air lift and reconnaissance, economic aid, and the expedited training of security forces, he simply would not commit the United States to the preservation of an independent, non-Communist South Vietnam.[107]

Kennedy's rationale for rejecting the commitment clause likely stemmed from his own assessment of the Vietnamese tangle as well as from concerns raised by aides and knowledgeable observers. The French experience in the 1940s and 1950s—which he condemned at the time—likely haunted him, both in what it said about militarizing a political struggle and fighting a limited conflict in Asia. The latter concern, which Gen. Douglas MacArthur had raised with him earlier that year, resonated with JFK, as did similar warnings from Mansfield, among others. Although Kennedy was prepared to support the GVN in halting the spread of communism in Southeast Asia—indeed, doing so was politically necessary at home and abroad—he was unwilling to make its preservation a vital interest of the United States. Advisory troops would deploy to assist the South Vietnamese, but combat troops would not intervene and Americanize the war.[108]

Almost immediately, though, senior officials began to misrepresent the president's position. It was not the first time they had done so, as several had stretched the meaning of Kennedy's commitment in the wake of the May decisions. Rusk, for instance, did not "visualize" sending combat forces to Vietnam, but a troop deployment "may become necessary later," as he suggested to French ambassador Hervé Alphand, or "some weeks hence," as he put it to British ambassador David Ormsby-Gore.[109] That message likely alarmed his counterparts, as neither the British nor the French regarded a U.S. troop deployment as wise; not only was this a war the South Vietnamese had to win themselves, but Saigon was far less vital to Western interests than Washington claimed.[110] It was a posture they would maintain throughout the Kennedy years, though de Gaulle would ultimately express his reservations more publicly and stridently than U.K. prime minister Harold Macmillan.

British and French sentiments had little bearing on Washington, however, as Rusk delivered a similar message to Nolting. Although the United States would not introduce combat troops at the present time, it might do so later if infiltration from North Vietnam continued unabated. In fact, the Pentagon would plan for a deployment, even as the objective of U.S. policy was to support the GVN with all means short of combat troops.[111] McNamara saw to it that such aid made its way to South Vietnam posthaste. Not waiting for a formal NSAM on the matter, he sought to implement the military assistance measures and the prepositioning of troops Kennedy had already endorsed, declaring that those actions "should be carried forward with all possible speed."[112]

Amid those exchanges, Galbraith continued to provide Kennedy with a contrarian view. The two had talked about the Taylor report and its implications repeatedly over the previous week, and Kennedy was keen to receive a fresh assessment. Galbraith's memo reached Kennedy while the ambassador was returning to Asia—on his way to Saigon, in fact, where he would update Kennedy en route to Delhi. Noting the difficulties of relying on Diem, Galbraith questioned the report's basic assumptions, troubling passages, and contradictory claims.[113]

Galbraith's interventions worried and angered several administration officials, many of whom sought to counter his influence with the president.[114] With Taylor having requested a follow-up meeting on Vietnam— ostensibly to move Kennedy off his no troops and no commitment pledges—aides acted quickly to hammer out their strategy and arguments.[115] The NSC's Rostow and Johnson feared "losing a strategic moment" for introducing U.S. troops, and Rostow assured JFK that conditions in Vietnam were better than those Galbraith described. Johnson acknowledged Kennedy's concerns, but thought it essential they should at least "decide now on the key question of whether we are prepared to introduce combat troops if necessary even if we are not going to introduce them now. That is obviously the ultimate test of whether we are prepared to prevent the fall of Viet Nam." If so, then they should communicate that understanding to Diem.[116] Rusk was already moving in that direction. Writing to Nolting prior to an NSC meeting slated for November 15, he sketched out the expanded program Kennedy was willing to endorse. Nolting was to inform Diem that the United States was "prepared to join the Government of Viet-Nam in a sharply increased joint effort to avoid a further deterioration in the situation in South Viet-Nam and eventually to contain and eliminate the threat to its independence." As for Diem's interest in U.S. troops, Rusk instructed Nolting to remind the GVN that "a substantial number of U.S. military personnel" would be on the way and that those troops would enhance Saigon's capacity to defeat the Communists.[117]

Kennedy approached the upcoming NSC session with the knowledge that key aides were troubled by his reluctance to make the major decisions they deemed necessary. Rostow captured their impatience in a note to Kennedy prior to the meeting. Resistance to a troop deployment, on top of negotiations to achieve a neutralized Laos, would induce "real panic and disarray," resulting in a "major crisis of nerve in Viet-Nam and throughout Southeast Asia." He thought Washington's actions in the Cold War demonstrated clearly that resolve and commitment served U.S. interests. But "if we act indecisively now, I fear we shall produce excessive fears on our side and excessive hopes on the other side," sentiments that might lead them to overreact to a deteriorating situation and heighten the danger of war.[118] Bundy, too, thought it time to give the president his frank advice. Like others, he recommended the dispatch of U.S. troops to Vietnam, but he wanted them to engage in combat and not just serve the symbolic function of raising morale. Most essential, though, was that Kennedy, and by extension the entire administration, acknowledge the significance of such a commitment prior to making it. Without that commitment, the entire program would be "half-hearted"; with it, the administration might not even need to carry it out—a belief also shared by McNamara, Rusk, Taylor, Rostow, and Vice President Johnson. Kennedy's reluctance to make that decision thus unsettled Bundy. Not only did key officials endorse it, he said, but the troop decision had "now become a sort of touchstone of our will."[119]

Those conversations and interventions came to a head on the morning of Wednesday, November 15. Signaling his discomfort with America's deepening engagement, Kennedy "expressed the fear of becoming involved simultaneously on two fronts on opposite sides of the world" and questioned the wisdom of escalating in Vietnam. Given the lack of clear aggression across the 17th parallel, as had been the case a decade earlier when North Korea drove south across the 38th, the support of allies would be even more important to avoid international criticism and domestic controversy. As for articulating a U.S. commitment to Saigon, Kennedy firmly rejected any pledge comparable to the one he had made regarding Berlin. Instead, he focused the discussion on what the United States would do now, rather than on whether Washington would become more deeply involved in the future. It would not be the last time the administration, and particularly the president, refused to confront the implications of the choices before them.[120]

Discussion about the precise course of action continued to percolate throughout the day and over the next week, though it seemed clear the administration would substantially augment its existing program. Officials persisted in lobbying for a firm commitment to South Vietnamese freedom and for the need to signal that commitment in unmistakable terms. Rusk, for instance, understood the risks involved and the prospects for success, but thought it essential to proceed, as Bundy told the president: "we *must* try to hold and must show determination to all concerned." The Secretary even suggested labeling the effort "a Rusk-McNamara Plan" and firing all involved if it failed to work out. It was vital that the United States "meet Khrushchev in Vietnam or take a terrible defeat."[121]

Galbraith again dissented. Writing to Kennedy on November 20, he remained dubious of the emerging program. Absent real reform within the GVN, which he thought unlikely, "the help we are now proposing will not save the situation."[122] Since U.S. troops "will not deal with fundamental faults" and provide sufficient security, those failures "could create a worse crisis of confidence" than the one they were being called upon to address. The "bright promise" of the New Frontier, Galbraith warned, was in danger of "being sunk under the rice fields."[123] As before, administration officials mobilized to neutralize him. Rusk discouraged Galbraith from meeting with a North Vietnamese representative visiting India, fearing it might result in the optics of a flagging American commitment, and Rostow told JFK that "the New Frontier will be measured in history" by how the United States met the challenge in Vietnam.[124] Their interventions likely had little impact on the president. Although Kennedy took Galbraith's memos with him to Hyannis Port over Thanksgiving weekend, he had already sanctioned the release of NSAM 111, codifying the administration's new approach to Vietnam.[125]

But a new policy required the right personnel to carry it out, and Kennedy was uncomfortable with the present alignment of people to program. The administration thus engaged in a "game of musical chairs," as Bundy put it, so the president could rely on officials "wholly responsive" to his desires. Averell Harriman replaced Walter McConaughy atop the State Department's Bureau of Far Eastern Affairs; George Ball took over for Chester Bowles as number two at State; Bowles assumed Harriman's post as roving ambassador; George McGhee left State's Policy Planning Staff to become under secretary of state for Political Affairs; and Walt Rostow moved from the NSC into McGhee's former slot as head of Policy Planning.[126] Dubbed the "Thanksgiving Massacre," the changes—which Kennedy endorsed with more than just Vietnam in mind—sidelined those officials deemed insufficiently loyal, unsupportive of his policies, or impolitic in their recommendations.

Implementing NSAM 111

As they formalized their expanded program, officials recognized that the influx of men and matériel would conflict with the limits Geneva placed on foreign troops in Vietnam. Washington had not signed the Accords, but it had pledged to observe them. Saigon had not signed them, either, though Abram J. Chayes, the legal adviser in the State Department, thought the GVN was bound by them nonetheless; since the French had signed on behalf of the French Union, which encompassed the State of Vietnam, Saigon was obligated to respect the limits on foreign forces.[127] But the United States was already dispatching assets to Vietnam in contravention of Geneva restrictions—actions it took prior to NSAM 111, even prior to the Taylor Mission. In mid-October, Kennedy had authorized the deployment of a "Jungle Jim" Air Force squadron to train the South Vietnamese in air-ground combat maneuvers.[128] By later that month, 86 of the additional 100 MAAG trainers Kennedy had authorized in April had arrived in South Vietnam, and scheduled deployments would bring the total MAAG force to 1,558.[129] With further deployments of air and helicopter support coming online, U.S. forces would soon rise to roughly 2,500.[130]

But Nolting remained concerned about Geneva, since it would be difficult to absorb those arrivals in a covert fashion. It was "urgent," he cabled home, that Washington decide on the embassy's preferred approach of "being more direct and forthright" about the larger numbers of U.S. troops in South Vietnam.[131] Ultimately, the Department passed along guidance that emphasized its determination to aid Saigon and help preserve its independence. It would make no admission of flouting the accords, even as it accused Hanoi of doing so through a State Department "White Paper." Compiled by William J. Jorden and released on December 8, the paper charged Hanoi with repeatedly violating Geneva by launching aggressive measures designed to swallow all of Vietnam. Hanoi's action thus absolved the United States from adherence to the accords, granting Saigon every right to ask Washington for assistance, per SEATO protocols. Kennedy and Diem exchanged letters to that effect in December.[132]

Against the backdrop of those diplomatic formalities, the Kennedy administration implemented the program it hashed out over the previous month. The interagency process coordinated its elements in Washington, while military and civilian officials handled more operational matters at Pacific Command headquarters in Honolulu. A series of "SecDef" meetings, convened by Robert McNamara, would take place once a month until at least March, so that the commander-in-chief Pacific (CINCPAC), key aides, and the U.S. Country Team in Saigon could confer with their counterparts based in the United States. As McNamara announced in December at the first such gathering, the task was to ascertain how the United States could improve the situation in South Vietnam and mobilize the resources to do the job. The group had great latitude, he explained, with the president insisting on one important caveat: "combat troops will not be introduced."[133] It was a stricture officials repeatedly hammered home. With McNamara and Lemnitzer injecting a sense of urgency to the proceedings—they wanted "concrete action that would begin to show results in 30 days"—they informed attendees that "we could have practically anything we wanted short of combat troops." The objective, McNamara said, was "to win in South Vietnam, and if we weren't winning to tell him what was needed to win."[134] Although barely articulated at the time, "winning" seemed to mean, at the very least, a reduction in the Communist military and political challenge to proportions the RVNAF and GVN could handle on their own.

Integral to that goal, therefore, was better performance from the South Vietnamese. Frustrations with the Diem government were longstanding, but they now grew in proportion to the expanded U.S. commitment. Lemnitzer acknowledged that Diem was proving difficult to work with and that "under such circumstances even U.S. combat troops could not solve his problem." McNamara, too, worried that Diem was "going to continue to be Diem," but "since he is all that we have, we must work with him."[135] The feeling was mutual, as the GVN made clear in the wake of the Taylor mission.[136] Discussions about Laos and neutralization continued to circulate in Saigon, leading the South Vietnamese to question the seriousness of the U.S. commitment—ominous signals from a government fearful of American betrayal. Ngo Dinh Nhu, Diem's brother and political counselor, went so far as to tell province chiefs that they would have to assume the burden of defending the country, as the Americans could "not be trusted over the long pull."[137] Those sentiments were commonplace in South Vietnamese circles and augured poorly for the limited partnership. By the middle of December, though, the U.S. embassy reported that "Anti-American themes" had largely disappeared in the local press, "reflecting apparent reestablishment [of] close working relationships between U.S. and GVN."[138] The signs were worrisome, nonetheless.

President Kennedy said little publicly about Vietnam in the weeks following NSAM 111. Given the changes he set in motion, his low-key approach to the conflict, which he sought to preserve throughout his term in office, reflected a keen interest in controlling the narrative. It would be a constant struggle, as the pressure to escalate—manifest during the spring discussions of Vietnam and Laos, as well as in the fall deliberations following the Taylor mission—ran counter to his instincts. Aides recognized the president's reluctance to talk about Vietnam, but there were dangers, too, in allowing others to define his program. Ted Sorensen, who as Kennedy's counselor had been with him longer than any White House official, urged the president to grab the mantle. He suggested a major speech on Laos and Vietnam to address the "wildly inaccurate speculation" about U.S. activities in Southeast Asia—actions that many feared could lead to another Korean War, with undesirable implications for American life and the Democratic Party. The president might even restate the themes he had emphasized in a mid-November address, highlighting the limits of American power. The United States, JFK said at the University of Washington, was "neither omnipotent or omniscient," nor could it "right every wrong or reverse each adversity." It was a sober statement of caution and restraint, one in contrast to the more dramatic rhetoric of Kennedy's inaugural. But it was no less emblematic of the president's impulses. Sorensen thought he should now stake out a comparable position on Vietnam.[139]

Kennedy chose not to do so. The farthest he went was to acknowledge the challenge of working with Diem, his administration's interest in GVN reforms, and the "discussion and controversy" those conversations had engendered.[140] It was not the only statement he made on the subject—the administration released letters from Kennedy and Diem acknowledging their joint partnership—but an exchange with journalists captured the tensions at work in the assistance effort.[141] Those involved ongoing friction with Diem over his autocratic leadership and his management of the counterinsurgency, but also clashes within Kennedy's administration over the shape and nature of the U.S. commitment.

At the center of those disputes was the disposition of American troops. Kennedy repeatedly rebuffed calls for their deployment and opposed their use in combat. While he sanctioned the introduction of military advisers for training and instruction, it was a far cry from what his senior advisers had recommended. Rather than Americanize the war, his administration sought to empower Saigon to fight it better on their own. Doing so would involve greater displays of Washington's resolve to convey the depth and breadth of the American commitment. Those measures included tangible assets that enabled Diem to conduct the counterinsurgency more effectively. But of signal importance was their symbolic content—the messages they conveyed about the U.S. commitment, and the impact of that commitment on Saigon's fighting morale.

2

Escalation

January 1962–June 1962

It had been a momentous first year on the New Frontier, full of the energy and activism JFK had promised as both candidate and president. The country had ventured into space and pledged to go to the Moon. It had extended a hand to the developing world, raised the minimum wage, and turned the White House into a cultural emporium. It was charting a course, as Kennedy foretold in his inaugural, toward "a more fruitful life for all mankind." But other developments, particularly in Cuba, Vienna, and Berlin, were cause for serious concern. So was the violence attending the Freedom Rides in the American South, which revealed the urgent need for social justice and the administration's halting pursuit of it. Collectively, those "disasters," as Kennedy described them, recalled the warnings he sounded early in his term, full of disturbing imagery and apocalyptic rhetoric.[1]

Kennedy thus used his first official State of the Union address to take stock of the past, reassess the present, and prepare for the battles ahead. Appearing before a joint session of Congress on January 11, 1962, Kennedy spoke to the providential mission of the United States. In so doing, he dispensed with the cautionary rhetoric of his Seattle address and returned to the dramatic cast of his inaugural. This nation, he intoned, "is commissioned by history to be either an observer of freedom's failure or the cause of its success." His actions in Southeast Asia would reflect that missionary impulse, as the preservation of South Vietnamese independence had become a more pressing concern of national policy. In conjunction with the GVN, Washington had "stepped up" its effort to combat the Communist "war of attempted subjection," an aggression, Kennedy pledged, that "will be resisted."[2]

But dissent about the mechanics, nature, and extent of that resistance—particularly from Congress—emerged just as Washington was expanding its advisory presence. During a closed session of the Senate Foreign Relations Committee (SFRC), Senator Wayne D. Morse [D-OR], who would become one of the war's most strident and consistent critics, warned that unilateral military action in Vietnam could hurt the administration. Morse's colleagues also wondered about Kennedy's program, asking Ambassador Frederick E. Nolting about the war's time horizon, the number of U.S. servicemen involved, and the administration's commitment to South Vietnamese freedom. The struggle was shaping up to be "a long, drawn-out, hard campaign," Nolting replied, and likely to take "five years or more." Averell Harriman, the newly minted chief of the State Department's Far Eastern division, compared the war to the one Britain had waged against Communists in Malaya. While it might not last the eight years it took London to win that fight, it nevertheless would be "a long, long pull." That message seemed to be getting through to lawmakers.[3] According to British diplomats in Saigon, Nolting was "surprised and pleased to discover a growing realization in the United States that the war would be a long one and that quick victories were not to be expected."[4]

Those sentiments also held sway throughout the U.S. defense establishment. Lt. Gen. Lionel C. McGarr, the head of the U.S. MAAG, recognized there would be "no quick, easy solution," though he presumed it would take fewer than the five years others had predicted to defeat the NLF—still longer, that is, than most of Washington's overseas engagements.[5] That was also the message Robert McNamara delivered at the second SecDef conference in Honolulu. Meeting with civilian and military officials in mid-January, he surmised that "the process of clearing and holding" would be "a long one," even as he sought to speed up the insertion of U.S. personnel.[6] The Secretary's remarks, along with those of lawmakers, policymakers, and military personnel, made clear that U.S. officials were under no illusion about the duration of the war in Vietnam.

Much of that perspective, Nolting relayed, was attributable to British counterinsurgency specialist Robert G. K. Thompson. Having won fame during the U.K.'s "police action" in Malaya, Thompson and his exploits had impressed Diem, whose extensive ties with Kuala Lumpur during the 1950s had led him to apply lessons from that conflict to his own war.[7] After almost eighteen months of discussion between U.K., Malayan, and South Vietnamese officials, Thompson made his way to Vietnam in September 1961, at Diem's invitation, as head of a British Advisory Mission (BRIAM).[8] Relations between BRIAM and the U.S. Country Team were rocky at first, owing to the Americans' belief that Thompson was exceeding his mandate and encroaching on U.S. prerogatives. But better coordination between U.S. and British military advisers, as well as between U.S. and British diplomats, emerged in the new year. Though differences in emphasis remained, both now agreed that the struggle would be a long haul.[9]

Regardless, it simply had to be undertaken. President Kennedy had repeatedly said as much, asserting that the United States was "determined" to prevent a Communist takeover of South Vietnam.[10] It was a pledge borne of the need to halt aggression in its tracks, lest the psychological dominoes begin to topple. As such, it drew on the 1930s and the lessons of Munich, which taught that aggression unchecked is aggression unleashed. Although the analogy was less operative for Kennedy than it would be for Lyndon Johnson, the need to confront belligerence and thereby forestall runaway dynamics—a blending of the Munich and domino analogies—was equally pertinent; hence, the need to stanch the insurgency in Vietnam.[11] British officials recognized the strength of the U.S. commitment, one that was likely to persist and even deepen. According to Harry Hohler, London's ambassador to South Vietnam, "American prestige was greatly, perhaps decisively, engaged in that cause."[12]

The U.S. military certainly thought so. Evaluating the strategic importance of Southeast Asia, Gen. Lyman L. Lemnitzer, chair of the Joint Chiefs of Staff, framed it as a vital interest in all but name. The United States, he told McNamara, "has clearly stated and demonstrated that one of its unalterable objectives is the prevention of South Vietnam falling to communist aggression and the subsequent loss of the remainder of the Southeast Asian mainland." While Washington could take positive action short of deploying combat units, Lemnitzer and the Chiefs saw "no alternative" to using them as a last resort.[13] Both positions remained at odds with that of the American president, as Kennedy had yet to convey a willingness to deploy U.S. troops. In fact, he had repeatedly resisted doing so, and he had rejected the categorical commitment his advisers wanted to make.

Beefing Up

But the signals Washington was sending testified to that commitment all the same. Its most significant expression came by way of the U.S. military presence in South Vietnam, a footprint expanding in both size and form. The Military Assistance Command, Vietnam—MACV, as it was known—came into existence on February 8, 1962. An upgrade to the MAAG that had coordinated U.S. support since 1950, the new organization, which emerged out of the Taylor Report and NSAM 111, heralded the expanding commitment to Saigon's defense. So, too, did the elevation of its chief, Gen. Paul D. Harkins, from a three-star to a four-star general, a development that magnified the importance of his command.[14] Nolting explained those developments to Saigon in instrumental terms, highlighting the need "to bring heavy and increasing MAAG activities and substantial US military operations" under a single authority.[15] But it was also intended as a much-needed boost to GVN confidence. As Lemnitzer observed, the reorganization served "to create in the minds of Diem and other Vietnam officials an awareness of the gravity of the situation, the increased support to be furnished by the U.S. and the necessity for greater acceptance on the part of the GVN of U.S. guidance, advice and counsel."[16] Press accounts struck similar notes. According to the *New York Times,* a "primary" rationale for the creation of MACV was "to manifest the determination of the United States to prevent a Communist takeover." Likewise, the *Washington Post* found that it "underscored this Nation's determination to win," with both the *Times* and the *Post* quoting an unnamed official who declared this "a war we can't afford to lose."[17] As with previous incantations, the imperative seemed self-explanatory; neither paper provided any explanation of why Vietnam was so vitally important.

But raising the visibility of U.S. actions was a double-edged sword. Although they sought to reverse a slump in South Vietnamese morale, those measures created optics that ran counter to the president's wishes. Kennedy was leery of drawing too much attention to the American commitment, and both the creation of MACV and the elevation of

Harkins, not to mention the impending arrival of thousands of U.S. servicemen, threatened to draw undesirable scrutiny. In conversation with the Chiefs on January 3, Kennedy stressed the need to play down the number of American forces in Vietnam as well as the need to avoid a deeper military engagement. Those troops would provide advice, training, and support, but they were not to engage in combat.[18] Publicity surrounding that mission was unavoidable, however, and revealed a dilemma at the heart of the U.S. project. Affirmations of the American commitment, whether rhetorical or tangible, served to bolster the South Vietnamese; in fact, the more public the pledge and the grander its expression, the more likely it would stiffen their spines. But those demonstrations also moved Washington closer toward the sweeping promise Kennedy sought to avoid. It was a tension that generated lasting discomfort, especially for the president.

Equally troubling were reports of what the commitment entailed. Coverage of the force expansion—what the Pentagon dubbed "Project Beef-Up"—depicted U.S. troops assuming combat roles in support of the counterinsurgency. American servicemen were "manning helicopters and small transport planes," the *Times* revealed, "and participating in coastal and river patrols by small, fast craft." Stories also suggested that the number of troops involved was vastly larger than the 685 allowed under the Geneva agreement, with between 2,000 and 4,000 U.S. forces in South Vietnam. In fact, journalists were citing figures closer to 5,000, with more on the way. While those troops were technically not engaged in combat, the Pentagon maintained they could return fire if fired upon.[19]

The disjuncture between government statements and media reports increased the pressure on the administration to come clean. A February 12 *New York Times* piece, for instance, relayed official concern about the likelihood of additional casualties "in what are now openly described as United States military operations against Communist rebels in South Vietnam."[20] With similar stories now appearing regularly in the press, policymakers tried to convince Congress and the public that this was a Vietnamese war and that Washington was providing only economic and military assistance.[21] The president himself minimized the extent of U.S. involvement. Just days after his State of the Union address, Kennedy denied that U.S. combat troops were supporting the GVN, though he stressed that the situation was "extremely serious" and that Washington had "increased its help" to Saigon. It was a line he delivered repeatedly to journalists over the next several weeks.[22]

But the administration also sought to obscure the scope and nature of that help. Kennedy himself said as much, declaring in a February 7 press conference that his administration—for prudential reasons, as he put it—would be less than fully forthcoming about the extent of U.S. activities.[23] It was an ironic admission, as JFK was embracing a practice he had once criticized Eisenhower for adopting; in April 1954, Kennedy demanded that the American people "be told the truth about Indochina," a pose easier to strike as a Democratic senator, with still grander political ambitions, than as a sitting president.[24] But obstruction and obfuscation were precisely what the Kennedy administration was engaged in, as several outlets reported. *Newsweek* highlighted the concealment in a mid-February cover story.[25] *New York Times* columnist James Reston went further, charging that the United States was now fighting an "undeclared war in South Vietnam," and rebuking the administration for not leveling with the American public.[26] Were the war to escalate and prompt open intervention from Hanoi, and ultimately from Moscow and Beijing, "the United States would find it difficult, if not impossible," the *Times* warned, "to withdraw from the fight[.]"[27]

Seeking to squelch that line of commentary, JFK used a February 14 news conference to steer a middle course between affirming U.S. support and downplaying its extent. He emphasized the seriousness of the situation, but he rejected the notion that combat units had deployed to Vietnam. Responding to press and partisan charges that his administration had been less than candid with the American people, Kennedy noted that members of both parties had been briefed on the dispatch of military advisers. American assistance had been relegated largely to logistics, he stressed, and the United States had "not sent combat troops in the generally understood sense of the word."[28]

But the president's remarks could not paper over concerns among the media or within the government. If stories were to emerge that Americans were "bombing and strafing Vietnamese villages," warned the State Department's Chalmers "Ben" Wood, "we would have serious political problems."[29] Carl Rowan, the deputy assistant secretary of state for Public Affairs, likewise feared the administration was "headed for a major domestic furor over the 'undeclared war' in South Viet-Nam," as well as a spat over secrecy protocols constraining American journalists. Indeed, news accounts and editorials warned that the administration risked "serious domestic political consequences" if it failed to establish better information policies. With the material *Life* magazine had scooped up, Rowan observed, "the press boys already have enough detailed information about troops and material to paint a disturbing picture of US involvement."[30]

Those concerns, as well as increasing unease about the Diem regime and its war-fighting moxie, led the administration to restrict the amount and quality of information flowing to the press. A joint directive, sponsored by State, Defense, and the U.S. Information Service (USIS), sought to shield reporters from developments that were potentially damaging to the American cause. In the words of Secretary Rusk, who established the policy on February 21, officials should reject the notion that this was a U.S. war and stress that "our participation is only in training, advisory and support phases."[31] Those instructions, however, would be of little use in countering speculation about the war's trajectory. A piece in *U.S. News & World Report* suspected that Washington's new level of engagement "may be only the beginning," as the American commitment was "bound to increase rather than slacken off." Ominously, the *New York Times*'s Jack Raymond doubted whether Americans were "ready to accept the idea of a long, drawn-out struggle," as "they might insist upon a quick, clean victory." With American troops receiving and returning fire, "all ingredients are there," according to *U.S. News,* "for another Korea if the Reds push too hard."[32] The Korean analogy, which had already emerged in discussions of Vietnam, would become more familiar both inside and outside the Beltway over the course of Kennedy's presidency.

Recognizing the politics at work in the growing commitment, the administration again took its message to the nation's lawmakers— discreetly—at the same time it sought to shape opinion on the war. Speaking in executive session before the Senate Foreign Relations Committee on February 20, Harriman claimed that no U.S. combat troops were serving in Vietnam, that he knew of no plans to deploy such troops, and that those serving in Vietnam were merely providing training and logistical support. Nevertheless, several senators, including Morse and Senator Albert J. Gore [D-TN], remained deeply uncomfortable with those developments..[33] The following day, legislators heard more about the extent of U.S. support from President Kennedy and senior officials at a White House briefing. MACV currently boasted approximately 5,000 U.S. military personnel, McNamara revealed, and its numbers would expand to roughly 8,300 by July. None of those troops, he emphasized, were engaged in combat operations; their role was to provide logistical support, training, and planning. But lawmakers were not to publicize those figures, as doing so might create problems for the ICC.[34] The attitude of official silence was indeed the public affairs policy of the Department of Defense. Not only would the administration hold that this was a Vietnamese war and that the United States was acting only in an assistance capacity, but that "specific numbers of Americans, numbers and designations of U.S. units, and type and amount of material introduced into SVN will not be provided."[35]

Members of Congress, in turn, came to the administration's defense. Mike Mansfield, the Senate's majority leader and generally accepted authority on the Far East, maintained that Kennedy officials had more than come clean on the scope of America's engagement in Vietnam. If anything, they had offered "a surfeit of information" on Vietnam and U.S. policy.[36] Other lawmakers offered more muted but no less vocal support of the administration's position. Through comments and articles they read into the *Congressional Record*, Senators Strom Thurmond [D-SC] and Gale McGee [D-WY] noted the value of preserving and even expanding the U.S. commitment.[37] Thurmond, in fact, was delighted with the administration's alleged admission, voiced by Attorney General Robert F. Kennedy, that the president was committed to "victory" in its tangle with the Vietnamese Communists. As reported in the press, the president's brother, who was refueling in Saigon during a tour of Asia and the Far East, had declared that the United States was going to "win" in Vietnam and that U.S. troops would remain there "until we do win."[38] Not all were cheered by the AG's maximalist stance. Senators Fulbright, Gore, and Morse were alarmed by its sweep; while eager to halt the spread of communism, they were hardly prepared to do so through the use of American combat units.[39] But Congress had generally recognized a president's prerogative to conduct the nation's foreign policy unhindered by legislative intervention—at least since the end of the Second World War. By and large, therefore, it supported the administration's commitment to Vietnam, a posture that involved resisting Communist aggression while having indigenous populations bear the primary burden.[40]

Nevertheless, as questions about the commitment began to mount, so, too, did opportunities for partisan advantage. Prior to 1962, Republicans had been generally quiet on the matter of Indochina. As *Newsweek* had pointed out in a September 1961 cover story, the GOP line on Vietnam had been consistent with a willingness among legislators to let the president take the lead in foreign policy.[41] Although Republicans had criticized Kennedy for the April 1961 Bay of Pigs fiasco, those attacks, which emerged most forcefully during the summer months, had since lost their sting; the president's handling of the Berlin crisis, along with his dramatic defense build-up, provided sufficient political cover. Indeed, opinion polls from early 1962 suggested that Kennedy and the Democratic Party were well positioned for the midterm elections later that year.[42]

By February, however, the GOP challenge had become apparent. Senior Republicans, including New York governor Nelson Rockefeller, Arizona senator Barry Goldwater, and Richard Nixon, the former vice president and 1960 presidential candidate, were criticizing Kennedy's management of foreign policy.[43] On February 13, the Republican National Committee blasted JFK for being "less than candid" in his description of American involvement in Southeast Asia. "Is the country moving toward another Korea," it asked, and starting a war that "might embroil the entire East?" With the influx of so many servicemen hard to disguise, the GOP urged Kennedy to "drop the pretense that the United States is merely acting as military adviser to South Vietnam."[44] Senator Kenneth Keating [R-NY] followed with a similar attack and claimed that the president's "made-in-Washington smoke screen" camouflaged the extent of U.S. involvement in Vietnam. Those critiques and others left Kennedy in a bind. As Fulbright put it, if Kennedy did nothing on Vietnam, he would be tarred for being soft on Communism; if he did act, he would be criticized for doing so without congressional consultation and in violation of the Constitution.[45] Politically, the Republicans had delivered a clever one-two punch.

But it was not terribly effective, for efforts to inject Vietnam into the midterm elections fell flat. At the very least, they did little to cut into Kennedy's approval rating, as his popularity increased during this period, rising from 77 percent in January 1962 to 79 percent in March.[46] Kennedy's numbers would dip to 73 percent the following month, but even so, they suggested the GOP attack was wide of the mark, with 63 percent of Americans regarding foreign policy, not domestic affairs, as the most important of the day.[47] Those figures also suggest that negative coverage in the press, despite Kennedy's ongoing concerns, did not unduly influence JFK's policy on Vietnam—at least not at that point in his presidency.

Counterinsurgency

Away from the public conversation about troops and secrecy, the administration was developing its strategy and tactics for unconventional war. Efforts to flesh out a new approach began early in its tenure, as Kennedy and his aides repeatedly stressed the need to rethink America's security posture and retool its military capabilities. The development of counterinsurgency (COIN) doctrine and training emerged largely through trial and error, with Vietnam serving as a proving ground for novel techniques and practices. Military and civilian officials repeatedly treated Vietnam as a workshop for a broad range of measures applicable to the brush-fire wars of the development decade. McNamara had been moving in that direction since at least August 1961, thinking Vietnam should be used "as a laboratory to develop organization & procedures for the conduct of 'sub-limited war.'"[48] He suggested that Fort Bragg establish "a special training facility devoted wholly to Vietnam needs" and additional measures to address language skills—the better to get "the first team" operational in Vietnam.[49] Kennedy also fixed on the importance of personnel; he asked the Chiefs whether they were sending younger officers to Vietnam, particularly those with specialized training in guerrilla and counterguerrilla warfare, "to participate in the present work, but also to be trained for other situations and other opportunities in the future." Since armed conflicts were increasingly likely to be unconventional, he was concerned about the apparent dearth of officers with the requisite knowledge and competence. Kennedy thus "directed that we 'make this a laboratory both for training our people, and for learning the things that we need to know to successfully compete in this area.'" Among the means devised for the competition were chemical defoliants and herbicides to deny food and cover to the enemy. Additional activities, developed by William Godel's Project AGILE, would further populate the test bed.[50]

Along with adopting new techniques and practices, U.S. officials refined their administrative approach to unconventional war. To Rusk,

Vietnam presented an "unparalleled opportunity . . . to demonstrate functioning inter-agency and international effort, which could serve as guidance in other free world struggles."[51] Those efforts found a bureaucratic home in the Special Group for Counterinsurgency (CI), an inter-agency outfit tasked with coordinating a government-wide approach to the matter. According to Maj. Gen. Victor H. Krulak, the Joint Chiefs special assistant for counterinsurgency, the group helped to "blot out the organizational lines" and allow the government to "function as a single matrix of power" by amalgamating the resources needed for "beating the Reds at their own game."[52] Its membership drew from key agencies, with leadership provided by Gen. Maxwell D. Taylor, the president's military representative, and by Attorney General Robert Kennedy—a selection testifying to the group's significance. Its writ included the development of internal security and police programs in the initial target countries of Laos, South Vietnam, and Thailand; specialized training in the techniques and history of counterinsurgency, including the establishment of a dedicated school for such activities; the development of country-specific counterinsurgency plans; personnel and operational enhancements for agencies involved in COIN activities; and the codification of a counterinsurgency doctrine to guide and coordinate all entities of the U.S. government.[53]

The most significant expression of that thinking came from Roger Hilsman, the director of the State Department's Bureau of Intelligence and Research (INR). Having fought in the Second World War in the China-Burma-India Theater, Hilsman fashioned himself as an expert on counterguerrilla warfare, a posture that would not endear him to the Pentagon brass. But it impressed the commander in chief. Kennedy subsequently asked Hilsman to attend the January SecDef conference before conducting an inspection tour of South Vietnam.[54] His findings indicated that the war had to be won on the village level by denying the Communists access to the people. Although he was silent on the precise definition of "winning," Hilsman intimated that it involved "eliminat[ing] the Vietnamese Communist armed-subversive force, the Viet Cong," to levels Saigon could control on its own.[55] He thus called for major expansions of the Civil Guard and the Self-Defense Corps—the country's provincial and local security forces, respectively. It was an approach fully in line with what BRIAM chief Robert Thompson was recommending.[56]

Hilsman developed his ideas more broadly after again visiting South Vietnam at Kennedy's behest that March. It was a fluid moment, as Saigon was just launching its Strategic Hamlet Program, the GVN's signal initiative in its war against the NLF. The program, which presumed to create thousands of fortified villages throughout the country, drew from Thompson's ideas as well as from concepts Diem had previously employed to isolate the Communists. Managed by Ngo Dinh Nhu, the program initially targeted the population-rich province of Binh Dinh along the central coast, a decision several U.S. officials thought unwise. A more effective approach, many thought, would be to achieve initial success in areas more conducive to those controlled experiments before seeping out in an "oil spot" fashion. But U.S. officials backed the idea of securing the villages and winning their allegiance, a theory Hilsman had earlier expanded into an overall strategic concept.[57]

As realized, however, the program suffered from more than just its geographic focus. Saigon failed to provide sufficient guidance and direction to those charged with its local management, uprooting too many communities and placing too many demands on them with too few resources to build the self-sufficient, pro-government, cohesive communities the Ngos envisioned. As historian Philip Catton relates, the hamlets were a "triumph of form over substance, and coercion over consent," generating too few gains for the GVN and too many converts for its enemies—developments that would become increasingly evident over time. At its outset, though, the Strategic Hamlet Program enjoyed broad support in Saigon and Washington, as well as in London, as the key to stanching the Communist insurgency.[58]

But the foundation of that partnership began to crack at the very moment it seemed to be flowering. Criticism of Diem, which had never vanished in the wake of a 1960 coup attempt, was appearing more frequently in the American press, questioning his ability to lead and the survivability of his government. His onetime friend and confidante Wesley Fishel, who had brought his Michigan State University Group to South Vietnam in the 1950s to help modernize the country's administrative organs, authored a scathing report on conditions in South Vietnam that found its way to President Kennedy. The timing of those critiques, coming just as Washington was boosting its assistance effort, could not have been less welcome. Worse, on February 27, two South Vietnamese air force pilots bombed the Independence Palace, the South

Vietnamese seat of government, with the aim of toppling the Ngo regime. Diem survived the attack, which he attributed not to popular and military unrest but to negative reporting in the press; he then demanded the departure of correspondents he thought responsible for creating the charged environment. Although U.S. officials convinced Diem to reverse his expulsion orders—the journalists eventually left when their visas expired—the episode escalated the Ngos' running war with the media at the very moment reporters were demanding more transparency from U.S. officials and greater access to South Vietnamese sources.[59]

The attempt on Diem's life thus heightened U.S. concern about the fate of his government and its ability to stanch the insurgency. It was too soon to tell if Project Beef-Up was having its intended effect, but Kennedy and the Joint Chiefs now thought it necessary to plan for the worst. In the wake of the failed coup, they talked about stepping up the pace of military operations. Given the apparent increase in PLAF forces, Kennedy probed the Chiefs about a possible escalation of U.S. activity. "What should we do next?," he asked. "Is our 8300-man operation a saturation point?" Hedging against a downturn, Kennedy wanted "a contingency plan" to deal with an emergency in South Vietnam, along with a separate plan for addressing infiltration from Laos. There was clearly a need, he said, "to develop a U.S. plan to hold key areas so that we do not lose all of South Viet-Nam." McNamara also wanted to "plan for the introduction of U.S. forces before the loss of the total interior of South Vietnam."[60] The president's military aide, Chester Clifton, suggested National Security Adviser McGeorge Bundy prod McNamara on or around April 1 about its readiness. As Kennedy indicated, "an important item in this planning is the timing of a decision for U.S. action and the factors that go into such a decision." Consistent with earlier concerns about the context of a U.S. troop deployment, officials continued to weigh the impact of those forces on the region, as the influx of American servicemen could reshape ongoing discussions about neutralizing Laos.[61]

Pushback

The uncertainties surrounding both Diem and the assistance effort led to a curious conjunction of events: just as Kennedy was asking about plans to introduce U.S. forces into Vietnam, he was learning of proposals to move in the opposite direction. The first such recommendation came from John Kenneth Galbraith, the U.S. ambassador to India, who had maintained a running dialogue with JFK over the fate of Vietnam and Southeast Asia. Since April 1961, Galbraith had written numerous memos on the subject and discussed his concerns with Harriman, Under Secretary of State George Ball, and Ambassador-at-Large Chester Bowles—men who, like himself, cast a jaundiced eye on America's commitment to South Vietnam. Galbraith's primary recommendation was to seek a diplomatic solution to the conflict. His contacts with Delhi left him ideally suited to explore such an arrangement; India, a leading member of the nonaligned movement, geographically proximate to Southeast Asia, and the neutral member on the ICC, was well-positioned to broker a deal. Galbraith's repeated cautions about further involvement in the war suggested—to him at least—that Kennedy should remain open to the possibility of a political settlement.[62]

But the ambassador's most significant intervention might well have come in early April 1962. Spending a Sunday with the Kennedys at their hideaway in rural Virginia, Galbraith spoke with JFK deep into the night about America's growing entanglement in Vietnam. Back in Washington the following week, he buttonholed McNamara and Harriman about the increasingly parlous situation, and, upon Kennedy's request, furnished the president with a memo summarizing his arguments. His paper outlined a negotiated settlement in Indochina—an approach, he claimed, shared by both McNamara and Harriman. The need to "keep open the door for political solution" meant that Kennedy had to "resist all steps which commit American troops to combat action and impress upon all concerned the importance of keeping American forces out of actual combat commitment."[63]

Almost at once, Kennedy sought to gauge the merits of those arguments. Upon Galbraith's suggestion, he met with Harriman to consider the possibility of seeking a joint de-escalation of hostilities.[64] Although Harriman rejected Galbraith's proposal for neutralizing Vietnam, he supported efforts to see whether the United States and "the Viet Minh" could mutually reduce their involvement; the ICC, which was soon to report on violations of the 1954 Geneva agreement, might be the vehicle for such an intervention.[65] But rather than wait for its finding, Kennedy again asked that Galbraith use his contacts with Delhi to probe Hanoi's interest in such an approach. He wanted the United States "to be prepared to seize upon any favorable moment to reduce our involvement, recognizing that the moment might yet be some time away." It was a telling remark. Coming less than five months after the start of Project Beef-Up and less than two months after constituting MACV, it is one of the earliest and most striking examples of Kennedy seeking to limit and even reverse America's involvement in Vietnam.[66]

Kennedy also directed that McNamara and the Pentagon review Galbraith's memo, a process that generated a uniformly negative response. The Chiefs rejected Galbraith's arguments and held that Washington should pursue its current policy "vigorously to a successful conclusion." JCS chair Lyman Lemnitzer declared that changing course "could have disastrous effects" on America's allies in Asia and around the globe—a transparent appeal to issues of credibility and resolve, and to the dynamics of psychological dominoes. Again misrepresenting the president's commitment to the war, Lemnitzer claimed that both Kennedy and McNamara had "recently and publicly affirmed the intention of the US Government to support the government of President Diem and the people of South Vietnam to whatever extent may be necessary to eliminate the Viet Cong threat."[67] The Pentagon's Office of International Security Affairs (ISA) also criticized the Galbraith memo along similar lines.[68] Those comments all found their way to the secretary of defense.

Yet McNamara never gave Kennedy a written assessment of the Galbraith memo, even though the president had asked for one.[69] Nor did Maxwell Taylor render a summary judgment. Upon receiving Galbraith's paper and a report of the president's meeting with Harriman, Taylor simply directed his naval aide to "see me."[70] The cryptic nature of those exchanges raises questions about whether Galbraith had exposed elements of planning that McNamara and Taylor thought better left unsaid—or at least uncommitted to paper. Given the hostility of military officials to a potential course correction in Vietnam, McNamara might well have kept his own counsel and shielded others at the Pentagon from learning of emerging efforts to rethink the disposition of American troops. But the informal nature of the Galbraith memo offers at least one clue to its bureaucratic treatment. As a "private communication" from Galbraith to Kennedy, it lacked the quality of an official contact, leading Harriman to believe it required no departmental staff work.[71]

Nevertheless, Galbraith's recommendations remained active within the upper reaches of government. On May 1, almost a full month after the ambassador lobbied for a neutralized Vietnam, the topic arose at a White

House meeting between the president and officials from State, Defense, and the CIA. Harriman, whom Galbraith regarded as a fellow traveler on Vietnam, now "vigorously opposed" neutralization, as did Roger Hilsman. Kennedy thus dropped the matter. As several officials argued, such talk might sap morale and lead Saigon to regard it as a first step toward an American withdrawal from South Vietnam, precipitating its ultimate collapse. In lieu of a diplomatic settlement, Kennedy would try to limit the U.S. military commitment and endow the GVN with the means to win the war on its own.[72]

Still, arguments for a lighter U.S. footprint were emanating from figures with far more credibility on military matters than Galbraith. Following the ambassador's recommendation, the second such intervention, and possibly the more significant one, came from BRIAM chief Robert Thompson, who was alarmed at the number of servicemen streaming into Vietnam. Although Britain had recognized the merits of publicizing the advisory and training mission, it also understood that U.S. forces were engaged in combat and thus "beginning to drift away from General Taylor's original conception."[73] Not only were American troops now more likely to come under fire, posing challenges for Kennedy at home, but they were creating difficult dynamics for the GVN. Already too great in number, those troops, Thompson told the Vietnam Task Force during a visit to Washington, were tarnishing Diem's image as a nationalist. As he put it, "the VC can develop a case that the US is running the show and have in fact replaced the French with all its implications." Fearing a more substantial land war in Asia, Thompson gave the administration a compelling reason to limit the scope of U.S. involvement. No one expected the United States to be out of Vietnam any time soon, however. Even Thompson thought it would take three to six years to defeat the Communists.[74]

But Thompson went further, raising the possibility of not only limiting American deployments but reversing their course. His suggestion fell flat, however, with British officials in Washington. With the United States having just established MACV and begun the escalation of its advisory commitment, the Kennedy administration was hardly disposed to moving so quickly in the opposite direction. In addition, worries that Hanoi might "call [the] American bluff," as British observers put it, left U.S. officials "apprehensive" about statements pointing toward troop withdrawals. Nor was Whitehall supportive of the idea. The Foreign

Office, whose reservations about the U.S. project in South Vietnam were already well known to their American counterparts, was wary of the proposal. Summing up the prevailing sentiment, Richard Ledward, the counselor at the British embassy in Washington, thought support for Thompson's idea "would only cause the Americans to doubt our enthusiasm and good sense."[75]

Yet Thompson had touched a nerve, for by the spring of 1962, Washington was even more upset about media coverage of its rapidly expanding commitment. As *Times* columnist James Reston relayed to Ball, the administration was "on a sticky wicket on the whole public policy of Viet-Nam," and Diem's actions had compounded the problem. Especially worrisome were stories that the war was beginning to look like a U.S. operation.[76] So concerned were administration officials that the State Department sent out a circular memorandum on April 11, reminiscent of the one it dispatched in mid-February, which sought to counter the image of an American war. As the directive maintained, this was a Vietnamese struggle. "They are fighting it," the dispatch ran, "and retain full responsibility for it."[77] To Kennedy, who was of two minds about his own program—committed to assistance but wary of its optics—those portrayals heightened his awareness of its potential for political trouble.

In truth, though, Vietnam sparked no such outcry of congressional concern. For virtually the entire month of April, no member of either party spoke about U.S. policy in Vietnam from the floor of the House or Senate. Only in committee testimony on military and economic assistance did legislative interest arise. Even then, criticism of administration policy was muted and confined primarily to the comments of Rep. Otto Passman (D-LA), who railed incessantly against what he regarded as wasteful spending. Kennedy therefore faced little pressure from Congress on his policies toward Vietnam. If anything, attitudes ran toward helping the South Vietnamese wage the war more vigorously. Indeed, it likely supported Lemnitzer's position, repeated in the press, that Washington would "provide 'whatever is needed' to defeat the Communists."[78] It was a point Harriman delivered as well. The United States was "absolutely determined to do everything we can to help the South Vietnamese retain their independence," even as he affirmed that no U.S. combat units were participating in the struggle.[79] Opinion thus allowed for considerable latitude with the assistance program, even as the administration prepared for more dramatic measures.

The Ball Speech

Notwithstanding those favorable circumstances, Kennedy officials were aware of Vietnam's potential impact on domestic politics. Their concern sprang from several additional media accounts, including a mid-April story in the *New York Times* declaring that Washington was shouldering a "sweeping commitment" in Indochina. So extensive was U.S. support for Saigon, the *Times* wrote, that it was "of decisive importance in the Vietnamese conflict."[80] Given the prevalence of those pieces in an elite, daily publication such as the *Times,* Under Secretary Ball believed the time had come for a more fulsome statement about America's posture and intentions. It was especially important, he thought, for the administration to establish its position before similar articles ran in the mass-circulation periodicals. *Life* had already published photographs of U.S. helicopters flying around Vietnam—a "mistake," as Harriman put it, that the administration should not have permitted—and made Vietnam its "Story of the Week" on March 16, maintaining that the United States had "committed to win" the war.[81] Ball thought it essential, therefore, to publicize the administration's position more widely. Informing Mc-George Bundy and President Kennedy of his desire to make its case, Ball endeavored to cast the war as a purely Vietnamese affair. Bundy thought it a "good thing to do," adding that Ball was nonetheless "a brave man to do it." Kennedy's "only guidance," Bundy relayed, was that public comment about Vietnam remain "in as low a key as possible—not excluding the notion that there would come a time we could back off if the others do."[82] It was a position fully in line with Kennedy's remarks to Harriman three weeks earlier.

Much to the administration's chagrin, the speech Ball delivered narrowed Kennedy's options rather than preserving them. Worse, it became a lightning rod for observers who wanted to see the administration make a more robust commitment. Writing in the *New York Herald Tribune,* Marguerite Higgins thought that Ball's April 30 address to the Economic Club of Detroit signaled the administration's complete engagement with Vietnam. "American retreat is unthinkable," she wrote, and the U.S. commitment "now irrevocable." Ball defended his remarks to the White House, lauding "responsible" reporting that emphasized "the limited nature of our involvement."[83] But his address left ample room for interpreting the U.S. commitment as deep and unbounded. Although the

United States was neither fighting nor running the war, the conflict was one, Ball had proclaimed, that "we must stay with until it is concluded." It could last as long as the eight years of the Malayan emergency, but the United States needed to see it through with patience.[84] Along with Robert Kennedy's statement two months earlier in Saigon, Ball's was the most categorical an administration official had made since the onset of Project Beef-Up—and one that contravened JFK's framing of the U.S. commitment.

Kennedy's reaction to the Ball speech offers a window into his thinking about Vietnam during the spring of 1962. His response—Bundy describes JFK as being "disturbed" by the Higgins article, fearing she had quoted Ball accurately—highlights Kennedy's sensitivity to the charge that Washington was fully committed to the fight.[85] Ball thus tried to set the record straight. Over the course of the next several days, he reworked the speech to bring it into line with the president's position and then release it as a pamphlet for public consumption.[86] Suggested edits from McGeorge Bundy and Averell Harriman point to Kennedy's ongoing desire to keep his options open. Most significantly, the revised version omitted the original passage about staying with the task "until it is concluded."[87]

But it would be going too far to suggest, as one scholar does, that the administration "approved Ball's speech as highlighting the move toward a scaled withdrawal from Vietnam."[88] That was not its intent, as Ball made clear when broaching the idea of delivering it. Instead, Ball aimed to reinforce the president's desire for a low profile by emphasizing the local and limited nature of the conflict. While it rubbed Kennedy the wrong way by "mak[ing] the news, rather than the situation itself making the news," it ultimately served Ball's larger purpose—one that, in the end, Kennedy might also have appreciated—of clarifying Washington's position and its intentions in Southeast Asia.[89] And that position, as several officials declared publicly and privately, was undoubtedly "limited," precisely the policy Kennedy had been pursuing since May 1961.[90]

As would be the case throughout the conflict, though, the administration never came to grips with the tensions of that posture. The desire for a limited and qualified commitment repeatedly clashed with rhetoric casting Saigon's fall in apocalyptic terms. Observers could well have been confused, therefore, as to whether the administration intended to "win" in South Vietnam—especially since its definition, in the context of the

Vietnamese struggle, was unclear. For Lt. Gen. McGarr, winning seemed to comprise "clearing the entire country of the communist guerrilla" once and for all.[91] For the State Department, it likely involved the less sweeping goal of eliminating the NLF as a subversive threat and reducing it merely to a manageable one. But either way, the administration failed to align its pursuit of those ends with the broad spectrum of means—military, economic, and political, among others—for securing them. That it did so owed much to the difficulty of the task, but also to the priorities of the president, who never fully embraced the GVN's defense as a vital interest of the United States.

The Origins of Withdrawal

Although newspapers featured the Ball speech prominently in the days following its delivery, it was not the primary focus of reporting on Vietnam. Its coverage in the *Washington Post,* for instance, ran under the headline "McNamara to Inspect Warfare in Vietnam," as developments in the country took center stage.[92] The Secretary's visit to Southeast Asia would be brief, lasting only two days; as biographer Deborah Shapley described it, the trip was "long remembered for the haste and zeal with which he rushed through it." Reviewing the Strategic Hamlet Program, the border regions of Laos and Thailand, and various metrics of military operations, McNamara left Vietnam generally satisfied with what he had seen. "Every quantitative measurement we have shows that we're winning this war," he said.[93]

It was during those meetings that McNamara first entertained the possibility of withdrawing U.S. troops from Vietnam. He reportedly broached the topic at the end of a briefing. After clearing the room of virtually all personnel, he asked Harkins for his thoughts on when Saigon would likely be capable of managing its own defense. Harkins was dumbstruck, as he was still consumed with expanding the U.S. presence and had not even considered the question. According to eyewitness George W. Allen, then serving as an intelligence officer in Vietnam, Harkins had "no idea" how long it would take the GVN to assume that responsibility. Undaunted, McNamara asked Harkins to devise a plan for South Vietnamese self-sufficiency that incorporated a timeline of three years for Saigon to achieve it. He then directed Harkins to present the plan at the next SecDef conference on Southeast Asia.[94]

McNamara's instruction likely took its cue from Kennedy's interest in reducing U.S. involvement when the opportunity for doing so presented itself. Indeed, scholars have maintained almost uniformly that Kennedy directed McNamara to begin the drawdown. They rest their case on the *Pentagon Papers,* the confidential study McNamara launched in 1967 to examine the history of U.S.-Vietnamese relations since 1945.[95]

But that planning also stemmed from bullish reporting about the war. Several officials, especially in the Defense Department, had noted encouraging signs, and press accounts largely reflected those positive assessments. As the Pentagon framed it, an "atmosphere of restrained optimism" seemed to obtain in every area McNamara toured, an attitude shared equally by U.S. and GVN personnel. Moreover, Defense officials held "a general conviction—first, that victory is clearly attainable through the mechanisms that are now in motion and, second, that hopefully, it will not take fifteen years fully to consummate it." Newspaper coverage of McNamara's visit reflected that cheery assessment. McNamara could now look back on months of work and derive a sense of accomplishment on the part of the U.S.–South Vietnamese effort, as well as harbor an expectation of continued progress.[96] Indeed, he had made a series of progressively optimistic statements over the previous three months, and he repeatedly invoked that theme of encouragement following the SecDef in May.[97] So, too, did line officers with responsibility for Vietnam. Rear Adm. Luther C. Heinz, who handled military assistance for the Far East, was increasingly optimistic about the U.S.–RVNAF working relationship.[98] Ben Wood, who was transitioning from his State Department post handling Southeast Asian affairs to directing the Department's Working Group on Vietnam, also discerned slow but steady progress. Conditions in the provinces were better than reports made them out to be, he maintained, and U.S. personnel were bypassing Saigon to further enhance the effectiveness of their operations.[99]

Other observers were not so sanguine. Concern, if not pessimism, was evident in Washington, where members of the interagency Vietnam Task Force were meeting just as McNamara was touring South Vietnam. According to Task Force director Sterling J. Cottrell, the administration was just now coming to realize that the entire Vietnam program had reached a critical juncture and that the GVN was failing to generate the progress necessary to win. Diem needed to take the appropriate steps to "get the job done," otherwise the possibility existed that "the large US investment will be of no avail."[100] Cottrell delivered a similar message to the Special Group (CI). Efforts to counter the insurgency had "reached bottom," leaving him dubious of "whether we have made the upturn yet." Absent illuminating metrics on the war, including the frequency of Communist attacks, the number of PLAF casualties, and the performance of South Vietnamese troops, there simply was no way to gauge how things were going.[101] Comparable assessments came from Walter G. Stoneman, who handled Vietnamese affairs for the Agency for International Development. A recent three-week visit to South Vietnam had left him more fully aware of Saigon's "disorganization and ineffectiveness." He was "amazed" at the lack of detailed and long-range planning for province pacification, a realization that challenged the more confident reports coming out of the McNamara meetings. The significance of Saigon's ineptitude, he said, was "now being comprehended on a wider basis in Washington."[102]

McNamara embraced the story of progress, nevertheless. As British observers explained it, the Secretary might well have been "genuinely optimistic" about the course of the war, as it was "easy in a short visit to see evidence of American aid which is impressive not only in quantity but in quality."[103] But McNamara also likely questioned that narrative, as the disparity between his public and private remarks suggests a concealed skepticism about the course of the war. Those doubts would grow over time, leading McNamara to adopt a quasi-manufactured optimism about events, one that enabled him to support and then sustain planning to withdraw from Vietnam. That "calculated posture," according to political scientist Aurélie Basha i Novosejt, allowed withdrawal to advance in an atmosphere of confidence—optics that were essential for American and South Vietnamese audiences. It was a position McNamara shared with BRIAM chief Robert Thompson, and perhaps even absorbed from Thompson. That outward sense of sureness, then—to some extent contrived—likely informed McNamara's decision to initiate a planning process for the drawdown of U.S. troops.[104]

Not that talk of an incipient withdrawal was to be made public. Nor, apparently, was it a topic of private conversation among officials responsible for Vietnam policy. As of late April, Cottrell would profess no knowledge of planning "to reduce the number of U.S. military personnel in Viet-Nam." If proposals toward that end were to move forward, "the course of the fight," he surmised, would "probably be the determining factor."[105] Outwardly, the administration was more concerned with reports that the American presence might be expanding. Officials remained adamant that there was still "no plan for introducing combat forces in South Vietnam," as McNamara himself affirmed in Saigon.[106] The Secretary even cast doubt on whether additional advisory troops would be necessary; U.S. aid to South Vietnam had actually peaked, McNamara told reporters, and now would start to level off. Although he offered journalists a positive assessment of the war, he stressed it would take "not months, but years."[107] In fact, within two weeks of his trip, he speculated that it would take "three to five, at a minimum."[108] But he offered no hint of any interest in troop reduction—and therefore no indication of whether the "course of the fight" would in any way shape a U.S. drawdown.[109]

The first six months of Project Beef-Up offered ample grist for optimists and pessimists as they appraised the war in Vietnam. The "limited partnership" of late 1961 provided for the flow of American troops and matériel into South Vietnam, and those soldiers had set to work advising and assisting their Vietnamese counterparts in the ways and means of counterinsurgency warfare. While the influx of men and the creation of MACV addressed the concrete needs of that campaign, they also served the abstract but no less vital aim of stiffening South Vietnamese morale—the first priority of the Presidential Program. The energy surrounding those developments thus generated a momentum that allowed for guarded optimism in the campaign. At the same time, senior civilian officials in the State and Defense Departments had come to accept that the war would be a "long haul." As Task Force director Cottrell put it in March, he was "encouraged by progress in the civic action programs," but it was "necessary to remember that we are engaged in an eight to ten year struggle."[110]

But the commitment was an ambiguous one, as it was far from clear that the administration was bent on total victory. To be sure, Kennedy had repeatedly spoken of maintaining its resolve; while he acknowledged the "very hazardous" dimensions of the assistance effort, the United States, he declared, "cannot desist in Viet-Nam." Likewise, he warned that withdrawal from Vietnam, as well as from elsewhere in the region, "might mean a collapse of the entire area."[111] But his reluctance to guarantee Saigon's independence came to shape perceptions not only of U.S. policy in Vietnam, but of Kennedy's Cold War posture more broadly. The optics of his approach to Laos, in the wake of his many first-year challenges, left the president open to charges of being soft on communism. With talks about neutralizing the kingdom stalled and Communist forces scoring victories over pro-Western units, Kennedy's policy looked increasingly feckless. His decision in May 1962 to shore up forces in and around Laos provided only a temporary respite, as it allowed negotiations to move toward a neutralization agreement, which concluded later that July.[112]

Republicans therefore sensed a political opportunity and pounced. Conservatives such as Senator Barry Goldwater were especially eager to criticize Kennedy, and administration missteps added fuel to the fire. Its members were pursuing a policy of "anything but victory," Goldwater charged, with its appeasement of communism so thorough that officials were prohibited from using the very word. The indictment had first emerged in March 1961, after it became known that the State Department had edited a speech by Brig. Gen. John W. White, replacing the word "victory" with the phrase "defeat of Communist aggression." In explaining its decision, the State Department maintained that "the word 'victory' has a militaristic and aggressive ring" and "implies an all or nothing approach leaving no room for accommodation."[113] The president took note of Goldwater's comments and was not pleased. In light of the administration's challenges in foreign policy, it hardly needed to open itself to such critiques.[114]

Kennedy tried to repair the damage, in part, via remarks that June at West Point. Echoing his administration's response to the "victory" affair, Kennedy sought to align the nation's military means with the novel threats it faced. The United States, he explained, was confronting "another type of war, new in its intensity, ancient in its origin—war by guerrillas, subversives, insurgents, assassins, war by ambush instead of by combat; by infiltration, instead of aggression, seeking victory by eroding and exhausting the enemy instead of engaging him." Those contests would not lend themselves to the decisiveness of "victory," and as emblematic of the struggles roiling the developing world, were "not susceptible of a final military solution." Nevertheless, they were "the kinds of challenges that will be before us in the next decade if freedom is to be saved," he said. They required "a whole new kind of strategy, a wholly different kind of force, and therefore a new and wholly different kind of military training."[115]

Kennedy was reluctant to test those theories and techniques in Laos, preferring to address the challenge through diplomacy. With the conferees at Geneva finally moving toward an agreement on the kingdom's political future, its contours were shaping up as "a good, bad deal," in the words of chief envoy Averell Harriman.[116] Indeed, its impact would continue to rattle the GVN, even as new initiatives sought to embolden South Vietnam in its fight for survival. The enhanced U.S. assistance effort and the Strategic Hamlet Programs had stirred hope that Saigon could mobilize effectively to thwart the NLF. But persistent questions about Diem's performance, along with Saigon's fears of American resolve, would shape the partnership as the Kennedy administration took its first steps toward a more comprehensive strategy for South Vietnam.

3

Formulation

July 1962–December 1962

The signing of the Geneva Accords on July 23 capped months of military threats, diplomatic wrangling, and bureaucratic maneuvering. Fourteen nations, including North and South Vietnam, decreed that Laos would be ruled by a coalition government headed by neutralist prime minister Souvanna Phouma, with Communist leader Prince Souphanouvong and rightist general Phoumi Nosovan as deputy premiers. Foreign troops, be they North Vietnamese regulars or U.S. military advisers, were to vacate the country within seventy-five days and cease their provision of military assistance. The agreement came just over two months after Kennedy had mobilized U.S. naval forces, sent six thousand U.S. air and ground troops to Thailand, and dispatched one thousand servicemen to the Laotian border. The deployment was designed to signal American resolve after the Pathet Lao had routed anti-Communist and government forces in early May. Kennedy had been wary, though, about inserting U.S. forces in great numbers. As NSC aide Michael Forrestal recalled, JFK wondered how he would ever withdraw them once dispatched. But with the Pathet Lao blunted and the Geneva talks nearing their conclusion, Kennedy moved to recall some of those troops, hoping to facilitate Communist cooperation while maintaining a credible threat of U.S. intervention. They began to leave during the last week of June, with their departure concluded by the end of July.[1]

Although the neutralization of Laos served Washington's immediate interests, it generated further concern in Saigon about Kennedy's intentions in South Vietnam. Members of the U.S. Country Team sensed that anxiety and it worried them. In late June, Joseph Mendenhall, the embassy's political counselor, remarked that "for the first time in my three years' service in Viet-Nam I had received serious indication that neutralization is beginning to be considered by some Vietnamese as a solution to the Vietnamese problem."[2] Opinion in South Vietnam was sufficiently fragile that key publics were liable to turn against the joint partnership. "If the war drags on with gradual deterioration and no hope of victory," the educated class in South Vietnam might switch "from strong anti-Communism to neutralism," a development that would be "disastrous" and lead shortly to a North Vietnamese takeover.[3]

Washington was similarly troubled. Averell Harriman, the State Department's chief of Far Eastern Affairs who had negotiated the agreement, had set out to calm nerves during the Geneva discussions, telling GVN foreign minister Vu Van Mau that the United States was committed to pursuing the anti-Communist struggle "to a successful conclusion," and that he anticipated no talks aiming at "a Lao-type settlement in Viet-Nam."[4] So serious were those concerns that Kennedy himself waded into the mix. In a letter to Diem, JFK defended the Geneva process by stressing that "the only alternative" to neutralizing Laos was to make an international battleground of it, a solution that would help neither the Laotians nor their neighbors. South Vietnam was different, he stressed, and assured Diem that the United States would "continue to help your country to defend itself."[5]

Planning for Withdrawal

Ironically, American officials began to undermine that commitment at the very moment they were seeking to bolster it. On the same day the accords were signed in Geneva, the Kennedy administration began to consider—formally and functionally—the merits of a phased withdrawal from Vietnam. It did so at yet another Secretary of Defense Conference in Honolulu—the sixth since December 1961—to review developments in the war. While conversations revealed substantial progress in the U.S. assistance program, McNamara wanted to transform the overall effort from one of "short term crash-type actions" to a "carefully conceived long-range program for training and equipping RVNAF and phase out of major US combat, advisory and logistics support activities."[6] It was a pivotal moment: Roughly eight months after U.S. troops started to deploy to Vietnam in greater numbers, they now would serve according to a trajectory that governed their departure as well as their arrival.

The planning for a U.S. troop withdrawal grew out of several dynamics, only some of which were directly connected to the war in Vietnam. McNamara reportedly began the process based upon an inference he drew from the administration's public position: that the U.S. objective was to train the South Vietnamese to defend themselves. "To me," he wrote in 1995, "that implied we ought to set a time limit on U.S. training support."[7] That public position largely mirrored the one Kennedy expressed in private. Indeed, it comports with the *Pentagon Papers* claim that the phased reduction was likely a genuine effort to turn the war over to South Vietnam. But it also stemmed from additional objectives and concerns, according to that study, including "contingency planning" to counter pressures for more "inputs"; a desire to subordinate Vietnam to the more pressing concerns of Berlin, Cuba, and Laos; fear the conflict might expand into a larger Asian land war; a way to leverage the GVN by putting a time limit on U.S. involvement; and a means to counter political resistance to American involvement, both at home and abroad.[8]

Those rationales deserve further expansion and amplification. Most significantly, withdrawal planning derived from an articulated sense of progress that allowed the Pentagon to anticipate a greatly reduced role for American advisers. Optimism had been building since the creation of MACV in February 1962, even if improvement was slow going. By June, the State Department could cite the heightened tempo of activities and "evidence of heartening progress in bolstering the fighting effectiveness" of South Vietnamese military and security units. Although "final victory" was likely years away and would occur "more by a steady erosion of Communist strength than by dramatic military success," signs were pointing in the right direction.[9] Especially encouraging were reports that the Strategic Hamlet Program and related military operations were advancing and "seem to promise good results."[10] McNamara himself embraced that narrative, albeit with likely less than full sincerity. While he repeatedly said it would be "years" before the war was over, he nevertheless assured the public that Saigon had improved its capabilities and would eventually defeat the Communists.[11]

Away from the spotlight, several officials were more circumspect in their assessments. To Ben Wood, who directed the Vietnam Working Group, they were "just about holding our own and an upward trend in our favor is not yet clearly in sight." A *Washington Post* story from early July included numerous accounts of U.S. soldiers characterizing the war as "fouled up," with the struggle likely to be a ten-year war of attrition.[12] But McNamara's view dominated the external and internal messaging. The Secretary exuded confidence at Honolulu, noting that "6 months ago we had practically nothing and we have made tremendous progress to date." Harkins was equally bullish. He had "no doubt that we are on the winning side," and assured attendees the advisory programs were "coming along well and in most cases are ahead of schedule."[13] That "can-do" mentality came to permeate the Pentagon's thinking about the war. According to Maj. Gen. William B. Rosson, the Army's special assistant for special warfare, it was in the wake of the July SecDef that he "came to appreciate the extent to which optimism could be institutionalized at the Washington level and within subordinate echelons." By the end of the year, that attitude had become the "recognized position" of the U.S. Army and the Kennedy administration, and was evident even within Congress.[14] Indeed, reports from the field, according to the *Pentagon Papers,* had "indicated a pattern of progress on a broad front," with the expected continuation of favorable developments generating a sense of "euphoria" and "the promise of eventual success."[15]

But domestic pressures were also pushing McNamara toward military disengagement. Some of them emerged from heightened interest in Southeast Asia during the spring and summer of 1962. Notably, Sen. Mike Mansfield, in a June commencement address at Michigan State University, faulted the United States for doing little to improve Southeast Asia. Even in Laos, which was then moving toward neutralization, U.S. aid had "produced scarcely a ripple," save for developments in its capital. As for Vietnam, years of support had left it "more, rather than less, dependent on aid from the United States."[16] Kennedy defended those investments in a press conference days later, suggesting the alternative would have been far worse.[17] But Mansfield had captured a growing uncertainty, if not unease, about the "limited partnership," leading McNamara to address the popular mood at Honolulu. Acknowledging that the GVN was "behind schedule" in building strategic hamlets and that it might take three years instead of one to protect the South Vietnamese population, he sought to "line up our long range program as it may become difficult to retain public support for our operations in Vietnam." Political pressure, he noted, would increase as American losses mounted.

Pressure was indeed building, but it had yet to burst into the open. Even with provocative articles in the press, American opinion indicated general approval of the administration's policy toward Vietnam. Over 50 percent said Kennedy was doing at least a "fairly good" job with Southeast Asia, while only 14 percent described his performance as "poor."[18] Still, Kennedy's overall support was falling. His approval rating had dropped from 79 percent to 69 percent, and Republican numbers were trending upward, particularly in the West and Midwest.[19] The defeat of administration bills on health care and farm aid, continuing fears about Berlin, and concerns about the outflow of gold and the balance of payments contributed to the shortfall in Kennedy's standing. So did a sluggish economy and a stock market plunge. Collectively, those developments stimulated interest in limiting and even reversing the flow—as the president evidently desired—of American troops in Vietnam.

Aside from political pressures and military rationales, bureaucratic dynamics also shaped the context of withdrawal planning. Up to that point in the war, American programs in Vietnam had been conceived and implemented as separate initiatives disconnected from each other. But McNamara had come to see the ad hoc and compartmentalized nature of those efforts as insufficient to the task at hand.[20] He therefore sought to inject greater rigor and purpose into the U.S. advisory mission and endow it with a more defined structure and trajectory. Doing so would allow him to schedule inputs and outputs more effectively and efficiently.

But the calendar for that planning was a matter of dispute. During the July talks at Honolulu, Harkins predicted it would take one year to eradicate the PLAF "as a disturbing force" from the point at which he could get the RVNAF, the Civil Guard, and the Self-Defense Corps "fully operational and really pressing the VC in all areas." McNamara suggested a more conservative timetable, presuming it would take "approximately 3 years to bring the VC in SVN under control." Likewise, he surmised that "wresting areas from VC control and protecting the population," a project to be accomplished through the Strategic Hamlet Program, would also take three years. He therefore directed Harkins to devise plans "for gradual scaling down of COMUSMACV during next

3-year period." Expanding upon a 1960 Counterinsurgency Plan, this new, comprehensive approach addressed the requirements of both U.S. and South Vietnamese forces. The two were to be mutually calibrated and reconciled so the RVNAF could fully manage the counterinsurgency in three years' time.[21]

The Fiscal Context

The CPSVN also reflected McNamara's desire to systematize defense policy in general. In fact, the impetus to transform the counterinsurgency from a series of ad hoc, makeshift responses to a deliberate, comprehensive approach took shape alongside a similar effort to revamp the entire defense budget according to more long-range, coordinated estimates. As McNamara made clear upon taking command at the Pentagon, he would rationalize its budget process, rein in wasteful spending, and impose sound business practices upon DoD operations.[22] The search for maximum efficiency also stemmed from innovations that Budget Director David E. Bell instituted for the entire federal government. Departing from the Eisenhower approach of devising budgets on a yearly basis, Bell instituted long-range fiscal targets developed alongside cost projections over a five-year time span. Such extended planning, which Kennedy sanctioned in April 1961, commenced with the preparation of the fiscal year (FY) 1963 budget, which meant that targets would begin to emerge in spring 1962. Bell refined the process that April, requiring departments to undertake a "spring program review" to focus on programs and budgets extending into 1967, as well as a summer and fall review of the same for FY 1964. The five-year planning schedule and the rigor it imposed aligned with McNamara's effort to inject greater discipline into Pentagon operations, including the advisory effort in Vietnam.[23]

It also marked a departure from prior DoD budgeting exercises. By lengthening the time horizon for adopting defense plans and allocating expenditures, McNamara's forward-looking fiscal strategy brought Pentagon operations in line with the practices of corporate America. Behind his approach lay a methodology familiar to the business world that had been adopted by researchers at the RAND Corporation, the Santa Monica think tank that previously employed several of McNamara's top aides. Known as PPBS, the Planning-Programming-Budget System sought to harmonize management and planning and would affect virtually all DoD operations during the McNamara years. Budgetary decisions would now be based on a Five-Year Defense Plan (FYDP)—a projection of costs and manpower devised alongside and commensurate with a projection of forces eight years out—with the reevaluation and refinement of those estimates taking place continually within five-year windows. Discussions about instituting the FYDP began in 1961 with an eye toward realizing its first iteration by July 1962, the very moment McNamara began to impose comparable discipline on U.S. assistance to South Vietnam.[24]

The first FYDP also coincided with a "Defense Department Cost Reduction Program" McNamara implemented to control departmental expenses. The need for such a program was rooted in the explosive growth of defense spending since the end of the Second World War, an increase in outlays that dwarfed other elements of the federal budget. Consistent with the budgeting guidelines Bell introduced, the cost-reduction program established a series of objectives McNamara sought to realize over a five-year time span. McNamara sent his proposals to Kennedy in July 1962—again, at the very moment he was moving toward a more integrated approach to stemming the Communist insurgency in Vietnam.[25]

More broadly, McNamara's fiscal and programmatic approaches took their cues from the economic health of the nation. Several developments were sapping America's vitality at the outset of JFK's term in office. A recession Kennedy inherited from his predecessor had capped anemic growth rates in the late 1950s. During most of Eisenhower's second term, economic expansion stood at 2.5 percent, down a full percentage point from the country's historic performance, and the unemployment rate had shot up to 6.7 percent—an almost 50 percent jump from where it stood in 1957.[26] Kennedy sought to reverse those trends, aiming for 5 percent growth and an uptick in hiring. Entering the presidency as a fiscal conservative and receiving advice from Treasury Secretary C. Douglas Dillon—a registered Republican, like several members of his Cabinet and White House staff—Kennedy resisted calls by more liberal economists, even those within his administration, for more assertive fiscal measures. But his re-evaluation of the country's defense needs and the dynamics surrounding Berlin led him to propose significant hikes in military spending, developments that contributed, eventually, to an economic expansion. Kennedy's early conservatism remained intact, however. Even with the rising cost of national security, he was wary of running deficits. By October 1961, Kennedy had outlined his funding priorities, committing the government to a balanced budget for FY 1963.[27]

The status of the nation's balance of payments compounded the challenge. An increasing outflow of dollars from the United States, owing to consumer imports, tourist travel, and foreign investment—and, significantly, defense spending abroad—had generated concern about the stability of the nation's currency. Kennedy himself was alarmed by the trend, and to a greater degree than many of his advisers, as he sought to align national security with financial security. Dangers continued to rise as foreign governments redeemed their expanding dollar holdings in gold, placing added pressure on U.S. gold reserves and the value of the currency. By the summer of 1962, those pressures had grown sufficiently for Kennedy to create a Cabinet Committee on the balance of payments, with McNamara and Dillon playing leading roles. McNamara's contribution involved scaling back Pentagon spending abroad and jawboning countries hosting U.S. troops into shouldering greater shares of their defense burdens. The tidier management of federal spending—and defense spending, in particular—thus became national priorities.[28]

One target for cost cutting was the Military Assistance Program (MAP), which had been a staple of U.S. defense policy, especially in the developing world, since its inception in October 1961.[29] Administration and military officials routinely cited MAP as essential to U.S. national security, as it sought to endow local governments with the capacity to resist Communist subversion. According to JCS chair Gen. Lyman Lemnitzer, who lobbied hard for MAP funding, the Communist threat was such that "we cannot successfully meet it by ourselves, or with only our own resources." Given Moscow's interest in aiding "wars of national liberation," the need to support friendly yet vulnerable nations via military and economic assistance was increasingly paramount.[30] Saigon was a prime candidate for the receipt of such aid. As McNamara put it in June 1961, South Vietnam was a "classic example" of a "double-threat" country, a nation that was "contiguous to or near the Sino-Soviet Bloc" that also faced "a direct threat from without and an indirect threat from within." Military assistance therefore played an "essential role" in the defense of Vietnam and all of Southeast Asia, for it helped in "furnishing arms and equipment and in teaching troops to operate, maintain, and use them."[31]

Notwithstanding the premium he placed on MAP and the challenge of the insurgency, McNamara was determined to gain a measure of control over expenditures in Vietnam. It was a position he shared with colleagues on the National Security Council. Recognizing that tensions over Berlin and Southeast Asia made it "an inappropriate time" to cut military aid, officials nevertheless believed they had to "move ahead with the longer-range process of reshaping our MAP policies to make them fully consistent with the needs of the 1960s."[32] Military aid to Saigon had expanded from $101.4 million in FY 1961 to a projected $179.4 million for FY 1963, an increase of 57 percent.[33] According to a DoD history of the era, McNamara "looked forward to early reduction of military assistance programs in South Vietnam," especially considering the global demands on U.S. forces as well as more general budgetary concerns. Overall MAP requests formulated during the Kennedy years would decline, falling from roughly $1.9 billion in FY 1962 to $1.1 billion for FY 1965.[34] Given that the drop coincided with continued worries over Berlin and Southeast Asia—as well as the situation in Cuba—McNamara's commitment to cost-cutting at the Pentagon is all the more profound.

At the same time, McNamara was adamant that cost consciousness not hamper the Vietnam program. In late 1961, he told CINCPAC Adm. Harry D. Felt and MAAG chief Lt. Gen. Lionel C. McGarr that the administration was prepared to go ahead "full blast" on Vietnam, minus the introduction of U.S. combat forces, and that "cost considerations particularly should be secondary in your search for new approaches." Money, as he put it, would "pose no problem."[35] He said much the same to the Senate Foreign Relations Committee (SFRC) in February 1962, noting that the Pentagon was treating Southeast Asia as a special case and "going all-out" to assist Saigon.[36] Given the shrinking pool of MAP resources, he was fully prepared to reallocate funds from within MAP to augment the pool of monies available for Vietnam. As a result, MAP funds for the Far East consumed progressively greater portions of the overall MAP budget, increasing from 41 percent for FY 1961, to 46 percent for 1962, to 48 percent for 1963.[37] Clearly, McNamara was grappling with competing demands: the need to lower the cost of U.S. aid to South Vietnam while providing the GVN with a virtual blank check for military assistance. While engaged in an ongoing effort to reduce DoD costs, he was inclined to exempt the war in Vietnam, for the time being, from such stringency.

McNamara's interest in reallocating resources also reflected strategic assumptions the administration had harbored since its outset. Doubting the relevance of nuclear weapons to the brush-fire wars of the 1960s—the dominant form of East-West combat the administration anticipated during the "Development Decade"—McNamara sought to shift the Pentagon's emphasis away from the bomb and toward counterinsurgency. The reorientation of priorities dictated a corresponding turn away from Europe and toward Africa, Asia, and Latin America. By Spring 1962, the contours of that strategy had become unmistakable. McNamara's speech that May to NATO officials assembled in Greece, which endorsed flexible response at the expense of massive retaliation, left little doubt as to where the administration was putting its energies.[38] Although it embarked upon a major expansion of nuclear and conventional arms, its strategic shift toward low-intensity warfare was clear. Indeed, the Secretary's approach toward strategy and budgeting were reciprocal, reinforcing each other. As political scientist Aurelie Basha i Novosejt observes, "McNamara supported a strategy of counterinsurgency and self-help because it promised an economically sustainable model for US leadership at a time when its responsibilities around the world were proliferating."[39]

The administration was wary, however, about making long-term, open-ended commitments to the developing world. The object lesson was South Korea, which the United States had been supporting with copious amounts of economic and military assistance since the end of the Korean War in 1953. Kennedy officials had become greatly concerned about the level of MAP aid flowing to Seoul, funds which continued to provide the resource base for arming and equipping South Korean forces. As McNamara told the Senate Foreign Relations Committee in February 1962, the Department of Defense was currently undertaking a major review of those commitments to determine the most appropriate level of future spending.[40] It could not come soon enough; by the summer of 1962, the White House would label South Korea "a ticking time bomb." If U.S. assistance could not "provide for a brighter economic and social future," there likely would be "an unpleasant reaction." A cut in South Korea's armed forces, which McNamara directed the Pentagon to review—with the president's support—would help redirect funds to more productive uses and defuse the explosive environment.[41]

The reduction was hardly popular with senior officials. Secretary Rusk was decidedly cool to the idea, as was Assistant Secretary of Defense Paul H. Nitze, who ran the Pentagon's office of International Security Affairs—the DoD shop that administered MAP.[42] So, too, was Gen. Maxwell D. Taylor, the president's military representative and incoming chair of the Joint Chiefs, who communicated his doubts directly to Kennedy in late September. Upon reviewing the aid program and options for paring back funds, Taylor came down squarely against a force cut. But pressure would build to bring the Korean program and other MAP schedules into line with broader administration objectives.[43]

It was against this backdrop of fiscal and strategic planning that the administration considered its commitment to Vietnam. Although the U.S. advisory program had developed a momentum all its own, it was encased in a budgetary and planning framework McNamara had implemented early in his tenure. Its respective elements—the Cost-Reduction Plan, the Five-Year Defense Plan, the Planning-Programming-Budgeting System, and the inchoate comprehensive approach to Vietnam—shared common principles of financial planning, program rationalization, and force reduction. Collectively, they led McNamara to impose greater discipline on the Vietnam assistance effort, a rigor that endowed its life cycle with a beginning, a middle, and now an end. His July 1962 directive to develop a long-range plan for U.S. aid to South Vietnam thus took shape according to these budgetary timetables, strategic adaptations, and programmatic innovations.

Yet none of those schedules were set in stone. The FYDP merely established a set of assumptions about the likely contours of various programs. It offered a reasoned, rational assessment of the costs the Pentagon was likely to incur in any planned venture, but it was a judgment always open to modification.[44] Likewise, the decision to begin "formal planning" for the phased withdrawal of U.S. troops from Vietnam was aspirational and subject to change. Such planning was to proceed on the assumptions that it would "require approximately 3 years to bring the VC in SVN under control" and that the RVNAF would gain the capacity to handle their own defense within that time frame.[45] The training of those forces, the success of the Strategic Hamlet Program, the provision of military equipment to the GVN—all were to take place within that three-year window, which itself was based on a forecast of military success against the PLAF. Although McNamara would later advocate for withdrawal regardless of the military situation in Vietnam, the viability of the reduction plan, at least initially, stemmed from a belief that a U.S. troop reduction and a Communist defeat would march in lockstep.

The Need for Speed

In aftermath of the July SecDef, the themes of progress in the counter-insurgency and rigor in the assistance program appeared more frequently in public and private communications. McNamara was their chief exponent, declaring that the effort was "paying off" and "the sign posts are encouraging." The RVNAF were "carrying the war to the Viet Cong with greater initiative and frequency," so the goal now was to sustain that momentum. The more systemized approach they hit upon would allow those measures to go forward, but it would also require patience from the American public. "Final victory over communist insurgency in South Vietnam may likely take several years," he told journalists. He therefore planned "to program future aid within the next fiscal year's budget so that over the long haul we will be putting material and support where it will do the most good."[46] His more disciplined program presumed that funding the war handsomely in the near term would allow Washington to reduce its commitments over time—and over a specific window of time. Action plans from both State and Defense invoked the three-year calendar he had proposed for training the RVNAF and withdrawing U.S. military advisers.[47]

Although Kennedy's knowledge of that schedule is hard to discern—evidence has yet to emerge that he acknowledged it prior to May 1963—Vice President Johnson became aware of it no later than mid-August 1962, when his military aide, Col. Howard L. Burris, summarized recent developments in official thinking. Noting that McNamara had "pursued the military effort with a great sense of urgency" and had "established a time factor" to neutralize Laos and secure South Vietnam, Burris characterized the withdrawal scenario as designed primarily for planning purposes. McNamara had "set forth the assumption that the present effort will be maintained for three years." Such specificity did not mean that "the effort will be terminated nor phased out in this period," Burris said, "but rather it is a realistic expression of a reasonable period during which success must be achieved or at least be in sight."The good news, Burris continued, was that "we appear to be just about turning the corner."[48]

Concerns about time—the period within which U.S. assistance was expected to generate results—were becoming more salient for U.S. officials. NSC aide Michael Forrestal expected that the war would heat up with the end of the rainy season in November, and U.S. soldiers would likely take more casualties. The American public would support those sacrifices if the overall effort was achieving results. But "we will be in for real trouble," he feared, if inefficiencies on the part of U.S. agencies or the GVN appeared to be thwarting progress. He therefore called for pressures on Diem "to be stepped up even at some risk."[49] Ambassador Nolting, too, recognized the need for speed. He regarded the next twelve months as crucial, suspecting that the acceleration of counterinsurgency measures and the intensification of social, political, and military pressures would result in either "great improvement" or in a "considerable deterioration" of conditions.[50]

But optimism continued to dominate official thinking about Vietnam. Military operations against the Communists seemed increasingly effective, and the Strategic Hamlet Program was accelerating and apparently resilient. Indeed, Communist archives have attested to that perceived early success.[51] Western officials in Saigon came to share that perspective, one evident within the diplomatic corps as well as among the military. Briefings for Gen. Maxwell D. Taylor, who visited Vietnam in September just prior to becoming JCS chair, bolstered that bullish view. BRIAM chief Robert Thompson was particularly encouraged and conveyed his sense of progress over the previous six months, especially in the Strategic Hamlet program. Taylor was eager to hear of such reports, given the political dynamics at home. He "obviously needed ammunition for dealing with Congressional Committees," Thompson told London, especially for "obtaining future funds for the American effort." Yet even with the expectations of continued progress, Thompson thought "it was still going to be at least a three-year job."[52] The challenge of retaining that support therefore remained significant.

Policymakers could meet it by demonstrating clear-cut progress in the war. The withdrawal of U.S. troops, Thompson thought, could serve as the requisite sign. He therefore resurrected the plan he raised with Washington back in April, and did so in light of broader concerns about

South Vietnamese morale. "We badly needed a genuine 'white' area if possible by next spring," he told Taylor, "to demonstrate to the people of the country and particularly the armed forces that we were winning." They could secure a pro-GVN locale, he thought, in one or two Delta provinces. Should it come to pass, he suggested making "a token American reduction, perhaps just as a bit of house cleaning, some time next year at a suitable opportunity." A withdrawal of that sort "should be entirely a unilateral move, well thought out and well timed, so that it achieved the maximum effect without taking any of the pressure off here. We had to think of both winning political advantages as well as military ones."[53] Taylor's reaction to the Thompson plan is unclear, but the general said nothing about it to Kennedy when the two reviewed Taylor's trip on September 25. He did, however, provide the president with an upbeat report about progress in the war.[54]

October SecDef

Although the summer of 1962 marked a significant moment for U.S. policy in Southeast Asia, developments in the region—or much of anywhere else in the global South—were hardly front-page news in the U.S. media. Except for stories about neutralism in Laos, self-rule for newly independent Algeria, and continued instability in the Congo, headlines focused primarily on events in Europe and the Soviet Union. Moscow had resumed its atmospheric testing of nuclear weapons in August, stalling further movement toward a test-ban treaty, while developments in Berlin threatened more significant trouble. The shooting of an East German *flüchtling* at the Berlin Wall revealed the face of Communist policy even as it highlighted the limits of Western power. American opinion, nevertheless, gave Kennedy high marks for his handling of Berlin, with 59 percent of the public finding his approach "good" or "very good," and only 17 percent rating it "poor."[55]

Closer to home, the campaign for social justice and constitutional rights continued to garner headlines, and troubling ones at that. By August, the yearlong effort to desegregate public facilities in Albany, Georgia, had stalled, with the movement having failed to achieve its objectives. Its closure nevertheless coincided with polling that supported Kennedy's handling of civil rights, with a combined 54 percent believing he was doing a "very good" or "fairly good" job at addressing the problems of segregation.[56] More volatile moments would come in late September, as efforts to integrate the University of Mississippi led to mayhem at its flagship campus in Oxford. Kennedy's belated intervention finally enabled James Meredith to enroll at Ole Miss, but not before the president deployed U.S. troops to stem the violence that claimed two lives.[57]

Notwithstanding those generally positive ratings, Kennedy was taking his lumps in the press. A *Newsweek* cover story on "Kennedy and His Critics" found the president suffering the "first real slings and arrows of his presidency," with former president Eisenhower describing Kennedy as "floundering." Media targets included the First Family and the president's policies, as well as Kennedy's dispute with U.S. steel manufacturers, a stock market plunge, and a stalled legislative agenda.[58] Kennedy's poll numbers reflected those concerns; whereas his marks in 1961 had hovered in the mid-70s—soaring to 80 percent in March 1962—they entered a steady decline that summer, falling into the low 60s by October.[59] A volatile domestic environment contributed to the downturn. Early that month, pollster Lou Harris told Kennedy he "had never seen the temper and mood change so drastically" as it had in the previous four weeks. Americans were expressing marked concern about civil rights as well as matters of war and peace. Kennedy's polling on Berlin revealed between 70 and 80 percent support—a significant climb from his August numbers—but opinion ran 62–38 against him on policy toward Cuba.[60] Those figures reflected ominous developments in the Caribbean. With Moscow announcing it would arm and train Castro's military, and with disconcerting reports of Soviet ship movements toward the island, the Communist outpost ninety miles from American shores once again became a focus of concern. Kennedy put the Kremlin on notice in early September: he would resist Moscow's effort to introduce offensive forces in the Western Hemisphere. It was a promise that would test the administration's credibility with allies and adversaries.

But its resolve in Southeast Asia had seemingly garnered significant public support, even as the media raised disturbing questions about America's commitment to South Vietnam. *Newsweek*, which was among the more critical journals, relayed "the uncomfortable truth" that despite spot successes in Vietnam, "bad policies and directions were driving out good ones." More troubling was the view that "the war in South Vietnam at the present time is a losing proposition."[61] *Time* magazine was more sanguine, parroting MACV chief Harkins's view that there was "a definite improvement" in the situation, even if the PLAF retained "the capability to strike when and where it likes."[62] But polling figures suggested a majority of Americans supported the effort. An August survey revealed that 51 percent regarded Kennedy's approach to the region as either "very good" or "fairly good," while only 14 percent thought it "poor."[63]

Against that backdrop, military and civilian officials conducted yet another SecDef conference on Vietnam, their first since initiating plans in July for a U.S. troop withdrawal. Gathering in Honolulu on October 8, attendees explored a host of subjects, including the augmented use of air and sea power; the metrics on operations, training, defoliation, and Strategic Hamlets; and a proposal from Harkins for an "explosive type operation" designed "to exert sudden and continuing pressure on known areas of VC concentration."[64] Harkins hoped the scheme, which he reviewed conceptually with Diem in September, "could be the basis for a bold plan to destroy the VC with one massive integrated all-out effort." Indicative of his perpetual optimism, the plan jibed with his belief that one year was all he needed to defeat the Communists. Hardly anyone in a position of responsibility shared that timetable, he acknowledged, including the GVN. Although Diem appreciated Harkins's planning and optimism, he thought it more appropriate to settle on three years instead of one.[65] So did South Vietnamese Secretary of State Nguyen Dinh Thuan, who accepted the three-year calendar as the "most optimistic estimate" for concluding the war.[66] But stepping up military operations made great sense, regardless. Even if officials doubted the likelihood that a single, climactic assault would stanch the Communist insurgency, the value of fighting it with greater speed and intensity—essentially, to boost South Vietnamese morale—was "becoming psychologically necessary," as Nolting put it.[67]

It would become even more necessary given the new trajectory of the American advisory effort. Previously, U.S. troops had provided that vote of confidence, as their growing presence served to convey Washington's commitment to the cause. But now that McNamara was scheduling their removal rather than their reinforcement, the question of American resolve became freighted once more. The friction between those imperatives was on full display at Honolulu. McNamara shot down the prospect of further air resources for South Vietnam, noting that recommendations for additional pilots would be received "coolly." Washington's objectives, he told Harkins, were "to help the Vietnamese fight their war and to reduce, not increase our own combat role."[68] Yet even as the conferees sought to compile a "progress report on [the] 3-year program for SVN," discussion of the schedule, and particularly its troop withdrawal elements, was absent from the proceedings. Harkins reportedly "did not have time to present his plan for phasing out U.S. personnel in Viet-Nam," though he noted that doing so would probably require large increases in U.S. military assistance and greater sums for the GVN defense budget, along with putting many more Vietnamese under arms.[69] Planning assumptions held that the war would remain demanding through mid-1965 but then decline in intensity, after which the insurgency would be brought "within acceptable limits" during the 1967 fiscal year.[70]

Yet no official—military or civilian—offered any compelling justification for how or why those developments would come to pass. They simply presumed that Diem and his armed forces would degrade the PLAF and NLF to allow for Saigon to control the country thereafter. It was a crucial assumption behind withdrawal planning—untested and, in time, grounded in the remarkable premise that the enemy would remain a static force. Nor was there any serious effort to determine the precise time frame for the provision of U.S. special assistance. The choice of a three-year window was simply a ballpark figure greater than the highly ambitious one-year schedule and less than a politically risky one of five years or more. For all the rigor and discipline McNamara imposed on his management of DoD operations, those qualities were absent in his planning for and conduct of the war itself.[71]

The presumption of GVN responsibility, moreover, continued to rest on the progress narrative, and McNamara sought feverishly to maintain that theme in the meeting's wake. Speaking to reporters upon his return to Washington, the Secretary stressed that the war was proceeding apace, as he had been trumpeting all summer and into the fall. It was a judgment Harkins expressed as well, noting that U.S. assistance was paying off, with "evidence that the tide of battle in Vietnam against the communists is turning." McNamara scoffed at the declaration. It was "too early" to make such a concrete appraisal or even "to predict the final outcome," but he did assert that "a tremendous amount of progress" had been made since the advent of the limited partnership. Indeed, he was more encouraged than ever about the course of the conflict. Yet even as he continued to push for an American withdrawal in three years' time, McNamara refrained from saying so publicly. Asked whether he was "sufficiently encouraged" by progress in the war to cite a date for bringing U.S. troops home, he responded curtly: "No, certainly not."[72]

Still, the notion of progress suffused internal deliberations as well as the administration's external messaging. Forrestal conveyed "cautious optimism" in relaying bullish reports to Kennedy in mid-September, all of which—on casualty metrics, crop prices, and village morale—seemed to be moving in the right direction.[73] Other quarters were even more effusive. The deputy chief of mission in Saigon, William C. Trueheart, said he was "tremendously encouraged by developments in South Vietnam," noting that progress in the war "had been little short of sensational," with comparable improvements in intelligence gathering.[74] A State Department summary from early fall was similarly upbeat, noting that Saigon and the RVNAF were "confident and anxious to get on with the job," with signs suggesting "that the people as a whole now believe the GVN will win[.]"[75] By December, State's Roger Hilsman would reference the 11,000 U.S. troops then in South Vietnam to illustrate that the United States had provided the GVN with a "considerable counterguerrilla capability." While Diem remained skittish about American advisers having extensive contact with South Vietnamese officials, evidence suggested that the heightened presence "has improved morale at all levels of the GVN administration."[76] Indeed, Ted Heavner, who now ran State's Vietnam desk, had "the distinct impression that many if not most civil servants believe the GVN will win in the space of a year or two."[77] This was precisely the kind of reporting that could validate McNamara's efforts to turn the war over to the South Vietnamese.

But the timing of the turnover was critical, as it shaped Vietnamese perceptions of the American commitment. The South Vietnamese needed to believe that "the Americans are in Vietnam at the invitation of the government," Nolting told Nhu, "and that they intend to continue to help until victory has been won. Then they would leave." The ambassador thought it vital to knock down any talk of Washington gravitating toward a neutral solution. Yet that was precisely the fear among locals— that the Americans would leave too soon, rather than stay too long, and "slip out through the door of neutrality."[78] It was a concern officials had repeatedly sought to quash since the onset of the Kennedy program in

May 1961, and which remained unsettled. Over eighteen months later, and after more than a full year of the "limited partnership," Deputy Under Secretary of State U. Alexis Johnson would report that Diem "constantly seeks reassurance that we are not going to be influenced by the French to seek a negotiated 'neutral solution' in South Vietnam."[79]

Such reassurance was warranted, as several U.S. officials were growing more dubious about the war. John Helble, the consul in Hue, was dispatching "relatively pessimistic" reports that were generating lots of interest, particularly from Averell Harriman and his deputy, Edward E. Rice.[80] Harriman acknowledged significant improvement since Washington had beefed up its programs, but he remained "concerned about the dangers of over-optimism in Viet-Nam."[81] Michael Forrestal told Robert Kennedy of his and Harriman's fear that the war was "not going as well out there as one might be led to believe," with the political challenges in South Vietnam "growing relatively worse." They were increasingly concerned about Diem and his inability to convince the South Vietnamese that they were better off with the GVN than with the NLF.[82]

Those conflicting reports made it exceedingly difficult for Washington to formulate policy. Optimists and pessimists alike populated all the key agencies and rendered contradictory judgments about the war. According to Taylor's naval aide, "considerable differences of opinion" existed within the Executive Branch, particularly regarding the Strategic Hamlet Program. While such differences were themselves not unusual, the "resolution of opposing views is difficult because of a paucity of information," with "doubters" existing in the Pentagon and at State, and with Mike Forrestal at the White House.[83] Maintenance of the U.S. commitment seemed essential, nonetheless. According to Heavner's team, defeat would be devastating, for "a Communist victory would have a strong impact on all of our allies by tending to devalue our commitments to them," a point he surmised rather than substantiated. Aside from providing North Vietnam with a steady supply of rice, the fall of Saigon would "add 14 million vigorous people to the Communist Bloc, and give the Bloc a strategic salient into the heart of Free Asia." Victory for the United States and South Vietnam, on the other hand, would prove that "underdeveloped nations can defeat 'wars of liberation' with our help, strike a telling blow to the mystique of the 'wave of the future', and save the tough and hard fighting Vietnamese people from the Communist regime they manifestly do not want."[84] Written in early October, that paper captured several dynamics informing policy: the obsession with credibility, the threat of falling dominoes, the volatility of modernization, persistent concerns about monolithic communism, the imperative of waging counterinsurgency warfare—collectively, the crosscurrents of national security on the New Frontier.

Come the third week of the month, though, all eyes turned toward the Caribbean and the showdown over Moscow's deployment of nuclear missiles to Cuba. Beginning on October 16, Kennedy and his national security team huddled in secret to hammer out an appropriate response. The crisis became public on October 22 as Kennedy quarantined the island, demanded the removal of Soviet offensive weapons, and delivered his own threat of offensive action. Six days later, after dramatic exchanges at the United Nations, public and private communications between Kennedy and Khrushchev, and frantic back-channel diplomacy, the thirteen days of the Cuban missile crisis ended with a Soviet promise to crate its missiles and return them to Russia. A more complete resolution, which did not materialize until November 20, awaited the removal of those and other weapons, the end of the quarantine, and assurances against a U.S. invasion of Cuba.[85]

By then, developments were already in train that would reshape U.S.-South Vietnamese relations. Senator Mike Mansfield was roughly midway through a fact-finding trip to Berlin and Southeast Asia—at Kennedy's request—that would play an outsized role in altering the limited partnership. What Mansfield found in South Vietnam was startling and disconcerting. He bemoaned the lack of progress since he had last visited the country "seven years and billions of dollars" earlier. Except for the cities, Vietnam was "still an insecure place which is run at least at night largely by the Vietcong." It was therefore unfortunate but necessary "to face the fact that we are once again at the beginning of the beginning." If the Strategic Hamlet Program and other measures did not bear fruit, then the United States might need to contemplate "going to war fully ourselves against the guerrillas—and the establishment of some form of neocolonial rule in South Vietnam." Mansfield therefore implored Kennedy to consider the extent and duration of support the United States was prepared to provide, but to reflect, first, on whether its interests in the country were "vital" or merely "essential." Answers to those questions would go a long way toward devising policy with the "realism and restraint" it required, two considerations that likely appealed to the president's own pragmatic posture.[86]

Kennedy was irked by Mansfield's report nevertheless. He had been receiving sunnier accounts of progress in the war, and so found himself "angry" with Mansfield—but angry mostly with himself, since he largely agreed with the senator's assessment.[87] His discussion with Mansfield about the trip, which took place in Palm Beach the day after Christmas, was a disappointing coda to the year, at least as far as Vietnam was concerned.

Developments in Southeast Asia and the Caribbean reflected the broader difficulties Kennedy faced as president. Sitting down with journalists from the major TV networks, JFK mused about the nation's troubles in a wide-ranging conversation earlier in December. What was needed, he stressed, was persistence and perseverance, themes he had long emphasized during his time in office. "I think our people get awfully impatient and maybe fatigued and tired," he conceded, with Americans wondering whether they could offload their collective burden in the Cold War. They simply could not "lay it down," he stated, "and I don't see how we are going to lay it down in this century." Still, they needed to address the country's struggles with realism and restraint. The challenges facing the country were not only more difficult than Kennedy had once imagined, but the nation's "ability to bring about a favorable result" was also more limited than he previously realized.[88] This, too, was a familiar refrain, harkening back to his remarks—delivered thirteen months to the day in Seattle—about the limits of American power and the rejection of policy extremes. His commitment to those principles would be tested early, and then repeatedly, in the coming year.

4

Modification

January 1963–April 1963

On January 2, 1963, after locating a PLAF radio transmitter roughly thirty-five miles southwest of Saigon, near Ap Bac, 1,200 ARVN troops and their American advisers set out to clear approximately 340 Communist guerrillas out of the area. Instead of reverting to form and retreating in the face of overwhelming numbers and firepower, the PLAF stood its ground. Over sixty ARVN soldiers and three Americans died in the daylong engagement, with the Communists losing about 100 of their own. Since the PLAF ultimately vacated the field, MACV deemed the operation a success—a plausible verdict if the war was a conventional one. But it was an unconventional one, with the conquest of territory less important than the allegiance of the population. Hanoi and the NLF thus learned they could hold their own in a pitched battle against the RVNAF and their American advisers as they looked to control larger portions of the countryside. For President Kennedy, who saw the images of downed U.S. helicopters in the press, it was an inauspicious start to the year, especially as it came only two weeks after he received the troubling Mansfield report about developments in South Vietnam.[1]

The Battle of Ap Bac took many by surprise and exposed worrying developments in the war. Key indices of Communist strength—capabilities, order of battle, operations, and casualties inflicted—had been rising since the onset of the Kennedy assistance effort. Although estimates of PLAF forces varied, they ranged from 22,000 to 24,000 "hard-core" members, an increase of between 5,000 and 7,000 since early 1962. Their supporting components, however, approached 100,000, and the Communists had little trouble in augmenting their ranks.[2] In fact, analyses of combined PLAF strength, later furnished by the Vietnamese Communists, pegged their full-time numbers at roughly 50,000, with several thousand arriving in South Vietnam through Laos and Cambodia via the Ho Chi Minh trail. By November 1962, moreover, they were implementing a "stand and fight" directive to engage GVN forces in the kind of battle that took place at Ap Bac.[3] In all, the PLAF comprised a growing, more confident, and increasingly lethal force.

At the same time, the RVNAF was suffering from defects that would continue to plague its performance. Poor leadership, corruption, a politicized officer corps, and a reluctance to take casualties stemmed from incentives that privileged loyalty to Diem over proficiency in combat. Their American counterparts knew of those flaws and ARVN's lethargic approach to battle, but remained largely mum, as they were loath to criticize the South Vietnamese and thereby add to frictions between Washington and Saigon. The reluctance to air serious concerns contributed to the losses at Ap Bac, which crystallized the deficiencies already in evidence. While the battle was not itself militarily significant, it highlighted alarming trends that affected the course of the war.

Equally discouraging were treatments of the battle in the American press. Commentary on Ap Bac savaged the South Vietnamese armed forces—the first major blemish on the U.S.-GVN partnership. The *New York Times* expressed repeated concern about Saigon's ability to manage the war. Worse, Arthur Krock reminded readers of Kennedy's own skepticism, expressed as a senator in 1954, about the folly of providing aid to a people not willing to die for their own independence.[4] More conservative publications, such as the *Wall Street Journal,* cast doubt on the U.S. assistance program altogether, with the *Chicago Tribune* recommending "disengagement" from Vietnam and from similar "commitments on the periphery."[5]

But the administration was likely to increase its commitment instead of abandoning it. According to the *Washington Post,* Americans could expect "stepped-up fighting and deeper United States involvement" throughout the course of 1963; reportedly, MACV chief Gen. Paul D. Harkins and CINCPAC Adm. Harry D. Felt were even contemplating the assumption of combat command over South Vietnamese forces.[6] Nevertheless, mass circulation outlets cautioned against too much pessimism, even as they recognized the problems at hand. *Time* and *Newsweek*, for instance, quoted U.S. advisers criticizing the RVNAF for having turned in "a 'miserable performance,'" with the South Vietnamese repeating mistakes they should have rectified.[7] Should those problems persist, the United States would find itself "ever more involved in the struggle for Southeast Asia," a struggle that had already claimed the lives of over sixty Americans.[8] But "to conclude from this experience that all is lost in Vietnam," as *Newsweek* put it, "is to be more darkly defeatist than a reasoned appraisal justifies." *Time* and *Life* argued much the same.[9]

Although Ap Bac drew considerable public attention to U.S. policy in Vietnam—scrutiny Kennedy had long sought to avoid—the engagement seemed to have little impact on the president's standing. His January numbers remained strong, especially in the wake of the Cuban Missile Crisis, with 74 percent of Americans approving of his performance, up from an October low of 62 percent. At least as significant, he received fewer negative marks, with his 25 percent disapproval rating of October dropping to 14 percent in January.[10] Kennedy's public silence on Ap Bac may have preserved those figures, but he did reference Vietnam in several statements later that month. He was particularly emphatic in his State of the Union address, declaring that "the spearpoint of aggression has been blunted in Viet-Nam," that the United States had "maintained the frontiers of freedom from Viet-Nam to West Berlin," and that the longing for independence was no different in Southeast Asia than it was in Central Europe. Honoring the memory of servicemen who had given their lives for the "cause of peace and freedom," Kennedy called on all Americans "to live up to their commitment." Days later, in his annual budget message to Congress, he cited the "need and importance" of maintaining U.S. assistance to Saigon. He did likewise in a *Look* magazine article that same week. "History is what men make it," Kennedy declared, "and we would be foolish to think that we can realize our own vision of a free and diverse future without unceasing vigilance, discipline, and labor" in Vietnam, as well as in other hot spots around the world.[11] Repeatedly, Kennedy made the case for patience and persistence in waging the Cold War, especially in fighting its hotter variant in Southeast Asia.

But a sense of urgency took hold among U.S. officials who were trying to figure out what really happened at Ap Bac and what it meant for the limited partnership. Central to their concern was the narrative itself and the need to control it, especially since fallout from the engagement was politically problematic. As congressional liaison Ralph Dungan put it, another such episode "could result in difficulties with Congress."[12] Those difficulties were likely to mount, regardless, as the Mansfield report was soon to become public. With legislators likely to assess Ap Bac against the backdrop of Mansfield's findings, the administration looked to reframe the encounter. Speaking to lawmakers at the White House, Secretary of Defense Robert S. McNamara maintained that the operation was successful, if poorly executed; media reports to the contrary were "incomplete," and journalists were "reporting untruths, as best we've been able to determine." Kennedy, too, thought press accounts were "much more harsh" on the South Vietnamese than circumstances warranted, and that those kinds of stories further complicated Washington's relations with the GVN.[13]

Privately, however, U.S. officials were critical of their allies. Gen. Maxwell D. Taylor, the JCS chair, received more "unfavorable" than "favorable" reports—certainly more than Kennedy received—even as he heaped scorn on reporting about the encounter.[14] That gap between rhetoric and reality reflected a dangerous dynamic at work, as British officials stationed in Saigon recognized. Both MACV and the U.S. embassy, they said, were "under increasing pressure from Washington to show results in return for the enormous investment in this country," a mandate made more difficult by the Ap Bac engagement. The resulting tendency to paint a "rosier" picture than circumstances warranted would undermine their messaging should further setbacks arise.[15] Away from the glare, MACV was "seriously worried by the failure of American advisers to insure that their advice was taken by the Vietnamese."[16] So was McNamara, who told Secretary Rusk that he had "been unhappy about progress in South Viet-Nam for some time"—not the message he was delivering publicly—and that he wanted each member of the Joint Chiefs to visit Vietnam once per quarter. Rusk, too, was "unhappy" and wanted to take a "fresh" look at the situation.[17]

Those assessments came in before the month was out. The military update came from Gen. Earle G. "Bus" Wheeler, the Army chief of staff, who reported in late January on progress in the counterinsurgency, the likely duration of the war, and the steps necessary to bring the effort to a "timely and successful conclusion." Writing to the president following his tour of South Vietnam, Wheeler described RVNAF planning and improvements as likely to provide the GVN with "an ever-increasing measure of control" over its land and people. At the moment, according to State Department intelligence, the PLAF controlled "about 20 percent of the villages and about 9 percent of the rural population" and was enjoying "varying degrees of influence among an additional 47 percent of the villages." Analysts also believed that the Communist presence had "almost certainly improved in urban areas" owing to subversion, terrorism, and propaganda.[18] But as long as the NLF chose not to escalate the conflict—an astounding assumption on Wheeler's part—he thought "the principal ingredients for eventual success" were in place.[19] Reviewing his findings with President Kennedy on February 1, Wheeler was confident that current efforts offered "reasonable prospects" for improving the situation. The United States, therefore, should neither pull out of Vietnam nor insert large numbers of forces but maintain its current level of support.[20]

A more nuanced assessment came from the NSC's Michael Forrestal and the State Department's Roger Hilsman. The two rejected Wheeler's "rosy euphoria" even as they surmised that the GVN was "probably winning" its war against the NLF. Success, however, would not come early. At the current rate, the war would last longer, cost more in terms of money and lives, and still not secure South Vietnam. Forrestal and Hilsman were particularly concerned about the byzantine nature of organizing and planning for the war. There remained "no single country-wide plan worthy of the name but only a variety of regional and provincial plans, some good and some not so good."[21] Such improvisation, Hilsman wrote separately, had generated "great confusion," with upwards of six competing plans operating simultaneously. Nor were military and political approaches implemented consistently. Individual agencies, particularly on the American side, were doing well, but the same was not true of the overall effort.[22]

The Comprehensive Plan for South Vietnam (CPSVN)—the first attempt to harmonize counterinsurgency planning since the advent of the Kennedy administration—sought to change all that. Incorporating a military scheme Harkins had devised to launch coordinated and countrywide attacks against the Communists—the so-called "Explosion," or National Campaign Plan—the CPSVN laid out a schedule of activities and expenses, in accordance with McNamara's instructions of July 1962, that would allow the United States to complete its program of special military assistance by 1965. As Felt described it, the plan aimed to bring the war to a successful conclusion, withdraw U.S. military advisers, and develop within the GVN a capacity to defend itself against the continuing Communist threat. Those three elements of the plan—winning the war, withdrawing U.S. troops, and building a self-sufficient South Vietnam—shared equal billing and envisioned a simultaneous American withdrawal and Communist defeat. It aimed, therefore, not just at progress in the war, but victory, which it defined as enabling the GVN to assert its authority over all areas south of the 17th parallel—though without a more granular understanding of what that authority looked like.[23]

To achieve those goals, MACV needed to intensify and accelerate its training of South Vietnamese security forces. That training, however, demanded an expansion of the U.S. troop presence. The GVN was unlikely to defeat the Communists on its own, so Washington would need to increase American personnel both to train the RVNAF and guide its war-fighting efforts before withdrawing U.S. forces.[24] That handover of responsibility—what subsequent administrations would refer to as "de-Americanizing" or "Vietnamizing" the war—also necessitated rapid increases in the delivery of vital equipment to South Vietnam and an uptick in the tempo of military operations. All of this would cost money, with more of it needed sooner rather than later. Officials therefore looked to revise their military assistance targets for South Vietnam, with the FY 1963 numbers requiring immediate attention. But restructuring U.S. and South Vietnamese force levels though the end of 1965 and beyond called for harmonizing the CPSVN with the entirety of the five-year Military Assistance Program cycle, from the 1963 fiscal year through FY 1968, and likely through the following year as well.[25] As envisioned in the CPSVN, dollar figures would peak in FY 1964 at $218 million, with U.S. troops in country falling from a maximum of 12,200 forces in FY 1965, to 5,900 in FY 1966, and to 1,600 and 1,500 in the 1967 and 1968 fiscal years, respectively.[26]

None of those plans made much sense, however, if they could not deliver a South Vietnamese victory. The Comprehensive Plan therefore built that presumption into its very framework, expecting the insurgency to be "under control at the end of three years[.]" That window, which stretched into December 1965, harkened back to the guidance McNamara had provided in July 1962. To meet the 1965 deadline, the RVNAF would require extensive support, both to defeat the Communists "and to prepare GVN forces for early take-over of U.S. activities." Ceilings on MAP aid, therefore, were no longer applicable; American and South Vietnamese forces would receive whatever funds were necessary.[27] Significantly, though, the plan was silent on the disposition of U.S. aid should the war turn sour. It simply assumed that a U.S. withdrawal and a GVN victory went hand in hand.

Indeed, projections about battlefield success and the future costs and manpower needs it depended on were no more than suppositions of how events might play out. As Felt indicated, the CPSVN had "been developed using factors based on in-country experience to date and is subject to change." Recalibration was thus an essential part of the process; officials would need to re-evaluate conditions on a semiannual basis, Wheeler recognized, to "make alterations in the Comprehensive Plan as indicated by the reassessment." Those alterations included the possibility—even desirability—of troop increases, meaning the Pentagon should consider additional troop requests "in a favorable light." All told, the CPSVN—including its estimates of the absolute number of U.S. forces and their timetable for withdrawal—was both fluid and flexible. It was not "a refined detailed program," Felt maintained, since fine-tuning would take place with the development and revision of the MAP.[28] As much as it marked a comprehensive effort to program the entirety of U.S. assistance, it was and would remain both provisional and presumptive.

In fact, within days of its receipt by the Joint Chiefs, military officials were emphasizing its contingent nature. They made clear that the drawdown of U.S. troops was dependent on the course of events; although withdrawal was a vital element of the Comprehensive Plan, it was less an ironclad commitment to leave the country than a general expression of policy preference. According to Rear Adm. L. C. Heinz, who helped refine both the MAP and the Comprehensive Plan at the Pentagon, the CPSVN was "not intended to be a detailed plan but rather a conceptual analysis of what would be required to turn over the war to the Vietnamese and control the insurgency in three years."[29] But even that goal seemed up for grabs. According to Maj. Gen. William B. Rosson, Wheeler's special assistant for special warfare, no Vietnamese with whom he had spoken thought the Communists could be neutralized within that time frame, and "only a handful of Americans harbored this belief." Col. Wilbur Wilson, the senior U.S. military advisor in the Saigon area, likewise regarded the withdrawal plan as "day-dreaming." So did Lt. Col. John Paul Vann, the senior U.S. adviser to the ARVN VII Corps—and eyewitness to the debacle at Ap Bac—who "denounced as being totally unrealistic those who believed that victory was at hand."[30] The CPSVN thus came off as flexible at best and foolish at worst.

Publicity

Given the tensions between the state of the war and the removal of U.S. advisers, managing public expectations became an even more central concern for Kennedy officials. While the circumstances were new—the trouble at Ap Bac, the impending release of the Mansfield report—the need to tell a better story was not. Coverage in weekly publications such as *Newsweek* or *Life* was more favorable than in the daily press, but generally, as Rusk maintained, the war was "going better than being reported to U.S. public."[31] That was precisely how the Special Group (CI) saw things. Its members were convinced Washington's policies were correct, but, according to the deputy director of the U.S. Information Agency, Donald Wilson, "you would never know it from the press coverage of Viet-Nam in this country."[32] The extent to which that coverage mattered was open to debate, for Americans seemingly cared little about the war. "Despite dramatic increase in American involvement," Nolting cabled from Saigon, "visiting editors and reporters repeatedly advise us that stateside public simply hasn't been stirred" by events in South Vietnam. Whether disinterest stemmed from Vietnam's remoteness, or from reports of progress, or from more dramatic developments elsewhere, Americans regarded the war as a sideshow. Uplifting stories got "little play," Nolting bemoaned, "while bad news often hits page one."[33] Wheeler, too, focused on the negative reporting. Public and congressional opinion was increasingly dubious of the RVNAF and fearful that the war was "misguided."[34] In recognition of those dynamics, senior press, information, and liaison officials met on January 21 to discuss how they might provide "favorable accounts" of developments "to the right press men under the right circumstances." Specifically, they sought to focus attention on upcoming news conferences from Felt and Wheeler, who would mouth the necessary party line.[35]

The administration got more than just positive spin, for it was in those appearances that word began to leak of an American withdrawal. The first hints came from Felt, who alluded to it at a Pentagon news conference in late January. Asked about winning the war within a "reasonable time period," Felt said that "three years is reasonable, and I think I can predict victory." The Associated Press described Felt's estimate, which followed his upbeat review of activities in Vietnam, as "the most optimistic yet voiced by any ranking U.S. official" since the advent of the limited partnership in late 1961.[36] Less than a week later, journalists asked Wheeler to comment on Felt's prediction at a presser of his own. "I certainly would not disagree with Admiral Felt," he said, "although I would prefer not to try to assess a time limit in months or days or years in a difficult war such as this." Nevertheless, when asked about a schedule for lowering the American profile, Wheeler conceded that there was indeed such a plan. "What we are really shooting for," he admitted, "is in about three years we would be in a position to start making some reductions. This again would have to be on a pick and choose basis."[37]

Those calendars conflicted with predictions of a long struggle. While U.S. and South Vietnamese forces were making progress in the counterinsurgency, victory—as the Americans were now defining it—would not come anytime soon. Wheeler himself had made that point upon his return from Vietnam. The war would still demand a "long, victorious effort," and while there was "reason for us to look forward to winning," it was "not yet time to form a victory parade."[38] Assistant Secretary of State Averell Harriman also had warned recently about making "over-optimistic statements to the press and to public officials," maintaining that "this will be a long struggle, with many frustrations."[39] McNamara, too, sought to emphasize the indeterminate length of the conflict. Speaking to the press in late February, the Secretary turned back suggestions that he and Wheeler were "optimistic" in their assessments of progress. "I don't believe I have ever indicated it would be other than a long, hard struggle extending over a period of years," he said. He was optimistic "in the sense that progress is discernible," but he was "not predicting the termination of the conflict. It will be a long, hard, dangerous conflict."[40]

The liabilities of a long war became further apparent with the publication of the Mansfield report in late February. Kennedy had been disturbed upon reading it in December, with its description of South

Vietnam as less stable and less responsive to its people than when Mansfield had been there in 1955. Analysts at State, moreover, feared that its hints of an American withdrawal "would probably undermine such improvement as had been previously registered."[41] Ultimately, its release on February 24 raised the very issues the administration feared most. The *New York Times* highlighted Mansfield's concern that the war was becoming Americanized, as well as the senator's call to reassess the U.S. assistance program. Suggesting that both President Kennedy and Attorney General Robert F. Kennedy had "publicly pledged" to what the Communists and the GVN "could only interpret as a fight to the finish," columnist Hanson Baldwin maintained that "the United States appears to be fully committed to continue massive aid to South Vietnam." Highlighting the dominoes in danger of falling, Baldwin thought "it would be very hard at this late hour to disengage in whole or in part in South Vietnam without dangerous political and psychological repercussions throughout Asia."[42] While the *Times* recognized the war was Saigon's to win, it supported Mansfield's finding that this was "no time for 'meat ax' cuts in aid to Southeast Asia nor for lessening our effort in South Vietnam."[43] The paper would continue to lobby for an enduring presence, maintaining that the U.S. effort in the region, and in South Vietnam in particular, must "continue to be resolute and extensive because of the deep American commitment."[44] The Mansfield Report thus tightened the knot surrounding U.S. policy in Vietnam, questioning the prospects for victory while prompting calls to stay the course.

The president agreed with the need to remain steadfast, at least in public. Asked about the Mansfield report roughly two weeks after its release, Kennedy confessed, "I don't see how we are going to be able, unless we are going to pull out of Southeast Asia and turn it over to the Communists, how we are going to be able to reduce very much our economic programs and military programs in South Viet-Nam, in Cambodia, in Thailand. I think that unless you want to withdraw from the field and decide that it is in the national interest to permit that area to collapse, I would think that it would be impossible to substantially change it particularly, as we are in a very intensive struggle in those areas."[45] Privately, however, Kennedy was souring on the commitment, and it was Mansfield himself who became privy to the president's growing disenchantment. Following a White House meeting with congressional leaders that spring, at which Mansfield questioned the administration's pursuit of the war, Kennedy ushered him into the Oval Office for a personal conversation. According to presidential aide Kenneth O'Donnell, who witnessed the exchange, Kennedy told Mansfield he shared the senator's concern and intended to pull U.S. troops out of Vietnam. But he could do so only after his reelection in 1964. Later, after Mansfield left the room, Kennedy explained his reasoning. If he withdrew the troops prior to the election, "we would have another Joe McCarthy red scare on our hands, but I can do it after I'm reelected."[46] The key, therefore, was to make sure he was reelected.

Revising the Comprehensive Plan

With the Mansfield report as backdrop, work on the Comprehensive Plan for South Vietnam moved forward during the late winter and early spring of 1963. Revisions centered on several components, all of which were intertwined, including the Military Assistance Program, the withdrawal of U.S. troops, and the establishment and evaluation of benchmarks to assess progress. Regarding the troop reduction, McNamara signaled his desire for a sharper draw down than originally conceived. Conferring with the Joint Chiefs in early March, he wanted U.S. servicemen to be used "strictly in an advisory role" in three years and for numbers to top out at between 500 to 700 personnel.[47] Those figures were only a sliver of the 12,800 U.S. troops presently in Vietnam, and which officials now expected to rise to between 15,000 and 16,000.[48]

But McNamara was confident that progress in the war would allow for a troop withdrawal. It was a confidence at odds with his January remarks to Rusk, suggesting that he reserved his more candid assessments for officials at his station or above. According to Assistant Secretary of Defense Nitze, guiding assumptions held that Washington and Saigon would "win the war" in that three-year period, allowing the United States to assume more of a "true" advisory role. McNamara's conception of "winning" did not mean that "every Viet Cong will be out," but the bulk of South Vietnam should be "under govt control in 3 to 5 years."[49] Early revisions of the CPSVN thus maintained its prior presumption that the removal of U.S. forces tracked alongside victory in the war.

The process of expanding and then contracting those forces meant officials needed to revise their military assistance requirements for South Vietnam. Training, equipment deliveries, and combat operations would need to accelerate if Washington and Saigon were "to defeat the insurgency by the end of 1965," which meant funding levels also needed to rise, with the greatest amount programmed for the 1964 fiscal year.[50] But with its onset only months away, the need to finalize the MAP and CPSVN was paramount; as Taylor put it, "all involved governmental agencies at the Washington level" now needed to sign on.[51] Yet McNamara refused to wait. Much as he had done following the Taylor Report in the fall of 1961, he authorized funds for augmenting the RVNAF prior to the full and considered agreement of the relevant U.S. officials.[52]

Despite his hurried acceptance of force totals, McNamara remained concerned about the broader contours of the CPSVN. The cost of intensifying and accelerating the counterinsurgency was proving to be higher than he imagined. Officials in the State Department were equally uneasy, not only about dollar figures, but about whether the scheduled drawdown of troops was too rapid. Washington therefore asked its embassy in Saigon for thoughts on whether to extend the phaseout. Its assumption was that doing so would reduce the costs planned for FY 1964, boost the chance that Saigon could take over the fighting in FY 1967, and lessen the risk of declining morale in the face of an early U.S. withdrawal. Each of those issues would be on the table at the next SecDef conference, scheduled for early May.[53]

In the meantime, the Pentagon sought to shape the Comprehensive Plan to ensure its responsiveness to battlefield conditions. It thus reinforced guidance that the withdrawal plan remain fluid and flexible. The Chiefs acted upon that presumption as they sought to calibrate RVNAF force levels to wartime contingencies. In April, they asked that Harkins provide semiannual reports "to support meaningful modifications" to the CPSVN, with an eye toward receiving his first batch of recommended changes in July.[54] Pentagon civilians also treated the plan as both elastic and aspirational; planning to achieve a drawdown of U.S. troops, they understood, hardly amounted to a coherent strategy for doing so. According to William P. Bundy, the deputy assistant secretary for International Security Affairs—and the McNamara aide most closely engaged with withdrawal planning—the CPSVN was "a highly generalized document, lacking detailed narrative and statistical backup upon which valid programming decisions might be made."[55] The extent to which it remained mutable awaited conversations in Honolulu, but it clearly originated as a prospective rather than a final schedule, and therefore remained subject to revision.

Its political value—never far from its founding rationale—also became more apparent as the administration struggled to realize broader policy goals, particularly with respect to the economic health of the nation. Kennedy had entered office as a fiscal conservative, committed to a balanced budget and a cautious approach to spending. But the economy had remained sluggish throughout 1961 and into 1962, a condition that endangered the national interest; as author Richard Reeves put it, all policy for Kennedy was national security policy, and an economically unhealthy nation was a vulnerable nation. The president himself maintained that if the country became weaker economically, "our influence abroad will be reduced."[56] To reverse the trend, Kennedy now shed his economic conservatism for the Keynesian approach his more liberal advisers were recommending. He thus proposed a demand-side tax cut in a January 1963 message to Congress to "speed the economy toward full employment and a higher rate of growth." He then stumped for the measure that winter and spring—in the face of stiff opposition from budget hawks—maintaining that there was "no more single fruitful or urgent business" before the Congress than tax revision.[57]

Kennedy's economic concerns extended to spending abroad as well as at home. The outflow of dollars from the United States had long been a source of worry, especially as foreigners redeemed those dollars in gold, which they were doing at alarmingly high rates, putting added pressure on the currency. American tourism and capital exports were two of the major culprits, but chief among them was the cost of stationing troops abroad—costs that seemed incommensurate with the strategy they were designed to support. Six U.S. divisions, comprising 257,000 troops, were deployed to Western Europe. Their mission was to hold at bay the Warsaw Pact armies for between sixty and ninety days in the event of hostilities. But with the West Europeans failing to contribute sufficient forces to sustain a ninety-day defense, and with NATO likely resorting to nuclear weapons within a much shorter time frame, Kennedy wondered about the strategic rationale for such a heavy U.S. troop presence, especially since he doubted whether Moscow would risk such a war anyway. He therefore wanted American forces "thinned out," unless and until NATO countries contributed their fair share. To rectify the imbalance, McNamara planned to withdraw between 50,000 and 70,000 troops from the continent.[58] The intersection of those strategic and economic interests bedeviled U.S. policymakers who sought to reassure Western Europe of Washington's commitment to its security while addressing economic insecurities of their own. By April, Kennedy had asked for deep cuts in foreign military expenditures, a measure that all recognized could come only through the redeployment of U.S. forces abroad.[59]

But officials also worried that the United States was spending too much on foreign economic aid. Kennedy was at pains to point out that Washington was doing so for hard-nosed reasons and not just humanitarian ones. To generate greater support, he wanted the Pentagon to "help sell Congress on economic assistance." Lawmakers were poised to "cut the heart out of the AID program," he warned the NSC in January 1963, and if they succeeded, "we would be in real danger."[60] The array of legislators who sought to slash foreign aid or refocus its impact cut across party lines. Republicans wanted those funds to pry open local economies to American capital, while Democrats had soured on aiding undemocratic, albeit non-Communist, regimes. The administration's $4.9 billion request was thus facing bipartisan trouble.

That coalition of conservatives and liberals prompted Kennedy to change his approach to securing those funds. He replaced the director at the Agency for International Development, Fowler Hamilton, with Budget chief David E. Bell, whose efforts to achieve efficiencies had won plaudits. To make the case for preserving current levels of support, Kennedy also enlisted the help of stalwart Cold Warrior Gen. Lucius D. Clay. It was not the first time JFK had called on Clay in a moment of need. As the Berlin Wall was going up in August 1961, Kennedy asked him to lead a military convoy through the East German corridor into West Berlin to highlight America's commitment to western access. The president had also relied on Clay to help win the release of anti-Castro Cubans captured at the Bay of Pigs. He now asked the general, a lifelong Republican, to head off a congressional revolt against foreign aid. Clay's "Committee to Strengthen the Security of the Free World" met in January and February and set its sights on AID, the Military Assistance Program, and the Alliance for Progress, as well as on the broader rationale for foreign support.[61]

The move backfired, as Clay criticized the assumptions, management, and outcomes of Washington's aid programs. Released on March 22, Clay's report damaged the administration's position, amplifying the common criticisms of foreign assistance. The United States had been "trying to do too much for too many too soon," it stated, pronouncing the nation "overextended in resources and undercompensated in result, and that no end of foreign aid is either in sight or mind."[62] Although the administration tried to soften Clay's language, its effort to secure an aid budget at the desired levels became a much tougher sell. Kennedy thus trimmed his sails, slashing $400 million from his original request.[63]

His preemptive strike did little to quiet congressional voices. Familiar foes, such as Otto E. Passman [D-LA], the longtime aid critic who chaired the House Appropriations subcommittee on Foreign Operations, vowed that "we are no longer going to be suckers." It was a refrain common to conservative lawmakers, Republicans and Democrats alike. But J. William Fulbright [D-AR], who chaired the Senate Foreign Relations Committee and was among the more thoughtful members of the upper chamber, also signaled that cuts were in the offing; so, too, had even more cerebral voices, such as political scientist Hans Morgenthau, who called for "tougher-minded selectivity" in disbursing foreign aid.[64] Although opinion was moving in Kennedy's direction—support for foreign aid had increased from 51 percent to 58 percent over the previous four years, while opposition fell from 33 percent to 30 percent—the administration was still in trouble.[65] *Life* magazine, which called for Congress to fund the program at a further reduced level of $4 billion, epitomized the emerging consensus. It hoped the program might still live up to its promise as a "tool of Western diplomacy," capable of serving the country's long-term interests.[66] The implication was that it had yet to do so.

A Token Withdrawal

In light of those difficulties, the opportunity to scale back foreign and military assistance, albeit prudently and responsibly, carried real appeal—even more so if it addressed the growing American footprint in South Vietnam. For that reason, Washington embraced the troop reduction that BRIAM chief Robert Thompson floated in April 1963. Thompson had already raised the idea with U.S. officials in April 1962 and again with Taylor that September in Saigon. By early 1963, he was determined to push for a symbolic withdrawal more widely and energetically. His opportunity came on an eagerly anticipated swing through the United States in advance of talks with Her Majesty's Government in London. Ben Wood, who chaired the Vietnam Working Group, was "delighted" to learn of the upcoming visit and proposed that Thompson meet with several audiences in Washington and at Fort Bragg. Ultimately, Thompson's schedule included four days of conversation with senior and midlevel officials throughout the U.S. government, including with Kennedy at the White House.[67]

Thompson made his pitch against the backdrop of presumed progress in Vietnam. Whereas he had been "cautiously optimistic" about developments in the spring of 1962, by March 1963 he could report that Saigon "is beginning to win the shooting war against the Vietcong." It was a position, he said, supported "by all members of the Mission."[68] Nevertheless, and conscious of the "war-weariness" within South Vietnam, Thompson stressed that "every effort should be made to prove to the people of the country (and to the world) that we are winning."[69] The United States, too, would benefit from such a display. He had detected "increasing American public dissatisfaction with the slow progress being made and with the poor return for an enormous American investment."[70] It therefore was necessary to "try and achieve a genuine and substantial white area not later than the end of August."[71] Stopping first in Honolulu, Thompson told U.S. military officials that "if things go right by end of 1963, we should take one thousand U.S. military personnel out of RVN at one time, make big production of this and publicize widely." Those moves "would show (1) RVN is winning; (2) take steam out of anti-Diemists; and (3) dramatically illustrate honesty of U.S. intentions." This "token" troop reduction "would have a beneficial psychological effect as an indication that we are enjoying success in bringing the insurgency to an end and that we intended to pull out as soon as the situation would permit."[72]

Thompson repeated those arguments in early April briefings for Kennedy officials in Washington. Meeting with Averell Harriman, Mike Forrestal, William Sullivan, and Ben Wood at the State Department, he indicated that McNamara had already inquired about the "advisability of reducing U.S. forces."[73] Thereafter, Thompson pushed the administration to consider an early withdrawal of U.S. troops. If progress continued throughout 1963, and if it were possible to establish a white area that summer, then "it might be wise to reduce U.S. strength by a significant amount, say 1,000 men."[74] Days later, he delivered a similar message to

Kennedy at the White House, maintaining that such a pledge could be made only on certain conditions: Saigon's prosecution of the counterinsurgency continued to show progress; it was possible to declare one or two provinces "white," or cleared of the NLF; and confidence of success continued to grow throughout the year. If circumstances "improved sufficiently to justify this reduction," then the administration would gain real advantages in making its "case to Congress and the American public."[75] Although meeting notes failed to capture Kennedy's reaction to the proposal, the president appreciated the conversation nonetheless, congratulating Thompson on his presentation "and on his very fine work in Viet-Nam."[76] Thompson then repeated the exercise for the Special Group (CI), targeting the middle of 1964 as the moment when the GVN might have "sufficient control of the population" to shield it from the PLAF—the only valid benchmark, he thought, for their combined efforts in Vietnam.[77]

The Thompson meetings were a triumph. Having visited with senior members of the administration, as well as with line officials formulating Vietnam policy, Thompson lifted their spirits and gave them a target to aim at. His "tremendous reception" owed much to his reputation, but also to his perceived judgment and expertise. According to Dick Ledward, who was leaving his post in Washington as counsellor at the British embassy, Thompson "is regarded here as completely infallible and indeed did a lot to restore some Americans' confidence in themselves."[78] Central to that restoration was Thompson's faith that "we are winning" and were "on the right" track in Vietnam. There would be no better expression of that progress than for Washington to pursue "unilaterally and without prior announcement" the removal of one thousand troops by the end of 1963.[79]

Thompson's proposal was so compelling that work on it moved forward almost at once. By mid-April, Ben Wood noted "very confidentially" that McNamara would order military officials "to cut their forces by 1000 at the end of this year," and would make clear to those officials that "large additional funds will not be available" for use. In communicating those directives to Roger Hilsman, now heading the Far Eastern bureau at the State Department, Wood noted the resistance they created within the military.[80] Harkins had "no sympathy with the idea and would oppose it," a stance akin to Wheeler's February 1963 admonition against an early reduction of troops.[81] Nevertheless, State began the preparatory work for implementing the thousand-man troop withdrawal. As part of its planning for the upcoming SecDef conference in Honolulu—McNamara's eighth since the advent of the joint partnership in late 1961—Rusk asked Nolting to reflect on whether the United States should offer to "substantially reduce" its contingent of military advisers in any province within ninety days of declaring it "white." For the time being, this was a matter for Nolting alone. He was not to discuss with the GVN either the token withdrawal or the larger drawdown scheduled for 1965.[82] The Diem government thus remained in the dark about both, a reality that accentuated the "limited" nature of the U.S.-Vietnamese "limited partnership."

McNamara initiated planning for the thousand-man withdrawal at the end of April. Raising the matter with the Joint Chiefs, he noted his particular interest was "in the projected phasing of US personnel strength," and told the Chiefs that during the upcoming Honolulu conference, he would "explore with Ambassador Nolting and State the feasibility of bringing back 1000 troops at the end of this year." He asked the JCS to develop a plan along those lines "on the general assumption that such course of action would be feasible."[83] According to Paul Nitze's notes of the meeting, McNamara wanted the administration to "make something out of it," presumably for publicity purposes. The idea would be to remove U.S. advisors "with plan for SV to take over." Strikingly, Nitze's notes suggest that President Kennedy was supportive of the approach—the earliest concrete evidence that Kennedy embraced the planning to effect a U.S. withdrawal from Vietnam.[84]

Reducing the American footprint took on greater urgency as the GVN raised the volume of its own campaign to lower the U.S. profile in South Vietnam. Diem's unhappiness with Washington spanned the entirety of the bilateral relationship and reflected conflicting positions on a range of political, economic, and military matters. But the escalation of the assistance effort had generated considerable friction and raised the stakes of those disagreements. At root was Diem's hold over the populace; as the United States elevated its presence and involvement in South Vietnamese affairs, and as contacts between Americans and South Vietnamese increased, Diem feared a diminution of political control. His latest concern arose over custody of a piaster fund to support projects linked to the counterinsurgency. Washington and Saigon began negotiating its stewardship in January 1963, but tentative agreements between the two fell apart in late March, largely at the urging of Ngo Dinh Nhu, Diem's brother and political counselor. Nhu had raised several questions about the future of U.S.-South Vietnamese relations, interpreting pointed stories in the American media, such as on the Mansfield Report, as a weakening of U.S. support. His suspicions about the American commitment thus led to waning enthusiasm for the piaster arrangement.[85]

But the greater irritant was the growing number of U.S. personnel in South Vietnam and their perceived impact on Saigon's political fortunes. Their presence in such large numbers—approximately 13,000—was fueling Communist propaganda that GVN officials were "American stooges." It therefore was likely, thought British ambassador to Saigon Harry Hohler, that the Ngos would try to "secure a reduction in the number of American advisers" during the course of the year. While Diem and Nhu would seek to preserve the pipeline for U.S. financial and material assistance, they "now earnestly desire and are likely to demand a reduction of American manpower" throughout the country.[86] By early April, Hohler learned that Diem wanted to remove one-quarter of U.S. troops.[87] In fact, the very day that Thompson raised the token withdrawal with Kennedy in Washington, Diem told Nolting of his wish to reduce the U.S. footprint in South Vietnam. The "number and zeal" of Americans, Diem said, was creating the impression that the country was becoming a U.S. "protectorate." There simply were "too many people here, advising in too much detail on too many matters," and the "remedy" was to cut back on their number. Although Nolting conceded the possibility of a modest withdrawal, he found the conversation disconcerting. Relations were now likely to spiral downward, he told Diem, forcing a change in American policy toward the GVN. Cabling Washington about the encounter, Nolting said it left him "gravely concerned and perplexed."[88]

Indeed, the demands of the Ngos highlighted Washington's dilemma, a dynamic that both helped and hindered the counterinsurgency. The Country Team, for instance, believed it vital that the United States "maintain the present depth of our involvement" for war-fighting purposes, even as that involvement conveyed an image of dependency that compromised the GVN.[89] Back in Washington, officials acknowledged Diem's desire to thin out the U.S. civilian and military presence "at the rice roots," and agreed that the "peak of U.S. numbers should be passed in 1963."[90] To assuage Diem's fears, Nolting proposed that the United States bring Diem into discussions about the plan to withdraw U.S.

advisers from Vietnam. He suggested doing so, however, only after reminding Diem that those advisors were adding tremendous value to the counterinsurgency; it was their presence, Nolting stressed, that had allowed the GVN to achieve a measure of progress in the war, and it was unlikely Saigon could win it without them "in roughly present density for the next year at least."[91]

By the spring of 1963, events in South Vietnam and the United States had intersected to make troop withdrawal an attractive policy. Some of those developments emerged from the war itself. Although numerous reports had painted a positive picture, the black eye of Ap Bac, the unsettling Mansfield Report, and multiple fact-finding missions suggested that U.S. aid and advice had yet to generate consistent and substantial returns. While South Vietnamese forces had racked up battlefield wins as well as losses, the war remained an escalating stalemate and unlikely to end anytime soon. Moreover, the very provision of U.S. foreign aid—to Vietnam or much of anywhere else—had come under fire, as Congress and the American public soured on extending it at levels Kennedy thought essential. The politics of foreign assistance thus tilted toward trimming, or at least better managing, American largesse.

In the case of Vietnam, those outlays included economic and military assistance, but also the stiffening and instructional functions of U.S. advisory troops, whose numbers exceeded 12,000. As was becoming apparent, their presence, while helpful militarily, was creating challenges affecting the counterinsurgency. A targeted withdrawal, therefore, could benefit both South Vietnam and the United States. On the one hand, it would remove a sticking point between the Diem regime and the Kennedy administration, and theoretically demonstrate Saigon's capacity to manage the war itself. On the other, it could underscore the boundaries of an American commitment and serve broader administration goals. The politics of an American troop withdrawal were thus coming into sharper focus.

5

Acceleration

May 1963–August 1963

In the early evening of May 8, in the old imperial capital of Hue, a crowd of Vietnamese Buddhists gathered outside the city's radio station to hear a presentation commemorating the birth of the Gautama Buddha. When it failed to materialize, the crowd became restless. One of the assembled climbed atop the building and replaced the South Vietnamese national flag with that of international Buddhism, flouting a recent decree banning the flying of religious flags and banners. GVN troops swung into action and in the ensuing melee killed and injured over twenty Vietnamese citizens. President Ngo Dinh Diem deflected blame for the incident and pinned it on the Communists, fanning the flames of Buddhist outrage. The confrontation between Saigon and the Buddhists—the country's majority if fragmented religious group, and now a mobilized political force—ushered in a new and more volatile chapter in South Vietnamese political life and a deeply divisive phase in U.S. relations with the GVN. Its impact would alter the partnership and ultimately reshape the American commitment to Saigon.[1]

For President Kennedy, the onset of the Buddhist crisis compounded the troubles flowing from Ap Bac and the Mansfield report. The image of America's ally engaging in religious persecution was likely even more worrisome than those earlier setbacks. But it was not the only crisis Kennedy confronted that May, as the events in South Vietnam shared headlines with those in the American South. Only six hours after the Buddhist incident, Kennedy took to the microphone for his biweekly news conference to address the horrors of Birmingham, Alabama, where White security forces had set police dogs and firehoses on Black citizens protesting the city's discriminatory practices. The shock of those images, relayed in the media, galvanized the American public, as the percentage of those who thought civil rights the country's most urgent problem jumped from 4 to 52 percent.[2]

Although Kennedy received generally high marks for his handling of civil rights—two-thirds of the country was "satisfied" with the way he was addressing the challenge—the politics of social justice were explosive and added to Kennedy's woes. By June, more than half of those polled thought Kennedy's approach was either "poor" or "only fair."[3] New York governor Nelson D. Rockefeller, at that point the favorite to win the Republican nomination for the 1964 presidential election, was eager to exploit Kennedy's failings. Rockefeller had made news in April 1963 by assailing JFK for aiding "freedom fighters" in Vietnam while "holding them back and preventing them from operating in Cuba." He then charged Kennedy with pursuing an "erratic and vacillating" course in foreign policy.[4]

His comments were part of an emerging critique that chipped away at Kennedy's favorable image. "For the first time since he entered the White House," wrote *Times* columnist James Reston, Kennedy seemed to be "on the defensive." The optimism of the post–missile crisis period had now vanished and been replaced by a sense of "frustration and stalemate." Journalists noted the "air of indecision" that permeated Kennedy's policies and the hollowness of the New Frontier as a political movement and philosophy.[5] While polls throughout the first half of 1963 gave him high marks, Kennedy's approval ratings fell from 74 percent in January to 64 percent in early May.[6] The slope of the trajectory was disconcerting. Although Rockefeller's star would fade because of decisions he made in his romantic life—decisions that would allow Barry Goldwater to emerge as a viable Republican candidate—Kennedy could now expect a bruising election campaign in 1964.

And then there was the war itself. Although the fighting in Vietnam was tough and getting tougher, it still seemed to offer rays of hope for a successful outcome. To be sure, prominent voices were criticizing the Diem government and casting doubt on reports of military progress. But

at that point, Saigon's challenges were pointing toward a lengthier conflict rather than an inevitably doomed one; those were the findings of
the Hilsman-Forrestal and Wheeler missions during the winter of 1962–
1963, as well as that of influential journalists stationed in Vietnam.[7]
The U.S. intelligence community came to similar conclusions, having
produced a guardedly optimistic forecast in mid-April. Although it refrained from expressing confidence in future developments, analysts surmised that the GVN could expand its control of the countryside and
contain the PLAF, barring massive support from Hanoi.[8] Nevertheless,
save for MACV chief Gen. Paul D. Harkins and his repeated expres-
sions of early triumph, most observers accepted that the war would be a
long, hard slog. A resulting and uneasy mix of "optimism and uncertainty," as historian George C. Herring describes it, characterized the
mood in both Washington and Saigon.[9]

Deteriorating conditions in neighboring Laos, however, threatened to
undermine even that equivocal position. Continued instability in Vientiane's coalition government, which had persisted since the signing of the
Geneva Accords in July 1962, had grown more pronounced following
the assassination of several officials, including the April 1963 murder of the
country's left-leaning foreign minister. The resulting mobilization of
Pathet Lao forces threatened to upend the shaky balance of power. Kennedy, in turn, dispatched a carrier task force to the region, the third time
in three years he scrambled U.S. forces to head off a Communist spring
offensive. At the same time, officials at State and Defense readied plans
for direct intervention should the president shed his long-held resistance
to using extensive lethal force.[10]

Each of those influences—the troubling developments in Laos, the
halting progress in Vietnam, increasing tensions with Diem, and political
challenges at home—set the stage for the pivotal SecDef conference of
May 1963, the first high-level interagency effort to assess and refine the
Comprehensive Plan for South Vietnam. McNamara approached it from
a bullish standpoint, believing that the training and outfitting of South
Vietnamese forces was proceeding apace. The Secretary "was very pleased
with the progress" and "said so several times," according to conference
memoranda. Planning for the withdrawal of U.S. troops thus moved forward in that spirit of optimism. McNamara instructed Harkins "to rationalize such departures with the Vietnamese Government on the basis

that we were winning and therefore U.S. strength could be reduced."[11] Apparently, U.S. officials were now ready to discuss their comprehensive strategy with the South Vietnamese—a noteworthy development, given that such planning was being undertaken ostensibly in their name.

While U.S. officials considered troop withdrawal against the backdrop of guarded optimism in the war, they approached MAP costs from a more pessimistic viewpoint. The politics of foreign assistance greatly affected planning for the Vietnam Military Assistance Program, especially given "the hardening of Congressional views" over the U.S. aid program, as McNamara put it. Policymakers, therefore, looked to scale down the level of military assistance flowing to the GVN. Still assuming the Communist insurgency would be "broken" by December 1965, McNamara indicated that MAP funds for Vietnam would fall from well over $200 million per year to between $50 and $100 million per year, and would undergo constant reevaluation "based on drastic reductions in dollar guidelines." But the projected shortfall in MAP support and the current difficulties with foreign aid were not to deter them. As he told the conferees, "we have over $50 billion in the U.S. Defense effort and we can not allow the limited availability of MAP funds to keep us from supporting the counterinsurgency war in Vietnam."[12] Concerns about U.S. aid therefore conditioned discussions about the limited partnership, even if they did not fully dictate funding for the war.

Yet even as McNamara sought to shield Vietnam from lawmakers' fatigue and frustration, he recognized that those currents would affect the assistance and advisory effort. He thus sought to inject a renewed and heightened sense of urgency into planning for Vietnam, a determination that dictated the shape of all resources—human, financial, and material—Washington provided. Defense officials would look to turn over U.S. equipment "as rapidly as possible" so the RVNAF could move swiftly toward a position of self-sufficiency.[13] Since plans for doing so were not in evidence, McNamara directed that the group retool and draw up schedules "that will permit us to start an earlier withdrawal of U.S. personnel than proposed under the plan presented."[14] The need for speed would now govern discussions about the training of South Vietnamese soldiers and the removal of U.S. armed forces.

As a result, the thousand-man withdrawal BRIAM's Robert Thompson had long been recommending, and which McNamara had recently championed, became a central focus of the meeting. It populated three of the four agenda items, with discussion addressing the composition of forces to be withdrawn, the timing of their withdrawal, the circumstances under which they would depart and—after their removal—the total number of U.S. troops to remain.[15] Most significantly, the thousand-man withdrawal now merged with the CPSVN as a means for addressing South Vietnamese morale, GVN autonomy, American assistance, and military escalation. Collectively, those concerns spoke to matters of perception—of confidence in Saigon's ability to run its own war and Washington's sense of proportion in the project. The thousand-man reduction thus emerged as an avowedly political device, keyed to audiences in South Vietnam and the United States.

But its effects were potentially troubling. For Diem, withdrawal could address the elevated American presence in South Vietnam, which had become a subject of deep concern, especially as it coincided with an uptick in Vietnamese nationalism. That chauvinism grew out of several problematic developments over the last few months: the Mansfield Report, which the GVN regarded as "a harbinger" of declining American support; U.S. policy toward Laos, which Saigon viewed as inconsistent with U.S. policy toward South Vietnam; and the advisory presence itself, which had engendered "jealousies and conflicts" and reputedly "tamper[ed] with Diem's political base."[16] Withdrawal thus acknowledged the detrimental effects of U.S. assistance and sought to ameliorate their impact. But by vacating the field, Washington threatened to aggravate fears of an American departure and deepen the crisis of confidence its presence was supposed to correct. Much depended, therefore, on convincing all involved that an American withdrawal was taking place in the context of military success.

It also depended on a fair assessment of RVNAF capabilities. As Nolting argued, "early withdrawal" should occur only when Saigon was "fully able to assume the responsibilities involved," including those handled by sector, province, and Special Forces advisors. Those were the forces whose advice encroached upon Diem's base, but they were also the troops most valuable to the war effort.[17] Although Diem and Nhu were "sensitive to our presence" and believed an American withdrawal "would be in the best interests of all concerned," any force reduction had to account for military realities. It could take place "only in those areas where the GVN is capable of assuming those functions," and therefore at some undetermined future date.[18]

American realities, particularly political ones, were equally in play, and McNamara couched the thousand-man withdrawal in terms of its impact on key publics. A plan of that sort was necessary, he said, "for two purposes—foreign and domestic—to give evidence that conditions are in fact improving."[19] But he was not unmindful of the connection between withdrawal and battlefield performance. In fact, he repeatedly characterized the reduction as contingent upon military success, and the withdrawal schedule CINCPAC Adm. Harry D. Felt developed focused on those forces "considered to pose least impact upon current operations."[20] Yet those two imperatives would coexist uneasily. While McNamara wanted Americans to come home "as the situation improves" or "if the situation allows," he also stressed the need for their removal "if we are to get continued US support for our efforts in Vietnam." Withdrawal thus became a domestic political imperative, even as its fate remained dependent on the course of the war.[21]

None of this sat well with U.S. military officials, who raised cautionary flags about the manner, timing, and number of troops to be withdrawn. Support services could be among the first to depart, McNamara suggested, proposing that MACV target two or three Vietnamese units for accelerated training—aircraft control, warning squadrons, or liaison squadrons came to mind—so their respective U.S. advisors could leave by December, preferably in a single package.[22] The schedule was problematic, though, as such training was itself part of the broader Comprehensive Plan. In fact, Harkins maintained that the training of many units "cannot be expedited over that now planned in view of lead-time requirements."[23] His comments betrayed a broader opposition to the thousand-man withdrawal. Two days before the conference began, during a discussion of what had been labeled "Mr. Thompson's plan," Harkins announced that he had "would oppose it."[24] He now elaborated, declaring he "did not want to gather up one thousand U.S. personnel and have them depart with bands playing, flags flying, etc." Such pomp "would have a bad effect on the Vietnamese, to be pulling out just when it appears they are winning." McNamara was unmoved. He acknowledged the psychological impact of such a scene, but thought it was no reason to shy away from withdrawal. Its execution would simply have to proceed carefully, through "an intensive training program" for South Vietnamese forces and the removal of U.S. troops as integrated units rather than as a collection of individuals. He thus directed that such a program be readied over the next two weeks.[25]

Aside from identifying the units most suitable for training and removal, officials sought to clarify the total number of troops from which those thousand were to be withdrawn. Those exchanges highlight several dimensions of the plan that demanded greater attention. First, the number of American forces deploying to Vietnam had been on the rise since the summer of 1961 and had increased dramatically following the Taylor mission that fall. As of March 1963, MACV reported a total of 12,822 U.S. military personnel in South Vietnam. But additional units were continually being programmed for deployment. CINCPAC thus called for reducing U.S. forces from an anticipated peak of 15,640, with one thousand troops returning to the continental United States "in sizeable increments about 31 December 1963."[26] Since reporters were using the figure of 12,000 as the approximate number of American troops in country, a thousand-man withdrawal that left a residual force in excess of 14,500 would create a public affairs embarrassment. That publicity challenge persisted as U.S. officials worked to refine the Thompson "token" reduction.

The specifics of the reduction remained a matter for McNamara to work through, but their generalities now rose to the level of presidential attention. Briefing Kennedy at the White House on May 7, McNamara offered a thumbnail sketch of the conversations just concluded in Honolulu. Their Oval Office exchange, which the president captured on his secret taping system, suggests there was indeed a strong link, particularly in Kennedy's mind, between military progress and troop reduction. McNamara framed the proposed withdrawal as one of his "major points" of the conference:

> **McNamara:** And secondly, I think that, as I've mentioned before, that both for domestic political purposes and also because of the psychological effect it would have in South Vietnam, we ought to think about the possibility of bringing a thousand men home by the end of the year. Now, I've asked them to lay out that plan, without at the present time making any decision to—

President Kennedy: That's right [*McNamara attempts to interject*]. Because in the case that—if it isn't in very good shape, you don't want to make—

McNamara: Absolutely.

President Kennedy: Yeah. Yeah.

McNamara: It would be . . . have a negative influence. But on the other hand, if we had two or three victories, this would be [*President Kennedy acknowledges*] just exactly the shot in the arm we ought to have. So they're going to do that."[27]

The reluctance to embrace a troop reduction without military progress, which Kennedy and McNamara expressed to each other privately in the Oval Office, mirrored the guidance Thompson shared at CINCPAC in March and in Washington that April. It would continue to inform planning for the remainder of the summer.

For the time being, though, McNamara would distinguish between planning for withdrawal, on the one hand, and implementing it, on the other. Since he wanted the Pentagon to execute a drawdown if conditions allowed for it, preparations moved forward even though U.S. and GVN forces had yet to score major victories against the Communists or declare a series of provinces "white"—two of the conditions Thompson attached to a token withdrawal. McNamara therefore directed that the Joint Chiefs, as "a matter of urgency," plan for the withdrawal of one thousand troops by December, grounded in "the assumption that the progress of the counterinsurgency campaign would warrant such a move."[28]

But preparations for the more comprehensive withdrawal, as McNamara now appraised them, were unrealistic and needed to be "completely reworked."[29] Its expenditures were too high, and its withdrawal of advisers too slow. With the 1963 and 1965 timelines now interlinked, McNamara directed that civilian and military officials move quickly and revise both the CPSVN and the MAP for fiscal years 1965 through 1969. Members of the Joint Staff, along with representatives of CINCPAC and Harkins's staff, thus began to formulate and assess the implications of three separate "dollar guideline programs" that would stretch from FY 1965 through FY 1969: one developed by CINCPAC, with a price tag of $585 million; one prepared by the Office of International Security Affairs at the Pentagon, costing $450 million; and one devised by McNamara himself, which ran to $365 million. The study would conclude on or about June 5.[30]

Regardless of which version emerged as the most fiscally prudent, Felt questioned the assumptions informing them. Not only did he doubt their premises about the war, but he was skeptical of the RVNAF's capacity to improve within the allotted time frame. He thought it "overly optimistic to assume that insurgency can be controlled as early as FY 65" as they had outlined. Saigon, moreover, simply could not produce enough trained personnel to allow for the early withdrawal of U.S. advisers.[31] Maj. Gen. William B. Rosson, the Army point person for special warfare, thought likewise. Rosson, who was in Vietnam exploring enhancements to air mobility, questioned the estimates guiding such planning. Neither senior RVNAF officials nor knowledgeable U.S. personnel thought "an early end to the war was in sight." Nevertheless, the Kennedy administration would plan for a U.S. troop reduction largely because McNamara had deemed it "desirable or necessary," rather than because it squared with events on the ground. Rosson thus concluded that the Comprehensive Plan was "unrealistic" and "based on day-dreaming as against justifiable optimism."[32] Although McNamara had made clear his intention to effect the withdrawal, the most senior soldiers directing the war, as well as others supporting their efforts, were hardly supportive.

Talk of a phaseout became more acute in the wake of the Honolulu conference. Discussions referenced not only the possibility of withdrawal but even a timetable for completing it. Arthur Sylvester, the Pentagon spokesman, affirmed that the United States would be able to reduce its advisory mission in one to three years. Declaring that "the corner definitely has been turned" in the war against the Communists, Sylvester couched the expected withdrawal within the framework of military success.[33]

The debate over troops became more widespread as two incidents heightened alarm about the advisory effort. Following the Buddhist incident on May 8 and criticism of Saigon in the American press, the Ngos turned up the heat of their campaign to lower the U.S. profile. On May 12, the *Washington Post* published a front-page story on Nhu's desire for the United States to reduce by half its 12,000 to 13,000 advisers serving in South Vietnam.[34] The piece expressed sentiments Diem and Nhu had harbored at least since publication of the Mansfield report in February. Thereafter, South Vietnamese officials began to speak more openly and disparagingly about the elevated American presence, culminating with Nhu's remarks in mid-May.[35] None of this sat well with the *Post*'s editors, who observed that 12,000 Americans were serving in South Vietnam and "dozens" of them had been killed "while the government holds its troops in check." How much longer, the *Post* asked, "must the United States help President Diem to lose his war and waste its money, to delay the reforms that alone might gather his regime the popular support that victory requires?"[36]

Although the duration of U.S. assistance remained an open question, Kennedy officials sought to allay GVN concerns about the American presence. It was a topic they had already discussed in Honolulu, but the publicity surrounding Nhu's complaint suggested U.S. troops were further complicating Diem's challenges.[37] While Saigon had made no formal request for a troop reduction, *Post* reporting highlighted a "compromise" the Americans had reached at Honolulu that resulted in an agreement to withdraw roughly one thousand forces in a year's time.[38] Five days later, on May 17, American and South Vietnamese officials issued a joint communiqué expressing the shared objective of drawing down the U.S. advisory mission—a statement that served to quiet calls for an immediate withdrawal.

But the reduction was to be contingent on improvement in the war. Current levels of assistance were still necessary, the agreement noted, but "as the security situation improves," the two sides "expected that the need for foreign assistance, both in terms of material and personnel, will be progressively lightened."[39] Indeed, McNamara told Congress that both governments would look to end U.S. assistance "at the earliest possible moment," consistent with the GVN's "national safety." While he was unwilling "to place any time limit on the termination of hostilities," he thought the GVN exerted more control over South Vietnam than it had six months earlier. Taylor, too, evinced a sense of optimism in the war. There was "no doubt in my mind," he said, "that we are going to win in South Vietnam if the domestic front here does not accept a tone of defeatism." The RVNAF were "winning in the military sense" and politically were "making constant progress."[40]

Still, Nhu's comments and the joint communique generated increasing chatter about Vietnam and forced President Kennedy to comment publicly on the prospect of a U.S. withdrawal. At a press conference on May 22, he stated that the United States would indeed withdraw troops if the GVN made such a request. He did hope to remove forces before the end of the year, but the administration "can't possibly make that judgment at the present time." There was still "a long, hard struggle to go. We have seen what happened in Laos, which must inevitably have its effect upon South Viet-Nam, so that I couldn't say that today the situation is such that we could look for a brightening in the skies that would permit us to withdraw troops or begin to by the end of the year. But I would say, if requested to, we will do it immediately. As of today we would hope we could begin to perhaps to do it at the end of the year, but we couldn't make any final judgment at all until we see the course of the struggle the next few months."[41] The similarities between those remarks and the ones Kennedy expressed to McNamara two weeks earlier are striking. On both occasions, Kennedy indicated his reluctance to withdraw U.S. troops in the context of adverse military conditions. His public comments thus mirrored his private ones, suggesting that a troop pullout, at least as originally conceived, was indeed contingent on "the course of the struggle."

Yet the evolution of the Buddhist crisis, then two weeks old, would alter that planning, as well as relations with the Diem government. Not only would the crisis force the administration to rethink its commitment to supporting and preserving Diem, but it would change the terms of the thousand-man troop reduction. Whereas it had once been a conditional withdrawal, based on battlefield realities, it now moved forward as a virtually unconditional one, irrespective of military progress. Its political benefits, including its signaling about prudent planning, a limited commitment, and even military success, were simply too great to forego.

The Influence of Korea

That transformation hinged on an additional concern shaping administration and popular attitudes toward the advisory effort: the object lesson of South Korea.[42] Washington had been supporting Seoul with substantial amounts of aid since the end of the Korean War in 1953, the last major engagement involving U.S. military forces prior to their arrival in Southeast Asia. Korea soon became ever-present in American thinking about Vietnam. It raised the specters of both limited war and hostilities with China, but also the political perils and fiscal drain of supporting a troublesome ally. Kennedy appreciated the analogy, which friendly critics brought to his attention. Mansfield had warned him in November 1961 that an expanded military commitment in Vietnam might lead to "an indecisive and costly conflict along the Korean lines." Galbraith had also worked it into his April 1962 memo, warning that a deepening commitment to Saigon would likely generate "a major political outburst about the new Korea and the new war into which the Democrats as so often before have precipitated us."[43] At that point, however, with the limited partnership in its infancy, the analogy conjured a set of risks looming further out on the horizon.

Those vistas came into clearer view during 1963, as observers grew increasingly worried about the similarities between that earlier war and the one currently expanding in Southeast Asia. Mansfield spoke anew of the war in Vietnam becoming a Korean type of conflict "paid for primarily with American lives."[44] Chester Bowles, Kennedy's roving adviser on the developing world, feared the escalating commitment to Vietnam, accompanied by more American casualties and domestic criticism, would generate, "as in the days of Korea," demands that the United States "either 'admit our error' and withdraw, or go after 'the real enemy,' which is China.'"[45] The parallels were ominous. "Where a decade ago there was full-fledged war in Korea," the *New York Times* editorialized in March 1963, "today there is guerrilla war in Vietnam."[46] In the *Washington Post,* Jack Anderson ventured that the United States may be on the cusp of "another Korean-scale war that may cost thousands of American lives."[47] The North-South partition of the two Vietnams, like the two Koreas, also pointed toward the presumed instability of a divided nation and the possibility of general war to resolve it.[48] As David Halberstam wrote in the *Times,* the United States had made "a deep commitment" to Vietnam that could "become even deeper," and observed that "the Americans do not, by a long shot, have control over the pace and price of this war."[49] For a president who chafed at the loss of control and who worried about a "Guns of August" scenario—he had read the Barbara Tuchman book the previous summer—the prospect of an unmanageable, runaway conflict such as World War I, or even such as Korea, was precisely what he most wanted to avoid.

Yet as with the Korean War, it was concern about the Chinese threat that loomed so large and led Kennedy officials toward greater engagement in Vietnam. Viewing the People's Republic as the locus of trouble in Southeast Asia, they surmised that the Sino-Soviet split would likely propel the PRC toward greater belligerence in the region and fuel its expansive tendencies. The administration pursued its assistance effort nonetheless, believing that any sign of accommodation would whet Beijing's appetite still further and tarnish Kennedy's credibility at home and abroad. Short of introducing combat troops, stepped-up U.S. aid, Washington believed, would deter China and moderate its aggressive intentions. Yet the assistance effort had the opposite effect, generating an escalatory spiral that sank Washington and Beijing deeper into the Vietnamese tangle.[50]

The political parallels between Seoul and Saigon also suggested trouble ahead. Continuing difficulties with Korean strongman Park Chung Hee, who was looking to enhance his power following his May 1961 coup, created dilemmas for the Kennedy administration, which was trying "to walk a narrow path between upholding the principle of civilian rule," as the *Times* put it, "and the prevention of violence in a region still not immune to Communist attack."[51] It was a dynamic with widespread applicability. As simmering discontent with Diem boiled over during the Buddhist crisis, the links between the two polities and the two conflicts became hard to ignore. "The situation in Saigon has taken on a sinister similarity to the last days of Syngman Rhee," the *Times* editorialized, with the "same kind of popular outbursts . . . being suppressed with the same kind of police brutality."[52] By late summer, the *Times* again opined that Washington faced in both South Korea and South Vietnam "a Government it can neither abandon nor support with unreserved good conscience." Both regimes depended on American support to protect them from Communism, yet both proceeded in a "dictatorial way in defiance of all Washington pressure."[53]

The Korean example was also on McNamara's mind at the SecDef conference in early May. Whereas public servants and media outlets had focused attention on the martial parallels between the two conflicts, McNamara focused on the fiscal ones. He warned that the United States "must avoid creating a situation that now obtains in Korea where we are presently spending almost a half billion dollars per year in foreign aid."[54] With Congress "likely to be tougher than ever on all foreign aid in the future," the government "surely didn't want to 'rescue' Viet-Nam and have a future $400–$500 million support problem as we now have in Korea."[55]

The Secretary brought those concerns back to Washington and expressed them directly to Kennedy in their Oval Office meeting the following day. Channeling the range of official and media comment on the similarities between Vietnam and Korea, McNamara railed against the excessive budgets he had seen for both the Military Assistance Program and the Comprehensive Plan. After suggesting that it "may take two or three years" to get the insurgency "under control," he told Kennedy that "we should now be looking to the time when we'll have a normal military program there. "Instead, they're proposing fantastic Military Assistance Programs. I think we ought to take 75 to 100 million [dollars] out of the '65, '66, '67 military assistance programs they're talking about and be looking to a normal relationship so we don't build up another Korea. When I look at what's happened to [South] Korea, in the way of U.S. aid, and how difficult it's going to be to scale that aid down, we certainly don't want to let another Korea develop in South Vietnam and we're well on the way to doing that."[56] McNamara's desire to limit the extent and duration of MAP support for Vietnam, even in light of the challenges then posed by the Communists, reflected his broader fear about making long-term, open-ended commitments to the developing world. For a defense secretary intent on rationalizing budgets and programs, and committed to cost reduction and fiscal prudence, South Korea stood as a cautionary tale. He therefore sought to ramp up U.S. aid to Saigon to scale it back down: the more money Washington devoted to fighting the NLF in the near term, the less it would have to shell out over the long haul. The Korean conundrum thus captured the economic and fiscal considerations shaping U.S. policy toward Vietnam.

Fiscal Pressures

A related concern was the outflow of gold and the balance of payments, which had worried Kennedy since entering office. His alarm over fiscal and economic considerations became more acute in 1963. It was "imperative" that all federal agencies "minimize their payments and maximize their receipts," according to Budget director Kermit Gordon. Agencies were to refrain from increasing their personnel or general expenditures without express approval from the Budget Bureau and to "assure that all possible actions are being taken to minimize the balance-of-payments costs of maintaining offices and missions abroad."[57]

The Defense Department was a prime contributor to that imbalance, though McNamara had already taken steps to rectify the problem. Among the most significant was the "Cost Reduction" program he instituted in July 1962. Its application had since trimmed over a billion dollars from DoD ledgers, a 25 percent increase over what he originally expected. His goal thereafter was to realize savings of $4 billion per year. Although he denied that those gains would come from reducing the nation's combat forces or withdrawing troops from Europe, he did note that the Pentagon was "continually adjusting our deployments" and that technological improvements would likely result in further personnel reductions.[58] In truth, troops were central to that discussion, a consideration with great relevance, especially to Korea and Vietnam.

Military assistance also remained a target for cost cutting. Budget director Gordon had asked McNamara to "conduct a critical review" of Military Assistance Advisory Groups, as well as military attachés and liaisons, "with the objective of minimizing net payments abroad."[59] The Joint Chiefs began the assessment in March 1963, but a May request to scale back MAAG expenditures, first from the Budget Bureau and then from DoD's Office of International Security Affairs, intensified the effort.[60] Resistance emerged throughout the global archipelago of MAAGs, however, as well as from command echelons. Opponents of the reduction ultimately prevailed in a battle that pitted cost control against security risk.[61] But the effort shaped policy, nonetheless, particularly in locales such as Vietnam. Guided by the need to "apply to maximum extent [the] principle of self-help" and to encourage host states to assume a larger share of their defense burdens, McNamara sought to rein in mounting expenditures, especially the ballooning commitment to Saigon.[62] The phased withdrawal of U.S. troops, as part of the CPSVN, was very much part of the plan.

Still, the challenges of reducing expenses without sacrificing capabilities remained, with McNamara wanting the capacity to project military power, and quickly. His search for a cost-effective solution led him to "substitute mobility for forward deployment on the periphery," a principle demanding political and technological dexterity. July discussions on the subject centered around trials to transport upwards of 40,000 troops from the United States to bases in Europe. Over the next several months, DoD planned to test those capabilities, an exercise that would raise additional questions about the political and economic costs of deploying troops abroad.[63]

The Buddhist Crisis

Those questions became increasingly salient as Saigon sunk deeper into political crisis during the summer of 1963. A "cycle of protest, repression, and mobilization" took hold, writes historian John Prados, as Buddhist leaders demanded redress in the wake of the May 8 incident. Although Diem sought to accommodate their concerns, Buddhists continued to rally against the GVN on virtually a daily basis, motivated by years of mistrust and their newly energized religious revival. Their protests culminated on June 11 with the self-immolation of Thich Quang Duc, a Buddhist monk who martyred himself in an expression of opposition to the Diem regime. Its impact was electric. The GVN and Buddhist leaders hammered out an agreement days later, raising hopes that the five weeks of mounting tension would subside. But mutual mistrust endured and intensified. Both sides adopted uncompromising positions, increasing the likelihood of more clashes to come.[64]

In the wake of Quang Duc's self-immolation and further calls for political reform, the Joint Chiefs' special assistant for counterinsurgency, Maj. Gen. Victor H. Krulak, embarked on a one-week inspection visit to South Vietnam.[65] Touring the country from June 25 to July 1, Krulak spent most of his time in the provinces and rural areas, talking with American and Vietnamese officials about a range of concerns. Weighing present realities against the backdrop of his earlier visits, Krulak reached several conclusions about the state of the war: the PLAF was on the defensive; Communist defections were on the rise; and the relationship between U.S. advisers and their Vietnamese counterparts was "efficient and mutually respectful." Most notably, the Strategic Hamlet Program was having a favorable impact, with roughly 60 percent of the rural population having been relocated into presumably fortified villages. While PLAF "hard core" strength remained between 22,000 to 25,000, its irregular forces had dropped from estimates of 100,000 in January to 80,000 in June. Collectively, those developments offered "reason for optimism," especially since the Buddhist crisis had yet to significantly impact the counterinsurgency. The United States and the GVN were "winning the war," and if they continued along the course they were on, they would "see the job done."[66]

The trip also allowed Krulak to comment on the withdrawal of U.S. troops from South Vietnam, the planning for which continued apace. Those efforts became freighted with increasingly political overtones following Nhu's remarks to the *Washington Post,* in which he called for a 50 percent reduction in American personnel. As the CIA observed, "the extensive US presence is setting in motion political forces in South Vietnam which could eventually threaten Diem's political primacy," and which were "likely to increase the GVN's desire to reduce that presence."[67] The confluence of a more volatile polity and the elevated U.S. profile conditioned Washington's appraisal of recent events. Impulses in both the United States and Saigon were thus aligning to speed the withdrawal of U.S. troops from South Vietnam, a departure that remained feasible, even as it found little favor among senior military officials.

But efforts to achieve a rapid withdrawal, particularly within the calendar year, failed to account for the conditions that sparked such planning in the first place. Its originator, British counterinsurgency expert Robert Thompson, held that a token withdrawal of one thousand troops should move forward only after the establishment of verifiably "white" areas in South Vietnam—areas that were demonstrably secure and likely to remain so. During the summer of 1963, however, Thompson acknowledged the absence of those conditions and the improbability they would emerge any time soon.[68] Although RVNAF operations were increasing and those of the PLAF decreasing, the intensity of military activity was rising, as were casualties on both sides. Indeed, there was no sign the GVN was any closer to finishing off the Communist insurgency, nor were any provinces on the cusp of being declared "white."[69]

Yet senior American officials ignored Thompson's proviso. While they factored the impact of troop withdrawals into their assessments of battlefield capabilities, the pacification of specific provincial areas played no role in calculations for reducing the U.S. footprint. McNamara and Kennedy, for instance, had expressed their reluctance to move forward with withdrawal if the situation "wasn't in very good shape," basing that position on the tempo of the war and not on the requirements Thompson stipulated. Civilian and military officials likewise shunned the geographic specificity Thompson thought essential. Krulak, therefore, believing that the training of the RVNAF had "passed its climax," thought the reduction of U.S advisers was, in principle, "a logical prospect." So did Harkins, who thought it "feasible" to move forward with the thousand-man reduction—contrary to what he said earlier—provided there was "no further deterioration" of the situation elsewhere in Southeast Asia. Indeed, he thought those troops could be withdrawn at that very moment "without affecting adversely the conduct of the war."[70] Although neither MACV, nor CINCPAC, nor the Joint Chiefs were enthusiastic about backing the token withdrawal, each ultimately found their way to supporting it.

They did so by trying to cushion its impact on the counterinsurgency. With "the shooting part of the war . . . moving to a climax," Krulak warned, "our help for the Vietnamese in logistic and tactical support is thus probably not susceptible of much reduction in the immediate future."[71] The technical nature of the activities, such as the training of pilots for helicopter, transport, and liaison squadrons, were such that those programs probably could not meet an end-of-year deadline. Not all activities were equally demanding, though, and units charged with less sophisticated tasks were much better candidates for early removal. CINCPAC had already recommended dividing those forces into separate classes: a "Category I list" of expendable troops, totaling 538 and comprised largely of headquarters personnel performing "housekeeping tasks," and a complementary "Category II list of units" playing more vital roles. Those latter units, however, "should not be withdrawn unless marked progress is attained in Vietnam." Harkins was fearful of making heavy unit withdrawals, even though their removal would convey RVNAF progress in learning key skills.[72] But any ratio exceeding a 50/50 split of units to individuals would begin to erode military effectiveness; he simply could not identify any unit not already scheduled for departure that could leave before the end of 1963 "without degrading our operational support capability." Felt also worried about skewing the ratio toward units and had suggested back in May that shortfalls in unit withdrawals be filled by transferring individuals to departing components "to swell the unit totals."[73] Doing so would allow the Pentagon to sanction the phaseout in ways that preserved operational effectiveness.

But handling withdrawal as a shell game was problematic since the publicity benefits of troop withdrawal would diminish if it looked like a ruse. Krulak thus joined others who had discouraged "any plan which employs a deception device, such as attaching individuals to a unit purely for the purpose of maintaining the 'unit withdrawal' or by creating a phantom unit." Harkins needed to "fully justify" any individuals withdrawn to reach the one thousand figure and to develop an associated public relations plan for their removal.[74] Compounding the challenge, McNamara had directed that the mix of units to individuals withdrawn target a ratio of 70/30, with a minimum acceptable breakdown of 50/50. For Deputy Chief of Staff A. E. Allemand, the whole exercise seemed "an unrewarding circle of increasing complexities in fabrication," especially since he knew that the starting point for the drawdown was rising to 16,732—far more than the figure of 15,000 troops that had been tossed around in planning documents.[75]

Incorporating those exchanges and observations, Felt submitted the thousand-man withdrawal plan to the Joint Chiefs on July 21, 1963. He did so in accordance with their May and June guidance that the reduction "will be ordered if progress in the counterinsurgency campaign warrants such action." The objective, he noted, was "to withdraw units rather than individuals to the extent practicable to gain maximum psychological impact rather than reach a predetermined in-country strength by end CY 63." The phasing of withdrawal should thus "take place in several increments, each large enough and sufficiently spaced for news prominence and cover," a schedule that suggested "3 or 4 increments." If decreed, withdrawal should move forward "with minimum impact on the combined US-RVN capabilities to bring counter-insurgency campaign to successful conclusion in shortest possible time." The decision to implement, therefore, should not be made prior to October 1 or after October 31, due to "several conflicting factors": continued instability in Laos; the return of servicemen to the United States by Christmas; the need to find appropriate assignments for all returnees; the implementation of an associated publicity campaign; and the imperative of being "least disruptive" to the counterinsurgency.[76]

While officials were refining those plans for transmittal to McNamara, public attention fixed on the deepening Buddhist crisis in South Vietnam. *Life* had joined other media in publishing pictures of Quang Duc's self-immolation and declared it "Time for Diem to Mend His Ways." *Newsweek* responded to the churning with a cover story on Laos and Vietnam, highlighting the "Peking-inspired 'dirty, disagreeable war'... that seems to have no end" but was nevertheless "vital" to win. *Time* lamented the multiple suicides stoking political fires, relaying concerns about their impact on the war "just when it is beginning to go well."[77] And both national and regional publications, such as the *New York Times*, the *Minneapolis Tribune*, and the *Denver Post*, maintained that regardless of the unrest and its impact on bilateral relations, "the U.S. must not pull out" of Vietnam. As the *Christian Science Monitor* put it, "The loss of Vietnam, unlike the loss of Laos, could not be absorbed without the most serious consequences for the entire future of the Cold War," a sentiment the State Department recognized as widespread.[78]

But the Cold War itself was evolving from the near apocalypse of the previous autumn. The installation of a Washington-Moscow hotline, progress on a test-ban treaty, and mutual concern over Chinese nuclear ambitions occasioned a more sober appraisal of U.S.-Soviet relations. Sharing that newfound appreciation of global realities, and with an eye toward finalizing the test-ban talks, Kennedy delivered a stirring message to the graduates of American University that June. Asking all Americans to reexamine their attitudes toward Moscow and the East-West conflict, JFK appeared to turn a page in the postwar confrontation that governed much of international relations. But novel as they were, his remarks largely centered on the danger of superpower conflict, and not on the broader contest between the two camps.[79] The erosion of Western influence in Southeast Asia—part of the "periphery" Kennedy had long regarded as a Communist target—remained of utmost concern. Its meaning, however, seemed to reside more in what it said about U.S. credibility than on the cold calculations of material and economic interests.

The president then doubled-down on the need for such resolve in remarks to journalists one month later. Following an escalation of the Buddhist crisis on July 17, when GVN security units clubbed and arrested protestors and barred entry into the pagodas, Kennedy went on the record about the crisis and its impact on the war. He did so by referencing the progress narrative, domino dynamics, and the strength of the American commitment. Kennedy thought it "unfortunate that this dispute has arisen at the very time when the military struggle has been going better than it has been going in many months." He hoped the crisis would be settled shortly, "because we have invested a tremendous amount of effort and it is going quite well." Indeed, it was imperative the GVN remain free and independent; the United States, therefore, was "not going to withdraw" from Vietnam, he stated flatly. An American departure "would mean a collapse not only of South Vietnam, but Southeast Asia. So we are going to stay there."[80]

The invocation of falling dominoes had a long pedigree in the Kennedy administration. Of primary concern was not the strength of regional Communist parties, but the accommodation of area states to Chinese pressure. Should the Americans leave the field, the susceptibility of those countries to Beijing's influence—particularly Thailand and Indonesia—would likely lead them to adopt a neutralist orientation, at the very least, or full-fledged alignment with the PRC.[81] Regardless, McNamara said two days later, the war was going well, as operations were "proceeding very satisfactorily" in spite of the political disturbance.[82] But opinion hardened against the GVN. Press support for Diem, according to State's analysts, was "severely shaken," with a smattering of editors deeming it "unfortunate" that the president saw fit to reaffirm Washington's backing of Saigon.[83]

Kennedy's remarks, coming just hours after the events that sparked them, suggest that his public optimism mirrored his private sentiments. Two weeks earlier, he told top officials at a White House meeting on Vietnam that things were going "pretty well" despite the Buddhist crisis, a judgment validated by Roger Hilsman and others from the NSC and the State Department.[84] Indeed, he had little reason to think otherwise. Although he had received troubling reports from Hilsman and Forrestal, both were urging greater skepticism about the military's "rosy euphoria" more than they were despairing of developments writ large; Mansfield had taken a darker view. Still, JFK greeted critical reporting from American journalists with a healthy dose of skepticism, believing they were prone to whacking unpopular allies and overstating military setbacks.[85] Although his appraisal of the war has been difficult to discern, evidence suggests he avoided both gloomy pessimism and can-do optimism.

Kennedy said little else about Vietnam during the height of the summer, as his attention prior to and following the July 17 events had been elsewhere. A late June trip to Europe included stops in England and Italy, but it would be remembered for his visits to West Berlin, where he pledged to preserve western freedoms, and Ireland, where he toured the haunts of his ancestral home. More policy-focused developments were also cresting and absorbing his energies. By the end of July, representatives from the United States, United Kingdom, and Soviet Union had finalized the Limited Test-Ban Treaty, banning nuclear testing above ground, under water, and in the atmosphere. It was a major achievement for Kennedy, who had come into office focused on arms control. Though its ratification by the Senate was hardly a forgone conclusion, it faced better odds than the civil rights legislation then taking shape. Dramatic incidents in mid-June—the enrollment of Black students at the University of Alabama and the murder of activist Medgar Evers—had rallied Kennedy to support a sweeping civil rights bill, which Black leaders mobilized to enact. But preparations for a late-August march on Washington alarmed the White House, which feared its potential impact on the city and on Congress.[86] Collectively, those developments contributed to a crowded presidential agenda, distracting the president from focusing more attention on Vietnam.

Nevertheless, planning to withdraw U.S. troops from South Vietnam continued to advance in the background, with preparations for the incidental reduction and the more comprehensive phaseout moving toward completion. Yet even with the acceleration of RVNAF training, none of the MAP plans under consideration allowed for sufficient troop withdrawals or the turnover of equipment before the end of 1963. Felt therefore programmed for removal those units "which can be released with least effect on operations," as well as "specially-formed 'service support units.'" Although planners recognized the downside of creating units for the purpose of withdrawing them, officials in the Pentagon's office of International Security Affairs deemed the approach "reasonable." There simply was "no good alterative, if the withdrawal is to be carried out by year-end, without reducing important capabilities, such as airlift." To further minimize its impact on military operations, the plan would not require final approval until the political and security situations were clearer.[87] Taylor thus asked McNamara to "approve the withdrawal plan for planning purposes," but to withhold a final decision until the JCS could review the situation in the fall, with a decision arriving on Mc-Namara's desk by October 20.[88]

What remained very much unclear, however, was guidance on the absolute number of U.S. troops in South Vietnam. Discussions about troop totals and their relation to a token reduction had picked up steam in the wake of the May SecDef and were now coming to a head. John Mecklin, the public affairs chief at the embassy in Saigon, sought authorization to inform journalists of their actual number so its disclosure would not overwhelm the eventual withdrawal announcement. Regardless, he thought any such announcement "should be deferred indefinitely." A public statement on withdrawal "could be distorted to look like U.S. disengagement and thus of faltering support for the GVN at a critical moment," a development that "could be exploited by both the Buddhists and the Viet Cong." Use of the 15,000 figure, though, could serve "as evidence of U.S. determination to press the struggle against the Viet Cong." Mecklin thus recommended that "there be no further public comment on our intention to make a token withdrawal until late in the year when it is to be hoped that the internal situation here will have improved."[89]

But American forces were now climbing past 16,000 and, along with civilians serving in the assistance mission, the official U.S. population in South Vietnam was set to reach almost 19,000—figures well north of what journalists were reporting and the Pentagon was confirming. As British officials noted, the true extent of the U.S. presence was "sufficiently widely known" to make it virtually impossible to suppress indefinitely. The Americans, therefore, were still looking for authority "to make a progressive and unattributable release of reasonably accurate figures."[90] But the very idea of withdrawing troops, whatever their actual number, struck British officials as curious. "Obviously this is an American problem," they noted, "but we had thought all ideas of a token reduction would be suspended in present circumstances," as "surely the idea of a reduction was to please the Ngo family particularly the Nhus."[91] Until more accurate figures were made public, a number that British diplomat Reginald A. Burrows accurately pegged at 16,700, "it is almost certain that a 'token reduction' exercise would blow back in their faces."[92]

Coup Talk

By the end of August, the more significant blowback was coming from Washington's political ties to Saigon. The United States had long accommodated itself to an uneasy relationship with Diem, but mounting displeasure with his rule had peaked with the onset of the Buddhist crisis. Although Diem had sought to placate Buddhist concerns through nominal reforms, opposition to his leadership was coursing through South Vietnamese civil society. It also emerged within the military, and, by the summer, had led pockets within the armed forces to coalesce around the idea of mounting a coup.

Kennedy officials had also begun to consider the possibility, even the need, of removing Diem from power. Not all were so inclined and the ensuing debate split key members of the administration. State Department officers connected with Vietnamese affairs, including Averell Harriman and Roger Hilsman, supported the search for new leadership; adherents also included Under Secretary George Ball and Michael Forrestal at the White House. Senior officials at the Defense Department and CIA, as well as officials responsible for managing the assistance and advisory programs, opposed those efforts, even as they grew frustrated with Diem's performance. There simply seemed no viable alternative to Diem, who had maintained his hold on power, at times against great odds, for close to a decade.

Into the breach stepped Henry Cabot Lodge Jr., whom President Kennedy had appointed in June as U.S. ambassador to South Vietnam.[93] It was a bold choice, with a high degree of risk and reward. A Republican with a prominent family name in American politics, Lodge had tangled politically with Kennedy for more than a decade—over a Senate seat in 1952, as well as over the White House as Richard Nixon's running mate in 1960. But Lodge spoke fluent French, had expressed deep interest in the challenges of Southeast Asia, and wanted to be of service. When Rusk floated his name as potential ambassador, Kennedy apparently jumped at the chance; the opportunity of saddling Lodge with the mess in Vietnam struck JFK, according to presidential assistant Kenny O'Donnell, as "irresistible." The bipartisan cover it offered to Kennedy was also appealing, even though Lodge's stature, arrogance, and imperial streak would likely create headaches.[94]

Diem viewed the move more darkly. He was reportedly "considerably disturbed" by the nomination and presumed it signaled Kennedy's willingness "to wield a 'big stick'" with respect to Saigon.[95] That readiness to get tough was evident in JFK's conversation with Lodge prior to the ambassador's departure for Southeast Asia. The president was prepared to regard Diem as a spent force, but evidence for Diem's failings was coming from journalists who were deeply critical of the Ngos and pushing their own agendas. Lodge would simply have to be the judge of whether Diem could hang on or whether the United States should consider a change.[96]

By the time he landed in Saigon, the ground had shifted once again. On the night of August 21, the GVN declared martial law, ransacked the pagodas, and arrested Buddhist and student protestors. Lodge thus arrived with tensions at their most feverish since the onset of the Buddhist crisis, and the climate more unstable than at any time since Diem had vanquished his political opponents in 1955.

Those events injected new energy into efforts at removing Diem, both in Saigon and in Washington. Taking advantage of a late-August weekend when senior Kennedy officials were scattered about the country, George Ball, Averell Harriman, Roger Hilsman, and Mike Forrestal—all of whom had fully soured on Diem—drafted a cable for Lodge that effectively authorized him to facilitate a coup. Although they sought concurrence in that message from leadership at State and Defense, as well as from the president, poor communication, misplaced assumptions, and bureaucratic cunning allowed the group to mount an "egregious 'end run,'" as Maxwell Taylor put it, around the highest-ranking officials in government. If Diem proved incapable of separating himself from the Nhus, the foursome made clear, "then we must face the possibility that Diem himself cannot be preserved."[97] That missive—Cable 243—launched the United States onto a new and even more uncertain path in South Vietnam.

By the time the Kennedy team returned to Washington on Monday, the atmosphere had reached crisis stage. Meetings took place daily, sometimes even multiple times a day, demanding the president's most sustained attention to Vietnam since late 1961. To manage its response, the White House reconstituted the Executive Committee of the National Security Council—the "ExComm" employed during the October 1962 Cuban Missile Crisis. Its sessions focused on the emerging coup's operational details, including the persons involved, its prospects for success, and Diem's countermoves.[98] Participants also debated—quite vigorously—Washington's overall posture in Vietnam, including its involvement in the scheme and its position in the country should the gambit succeed or fail.

Rarely, however, did they dig more deeply to rethink assumptions behind the basic commitment itself. Dean Rusk seemed the most willing to consider the implications of their actions. If Diem and Nhu prevailed in the contest, the United States would either have to "get out and let the country go to the Communists" or "move U.S. combat forces into

South Viet-Nam and put in a government of our own choosing." According to Hilsman's memcon of the meeting, "there was no dissent from the Secretary's analysis."[99] But there was also no willingness to engage it, either. Once again, senior officials, including the president, failed to answer the most basic question of whether South Vietnam was sufficiently vital to warrant the deployment of American combat units. Instead, they continued to punt, believing the situation would resolve itself or that the time for harder choices lay further down the road.

Those strategic considerations soon took a back seat to more immediate tactical ones. By Wednesday, August 28, the CIA station in Saigon believed the situation had "reached point of no return," with the city having become an "armed camp" and the Ngos "dug in for last ditch battle." Ball and Harriman thought they were "already beyond the point of no return," with the question now being, "how do we make this coup successful." Failure was simply not an option, the CIA warned, as it would lead Diem to "sharply reduce American presence in SVN" or mobilize Congress, American public opinion, and world opinion to "force withdrawal or reduction of American support" for South Vietnam. Harriman thought Washington should pull out if the coup did not materialize. "We put Diem in power," the Under Secretary charged, and "he has doublecrossed us."[100] Lodge, too, thought they had reached a threshold. "We are launched on a course from which there is no respectable turning back," he said the following day: "the overthrow of the Diem government." The United States had now committed its prestige to the coup, as there was no prospect, he believed, of winning the war with Diem.[101]

Although President Kennedy signaled his willingness to dispense with Diem, he emphasized repeatedly that he would support a coup only if it were likely to succeed. He also made clear that he would pull back from a coup if its prospects were faltering.[102] Exercising that option seemed all the more likely, for by Wednesday, August 28, intelligence assessments indicated that "Diem held the balance of power."[103] The following day, Kennedy clarified his prerogative for Lodge: "Until the very moment of the go signal for the operation by the Generals," he declared in an extraordinarily sensitive letter, "I must reserve a contingent right to change course and reverse previous instructions." Referencing his own troubled past with coup plotting and covert action, Kennedy noted the stakes involved. "While fully aware of your assessment of the consequences of such a reversal, I know from experience that failure is more destructive

143

than an appearance of indecision. . . . When we go, we must go to win, but it will be better to change our minds than to fail. And if our national interest should require a change of mind, we must not be afraid of it."[104]

The need for such courage dissolved, for by Saturday, August 31—one week to the day since the dispatch of Cable 243—the coup had fizzled. The South Vietnamese generals plotting Diem's demise "did not feel ready and did not have sufficient balance of forces," wrote Harkins.[105] The administration therefore confronted the prospect of mending fences with Diem, or at least clarifying for him the difficulties of maintaining unqualified support. Either way, the future of the advisory effort was uncertain, as the Ngos would likely revive their effort to push Americans out of the provinces. Diem and Nhu ultimately pursued a more ambiguous policy of courting Lodge while tarring lower-level U.S. officials— part of an effort, according to historian Edward Miller, to renegotiate, albeit clumsily and foolishly, the terms of the limited partnership.[106]

But given presumptions about Saigon's increasing distrust of Washington, and Washington's increasing doubt about Saigon, maybe the best move was to seek an honorable withdrawal from Vietnam. Better a dignified retreat, argued the State Department's Paul Kattenburg, than getting thrown out of the country in six to twelve months.[107] That position found few takers. Nolting thought the United States had "done a tremendous job toward winning the Vietnam war," and doubted the likelihood of such public opprobrium. Rusk also objected, treating Kattenburg's argument as "largely speculative." They had been succeeding, he claimed, and now should move forward on the "firm basis" of two principles: "that we will not pull out of Vietnam until the war is won, and that we will not run a coup." The secretary of defense, who was then in the process of finalizing plans to withdraw one thousand U.S. troops by the end of 1963 and virtually all of them by the end of 1965, agreed.[108] So did the vice president. Lyndon Johnson rarely spoke at such gatherings, but Kennedy's absence at the meeting left him seemingly liberated to voice his approval of Rusk's position. He then disclosed his "great reservations" about the coup, largely because he saw no alternative to Diem. The United States might need to reduce its aid to the GVN and demand it take certain actions, but a coup was out of the question, as was an American withdrawal. "We must reestablish ourselves and stop playing cops and robbers," he said, and "once again go about winning the war."[109] That effort, however, would now move forward in an altered political environment—one steeped in mistrust—in both Saigon and in Washington.

It also would involve more aggressive diplomacy if the Americans were to coax Diem into adopting their desired reforms. Leverage, and the best means for securing it, became ExComm's quest in the waning days of the aborted coup. McNamara wanted to avoid withholding funds as the opening move, but officials eventually gravitated toward it, nonetheless. Lodge ultimately received authorization, as Rusk put it, "to announce suspension of aid through Diem Government at a time and under conditions of your choice." The ambassador wondered whether Congress would mount its own pressure campaign. It might be helpful, he mused, for the House to cut the foreign aid appropriation for South Vietnam, a measure that "could have certain advantages." Rusk, too, thought it worthwhile, suggesting that Lodge, in reopening talks with Diem, highlight the challenge of sustaining congressional support for Saigon. Kennedy himself advised tying aid to performance. Developments in South Vietnam had already resulted in congressional cuts to foreign aid, with more to come unless the GVN mended its ways. Should Diem fail to take appropriate measures, the United States "simply would not have resources to sustain massive present level of support."[110]

Over the next several weeks, Congress and the White House, both separately and jointly, would consider ways to press the point. While lawmakers were more vocal in applying that pressure, it was the administration that produced the more dramatic and consequential response.

6

Declaration

September 1963–October 1963

With the coup in Saigon having collapsed, the Kennedy administration was now in a precarious position. Not only did it fail to remove
the Ngos from power, but the United States was now exposed as a co-
conspirator in the plot. The GVN undoubtedly knew of Washington's
role in the episode and so had even more reason to resent America's
presence in South Vietnam. The administration, therefore, entered September tied to a partner it acknowledged as expendable, with its partner
openly doubting the value of the partnership. All the while, it remained
committed to thwarting the NLF's bid for victory in the South—a victory it regarded as highly damaging to American interests. Those interests continued to turn on matters of credibility and resolve more than
on material or economic concerns. For senior officials, the loss of South
Vietnam, even in light of Sino-Soviet tensions, threatened to bolster
international communism at the expense of western democracy. The administration thus feared it had few alternatives but to work with Diem
until a new coup emerged, if it ever did, and to hope in the meantime
that the GVN could mobilize effectively to win the war.

Further complicating matters, French president Charles de Gaulle
now inserted himself into the volatile mix. De Gaulle had frequently
chided the Americans for their handling of Vietnam, but he had done
so largely in private. He now went public with his critique, declaring on
August 29 his interest in helping the Vietnamese unify their country and

achieve "independence from exterior influences." De Gaulle's gambit to neutralize Vietnam was a pointed attack on Washington's militarization of the crisis, and Kennedy officials chafed at his intervention.[1] Secretary of State Dean Rusk made clear to French diplomats that a "truly neutral" Vietnam was not yet possible and that a "false neutrality" would pose great dangers to the region.[2] Equally alarming were indications that de Gaulle had taken his lead from Ngo Dinh Nhu, who U.S. officials feared was conspiring with Hanoi to eject the United States as part of a deal with the North.[3] De Gaulle's maneuver, following his rejection that January of Britain's bid to join the European Economic Community, as well as his increasingly harsh words about Washington's dominance of the Atlantic alliance, further strained Franco-American relations. They also carried worrying implications for developments in Asia and the Cold War writ large.

Kennedy countered with public remarks of his own. Three times in a ten-day stretch, from September 2 through September 12, JFK affirmed his commitment to the struggle in Vietnam. Sitting for a wide-ranging interview with CBS news anchor Walter Cronkite, Kennedy maintained that the war was Saigon's to win or lose. The United States could provide equipment and military advisers, "but they have to win it, the people of Viet-Nam, against the Communists." While the odds of prevailing were diminishing—a function of the political crisis, Kennedy intimated, as he was silent on the military balance—all was not lost. "With changes in policy and perhaps with personnel," Diem could still regain popular support; absent those changes, "the chances of winning would not be very good." Regardless, Kennedy repudiated those who called for the United States to pull out of Vietnam. "That would be a great mistake," he said. Yes, the war was difficult and close to fifty Americans had been killed, "but this is a very important struggle even though it is far away." Nor would his administration try to neutralize South Vietnam "and leave the world to those who are our enemies." The United States would remain there to help the GVN win its war against the NLF.[4]

Speaking with NBC's Chet Huntley and David Brinkley one week later, Kennedy seemed even more committed to the fight. The effort required the steely determination not only of his administration but of the American people, a refrain the president turned to several times during the conversation. "Americans will get impatient," he acknowledged, "and say because they don't like events in southeast Asia or they don't like the government in Saigon, that we should withdraw." But that would only make it easier for the Communists. "I think we should stay," he said, and try to influence the course of action as best as possible, "but we should not withdraw."[5] Parrying questions days later about the U.S. relationship with Saigon, Kennedy fell back on the now familiar mantra that "what helps to win the war, we support; what interferes with the war effort we oppose." The most he could say about U.S. objectives was that "we want the war to be won, the Communists to be contained"—a locution that effectively lumped Vietnamese Communists with Chinese Communists—"and the Americans to go home," policy goals shared by the GVN. But the United States was not in Vietnam "to see a war lost."[6] Although Kennedy had grown increasingly impatient with the conflict and was open to various means for prosecuting it, his commitment to the cause could not have been clearer.

So was the strategic rationale behind it. Defeat in Vietnam would lead the dominoes to start falling, Kennedy told NBC, thrice affirming his belief in that image of Communist expansion. Saigon's collapse would not only improve Beijing's geopolitical position, but "give the impression that the wave of the future in southeast Asia was China and the Communists."[7] It was not the first time Kennedy had warned the public about falling dominoes. Anticipating President Eisenhower's use of the metaphor, Kennedy had argued in January 1954 that the loss of Indochina would lead several regional states, as well as other independent countries, to "fall under the control of the Communist bloc in a series of chain reactions."[8] As president, he accepted the validity of domino thinking, even if he questioned its mechanistic application. Speaking to journalists in April 1963 about renewed fighting in Laos and its impact on neighboring states, Kennedy recognized "an interrelationship in these countries" which led his administration to seek stability in Southeast Asia. The effects of that dynamic extended beyond its regional impact. Consumed with issues of international credibility, where the image of a wavering Washington could negatively affect relations with allies and adversaries, Kennedy and his advisers thought the psychological dominoes were at least as relevant as the geographical ones. Demonstrations of American resolve, therefore, remained cornerstones of Kennedy's geostrategic thought.[9]

Coming on the heels of the failed coup in Saigon and the public handwringing attending it, the president's media blitz sought to convey the image of an administration regaining its footing. The White House and State Department thought the campaign highly successful.[10] But pundits and media outlets were less charitable and laid into Kennedy over the following two weeks. Walter Lippmann criticized the pursuit of victory in Vietnam; its price was "higher than American vital interests can justify," especially since Vietnam comprised "an important secondary interest" of the United States and not a "primary vital" one. If that was indeed the case, and if the war was for Saigon to win, then why was the United States, asked Arthur Krock, "spending American lives and billions of dollars in a war that is not ours?"[11] *Time* also panned Kennedy's television diplomacy, labeling it "a lamentable failure" that would "increase tensions and animosities between two governments that must continue working together for their mutual security." *Newsweek* wondered about the commitment itself, running a critical cover story on the Nhus and a piece comparing South Vietnam's ruling clique to those of Chiang Kai-shek in China, Syngman Rhee in South Korea, and Fulgencio Batista in Cuba—doomed regimes, all.[12] The administration, it charged, was simply "flailing" about with no semblance of a coherent policy.[13] Journalists highlighted the disarray seemingly on a daily basis, making repeated reference to rifts between U.S. officials in Washington and Saigon, and among others within the Defense Department, the State Department, and the CIA. The *New York Times* feared those splits and hostilities were so profound that the confusion they engendered could lead to "disaster." Pleading with the administration to find and follow a more consistent line, the *Times* maintained that "any policy is better than no policy at all or a dozen policies operating at cross-purposes."[14]

If there was one policy the press supported, it was a firm commitment to remain in Vietnam. According to analysts at the State Department, the notion that Washington might pull out was "rejected by most," with media outlets believing withdrawal would simply hand that corner of the world to America's enemies.[15] Leading commentators on politics and foreign affairs shared that view. Arthur Krock thought withdrawal would lead to the fall of Southeast Asia. Chalmers Roberts admonished "not the ugly American abroad but the impatient American at home," and held that Kennedy's "'win-the-war' and then bring-the-boys home" approach would only encourage further impatience. Even Walter Lippmann, who supported a neutralized settlement, thought there was "no way in which Washington could disentangle itself in South Viet-Nam without inviting some kind of disastrous landslide in Southeast Asia." The United States, therefore, had "no choice but to stay in South Vietnam" and maintain its support of Diem.[16] The sentiment was hardly uniform, as scattered voices encouraged Kennedy to disengage. But majority opinion, as the administration understood it, firmly backed the effort to stand with Saigon in its struggle against Communism. As pollster Lou Harris discovered, a whopping 72 percent of Americans supported U.S. policy, with only 28 percent opposed. While attitudes would turn more ambivalent in 1964 and 1965, opinion in the summer of 1963 favored the Kennedy commitment to preserve an independent and non-Communist South Vietnam.[17]

Congress

With the administration at loggerheads over how best to support the GVN, Congress became more engaged in Vietnam policy than at any time during Kennedy's presidency. Its involvement had been building throughout the summer as legislators expressed increasing displeasure with Saigon and its handling of the Buddhist crisis. But threats to exert leverage at home and abroad accelerated in the wake of Diem's August 21 declaration of martial law. Lodge welcomed the lawmakers' outrage and energy. "Nothing better has occurred to me on this score" than the idea of an aid cut for Vietnam, he wrote, even as he suspected that Diem and his circle had little understanding of the political headwinds lashing Washington.[18] They were particularly strong in the Senate Foreign Relations Committee, whose members gave Roger Hilsman an earful when he appeared before its Far East Subcommittee on September 5. The two-hour conversation "revealed far-reaching doubts" about Diem and Nhu, he said, but also about "continued US participation in Viet-Nam war." The mood "augur[ed] heavy sledding" in the upcoming Senate debate over foreign aid, as well as the "introduction of resolution condemning further US support for GVN."[19]

That legislative maneuver became more likely the following day when Senator Frank M. Church [D-ID] floated a resolution to halt U.S. support for Diem if GVN reforms were not forthcoming. Journalist Chalmers Roberts noted high-level backing for the measure, which it saw as helpful in reforming the Diem regime and, in turn, preventing calls for disengagement. "The Administration is totally opposed to pulling American forces out of Viet-Nam," Roberts wrote, but without a solution to the RVN's political crisis, U.S. officials expected that "pressures to that end will begin to exert themselves in Washington."[20] Attorney General Robert F. Kennedy even suggested "get[ting] out now rather than waiting," especially if the war could not be won—a recommendation that occasioned far less pushback than when Paul Kattenburg voiced similar thoughts the previous week. But the presumed leverage of withdrawal went only so far. It would be "very serious to threaten to pull out of Vietnam," said Secretary of State Rusk, for if the Vietnamese Communists took over in Saigon, "we are in real trouble." Indeed, if the situation continued to deteriorate, he feared they might have to mount "a massive U.S. military effort."[21] Neither of those options were attractive, so Rusk directed Lodge to "initiate dialogue with Diem soonest" to indicate the depth of Washington's concern, and suggested the ambassador invoke Senate statements threatening an aid cut unless reforms were forthcoming.[22] It was a high-wire act, with the administration trying to maintain public support for the war while pressuring America's client state to do a better job of waging it.

As much as those maneuvers sought to marshal leverage against Diem, they also made it difficult to confront Saigon with a unified position. Open discussion of a potential aid cut threatened to reveal cracks within the government that others could exploit. Roger Hilsman thus worked with Church to fashion a resolution more amenable to administration tastes. Joining forces with Church seemed increasingly necessary, as another Diem detractor, Sen. Wayne L. Morse [D-OR], was considering an even more dramatic approach: amending a foreign aid bill not only to bar further aid to Saigon, but to force Washington to "get out" of Vietnam.[23] More conservative and centrist lawmakers pushed back. Senator Barry M. Goldwater [R-AZ] railed against the defeatism of those who renounced their support of Diem. So did Senator Henry M. "Scoop" Jackson [D-WA], who criticized calls for withdrawing troops and endorsed a Veterans of Foreign Wars statement urging Kennedy "to take whatever steps are necessary to win" the fight. Senator Stuart Symington [D-MO] followed suit, embracing a *St. Louis Globe-Democrat* editorial that scored the "folly" of retreat from Southeast Asia.[24] In general, though, commentary on the Church statement highlighted the confusion surrounding administration policy.[25]

The president himself contributed to it. Aid cuts to South Vietnam "would not be helpful at this time," he told Huntley and Brinkley on September 9, as they would hurt the GVN and benefit the Communists—a dynamic not unlike that which doomed the Nationalist government in China following the Second World War.[26] It was a position seemingly out of step with maneuvering behind the scenes, for Church was using the administration's own language in his resolution.[27] When the Senator finally introduced his motion on September 12, with the backing of twenty-one lawmakers from both sides of the aisle, Kennedy appeared to pivot once again. "I have indicated my feeling that we should stay there, and continue to assist South Viet-Nam," he said, but such assistance "should be used in the most effective way possible."[28] What was most effective, he thought, was the use of that aid as implied leverage; the administration preferred the resolution remain pending rather than have it come to a vote, so other senators could continually attach their names to it.[29] That was precisely how Lodge thought he might use it. Church's talk about an aid cut had "shaken" Nhu, and when meeting with Diem on September 9, Lodge referenced Senate statements about a possible suspension of aid to South Vietnam. More foolish speeches from the incendiary Madame Nhu, he said, could add even more signatures to it.[30]

Withdrawal Planning

Amid that public and private diplomacy, preparations for withdrawal moved closer to fruition. On September 3, Secretary of Defense Robert S. McNamara approved "for planning purposes" a schedule to realize the 1963 withdrawal of one thousand U.S. troops from Vietnam. The timetable remained contingent—as far as the Joint Chiefs were concerned—on developments in South Vietnam. The JCS would not finalize it until late October, when they would evaluate the political and military situation and forward their judgment to the Secretary. An October deadline would allow enough time to draw down U.S. troops in Vietnam before the end of the year, while ensuring that those withdrawn would not compromise the counterinsurgency.[31]

Maintaining its effectiveness was essential, even as present realities offered a mixed bag. The intensity of the war continued to ratchet upward, with the Mekong Delta still under Communist control.[32] U.S. estimates of PLAF strength remained comparable to summer numbers; "hard core" fighters numbered in the ballpark of 21,000, but irregular forces had presumably shrunk from 85,000 in June to 70,000 in September.[33] More worrisome were State Department figures on rates of infiltration. While estimates held that roughly 3,500 had arrived from North Vietnam since early 1962, the growth in both PLAF casualties and PLAF fighters suggested the NLF was having considerable success recruiting from within South Vietnam.[34] Nevertheless, the Strategic Hamlet Program—the signal initiative in the counterinsurgency—appeared to be advancing. September figures diverged on the percentage of South Vietnamese living in those fortified villages, with reports suggesting between 72 and 96 percent of the rural population were ensconced within them—a range that should have raised more eyebrows at the time. Nevertheless, BRIAM chief Robert Thompson reported that "steady progress" had been made in the southern part of South Vietnam, with GVN authority having been restored and security provided "for greater numbers of the population."[35] Collectively, those figures suggested that planning for a U.S. troop reduction would continue to move forward in a climate of guarded optimism.

At the same time, preparations for withdrawal reignited internal discussion about how many forces would remain in South Vietnam after those first thousand came home. Troop levels were actually scheduled to rise from a late-August figure of 16,201 to a peak strength of 16,732 by October 30, the result of deployments "critical to current operational and training needs in Vietnam," as JCS chair Maxwell D. Taylor put it.[36] Accordingly, CINCPAC Adm. Harry D. Felt settled on a year-end strength of 15,732, with the first withdrawal increment of 276 leaving in November and the remaining 724 departing in December.[37] McNamara's review of the plan, however, led him to question the wisdom of "creating special holding units if their only purpose is for withdrawing individual advisors and headquarters personnel." The Chiefs therefore wanted "a detailed public affairs plan treating the withdrawal as a package operation." The plan would need to emphasize Saigon's progress in the war and MACV's success in training the South Vietnamese military, so the RVNAF could "assume the functions of certain US units thereby permitting their withdrawal."[38]

Beyond the thousand-man withdrawal, the Pentagon was refining plans for the broader withdrawal two years hence. Those efforts included changes to the Military Assistance Program for Vietnam. On 6 September, McNamara approved what came to be known as the "Model Plan" for MAP aid.[39] It was one of five such plans the Pentagon developed that summer—two more than it originally envisioned—covering FY 1965 through FY 1969. Ranging from $385 million to $585 million, they addressed matters such as South Vietnamese troop strength, weapons costs, the GVN defense budget, equipment turnover, and an inventory of U.S. advisory forces. Coming in with a price tag of $400 million, the "Model Plan" sought to maximize the advantages and minimize the disadvantages of the other four schemes. According to CINCPAC, it provided the best mix of operational capability, economic feasibility, and political acceptability, all with a range of measures designed to neutralize and contain the Communist insurgency.[40]

Pressures and Persuasion

Although planning for withdrawal seemed to be moving forward without a hitch, options for leveraging the Ngos into better performance remained elusive. Kennedy and key aides addressed those measures in a September 10 briefing from Maj. Gen. Victor H. Krulak and the State Department's Joseph A. Mendenhall, who had recently conducted a fact-finding trip to South Vietnam. The mission emerged out a White House meeting days earlier that revealed deep uncertainties about Diem's ability to prevail against the Communists.[41] To Kennedy's chagrin, the mission's findings proved no more enlightening and failed to satisfy the need for clarity that prompted the visit in the first place. In fact, its depictions of the war were so disparate, with Krulak offering an encouraging account of fighting in the countryside and Mendenhall a scathing report on politics in the cities, that Kennedy wondered whether the two had visited the same country.[42]

Additional voices clouded the image even further. Rufus Phillips, who headed the rural affairs operation in South Vietnam and had returned to Washington with Krulak and Mendenhall, noted the "crisis of confidence" pervading the body politic and the impossibility of winning the war with the Nhus still involved. Phillips recommended that Ed Lansdale go to Saigon to help turn things around, a move Lodge endorsed. Further suggestions came from John Mecklin, the public affairs chief at the embassy in Saigon, who offered the most hawkish advice of all: support a coup to oust the GVN and introduce American combat troops. It was a deployment senior aides had suggested back in the fall of 1961, the last such fluid period for policymaking on Vietnam. Kennedy embraced none of those options, but he did ask Hilsman to flesh out actions they might take in the event they "decided to go up the aid route."[43]

Confusion over policy reemerged during a session that evening at the State Department. Seeking to resolve the differences between Washington and its embassy in Saigon, National Security Adviser McGeorge Bundy sparred with McNamara and Assistant Secretary of State Averell Harriman over just what was on the table—whether to work within the statements Kennedy had made or seek wholly new departures. McNamara found the present policy "barren" and said he was willing "to support any proposed position if it exhibits strength," including working with Diem or dumping him, or pursuing both at the same time. Grasping at straws, Hilsman now resurrected Mecklin's gambit from the morning session and raised the possibility of introducing U.S. combat troops, an option Taylor vigorously opposed. Having failed to settle the dispute, Bundy called for a subsequent meeting to review Hilsman's papers. They would cover U.S. objectives in Vietnam and "a program of pressures against Diem with the aim of forcing him to meet our demands."[44]

Those pressures were precisely what Lodge was recommending, as he saw little else that might alter Diem's approach. If the administration could devise effective sanctions, it should apply them "to force a drastic change in government," and in short order. A "wait-and-see approach," especially if Diem seemed incapable of winning the war, would simply leave Washington with fewer options. Lodge's cable struck a chord with the president—reportedly, the "most powerful" message JFK had seen on the developing situation in Vietnam. The Pentagon was less impressed. Neither McNamara nor Taylor supported sanctions, nor did they "buy the assessment this is going to get worse and something serious must be done," as Bundy reported.[45] Bundy himself was deeply troubled. Aides found him "visibly disturbed by the way things are going in Vietnam" and, uncharacteristically, "at a loss about what to do." Deepening his puzzlement, he found Mme. Nhu's recently announced plan to visit the United States simply confounding. Her behavior, along with that of her husband and brother-in-law, marked "the first time the world had been faced with collective madness in a ruling family since the days of the czars."[46]

Madness or not, the Kennedy administration was no closer to devising an effective policy for dealing with the Ngos. Papers from Hilsman and the NSC's Michael Forrestal presented options for either maintaining the status quo or pressuring Diem to reform. Proposed measures included exiling the Nhus, holding new countrywide elections, fostering reconciliation between the GVN and the Buddhists, and, of primary importance, prosecuting the war more vigorously. Hilsman even entertained "the quiet removal" of individuals "who may have become anathema" either to the GVN or to the United States—essentially acknowledging Nhu's concerns about the elevated profile of Americans in South Vietnam.[47] None of those measures commanded much popular support. American opinion, as refracted through editorials in the press, seemed evenly divided between whether the administration should "get tough or ride it out," as Forrestal put it—a darker vision than the more favorable Harris poll just weeks earlier. But the real question, as he posed it, was "whether U.S. domestic opinion will allow us sufficient time to determine whether the Vietnamese can solve their own problems."[48] Senior officials, therefore, had a range of options to review, all of which presumed a continued American presence in South Vietnam.

Their discussion on September 11 revealed an aversion to asking hard questions and a reluctance to answering those on the table. But it also highlighted the difficulty of the task at hand. Rusk articulated the conundrum, maintaining that Washington "should not abandon Vietnam," but neither should it "apply force to achieve our objectives." The administration had several paths open to it "before we have to choose between getting out or sending in U.S. combat troops." If there was any consensus among senior officials, it was that time was on their side. Rusk thought the calendar for action would be measured in weeks, not days, as did McNamara, Taylor, and Bundy; Hilsman and John McCone, director of Central Intelligence (DCI), thought the critical moments would come even further down the road, perhaps as many as three months hence. The group therefore rejected Lodge's call to precipitate the fall of the Diem government, seemingly marking the end of coup plotting. Instead, it wanted Lodge to seek frequent contact with Diem while it considered "concrete moves" to give him "additional leverage" with the GVN. Those included the evacuation of dependents and deft use of the Church resolution.[49] Lodge thought it "obvious" the United States "must not leave" South Vietnam, "but the question of finding a proper basis for remaining," he confessed, "is at first blush not simple."[50] Collectively, those conversations, which consumed the better part of two weeks, highlight the persistent disarray plaguing the administration in its handling of Vietnam—a chaos borne of the tension between the presumed need to remain in Vietnam and its chosen means for doing so.

Policymakers inched closer to a coherent position as Hilsman used the weekend of September 14 and 15 to develop alternate approaches to the Diem regime. The less disruptive involved a "Reconciliation Track" which sought to work with the Ngos and, through a series of political, legal, press, and religious reforms, repair their standing in South Vietnam and the United States. But Hilsman favored a "Pressures and Persuasion Track," based upon the assumption that Nhu had "already decided on an adventure" that would involve the departure of U.S. civilian and political advisors, at a minimum, and the withdrawal of the remaining Americans as part of a deal to secure a "neutralist" South Vietnam.[51] Nhu was still condemning the elevated profile of Americans in Vietnam, maintaining the rhetorical campaign he had waged against the United States over the previous six months.[52]

More ominously, Nhu was at that point in contact with Hanoi, a parley that was an "open secret" in Saigon diplomatic circles. Interpretations of his strategy differ and hold that he was either seeking leverage over Washington, or willing to cut a deal with Hanoi, or even expecting to negotiate a victorious peace over his enemies. Whatever the case—and his intentions remain obscure—each of those scenarios looked toward the removal of U.S. forces from South Vietnam.[53] But efforts to sideline Nhu might prompt the same result; aid cuts to pressure the Ngos could create an "unpredictable and uncontrollable situation," as DCI McCone put it, and if they provoked an unsuccessful coup, the United States would likely face an "invitation out of SVN." Days later, Thomas Hughes, the State Department's intelligence chief, raised similar concerns, citing Nhu's frequent calls to reduce the American presence. Hughes was particularly troubled that reports of Nhu angling for a negotiated settlement with Hanoi had become "so credible and widespread as eventually to undermine morale in the army and bureaucracy, regardless of their current accuracy."[54]

Those reports were even more worrying as Nhu likely now held greater power than Diem. Indeed, the administration believed that Nhu had played a key role in De Gaulle's August 29 statement, even if he professed opposition to a neutralized South Vietnam.[55] His impact on Saigon, therefore, would continue to be malign. While fears remained that a policy of coercion might lead Nhu to order U.S. advisers out of the country, Hilsman sought to implement one "in such a way as to avoid triggering either civil violence or radical move by GVN to make deal with DRV and remove US presence."[56]

Whatever option Kennedy chose, the time for choosing was at hand. U.S. policy had been rudderless over the previous several weeks—if not months—a reality that was making Washington a prisoner of events. True, Kennedy's engagement with Vietnam, which had been episodic at best, was now more sustained. But recognizing that the administration had reached "a position of stall in our attempts to develop a Washington consensus," Forrestal concluded that "the governmental situation here requires Presidential guidance." He thought Kennedy might implement the first phase of Hilsman's "pressure" plan, especially since it was comparable to the initial phase of the "reconciliation" track, after which they would have an opportunity to evaluate next steps.[57]

But Kennedy still seemed reluctant to act, a reticence that signaled his desire to avoid any course that narrowed his options. A series of domestic developments might also have slowed his selection of a policy position. On Sunday, September 15, a church bombing in Birmingham, Alabama, killed four young girls; two boys would die that day as well, shot down in that city's streets, increasing the stakes of the civil rights struggle the administration was now supporting with legislation. Kennedy was also consumed with ratification of the Limited Test-Ban Treaty; a vote loomed in the Senate, though its passage looked likely. Still, the magnitude of its importance likely absorbed more of the president's energy and attention. News from Vietnam did emerge over the weekend—not all of it bad, as Diem signaled the end of martial law by noon on Monday, September 16. But Vietnam was absent from Kennedy's agenda as the new week began, with no decision on Hilsman's "tracks" in the offing.[58]

The McNamara-Taylor Mission

Instead, Kennedy chose to send yet another factfinding team to Southeast Asia, this time headed by two of his most senior national security officials. On Tuesday, September 17, he asked McNamara and JCS chair

Taylor to see Lodge in Vietnam and "get his whole feeling about this thing." They were to form "their best judgment of how the war is going" and find out "whether the infection is spreading out of Saigon, and all the rest." Not only would the visit allow the administration "to operate ourselves with a little better judgment," but its domestic benefits, because of Taylor's participation, "would look well here." It was Taylor's 1961 visit, after all, which resulted in the "limited partnership," and his on-the-spot military assessment would help greatly with Congress and the public.[59]

Although the mission granted Kennedy still more time to ruminate over options before making a definitive choice, it continued to steer the administration away from the coup plotting of late August. That it stood as a rebuke to the anti-Diem crowd was not lost on its members, as several of them recognized; there simply was "no good opportunity for action to remove present government in immediate future," Kennedy wrote Lodge. "Therefore," he continued, "we must for the present apply such pressures as are available to secure whatever modest improvements on the scene may be possible." Those included the prerogative to tell the GVN that "all U.S. assistance is granted only on your say-so," as well as the power "to apply any controls you think helpful for this purpose." Lodge himself could decide whether to publicize those moves. Most essential, though, was that the trip allow Kennedy to make the case to Congress for continued prosecution of the war, and it was for that purpose the president had decided to send McNamara and Taylor to Vietnam.[60]

Planning for the trip moved forward with meetings on September 19 to hammer out details. As Kennedy made clear in an off-the-record session he secretly recorded, he wanted an assessment of current as well as future prospects for the war.[61] If it was faltering, then the administration had to decide "what it is that is really essential to make the war go well and then figure out how we're going to accomplish it"—or, as he later put it, "what is it we should do to make them do what they have to do." As for their approach to Diem, Kennedy signaled that McNamara and Taylor should be guided by their findings. If the "rot really was setting in," he said, "then I think you just give it to him as tough as you can and just—and tell him—just decide on two or three things that you think we could get him to do, which would not dismantle his whole operation and could make a serious difference. And just say this is what you got to do. Because he's going to lose the war!"

To leverage Diem into better performance, Taylor wanted to confront him with the prospect of an American troop withdrawal by 1965. "It's not only that we have to win with you," Taylor envisioned telling Diem, but "we have to win very soon." Bundy and McNamara also thought the timeline could serve as a helpful inducement:

> **Taylor:** We just cannot be an indefinite proposition. Hence we oppose [*unclear*]—we have a feeling that many of your measures are indeed slowing up victory, and we just can't continue on this basis, because the pressure for—being generated at home.
>
> **Bundy:** You don't have forever. We're not here forever and [*unclear*]—
>
> **Taylor:** We're not here forever.
>
> **Bundy:** On a fixed basis.
>
> **Taylor:** And furthermore, just to show you [*Bundy attempts to interject*], we have a plan, which the Secretary has, showing how we expect to phase out of here. And we need to do this in a—in some finite period of time. This isn't forever.
>
> **McNamara:** I particularly (*sic*) to tell Diem that at some point. I suspect we're going to have to see Diem several times. [*President Kennedy acknowledges.*] And one of these occasions, I'd like to show him that we do have a plan for getting out of there. That's the time for success . . . that we have. We worked it out in some detail.

Evidently, and remarkably, the administration still had not informed the GVN about planning undertaken ostensibly in its name, the central feature of which involved a U.S. troop withdrawal. Fifteen months after that planning had begun, and six months after Nolting suggested he disclose it to Diem, the GVN was still in the dark about Washington's strategic calculus—a reality that again exposed the limits of their partnership.

Even so, the virtues of withdrawal were coming into view. While Taylor and Bundy hinted at its coercive value, McNamara seemed to construe it as a way to accommodate Diem—an acknowledgment of Diem's sensitivity to the elevated American presence in South Vietnam.

Although Diem and Nhu recoiled at that presence, senior U.S. officials regarded Diem, at least, as worried about its progressive diminution. To address his concern, McNamara instructed Krulak, who, along with Bill Bundy, would assemble the "Black Book" for the trip, to "get withdrawal plan in shape for presentation to Diem" at some point during the visit.[62]

Kennedy, however, remained silent on the merits of revealing it to Diem. Presumably, he understood its generalities if not its particulars, though outside of Paul Nitze's late April notes and the May 7 White House conversation with McNamara, no record exists of JFK receiving a briefing on it. His silence is more understandable in light of his conversation with McNamara and Taylor just prior to their departure on September 23. Two days earlier, Kennedy had maintained that the "question of progress" in the war was a matter "of the first importance," since he needed "to have the best possible on-the-spot appraisal of the military and paramilitary effort to defeat the Viet Cong."[63] For Taylor, though, the question was "not only to detect whether we're making progress, but are we making progress fast enough." He wanted Diem to know the United States was "not going to do anything to carry forward this enterprise indefinitely."[64]

Now, on September 23, Kennedy rose to the bait. He was skeptical of threatening Saigon with a possible U.S. withdrawal. Diem had been hearing versions of that threat for ten years, he said. The better approach was to tell Diem that the GVN was going to lose the war, if indeed signs were pointing in that direction. McNamara came to Taylor's defense, suggesting they tell Diem that "we have plans for withdrawal of our forces when military success warrants it." If Diem wanted to get them out, as McNamara put it, "why don't you see about getting them out? We hope that before the end of the year, we can withdraw military (*sic*), [if the] situation improves. We hope—believe we can." It was the clearest indication yet, from the individual most closely associated with withdrawal planning, that the troop reduction was contingent on military success.[65]

Again, though, Kennedy sought to shift the focus away from that planning and toward arguments he thought more compelling. Instead of focusing on withdrawing troops, Taylor should convey Washington's concerns in the spirit of a ten-year relationship that involved significant amounts of U.S. aid. Theirs was a partnership with a common goal, for what really mattered was Diem's ability to prevail in the counterinsurgency. This was not a "struggle" between Washington and Saigon, the president said. "We're not—we don't care what the hell he does out there, really. We're not demanding—we're not getting into a moral judgment about the Buddhists, their pagodas, and all their arrests—we're getting into a—my better judgment, whether—helps with the war." Again, he questioned the value of leveraging better performance out of the GVN by warning of a reduction in economic and military assistance. "I think probably it isn't much use to threaten them on the aid," Kennedy maintained. Bundy agreed, believing it "better to let those things happen than to talk about that [*unclear*]." Taylor continued to advocate for pressure, though, and preferred to emphasize the planned reduction in force. "I'd much rather lay out a schedule" and highlight "our plan to withdraw and say this is what we're going to [*unclear*]. We have to win this war in this timeframe." Once more, Kennedy sidestepped the matter of troop withdrawal, focusing on a proposed recommendation to Diem. If Taylor and McNamara concluded that Diem's approach was bound to result in "inevitable defeat," then they would need to see both Diem and Nhu and give them "a military judgment that they're not going to win," and "therefore they got to do something else." The troop withdrawal was simply not worth raising with Diem, and Kennedy's repeated reluctance to consider its virtues reflected his skepticism about its coercive or persuasive impact in Saigon.[66]

But it might have some political value in Washington. Kennedy was therefore eager for the trip to depart, since troop withdrawal, as part of a broader review of Vietnam policy, allowed him to address several challenges at home. Republicans, with an eye on 1964, were likely to use Vietnam to chip away at Kennedy's performance and popularity, even with the Lodge appointment that summer.[67] Of more immediate concern was Kennedy's foreign aid package and the recognition that lawmakers were holding it hostage to Vietnam. Taylor understood the linkage and, in a note to Harkins, stressed that he and McNamara, upon their return, would need to give "an eye-ball account of situation in South Vietnam to an increasingly critical Congress." Foreign aid had been "endangered by recent events," he said, and legislators would want assurance that "the war can be won in a finite period."[68] The connection was foremost in Lodge's mind as well, as he sought to tie support of Diem to congressional concerns about his rule. Invoking Church's maneuvering, Lodge told Nhu that more senators had added their name to the impending resolution, "and that it would not be difficult to get enough sig-natures to guarantee a majority." Were those signatures to materialize, it would constitute "a body blow to foreign aid" and thus a blow to sup-port for South Vietnam. Nhu should leave the country, he recommended, until Congress could pass its appropriation for foreign assistance.[69]

Church, in fact, had maintained his pressure campaign on Vietnam, as had other colleagues who were looking to assert a congressional role in policymaking. The senator from Idaho had repeatedly entered into the record articles and editorials critical of U.S. policy, including a piece from the *Salt Lake City Tribune* calling on Kennedy to disengage from Vietnam.[70] It was a position gaining more adherents: on September 26, Senator George S. McGovern [D-SD] urged Kennedy to withdraw, making him the second senator after Wayne Morse to do so.[71] The drum-beat for withdrawal ended there, however. Neither Morse nor Mc-Govern lobbied the president directly, and, aside from Church's pending resolution, members of Congress remained generally silent on the ques-tion of withdrawal. But the resolution itself posed problems. If it received less than virtually unanimous approval, "it pulls the rug out from under us," as Hilsman framed it.[72]

At least as worrisome was the prospect that it might get attached to the administration's foreign aid bill, which remained in deep trouble.[73] Lawmakers on both sides of the aisle were in the process of slashing Kennedy's original $4.9 billion request by over 25 percent; conservatives had tired of sending U.S. dollars to statist economies, and liberals had soured on outfitting dictators with military support. Both groups thought such assistance should be administered more frugally and responsibly.[74] Senate Foreign Relations chair J. William Fulbright [D-AR] ultimately agreed to postpone hearings for the bill, as he feared that Vietnam would further complicate its prospects. Ironically, the effort to link Diem's ac-tions to congressional support threatened the broader program upon which it rested. The McNamara-Taylor mission thus opened a route toward passing the aid request as well as maintaining the Vietnam as-sistance effort.

Once in South Vietnam, McNamara and Taylor conducted interviews and sat through briefings with U.S. civilian and military personnel, as well as with GVN officials and RVNAF commanders.[75] Among the more consequential were two sessions that conveyed the increasing gravity of the situation. An exchange between McNamara and CIA station chief John Richardson highlighted the tenuous ties between U.S. advisors and their South Vietnamese counterparts. A pervasive sense of suspicion could doom their collaboration, especially at lower levels, even though they presently shared good working relationships. As for the higher echelon of Vietnamese soldiers, Richardson feared that many of them "have been turned against the government." The toxic environment, marked by widespread arrests, kidnappings, and hatred of the Nhus, could only "lead to disaster." In all, Richardson found the future "so uncertain" that he could offer no prediction of what would happen.[76]

McNamara's talk with Patrick J. Honey, a Southeast Asia specialist based at the University of London, was even more disturbing. Having once believed that the Americans could work with Diem, Honey had now come to think otherwise; Diem was a failing force, was incapable of changing, and was totally dependent on Nhu, who had spread fear throughout all of Saigon. But any coup or assassination that overturned the regime—the only viable routes toward a new government, he reckoned—offered no more than a 50 percent chance of "getting something better." Yet that something better was essential if the war was to be won. Were the Communists to gain control of South Vietnam, "not another political leader in all of Asia will place any confidence in the world (*sic*) of the West." In fact, Honey warned, "the loss of confidence will not be limited to Asian leaders."[77] The psychological dominoes, as Honey framed them, were thus ripe for falling—a lurid vision of the future.

It was in this context that McNamara and Taylor considered the prospect of lowering the U.S. profile and operationalizing withdrawal. Reductions in force, however, would come only in the context of progress in the counterinsurgency. Indicators of success in the advisory effort, which the mission presumed would appear "in measurable degrees" during 1964, included a slowdown in PLAF military activity, increases in PLAF defections, and Saigon's reclamation of areas formerly held by the NLF. Furthermore, between 15 and 25 percent of operations against the PLAF would need to arise out of information provided by the populace, and 90 percent of key areas of South Vietnam would need to be under Saigon's control for the reduction to move forward.[78] Projected U.S. force strengths would then top out at just over 15,000 for FY 1964 and fall to under 2,500 by FY 1969.[79]

As for the thousand-man withdrawal, mission documents placed conditions on the removal of those forces as well. Guidance still held that any such reduction "should take place with minimum impact on the combined US-RVN capabilities to bring counter-insurgency campaign to successful conclusion in shortest possible time." CINCPAC had now structured it so that 526 personnel would pull out in dedicated units, with the remaining 474 coming from elements of MACV, MAAG, and other U.S. agencies. But the removal of units, it held, "depends on the progress of the counter-insurgency effort." Restructuring the mix to satisfy the preferred 70/30 ratio of units to individuals would be difficult "without seriously reducing the capabilities of the commands."[80] Both reductions, then—the thousand-man drawdown of 1963 and the comprehensive phaseout by 1965—were still envisioned as conditions-based withdrawals, dependent upon battlefield realities in the war against the Communists.

But the mission failed to communicate those plans to the GVN, stripping them of any coercive or persuasive power they might have held. The closest it came to sharing them was at the end of the visit, when McNamara and Taylor conveyed to Diem their "confidence in being able to cope with the Vietcong military threat by 1965," provided that Diem implemented the military and political reforms they now were recommending.[81] Taylor reaffirmed that confidence in a letter to Diem. Assessing the military situation, he defined victory as "the reduction of the insurgency to proportions manageable by the National Security Forces normally available to your Government." Taylor thought the GVN could still win its war, "providing there are no further political setbacks." Military indicators were "generally favorable and can be made more so by actions readily within the power of your Government." Taylor then closed with his "most important overall impression" of the war: "Up to now, the battle against the Viet Cong has seemed endless; no one has been willing to set a date for its successful conclusion. After talking to scores of officers, Vietnamese and American, I am convinced that the Viet Cong insurgency in the north and center can be reduced to little more than sporadic incidents by the end of 1964. The Delta will take longer but should be completed by the end of 1965."

Those were the key assumptions driving the Comprehensive Plan, though Taylor said nothing about the American withdrawal that was central to it. Rather, he implored Diem to energize his agencies, ramp up their activities, reward effective officials, punish deficient ones, and restore a political environment conducive to waging war against the Communists. "Both of our countries have put too much into this war to be satisfied now with less than a victorious conclusion."[82]

By the time Diem received the letter, the mission was aloft over the Pacific, stopping first in Honolulu before continuing on to Washington. Its members began writing their report in South Vietnam and continued working on it during their twenty-seven-hour flight east.[83] In the words of chief drafter William P. Bundy, it was "a very poor way to conduct the top business of the U.S. Government." Bundy slept just two hours on the flight and McNamara only a few hours more, compromising the coherence and clarity of the finished product. As Bundy later put it, the frenetic pace at which the mission was conducted and the report written reflected "the almost desperate urgency at which the president sought to resolve the policy issues and differences in his Administration."[84]

Accordingly, the report assessed South Vietnamese political dynamics, the effectiveness and staying power of the Diem government, U.S. policy toward the GVN, and the state of the war. While the battle varied widely within and between areas and provinces, McNamara and Taylor concluded that "the GVN military program has made great progress in the last year and a half, and that this progress has continued at a fairly steady rate in the past six months even through the period of greatest political unrest in Saigon."[85] The turmoil could spread, however, and ultimately derail the counterinsurgency. Washington should therefore "work with the Diem government but not support it." The time for reevaluating its position would likely come within two to four months, when the administration would need to decide "whether to move to more drastic action or try to carry on with Diem even if he had not taken significant steps."[86]

Based on those conclusions, McNamara and Taylor called for the "application of selective short-term pressures, principally economic, and the conditioning of long-term aid on the satisfactory performance by the Diem government in meeting military and political objectives which in the aggregate equate to the requirements of final victory." Those pressures included the suspension of loans for waterworks and electric power projects, the withholding of funds for a special forces unit responsive chiefly to Nhu, and a continuing freeze of the Commodity Import Program, which had been suspended initially in late September.[87]

McNamara and Taylor also used the report to operationalize planning for the U.S. troop withdrawal that McNamara, at least, had long sought to implement. Seeking firmer control over the growing U.S. military presence in South Vietnam, and even leverage over the Diem government, they recommended "a program be established to train Vietnamese so that essential functions now performed by U.S. military personnel can be carried out by Vietnamese by the end of 1965." As part of that program, they recommended that Harkins review with Diem the changes necessary "to complete the military campaign in the Northern and Central areas (I, II, and III Corps) by the end of 1964, and in the [Mekong] Delta (IV) by the end of 1965." Those changes involved a shift of operational focus to the Delta, the ratcheting up of activity in all corps areas, an emphasis on "clear and hold" operations rather than territorial sweeps, the accelerated training and arming of local militias, and a more prudent approach to building and securing strategic hamlets.[88]

Of all the assumptions and recommendations contained in the report, the withdrawal clauses generated the most pushback from members of the mission team. William H. Sullivan, an assistant to Harriman and the State Department's representative on the trip, complained bitterly to McNamara when he saw those passages during the drafting in Saigon. "I just can't buy this," Sullivan said, characterizing the withdrawal pledge as "totally unrealistic." The United States was not going to remove its troops by 1965, he maintained, and therefore "we mustn't submit anything phony as this to the president." Although McNamara allegedly convinced Taylor to strike that language from the draft report, Taylor's frustration with Diem got the better of him. On the flight back to Washington, he made the case for withdrawal as a form of leverage against the GVN. "'Well, goddamnit,'" he exclaimed, "'we've got to make these people put their noses to the wheel—or the grindstone or whatever,'" as Sullivan recalled their exchange. "If we don't give them some indication that we're going to get out sometime, they're just going to be leaning on us forever. So that's why I had it in there.'" Sullivan acknowledged Taylor's motivations but cautioned that "if this becomes a matter of public record, it would be considered a phony and a fraud and an effort to mollify the American public and just not be considered honest."[89]

Sullivan came away from the conversation thinking he had kept the clause out of the report. He was mistaken. McNamara and Taylor likely reinserted the passage when they met in Taylor's office on the morning of October 2, roughly three hours after landing in Washington and a mere eighty minutes before they were to meet with the president.

Fifteen months of planning to remove U.S. troops from Vietnam thus made its way to Kennedy's desk as a result of Taylor's pique and the last-minute machinations of Pentagon leadership.[90]

The thousand-man reduction also found its way into the McNamara-Taylor Report. Framing it as part of the comprehensive phaseout of American forces, its authors recommended that the Pentagon announce the initial drawdown "in the very near future" as part of the broader effort "to train progressively Vietnamese to take over military functions" presently being carried out by U.S. advisers. This first withdrawal, they noted, "should be explained in low key as an initial step in a long-term program to replace U.S. personnel with trained Vietnamese without impairment of the war effort."[91] Central to both the incidental and comprehensive withdrawals were concerns about South Vietnamese morale. In the end, Saigon had to run the war on its own, and the continued presence of U.S. advisory forces in Vietnam "beyond the time they are really needed" would compromise the "independence" and "initiative" of the South Vietnamese. In fact, McNamara and Taylor thought a limited transfer of responsibility could take place at that very moment "without material impairment of the total war effort." But beyond the return of those one thousand troops, they held that "no further reductions should be made until the requirements of the 1964 campaign become firm."[92] The comprehensive withdrawal would thus depend on military conditions, while the thousand-man withdrawal would now proceed in spite of them.

In addition to those and other recommendations, McNamara and Taylor proposed a four-paragraph statement they thought could serve as a policy position and be available for use in public settings and congressional testimony. Its contents highlighted progress in the war, concern about South Vietnamese political and military developments, and the use of sanctions—both economic and rhetorical—to improve Saigon's overall performance. It also included a declaration that "the security of South Vietnam remains vital to United States security," a clause that elevated Saigon's importance to U.S. interests. Consistent with that position, the declaration further held that the administration was committed "to the overriding objective of denying this country to Communism and of suppressing the Viet Cong insurgency as promptly as possible."[93]

As for the expected duration of the commitment, the proposed statement affirmed that "the U.S. part of the task can be completed by the end of 1965, the terminal date which we are taking as the time objective of our counterinsurgency programs."[94] Although it did not explicitly reference the withdrawal of all U.S. troops by that date, the implication was clear enough: those forces would leave when they had trained the RVNAF to run the war. Moreover, their departure was expected to co-incide with Saigon's victory over the NLF. Defining "victory" as "the reduction of the insurgency to something little more than sporadic banditry in outlying districts," McNamara and Taylor held that success in the northern three military corps in South Vietnam could come by the end of 1964, with "victory" in the fourth corps—essentially the Mekong Delta region in the south—taking longer, "at least well into 1965." Those judgments, they pointed out, "necessarily assume that the political situation does not significantly impede the effort."[95]

But that was precisely the problem with the McNamara-Taylor Report. Its military judgments hinged on its political judgments, but its political judgments cast doubt on Saigon's ability to stabilize the country sufficiently for the war to advance—rendering the future of the U.S. assistance program a dubious proposition.[96] Neither McNamara nor Taylor followed those premises to their logical conclusion when they reviewed the report with the president on the morning of Wednesday, October 2. Nor did any of the other officials attending the White House briefing, including the State Department's George Ball and Averell Harriman, DCI John McCone, AID administrator David Bell, National Security Adviser McGeorge Bundy, and, for the first twenty-five minutes, Vice President Lyndon Johnson.[97] While they recognized the influence of political conditions on military progress, they never fully confronted the likely impact of Diem's continuing rule, and thus its probable impact on the counterinsurgency.

But they did engage the matter of withdrawal, a topic that emerged early in the meeting. McNamara began the discussion by suggesting that Kennedy first glance through the report, a recommendation the president brushed aside, asking McNamara for his thoughts on the journalists covering the war.[98] "Miserable," McNamara replied, attacking them en masse for "allowing an idealistic philosophy to color all their writing," and singling out the *New York Times*'s David Halberstam and United

Press International's Neil Sheehan for censure. Once the president turned to the substance of the report, he focused on the proposed thousand-man withdrawal slated for December 1963. His skepticism was apparent:

Kennedy: You think this thousand reduction can really . . .

McNamara: Yes, sir. We—

Kennedy: Is that going to be an assumption that it's going well, but if it doesn't go well [*unclear*]—

McNamara: No. No, sir. One of the major premises—two major premises we have. First, we believe we can complete the military campaign in the first three corps in '64, and the fourth corps in '65. But secondly, if it extends beyond that period, we believe we can train the Vietnamese to take over the essential functions and withdraw the bulk of our forces. And this thousand is in conjunction with that and I have a list of the units here that are represented by that thousand.

The two withdrawals—the thousand-man withdrawal planned for 1963 and the more comprehensive withdrawal scheduled for 1965—now intersected as a matter of state policy. Although they were devised at different times for mostly different purposes, with the comprehensive withdrawal emerging out of bureaucratic and policy concerns in July 1962 and the thousand-man withdrawal originating mostly for political reasons in April 1963, they now combined formally and functionally as part of the U.S. program in Vietnam.

Not all were sold on the idea, for as soon as McNamara described its contours, McGeorge Bundy forced him to defend it. "What's the point of doing it?," Bundy asked. McNamara responded in unambiguous terms. "We need a way to get out of Vietnam. This is a way of doing it. And to leave forces there when they're not needed, I think, is wasteful and it complicates both their problems and ours." McNamara's search for an exit ramp from Vietnam, voiced in desperate tones on the recording Kennedy made of the conversation, was an extraordinary plea from the man who later welcomed the struggle being known as "McNamara's War."[99] Indeed, his commitment to withdrawal and his fervid support of it further amplifies the distance between his public statements and his private beliefs—gaps already in evidence that would widen with time.

Following their brief discussion of withdrawal, the conferees addressed other elements of the trip report. These included Hanoi's order of battle and rate of infiltration, Washington's options for inducing Diem to be more effective, and the challenge of engaging Diem personally. Kennedy and his aides then zeroed in on the actions McNamara and Taylor were recommending. For Bundy, "the most immediate" involved clauses designed as policy positions for use in congressional testimony and public statements. It was the announcement of withdrawal that concerned him most, which Taylor sought to explain and defend:

> **Taylor:** Well, it's something we debated very strongly. I think it is a major question. I will just say this: that we talked to 174 officers, Vietnamese and U.S., and in the case of the U.S., I always asked the question, "When can you finish the job, in the sense that you will reduce this insurgency to little more than sporadic incidents?" Inevitably, except for the Delta, they would say '64 would be ample time. I realize that's not necessarily . . . I assume there's no major factors—new factors entering [*unclear*]. I realize that's—
>
> **Kennedy:** Well, let's say it anyway. And then '65, if it doesn't work out, we'll get a new date.
>
> **Taylor:** '65 in the Delta.
>
> **McNamara:** I think, Mr. President, we must have a means of disengaging from this area. We must show our country that means. And the only slightest difference between Max and me in this entire report is in this one estimate of whether or not we can win the war in '64 in the upper three territories and '65 in the fourth. I'm not entirely sure of that. But I am sure that if we don't meet those dates, in the sense of ending the major military campaigns, we nonetheless can withdraw the bulk of our U.S. forces, according to the schedule we've laid out—worked out— because we can train the Vietnamese to do the job.

These passages are among the most significant of Kennedy's records on the war, as they contain some of the only instances in which JFK comments privately on the current and future status of American troops in Vietnam. His willingness to revisit the 1965 withdrawal date "if it doesn't work out" suggests a disposition to delay the removal of U.S. troops; neither his language nor his tone betray any impatience with the struggle or an inclination to abandon it. By contrast, McNamara's rejoinder conveys a sense of urgency about reducing American involvement. With Kennedy tying the proposed withdrawal to military progress, the end date for U.S. participation became more flexible. Kennedy's Vietnam War, then, by his own admission, was likely to continue through the election of 1964, into the first year of a presumed second term, and perhaps beyond.

Yet neither Kennedy nor his team came to grips with either losing in Southeast Asia or extending their involvement. It was not for want of trying, as officials had pushed them to consider those possibilities over the previous few weeks. DCI John McCone now revisited the matter, suggesting that Hanoi could up the ante and commit more troops to the fight. Taylor and McNamara rejected McCone's premise, with Taylor resting his case on the Strategic Hamlet Program; if that initiative was as successful as its designers intended, then Saigon would be "creating an obstacle to any great addition to the North."[100] It was a massive presumption, particularly with so much riding on the program's success. But tales of progress, at least in the northern three corps, had been largely bullish, as they had been in field reports and conversation among senior officials. Discussions dating back to the aborted coup in August also included claims that the war was advancing satisfactorily, with memos from civilian and military advisers attesting to the same. Taylor had been particularly upbeat, informing Kennedy of "favorable trends in all military activities" during August, "despite Saigon's preoccupation with the unstable political situation."[101] By the time the president met with McNamara and Taylor on October 2, he had received a steady stream of data indicating progress in the counterinsurgency—a precondition he and McNamara had previously established for the December 1963 pullout of one thousand troops, if not for the more comprehensive drawdown scheduled for 1965.

Still, trouble was brewing, and the president took notice. While Hilsman detected "no let-up in the war effort" in the aftermath of the Buddhist crisis, "disturbing signs" had emerged since the events of August 21, suggesting "the war effort may be affected."[102] Kennedy acknowledged those concerns in dispatching McNamara and Taylor to Vietnam in late September. Events since May, he stated, "have now raised serious questions both about the present prospects for success against the Viet Cong and still more about the future effectiveness of this effort unless there can be important political improvement in the country."[103] While McNamara may have discerned sufficient progress to accelerate the time-table for withdrawal, Kennedy's increasing unease about the counterin-surgency was evident in the extra attention he was devoting to it.

Nevertheless, the originator of the thousand-man withdrawal believed its operative conditions no longer held. Visiting the Mekong Delta that summer, BRIAM chief Robert Thompson saw glimmers of hope, noting that GVN authority "was gradually being restored over large areas of the country" and that Saigon had made "steady progress" over the previous six months in building strategic hamlets. But the program had overex-tended itself and needed to proceed more methodically. "The greatest mistake," he said, would be "to try and go too fast." He therefore warned against setting target dates for completion, as they "only encourage Prov-ince Chiefs to 'cut corners' and to create hamlets which are strategic only in name." Significantly, he warned against trying "to rush the es-tablishment of a white area in Vinh Long," the most promising area for that achievement, "even if it takes well into 1964." The first area declared "white"—a condition Thompson attached to any token withdrawal they might make—had to be "absolutely secure." It was still possible to achieve great progress in the Delta by the end of 1965, but it was essential the GVN now consolidate the program's gains.[104]

Ironically, then, the decision to move forward with the thousand-man troop reduction, despite the provisos Thompson had stressed in April and September, and McNamara and Kennedy had embraced in May, trans-formed a conditional withdrawal into an unconditional one. That it did so owed much to political imperatives in the United States and to mil-itary realities in Vietnam. With foreign aid and Vietnam policy under attack at home, and with those thousand troops having little bearing on operations in the field, their withdrawal became much more plausible, especially as political capital for sustaining the Vietnam program and waging the aid fight. As for the 1965 withdrawal, Kennedy had little trouble supporting it as an aspirational goal, as much could happen in the span of two years to change his posture. JFK thus turned that seemingly unconditional withdrawal into a more conditional one. After all, they could always "get a new date" if battlefield realities warranted it. Taken together, those developments suggest an even greater irony at work: Rather than signal a growing interest in leaving the war, the proposed withdrawals allowed Kennedy to remain very much engaged in fighting it.

7

Implementation

October 1963–November 1963

Until October 1963, the planning to withdraw U.S. troops from Vietnam had taken place in secret—or, at least, in the classified world of departmental meetings, privileged conversations, and government memoranda. It had run for fifteen months, involving extended consideration from MACV, CINCPAC, and the Office of the Secretary of Defense. Officials at the State Department were aware it, though not heavily involved, save for perhaps the Country Team in Saigon; neither Averell Harriman nor Roger Hilsman, the two chiefs of the department's Bureau of Far Eastern Affairs during the period in question, left a significant paper trail on the matter, nor did the interdepartmental Task Force Vietnam seem to be comparably engaged. White House knowledge of that planning is also obscure. Kennedy apparently knew of its contours, but the record is silent on whether McGeorge Bundy and Mike Forrestal had such knowledge prior to preparations for the McNamara-Taylor mission in September. The circle would widen dramatically following its return home, as senior officials converted its trip report into administration policy. Those efforts moved the planning for withdrawal from declaration to implementation, a process that generated considerable opposition internally and externally—and ultimately altered relations with Saigon.

The declarative phase commenced on the morning of October 2, as the president and his most senior advisers sought to turn the McNamara-Taylor policy statement into a public White House position. Like much of the mission and its immediate aftermath, that process was highly improvised, as officials massaged the announcement and prepared for its release. Kennedy was most interested in hedging his bets and deflecting it from himself. Instead of preserving McNamara and Taylor's formulation that "the U.S. part of the task" would be over by 1965, Kennedy altered it so that the "major part of the U.S. task" would be completed by that date. He also looked to pin that judgment on McNamara and Taylor. "Let me just say I think this ought to be *their* statement, and I will support it then at a press conference, and so on." With Taylor describing the passage as a policy position and not a public statement, Bundy and Kennedy proposed the group develop a statement based upon that paragraph; McNamara and Taylor could then invoke it early the following week when they briefed Congress on their trip. But they needed to act swiftly, lest the entire report begin to leak, and suggested the NSC meet by Friday, October 4, to draft the statement. Harriman thought it unnecessary to wait two days and proposed the NSC meet that very evening, an idea Bundy, McNamara, and the president endorsed. When Kennedy recommended that the ensuing statement come from the NSC itself, Harriman and Bundy further qualified that approach, suggesting it emerge out of the military recommendations McNamara and Taylor made to the president, which, with the advice of the NSC, the president then approved. That way, all elements of the national security bureaucracy would have played a role in crafting a public position that bound the government together. Once they had done so and the relevant players had signed on, the administration's "civil war," as Bundy termed it, would come to an end.[1]

But there was still some skirmishing ahead, as revisions to the statement generated significant pushback. One such edit downgraded Vietnam's importance to U.S. national interests. Whereas the statement once held that "the security of South Vietnam remains vital to United States security," it now treated Saigon's defense as "a major interest of the United States as of other free nations."[2] That diminution of importance, along with a distribution of responsibility, struck at a recent public comment from the president himself. Just one week earlier, Kennedy had described Vietnam, along with Laos and the Congo, as "matters of the greatest concern, where the interests of the United States are vitally involved[.]"³ The less dramatic formulation of October 2 would survive the evening NSC review and appear in the statement released to the press.

More contentious edits involved the withdrawal deadlines themselves. Resistance to the 1965 end date had already emerged during the writing process and on the flight back to Washington, but opposition now grew as the 1963 withdrawal joined the 1965 timetable as part of the proposed public statement. It remains unclear how this melding occurred.⁴ What seems to have happened is that Kennedy ushered McNamara and Taylor into the Oval Office following the morning meeting to work out language he found acceptable. McGeorge Bundy likely began drafting the statement while McNamara and Taylor were meeting with the president, after which the two of them joined Bundy in his basement office.⁵ With the 1963 drawdown now affixed to the public statement and a bracketed passage added to qualify the 1965 reduction, both withdrawals emerged as contingent: "[If military progress continues,] the major part of the U.S. military task can be completed by the end of 1965, although there may be a continuing requirement for a limited number of U.S. training personnel. By the end of this year, the U.S. program for training Vietnamese should have progressed to the point where 1,000 U.S. military personnel assigned to South Vietnam can be withdrawn."⁶

Several officials were deeply upset with those amendments. Many of them agreed with William Bundy's later depiction of those clauses as "extraordinarily unwise."⁷ Their dismay seems to have stemmed not so much from opposition to the withdrawal schedules—though officials did question the wisdom of citing an end date for military involvement—but to plans for making them public. Chester Cooper, who headed the CIA's South Vietnam Working Group, maintained that "the available indicators do not provide an adequate basis for fixing a definite date (i.e. the end of 1965)," and he doubted "whether this is necessary or prudent in a public statement." Recognizing, however, that a withdrawal clause would likely remain in both the trip report and its associated pronouncement, Cooper suggested it might be "carefully qualified along the following lines: 'If present military progress continues, we believe that the US part of the task might be completed by the end of 1965.'"⁸ The Bundy brothers also opposed the withdrawal language, but when McGeorge persisted in questioning the wisdom of retaining it, Bill reportedly shot back, "Look, I'm under instructions!" Apparently, the national security adviser then took his case to the defense secretary, to no avail. As Cooper relates, "McNamara seemed to have been trapped too; the sentence may have been worked out privately with Kennedy and therefore imbedded in concrete."[9]

While it remains unclear how those passages found their way into the proposed statement, McNamara was adamant they remain there. He hardly came to that position belatedly, as he had been the driving force behind withdrawal planning for well over a year. According to William Bundy, McNamara was consumed during the recent mission by the question of whether the United States could reduce its advisory presence and withdraw the bulk of its forces within a three-year window.[10] Real-time evidence corroborates not only his focus on the question but also his guidelines for answering it. As was the case in his pre-trip meetings with the president, McNamara continued to tie an American troop withdrawal to military success. "Can Diem and Nhu provide the leadership," he asked the mission team, "to reduce the Viet Cong threat to proportions which will permit a diminution of the U.S. financial, material, and personnel investment in the war?" Or, as he put it in handwritten notes, "What degree of military success would justify the beginning of withdrawals of US forces," a question he phrased without a question mark attached.[11] McNamara had thus framed the proposed troop withdrawal, at least in advance of the trip, as contingent on progress in the war.

But his conversations in Vietnam apparently pushed him closer toward viewing withdrawal in unconditional terms. The Richardson and Honey interviews were particularly troubling, but so, too, was a briefing from junior U.S. officers in Can Tho, as was a conversation with South Vietnamese defense minister Nguyen Dinh Thuan.[12] Those encounters suggested to McNamara that the political and even military situations were more severe than he had previously grasped, and that their further impact on the war was likely to follow. McNamara had thus "changed his views considerably," according to Gordon Etherington-Smith, Britain's ambassador to South Vietnam," and "now had no illusions as to seriousness of political situation nor did he see how it could fail to affect anti-Communist effort." Indeed, Roger Hilsman sensed much the same about McNamara, regarding him as a changed man upon his return.[13] Those changes were in evidence during the morning briefing on October 2 and in the NSC session that evening.

Kennedy began the NSC meeting by stressing his desire for the group to approve a statement that would bind the government together. "I don't think it does the war any good; it doesn't do the government any good to appear that there's division in any way between State and Defense and CIA," so he hoped they could fashion a position that all could endorse.[14] McGeorge Bundy led the group through the proposed position by highlighting the president's suggested changes, each of which distanced Kennedy from the trip report and distributed ownership for its conclusions and recommendations to the NSC, and particularly to McNamara and Taylor. It was a tactic designed for political cover, especially given the state of the Saigon regime.

More significant edits involved the withdrawal schedules themselves. The following exchange between McGeorge Bundy and McNamara touched on the 1965 end date and the context for including it:

Bundy: Then on page one of the draft statement itself, the President is concerned about this sentence about "the major part of U.S. military task can be completed by the end of 1965," and asked whether we wouldn't do better to say that that is the judgment reported by Secretary McNamara and General Taylor.

McNamara: I would like that.

Bundy: Because we don't want to be in a position where we—

McNamara: I think that's—

Bundy:—are terribly—so that what we might say is, "Secretary McNamara and General Taylor reported their judgment *that* [*with McNamara acknowledging*] the major part of U.S. military task can be completed." Then, in the—paragraph four, the President's suggestion is—

McNamara: And that, Mac, eliminates this military [*unclear*]—

Bundy: Then you don't need that clause.

McNamara: Right. Right.

The clause they proposed to remove was the bracketed passage, "If military progress continues," which placed an explicit condition on the withdrawal statement. Instead, they pinned the timing of withdrawal on McNamara and Taylor's judgment that the United States could complete its military task by 1965. Taylor certainly believed the war could be won by then; his remarks earlier in the day, in which he maintained the United States could "finish the job" by December two years hence, suggest that for him, withdrawal would come when the insurgency had been all but fully vanquished.

McNamara was cagier. He thought the advisory part of the task could end by 1965, regardless of whether the insurgency had been defeated. Again, that was not the only position he had taken. His pre-trip remarks to Kennedy, as well as his memos to Pentagon officials, drew a direct connection between withdrawal and military conditions. Moreover, both he and Taylor acknowledged that RVNAF training was dependent upon the state of the war. If the counterinsurgency did not go as well as they hoped, particularly in the Mekong Delta, then merely training the RVNAF by December 1965—especially in a deteriorating military environment—might not be possible. The question remains, therefore, whether an inability to complete that training—the bare minimum McNamara was proposing—would still have left him pushing for unconditional withdrawal.[15] His reflections on that hypothetical, as well as on how the president and the country might have navigated it in the face of defeat, are absent from the existing record.

Aside from ownership of the military judgment, the NSC addressed the key dynamic informing it: the relationship between South Vietnamese domestic politics and progress in the war. Saigon's turbulence had yet to compromise the military effort, as Kennedy recognized, though it might well do so in the future. But the president wanted to downplay the GVN's repression and U.S. revulsion to it. He wanted all to know that "the object here is to win the war," as Bundy phrased it, and therefore "didn't want to have it said that we were just Pollyannas and couldn't stand a little authoritarian government." The State Department pushed back, but Kennedy was undeterred. "I'd rather tie it—I think we got a major problem in the United States," he said, and thought it "better to make it our objection, our big problem with this thing, and if it's so, it's because it's going to hurt the military." The war—not democratic niceties, not social reforms, not moral qualms—was Kennedy's primary concern, as it had been throughout. While its national security dimensions remained paramount, its management as a domestic political matter remained equally salient.

Having settled on language for the 1965 withdrawal and the circumstances surrounding it, the group turned to the thousand-man reduction and the virtues of publicizing its due date. Kennedy did not object to its inclusion, but he did question its prudence:

Kennedy: My only reservation about it is that it commits us to a kind of ch—if the war doesn't continue to go well, it'll look like we were overly optimistic, and I don't—I'm not sure we—I'd like to know what benefit we get out at this time announcing a thousand.

McNamara: Mr. President, we have the thousand split by units, so that if the war doesn't go well, we can say these thousand men would not have influenced the course of action.

Kennedy: And the advantage of—

McNamara: And the advantage of taking them out is that we can say to the Congress and people that we *do* have a plan for reducing the exposure of U.S. combat personnel to the guerrilla actions in South Vietnam—actions that the people of South Vietnam should gradually develop a capability to suppress themselves. And I think this will be of great value to us in meeting the very strong views of [Sen. J. William] Fulbright [D-AR] and others that we're bogged down in Asia and will be there for decades.

Kennedy thus conveyed to this larger group what he had said privately to McNamara in May: the withdrawal of American troops from Vietnam was, in his mind, dependent upon progress in the war. Through all the improvisation of that planning, especially over the previous twenty-four hours, the focus on battlefield conditions had remained a constant; withdrawal and military progress went hand in hand. But Kennedy remained open to arguments suggesting otherwise, especially if they offered a net gain in political advantage.

To give the president even more cover, Bundy sought to put distance between Kennedy and the thousand-man withdrawal clause. Along with the 1965 withdrawal, the decision to remove one thousand troops by the end of 1963 would again rest on McNamara and Taylor's judgment that it made sense to do so. Kennedy still had doubts about the 1965 date, though, and wondered whether they should tie it to Saigon's vigorous pursuit of the war, a proposal McNamara discouraged. "As to whether it's vigorously pursued or not," McNamara said, "we'll have a training program such that we can take them out, and we ought to be charged with the responsibility of doing that."[16] It was a position consistent with his newfound willingness to remove those troops regardless of military success.

The NSC next turned to the sanctions they would impose to elicit the desired GVN response. A working group would flesh them out over the next several days, but they were to be embargoed, at least until the group had agreed on them before reporting back to the president. Press discipline was paramount, as attendees were discouraged from discussing the report and its effects. Most importantly, they were to maintain a common front. Indeed, securing that government-wide position had been the whole point of the exercise—the McNamara-Taylor trip and the public statement. Having apparently succeeded in the effort, Kennedy framed their achievement near the end of the session. "As of tonight," he said, "we have a policy and a report endorsed by all the members of the National Security Council."[17]

The Public Reacts

If the administration thought its messaging would quiet concerns about Vietnam, it was sorely mistaken. The White House statement, which Kennedy press secretary Pierre Salinger and Pentagon spokesman Arthur Sylvester delivered to journalists after the meeting concluded, seemed to raise more questions than it answered. Neither Salinger nor Sylvester would cite the number of U.S. troops in South Vietnam, nor would they clarify whether the military effort would end in 1965, nor would they say how many troops beside the thousand scheduled for removal in 1963 would come home. It was a frustrating exercise for all involved, and an inauspicious start to the administration's publicity campaign.[18]

Reaction around the country was hardly more reassuring. Press comment, as captured by State Department opinion watchers, was swift and scathing. The administration's "overly-optimistic" statement did nothing to dissipate "the confusion and dissatisfaction which exists with regard to U.S. Viet-Nam policy," nor was it "the frank accounting the American people deserve."[19] Government statements on Vietnam had long been "lacking in candor," charged the *New York Times,* and were evidently "still far from frank," sentiments also expressed by the *Wall Street Journal.*[20] Martin Agronsky, the host of NBC's *Meet the Press,* reached out personally to Averell Harriman, phoning him on the morning of October 3 to relay widespread confusion about U.S. policy and a sense that McNamara's evaluation of the situation was "fantastically optimistic." The forecast of a U.S. troop withdrawal by 1965 featured prominently in national headlines and came in for especially harsh treatment. That "groundless prophecy . . . isn't worth the paper on which it is written," opined the *Washington Post,* which further cast the statement as a "reckless" disclosure of military planning.[21] Similar appraisals came from *Newsweek,* the *Los Angeles Times,* the Scripps-Howard papers, the Knight papers, the *Chicago Tribune,* and the *New York Herald Tribune,* with the latter chiding the White House for assuming the political situation would not worsen.[22]

Criticism was not universal, however. Newspapers and journals supportive of the White House statement, such as *Time,* the *Christian Science Monitor,* and the *St. Louis Post-Dispatch,* thought it signaled that Washington would now exert "quiet but steady and substantive pressures" on Diem. Other outlets, such as the Hearst Press and the *Des Moines Register,* believed it revealed "no change" in U.S. support of the GVN, while the *Louisville Courier-Journal* thought it allowed the administration latitude "to change its policies as conditions change."[23] In fact, William S. White, Charles Bartlett, *Life,* and the *L.A. Times,* among others, argued for staying in Vietnam come what may, even as they were confident that "victory is still within our grasp." That position mirrored popular sentiment. A recent Lou Harris survey found that support for the U.S. commitment had dipped only marginally, as those who approved of assistance to South Vietnam still numbered more than two to one. Nevertheless, as George Ball noted, several outlets urged the United States to withdraw its aid and forces. As evidence, Ball cited the *Salt Lake City Tribune,* which argued that "withdrawal would be defeat for US, but not nearly as disastrous as continuing hopeless struggle."[24]

More troubling assessments came by way of British and American officials stationed in Saigon and Washington. London's ambassador to South Vietnam, Gordon Etherington-Smith, thought the mission report was "very cool," and quoted Lodge as stating it "would have been considerably cooler and more outspoken had it not been phrased with an eye to effect on Congress and the continuation of aid appropriations."[25] As for the withdrawal itself, David Ormsby-Gore, Britain's ambassador to the United States, thought it was clearly designed "for public consumption," and that removing those thousand advisers would, in the eyes of Robert Thompson, "have an encouraging effect on South Vietnamese morale and a correspondingly depressing effect on the Viet Cong." Its value was also evident to the Joint Chiefs, though they thought it was targeting a different audience. As recorded in their official history of the era, they understood that the White House statement was "obviously made with the U.S. Congress and public in mind," and thus constituted a political as much as a military judgment—as indeed it was.[26]

Implementation

In the wake of the White House statement, Kennedy officials developed the program of economic and political pressures outlined in the McNamara-Taylor Report. Those measures aimed to signal American "displeasure" with the GVN and generate "uncertainty" in Saigon over Washington's future intentions without compromising the counterinsurgency. Ultimately, they were designed to mobilize Vietnamese popular support for winning the war and reduce the strain in relations between Washington and Saigon.[27] While those actions could lead to vastly different outcomes—either fostering a reconciliation with Diem or precipitating his overthrow—McNamara expected Diem to respond in ways that would "improve the political situation and therefore improve the military effort."[28] Working sessions on October 3 and 4, which essentially reconstituted the Executive Committee of the National Security Council (ExComm), set the stage for an off-the-record meeting with the president on Saturday morning, October 5. Kennedy went into the conversation knowing that press treatment of the White House statement had been none too kind. The Saturday meeting thus provided an opportunity not only to flesh out their program but to further bind the government around a common approach recognizable to the American public.

That program amounted to a sanctions regime which maintained existing measures and imposed new ones. It preserved a halt in the Commodity Import Program, suspended loans for key infrastructure projects, modified deliveries of surplus U.S. food, and held up funds for a Special Forces outfit responsive to Nhu. It also called for a series of military and political changes, such as shifting the war to the Mekong Delta, increasing the tempo of combat operations, emphasizing "clear and hold" tactics, reopening the universities and releasing detained students, repairing the pagodas and freeing Buddhist protestors, and restoring civil liberties. While Kennedy probed the ExComm on each, he was particularly interested in the way Saigon would learn of those demands. They would have the greatest impact, he thought, if "they come out as they arise rather than as a formal statement by either you, or an informal one by your staff, or any formal statement by us. They ought to just come as the situation arises. Seems to me that has a little more clout than looking like we're trying to put on a public squeeze on him." It was a point he repeated for effect. The United States would achieve its objectives "if the Vietnamese learn about these restrictions as they come up, and not as a rather formal action to put public pressure on them. I mean, then he's— then it doesn't have any impact, that he has to resist us." The low-key approach was thus critical to the process.[29]

Those considerations resurfaced near the end of the session when the group turned to the thousand-man withdrawal scheduled for December. It was a matter the Attorney General had raised at an ExComm meeting the previous day, when he asked about "the logic of making known the plan to withdraw U.S. soldiers." McNamara repeated the arguments he made on October 2, maintaining that it made no sense to leave U.S. forces in Vietnam "when their presence is no longer required, either by virtue of the Vietnamese having been trained to assume the function, or the function having been fulfilled."[30] But now the president, too, wanted to revisit the policy, and he addressed it near the end of the October 5 meeting. McNamara stood firm, maintaining that those thousand forces were "just not needed out there":

McNamara: We've trained the Vietnamese to carry on certain functions. There's no reason . . .

President Kennedy: Well, I think the only thing is, if it's going horribly, just from the public point of view, withdrawing would seem illogical. It's going to have to be formally announced rather than just do it by attrition, if you really are doing it. I'd say if we're doing it for some impact, then I think we can't do it unless the war is, seems to be succeeding. Otherwise, we ought to just do it by rotation [*unclear*]—

McNamara: That's the way we [*President Kennedy attempt to interject*] [*unclear*] to do it.

President Kennedy:—rather than any formal . . . "we will announce in the near future." I think . . . I think it best maybe just—

McNamara: Or we could do it just through normal attrition.

President Kennedy: That's good.

McNamara: Normal rotation.

[*Unclear exchange.*]

President Kennedy: But the only thing is we're talking now about shortly—let's just go ahead and do it without making a formal statement [*McNamara acknowledges*] about it.[31]

Kennedy's approach to publicizing the thousand-man withdrawal thus mirrored his sanctions strategy more broadly. The sensible way to handle the proposed aid cuts and troop reduction would be to treat both in a "low key" fashion, as the quieter approach was likely to be the more effective one. The more public the talk about sanctions, the more likely Diem would resist U.S. pressures. And the more public the withdrawal announcement—particularly in the face of dubious military progress—the more likely it would seem nonsensical. Indeed, Kennedy's impulse to downplay withdrawal, and McNamara's concurrence in that posture, suggests a recognition that progress in the war was, at the very least, uncertain, and conditions could well deteriorate in the near future. The Saturday session thus ended with a presidential directive that "no formal or public statement" about the thousand-man withdrawal "should be made at the conclusion of the meeting."[32]

While Kennedy spent the rest of the weekend at Camp David, his senior aides remained in Washington, hammering out instructions for Lodge and delivering them to Saigon. They did so in two notes: a procedural cable from McGeorge Bundy and a substantive one from Dean

Rusk. Bundy's highlighted the president's desire for a low-key approach to managing Diem. Lodge should send no signals that the United States was squeezing the GVN with a program of pressures and demands, since public knowledge of those measures would only stiffen Diem's resistance.[33] Rusk's cable to Lodge, No. 534, transmitted the decisions and instructions ExComm formulated earlier in the day. Its goal was "not to lay down specific hard and fast demands or to set a deadline, but to produce movement" in Saigon to facilitate a better relationship with Washington, a more propitious domestic climate in South Vietnam, and, most importantly, more effectiveness in fighting the Communists.

Remarkably, the benchmarks for measuring success were not only ill-defined, but undefinable. "It is not possible to specify with precision," the cable read, "the criteria that we should use in determining whether this proposed course of action has brought about adequate changes in performance of Diem Government and should, therefore, be modified or withdrawn, or whether on contrary response of the Diem Government is clearly inadequate so that more drastic action should be considered." Thwarting the Nhus, who together were "a symbol of authoritarianism," would go a long way toward restoring confidence in the government. But it was far from clear how they were to achieve that objective—or even to know whether they had done so.[34]

As cable No. 534 was wending its way to Lodge, the Joint Chiefs were delivering their own instructions on the war and the disposition of U.S. forces. Designed to improve battlefield conditions in South Vietnam, those guidelines also directed that the GVN be apprised of Washington's intentions regarding troop withdrawal. Copying them to CINCPAC and to Saigon, the Chiefs directed Harkins to review with South Vietnamese officials those actions needed to "complete the military campaign in the Northern and Central areas (I, II and III Corps) by the end of 1965." U.S. officials were also to accelerate the program to train the RVNAF "to insure that all essential functions" required for the war, including those performed by U.S. troops, "can be assumed properly by the Vietnamese by the end of calendar year 1965." Indeed, "all planning" would now be "directed toward preparing RVN forces for the withdrawal of all U.S. special assistance units and personnel by the end of calendar year 1965," with any exceptions needing to be "specifically justified." The Chiefs directed that Felt revise the Comprehensive Plan with those objectives in mind and "reduce planned residual (post 1965) MAAG strengths appropriately." His deadline for resubmitting the CPSVN with those changes was November 15.[35]

Taylor also provided the operative language for the thousand-man reduction, directing Felt to "execute" the plan to withdraw those troops by the end of 1963. Its publicity, however, would now change. No longer would it assume a triumphal cast, as originally envisioned; rather, it now would move forward in a "low key" fashion. Taylor also mandated that Harkins establish checkpoints for monitoring progress in achieving both the military and training goals, which officials were to review quarterly. Those reports would "provide the basis for continued leverage on the GVN to maintain the required rate of progress."[36]

Making the Case

Having devised a policy position and delivered instructions to the Country Team in Saigon, senior Kennedy officials made their way to Capitol Hill to explain their strategy to Congress. Although the media subjected it to intensive scrutiny, lawmakers asked virtually no questions about a key element—troop reduction—when McNamara and Taylor appeared before the Senate Foreign Relations Committee on October 8.[37] Taylor raised the matter in his testimony nevertheless. Confessing that they "obviously were considering all the time" whether they could "put a time limit, a time objective on our efforts," he reiterated the withdrawal dates for the end of U.S. special assistance. Not all military advisers would return by 1965, he admitted, as some would remain to handle specialized tasks. But if "victory" constituted a diminution of the Communist insurgency to proportions the South Vietnamese could handle on their own, then "we have the resources over there now that are probably sufficient to attain victory" in just over two years' time. All bets were off, though, if any new developments intervened, such as "any serious political upset," including "an overthrow of the government, for example," or some massive infiltration of North Vietnamese.[38] Again, given recent history, it was a remarkable hedge.

For some committee members, the United States was already in too deep. Senator Albert Gore Sr. [D-TN] thought the assistance effort "an impossible burden" and that Washington should promptly pull its troops out of the country. McNamara begged to differ. Not only was it a burden they currently could finance, but one they could see shrinking in the future. "We do believe it will be possible to bring back a thousand of the men that we presently assigned there before the first of next year," he maintained, because those men will have "fulfilled their function." Regardless, Taylor said, this was a war "we must win and we can win," an imperative McNamara reinforced through popular imagery. "If South Vietnam loses this struggle," it was almost certain "that there will be a domino effect throughout not only Southeast Asia but extending both east and west" of the region. In fact, the ripples would extend "clear to the borders of Turkey on the west and Japan on the east."[39] Those were among McNamara's most categorical and alarmist comments yet on the importance of Vietnam—statements clearly designed to keep wavering senators on board with administration policy.

They also flew in the face of his White House remarks about an unconditional U.S. withdrawal from Vietnam. If the impact of Saigon's fall was likely to be so damaging, then why was McNamara lobbying for a defined departure date regardless of progress in the war? Surely not because of confidence in the GVN's capacity to prevail against the NLF. Most likely, McNamara needed a formula that both dramatized the ongoing need for U.S. assistance and projected a GVN victory in two years' time. Had the McNamara-Taylor report been as pessimistic as the defense secretary reportedly felt, the tensions between its findings and the public statement would have been that much greater. In all likelihood, McNamara was triangulating between the political needs of both sustaining and qualifying the U.S. commitment to Saigon. But those tensions remained, as neither policymakers nor legislators seemed willing to probe them sufficiently. No senior official seriously challenged a policy that framed the assistance effort as conditional and yet cast its failure as unacceptable. Whether that negligence stemmed from myopia, denial, or the pressures of the moment, it was a failure of the first order.

Beyond the internal logic of the commitment, lawmakers weighed the merits of its necessity. Again, Gore led the questioning, observing that South Vietnam possessed no material resources vital to U.S. national interests. Taylor and McNamara conceded the point; the value of the assistance effort lay not in securing any tangible resources but in standing up to international communism. Citing Khrushchev's "wars of national liberation" speech as the template for communist strategy, Taylor appealed to the dictates of image and credibility and the workings of the Communist monolith. It was incumbent on Washington to "prove by our democratic method" that Khrushchev could not win those brushfire struggles. Vietnam thus represented "a great test" in which the United States needed to prevail. McNamara amplified that theme, emphasizing the inherent value of helping states resist communist encroachment. If Saigon ultimately lost its fight "despite our assistance," then the dominoes would surely fall.[40] Although the imagery failed to move Gore and committee members Wayne Morse [D-OR], Frank Church [D-ID], and Frank Carlson [R-KS], the majority of those present either supported claims of progress or refrained from expressing their views on the war.[41]

A more public opportunity to consider that policy arose the following day, October 9, when Kennedy held an early evening press conference in the State Department. Asked for an update on Vietnam in light of his early September call for GVN reforms, Kennedy confessed he had seen no "significant changes" over the last month. But aside from fielding questions about potentially rogue CIA actions in South Vietnam—a major focus of news reporting and the Senate hearing the previous day—not one reporter asked Kennedy about withdrawal.[42]

Still, the White House statement remained a matter of public comment over the ensuing days and weeks. Pieces from Joseph Kraft and the *New Republic* speculated that the policy aimed at disengagement, with Kraft surmising that public pressure might lean in the opposite direction toward a "win-the-war commitment."[43] Papers such as the *Christian Science Monitor* and the *Oklahoma City Oklahoman* worried about a move toward neutralization, particularly as the Laotian model seemed to be faltering. Other sheets, such as the *Washington Star* and the *St. Louis Globe-Democrat,* were wary of economic sanctions, fearing they would hurt the military effort. Still other voices, including Joseph Alsop and William S. White, thought the United States had little choice but to rely on Ngo Dinh Diem.[44] To clarify the administration's position, the State Department's Roger Hilsman appeared on NBC's *Today* show. Responding to questions about the 1965 end date, Hilsman said it meant neither that the war would be over by then, nor that Washington would discontinue its aid past that date, nor that the United States would abandon the fight. As the RVNAF became able to handle those advisory and training duties, U.S. troops presently performing them could "be pulled out."[45]

Privately, U.S. and British officials were more critical. Chester Bowles, recently installed as U.S. ambassador to India, added his voice to those who disapproved of the White House statement. Bowles characterized as "rather reckless" the presumption that the war would be "relatively under control" by 1965; Hanoi could easily upset planning by augmenting the PLAF order of battle.[46] A similar sense of skepticism—or worse—ran through Americans stationed in Vietnam. According to Col. H. L. Lee, Britain's military attaché in Saigon, numerous U.S. officials were "caustically critical of the optimistic statements which are being made on the conduct of the war" and "can now see no end to the fighting."[47] But withdrawal enjoyed support among key officials in Washington. Those in favor appeared to be McNamara and Taylor, along with Hilsman. The president seemed, at best, a distant fourth.

But those numbers would grow. With fallout from the McNamara-Taylor Report and the White House statement still percolating within the upper reaches of government, McGeorge Bundy looked to ensure adherence to the newly established policy. Speaking at a White House staff meeting on October 7, Bundy expressed surprise that the projected 1965 pullout had come off as "pollyana-ish." He thought the two-year window "was really a long time, considering that by then the war would have lasted four years—or longer than most wars in US history." He thus reiterated the line that "in two years the Vietnamese will be able to finish the job without US military forces on the scene," a position that all attendees considered reasonable. It was yet another step toward embracing the view that victory and training—that is, both winning the war and enabling Saigon to win the war—went hand in hand.

Bundy then moved to codify the administration's program through the issuance of NSAM 263.[48] Its components were already moving forward via the State Department's cable No. 534 to Lodge. But the NSAM altered policy surrounding the 1963 reduction, directing that "no formal announcement be made" of plans to implement it—a qualification stemming from Kennedy's exchange with McNamara on October 5. The thousand-man withdrawal would simply result from the attrition or rotation of U.S. personnel out of South Vietnam.[49] Kennedy's decision to forego such an announcement likely arose from a desire to play it safe. With the war and the political situation still churning, and with the proposed pullout still roughly three months away, it was far more prudent to wait on events before making any such declaration.

Yet preparations for the thousand-man reduction highlighted ongoing differences between administration decrees and military desires. While the NSAM signaled a firm decision to implement the pullout, CINCPAC still wanted to make the 1963 withdrawal contingent on battlefield success. It continued to talk about benchmarks for implementation, the timing and number of increments involved, the ideal mix of units to individuals, and the absolute number of troops prior to phaseout. The reduction would take place, Felt wrote, "if progress in the counterinsurgency campaign warrants such action." In the event it could move forward, it should commence "with minimum impact on the combined US-RVN capabilities to bring counter-insurgency campaign to successful conclusion in shortest possible time." The window for making that decision was closing, however, with October 31 representing the cutoff date.[50]

Shifting considerations about publicity also affected its timetable. To maximize its public relations value, Felt continued to lobby for bringing troops out of Vietnam in four increments, with target dates of November 25 and 29, and December 2 and 5.[51] Each contingent, he argued, should be "large enough and sufficiently spaced for news prominence and cover." The first one—"clearly the most important"—should "contain colorful elements, wide spectrum of skills and representation of all services," and consist entirely of troops headed to the United States.[52] But those recommendations ran counter to the "low key" approach the administration adopted in NSAM 263, as did Felt's conditions-based withdrawal. Taylor thus informed Felt in late October that the withdrawal would proceed without fanfare "as the initial increment of U.S. forces whose presence is no longer required."[53] Before the month was out, though, Harkins would announce publicly that "at least" one thousand troops would be heading home within two months—the most explicit and definitive statement yet on the plan to withdraw U.S. forces by the end of 1963.[54] With no pushback from the White House, the statement evidently satisfied the desired low-key approach.

The number of servicemen remaining in Vietnam was still an open question, however. According to Paul Kattenburg, who now chaired the interdepartmental working group on Vietnam, this would be the first time DoD had "officially announced a total figure for U.S. military personnel in South Viet-Nam," even though the administration had recently been citing numbers in the neighborhood of 15,000. An October 18 draft press release indicated that the drawdown would pull from roughly 16,730 U.S. military personnel in South Vietnam and would take place in

November and December.[55] Lodge subsequently learned that Washington would begin to leak a figure of 16,500 on October 21 and that he could disclose it as well. "No further announcement is contemplated on 1000 men withdrawal plan," the State Department informed him. Yet given Harkins's statement ten days later about the impending withdrawal, confusion evidently continued to govern the policy's implementation.[56]

Aside from publicity concerns, the Pentagon needed to determine precisely which soldiers would be departing. Initially, McNamara directed that the bulk of those returning do so as part of cohesive units—the better to suggest that the RVNAF had mastered a specific function for which U.S. support was no longer necessary. But in mid-October, Harkins produced a troop mix informed by his own assessment of the situation, as well as by "personal guidance" from the secretary of defense. That configuration not only departed from the desired 70/30 ratio of units to individuals and the minimally acceptable 50/50 mix, but flipped the initial skew on its head.[57] The director of the Joint Staff, Vice Adm. Herbert D. Riley, asked Taylor if he knew what "altered guidance" McNamara had provided so he and the Staff could adhere to it. While McNamara "recalled having given no additional guidance on this subject during his most recent trip to Vietnam," he indicated, nevertheless, that "the JCS should pursue that plan for withdrawal which the Chiefs consider most advantageous."[58] Harkins therefore structured the withdrawal to minimize its impact on the war; his decision to exclude "combat area battalion advisers" from the mix appealed to Felt, who recommended the Joint Chiefs approve the new 30/70 ratio.[59] Taylor himself supported the revised percentages, as he thought the new plan would "have less impact on operational effectiveness."[60] The Chiefs subsequently approved those recommendations on November 4, and discussed them with McNamara before informing Felt on November 5.[61] The defense secretary was thus firmly in the loop on the decision to alter the troop composition.

In fact, McNamara's recommendation that the JCS fashion a withdrawal plan they believed "most advantageous" suggests he had little concern about the Chiefs gutting the thousand-man withdrawal, as one scholar has described their actions.[62] Indeed, the premium on operational effectiveness, according to the McNamara-Taylor Report, was integral to the overall reduction plan, as the withdrawal of those thousand troops was a first step toward replacing U.S. servicemen "without impairment of the war effort."[63] Nor was this a matter of great concern to President Kennedy, for whom the thousand-man withdrawal was an exercise in public relations—as it always had been. Both Kennedy and McNamara acknowledged in the October 5 meeting that they could achieve it by "rotation," as Kennedy put it, or by "attrition," as McNamara framed it. While some of those troops would indeed return because their service was no longer necessary, others might do so merely because their tours had ended.[64] Either way, the White House and Pentagon could trumpet those reductions as signs of progress, if such progress was forthcoming, or simply proceed with a low-key withdrawal in its absence.

But all that maneuvering failed to pay dividends, for despite the October 2 statement and the subsequent slate of pressures, Kennedy derived few domestic benefits from the new Vietnam policy. Although the more heated rhetoric surrounding the Church resolution had cooled, the McNamara-Taylor mission hardly eased concerns about foreign assistance. Democrats who once supported those outlays now turned their backs on a robust aid package. Closed-door hearings of the Senate Foreign Relations Committee featured charges that the country was "fed up with foreign aid," and reports of "waste, inefficiency, and maladministration" signaled that the administration's aid request was in deep trouble.[65] Adding to Kennedy's woes, committee chair Fulbright thought the program was nearly "obsolete," even as he advised his colleagues against imposing significant reductions.[66] When Budget Director David Bell relayed those developments to the president, he warned of a potential "heavy blow to the program," which "would have very damaging effects upon our ability to carry out existing U.S. foreign policy."[67] Kennedy's new Vietnam policy, therefore, would have to sink or swim on its own merits and not as a means toward realizing broader administration objectives.

Nor did the policy seem to be having much of an impact in Saigon, at least not initially. Lodge cabled home in mid-October that the administration was "getting virtually no effect from our actions under Deptel 534," though he recognized it was still early in the process.[68] Nevertheless, DCI John McCone feared the impact would be soon in coming and that it would be explosive. Lodge came to share that belief; by the third week of October, he had heard that Diem was "worried." While the South Vietnamese president still had not contacted the American ambassador, U.S. actions were unsettling GVN officials, roiling the business community, and "creating favorable conditions for a coup" that might coincide with South Vietnam's national holiday near the end of the month.[69] Although the GVN had taken several steps consistent with U.S. desires, such as reopening the university in Hue and shifting military operations toward the Mekong Delta, Diem and Nhu, according to the CIA, seemed "fully prepared to face prolonged and significant cutbacks in American aid."[70]

It was a troubling development, for while the South Vietnamese regime seemed to be holding firm, its military was wobbling. That realization inverted the presumed course of events McNamara and Taylor had foretold: Saigon's chances of winning the war were now tanking faster than the country's political climate, a prospect the State Department flagged in late October. Using the Pentagon's own metrics, State detected "a number of significant and unfavorable changes in the military situation in South Vietnam" since July, concluding that Saigon's military position "may have reverted to the point it had reached six months to a year ago."[71] By the end of October, the CIA reported that "statistical trends" in the war were "becoming disturbing, and various indicators suggest a lowering of morale in the Vietnamese armed forces." McCone had become despondent, telling the president back in September that victory in Vietnam was "doubtful if not impossible," a position he maintained into November.[72] The Pentagon fought back, maintaining that the war continued to progress favorably and that State Department reporting, including from Lodge in Saigon, was unduly pessimistic—and likely tied to State's continuing interest in dumping Diem.[73]

Kennedy's appraisal of those trends is difficult to discern. His public and private remarks during the late summer and fall of 1963 reveal increasing discomfort with Diem, with the course of the war, and with the depth of the American commitment. Administration officials had repeatedly given him conflicting assessments, a pattern that persisted following NSAM 263 and its establishment of a government-wide position. On the one hand, the McNamara-Taylor report highlighted continuing progress in the war, even if the political situation threatened its prospects; additional Pentagon reports maintained that line. Lodge would not go that far, writing in an "eyes only" cable for Kennedy that the military effort was "not doing much more than holding our own."[74] Given the thrust of those communications and Kennedy's own recorded comments on the war, historian David Kaiser maintains that JFK never suspected that the counterinsurgency had deteriorated, and that the president likely traveled to Dallas in late November thinking the military effort was still going well.[75]

On the other hand, Kennedy had heard multiple accounts of troubles in the war. In mid-September, he received a summary of Robert Thompson's views, to which Lodge applied a negative spin and the media reported as similarly pessimistic.[76] Even more disturbing reports were arriving by the middle of October, painting a grimmer picture of developments. Several scholars therefore claim that Kennedy knew the war was a losing proposition, so much so that he was now committed to withdrawing the United States from it.[77] Indeed, Kennedy had reason to doubt the believers and side with the skeptics, and he likely gravitated toward that more pessimistic perspective. But his public and private commitment to comprehensive withdrawal—calculated, conditional, and arguably tepid—reflected a more complex reality than whether Washington and Saigon were winning or losing in Vietnam.

Coup

Losing or not, the explosion McCone feared and U.S. officials had been anticipating finally occurred on November 1. South Vietnam's leading generals launched their coup against the Ngos that afternoon, prompting sporadic fighting and the flight of Diem and Nhu from the Gia Long Palace. The two were picked up in the Saigon suburb of Cholon the following morning, placed in the back of an armored personnel carrier, and murdered. U.S. officials had been monitoring the putsch as it coalesced during the last week of October, but they had been aware of its development early that month. Indeed, while plans for removing Diem were gathering prior to the October 2 White House statement, Gen. Tran Van Don told Lodge that "the coup was a Vietnamese movement for which the U.S. decision to suspend aid created the climate."[78] But more than just sanctions hardened the generals' resolve. Days before the coup, General Don told Lodge that "the only way to win before the Americans leave in 1965 was to change the present regime."[79] Evidently, the pressure Taylor hoped to apply via the 1965 withdrawal had generated sufficient movement in South Vietnam to alter the GVN's approach to the war—even if it produced the less desirable outcome of altering the GVN itself.

The U.S. media were generally "cautious" in their assessment of the new government and cognizant of the challenges ahead. Most sources recognized that the war was unlikely to be over soon but thought the new regime could inspire hope through its emergence as a responsible force, better relations with its neighbors, and its prosecution of the war. Outlets suspected that the Kennedy administration might now feel an even deeper sense of responsibility for the future of South Vietnam.[80] As analysts relayed, an upcoming meeting in Honolulu of U.S. military and civilian officials—comparable to the SecDef meetings McNamara had previously held—marked "a good time for appraising what we want in Vietnam," including whether those aims were "reasonable" and "achievable." To various publications, including the *New York Times,* a negotiated settlement remained a viable option, even one that pointed toward neutralization—a shift from its earlier stance.[81]

That position worried Kennedy officials who thought it necessary to support Saigon in resisting what they considered to be northern aggression. Rusk rejected calls for neutralization and the imposition of "far-reaching changes" on South Vietnam without forcing comparable conditions on Hanoi.[82] Aides likewise called on Kennedy to rebuff those recommendations, especially given their potential impact on GVN sensibilities. At the same time, they urged him to reiterate the goal of withdrawing U.S. forces as soon as the GVN was able to defend itself.[83]

Kennedy obliged twice in the span of two weeks. The first came in an October 31 news conference, in which he presumed to withdraw "a thousand" troops before the end of the year; the second, in a post-coup press event on November 14. Clarifying the purpose of the upcoming Honolulu meeting, Kennedy described it as an "attempt to assess the situation: what American policy should be, and what our aid policy should be, how we can intensify the struggle, how we can bring Americans out of there." That was their goal, he said, "to bring Americans home, permit the South Vietnamese to maintain themselves as a free and independent country, and permit democratic forces within the country to operate—which they can, of course, much more freely when the assault from the inside, and which is manipulated from the north, is ended." Asked whether the coup had altered his thoughts about the thousand-man withdrawal, the president vowed to "bring back several hundred before the end of the year," not the thousand he had referenced earlier, though the precise number needed to await the results of the Honolulu meeting.[84]

Those were the most intentional statements Kennedy had made about troop withdrawal since the October 2 White House release, both of which, in their broader context, continued to couch its implementation in the framework of military success.

Planning for Honolulu began immediately after the coup and against the backdrop of vigorous debate about America's foreign commitments.[85] Among the most immediate concerns was the difficulty of securing foreign aid at anything close to the level Kennedy deemed sufficient. The president vented his frustrations in his November 14 press conference, describing lawmakers' actions as "the worst attack on foreign aid" since the Marshall Plan. "Are we going to give up in South Viet-Nam?," he asked. "Are we going to give up in Latin America?"[86] Presuming the answers were clear, Kennedy realized that continued support of Saigon still mandated that the administration keep a lid on expenses—even as his Vietnam policy failed to serve his foreign aid goals. The challenge was evident to those gathering in Honolulu. Briefing materials for the conference indicated that further assistance to Vietnam needed to incorporate "the increasing difficulty in securing aid appropriations."[87]

Those difficulties pushed the administration to consider additional means of cost-cutting. Consistent with its long-standing efforts to rationalize planning and reduce outlays, it engaged in a form of retrenchment, searching for efficiencies without compromising effectiveness, particularly within the Defense Department. One such method involved the substitution of military forces stationed at home for those deployed abroad. The test of that approach came with "Operation Big Lift," which sought to transport the 2nd Armored Division, in rapid fashion, from Ft. Hood, Texas, to bases in Europe. McNamara believed a successful demonstration would prove he could reduce U.S. forces on the continent without weakening NATO's capabilities. Doing so would allow him to keep dollars at home, rectifying the balance of payments and the outflow of gold while still providing for U.S. security. To embed the concept in Pentagon planning, preparations were also underway for Big Lift operations to South Korea and possibly the Middle East as well.[88] Collectively, the effort to increase mobility, cap expenditures, and husband bullion satisfied government-wide objectives, but it was tied to regional concerns as well. If McNamara could demonstrate its viability for

Europe, the need for stationing extensive forces elsewhere, including in Southeast Asia, was arguably less pressing.

Nevertheless, host countries perceived the operation as a prelude to an American withdrawal from Asia, even from the Cold War itself. Alongside a late-October speech from Deputy Secretary of Defense Roswell L. Gilpatric, who acknowledged the need to reduce Washington's "heavy overseas military expenditures," Big Lift stirred a multitude of worries. Kennedy had tried to soften its impact in his October 31 press conference—even suggesting that shortfalls in Vietnam could be balanced through Big Lift mobility—but concern among America's allies grew.[89] According to U.S. diplomats in Taipei, the Taiwanese were "beginning to feel letdown," with the combination of Big Lift and the Test Ban Treaty leaving some to wonder whether the United States was "going soft on Communism."[90] The Thais likewise worried that a departure from Southeast Asia signaled U.S. "disengagement with Sino-Soviet bloc."[91] Projected cuts in South Korea gave rise to similar fears. Force reductions in U.S. and local troops offered a means of holding down Seoul's defense budget and controlling inflation. But withdrawing troops would increase its reliance on the U.S. nuclear deterrent and possibly compromise South Korea's will to resist external aggression, turning a local conflict into a "world-wide nuclear engagement."[92] As much as the reductions served the administration's broader goals, their psychological impact endangered the very security they sought to uphold.

McNamara addressed those challenges through a bureaucratic maneuver designed to ease the pressure on foreign aid. His target was the Military Assistance Program, which Congress had been funding through the Senate Foreign Relations Committee (SFRC). By 1963, with its members launching broadsides against Vietnam policy and foreign aid more generally, McNamara shifted the funding of MAP, and thus assistance to Vietnam, to a more amenable body: the Senate Armed Services Committee. The switch allowed him to shield MAP and Vietnam costs from an increasingly skeptical group of legislators, effectively burying both in the military service budgets. But McNamara also used SFRC worries to accelerate the training of South Vietnamese forces and the removal of U.S. troops. The more aggressive the assistance program, the sooner the Americans could withdraw. Budget ceilings for MAP in the 1964 fiscal year rose accordingly. It was a shrewd move, as McNamara leveraged lawmakers' wariness over foreign aid and Vietnam to address objectives on both.[93]

Collectively, those concerns about foreign aid, rapid deployment, and troop withdrawal generated great interest in the November 20 Honolulu conference, the first high-level gathering of U.S. civilian and military officials since the coup in Saigon. Media comment was both hopeful and skeptical of what might transpire, with major outlets suggesting that the coup offered glimmers of hope, even if the goal of bringing the boys home was a "long way off."[94] Indeed, participants came into those talks with a sense of guarded optimism about the war.[95] Documents for the meeting noted that "the counter-insurgency effort in the countryside proceeded on an only slightly reduced scale during the September-October crisis period," and that daily operations remained unaffected by the "leadership crisis" in Saigon.[96] While it remained difficult to judge whether post-coup personnel and organizational changes had improved the quality or coordination of military operations, neither the coup nor the subsequent imposition of martial law appeared to be having a significant impact on military activity.[97] Moreover, hope still remained that the ruling junta would prosecute the war more effectively. As McNamara put it to journalists on the eve of the conference, the prospects looked "more promising" than under the previous regime.[98] Meeting attendees thus considered the partial and comprehensive withdrawals from that optimistic perspective.

Yet the press wondered whether the thousand-man withdrawal would, in fact, move forward. Reporters had fixed on Kennedy's November 14 remarks that "several hundred" of them would return, highlighting that altered language and relaying "speculation" that Washington might now "drop its withdrawal plan."[99] The Army's own paper, *Stars & Stripes,* went so far as to claim that Kennedy had "abandoned" plans to pull out those thousand troops before the end of the year.[100] But just one day after Kennedy's statement, Maj. Gen. Charles J. Timmes, the head of the U.S. Military Assistance Advisory Group in Vietnam, announced that one thousand U.S. troops would begin to leave in early December.[101] In fact, on November 20, the Defense Department "reaffirmed" its plans to bring home "about 1,000 of its 16,500" troops by January 1, with the first 300 leaving Vietnam on December 3.[102] For the moment, then, the skeptics on withdrawal were proved wrong: the coup in Saigon had no effect on the decision to remove U.S. troops from South Vietnam.

The challenge remained, however, to decide which 1,000 troops would leave. Whereas the CINCPAC proposal comprised 496 soldiers in units and 507 as individuals—the minimum 50/50 split McNamara desired—the subsequent plan, which McNamara approved, tilted those numbers toward 284 forces in units and 716 as individuals.[103] But it still needed to proceed with "low key" publicity. As for the 1965 drawdown, conference attendees considered accelerating its schedule by six months, from June 1966 to December 1965 "as the date for completion of all turnover actions."[104] That objective remained contingent on the course of the war, however. Grounded in a belief that the insurgency would fall to a level the South Vietnamese could manage, the plan laid out a schedule for enlarging the RVNAF and reducing U.S. forces "as the tempo of the war diminishes." But conversations between U.S. and GVN officials about ramping up South Vietnamese forces and scaling back U.S. personnel still had not taken place—even though Harkins received a directive to that end in early October. In fact, McNamara stated that "we were a long way from talking to the Vietnamese Government since we had not developed an over-all plan approved by the U.S. Government."[105]

The prospect of an American withdrawal had seemed to move the GVN nevertheless. Although Kennedy had questioned its value as leverage, several U.S. officials believed it had influenced the course of recent events. Taylor had repeatedly sought to use withdrawal as political pressure; the CIA's Chester Cooper hinted at doing so as well; and even McNamara, in the September 23 Oval Office conversation with Kennedy, had discussed withdrawal as a form of inducement.[106] So did Lodge, who thought the movement produced by the October 2 statement was so profound that U.S. officials should consider laying down similar schedules for U.S. Operations Mission and U.S. Information Service programs. "We can always grant last minute extensions," Lodge reasoned, "if we think it wise to do so." But the general value of establishing such benchmarks made great sense. As he told attendees at Honolulu, the administration "should keep before us the goal of setting dates for phasing out U.S. activities and turning them over to the Vietnamese," with calendars for each of those programs—military, economic, and psychological—continually reevaluated in light of changing circumstances. The 1965 date, Lodge said, "had—and is still having—a tonic effect."[107] Whether it was the effect they all had intended, given their differences over dumping or preserving Diem, is doubtful.

Nevertheless, reporting suggested the administration was pleased with its results. According to the *Times,* attendees at Honolulu believed the war "had taken a decided turn for the better[.]"[108] The *Post* likewise found that "a mood of hopefulness and cautious optimism" had replaced one of "tension and frustration"—some of the "happy developments" that had transpired since the coup.[109] That was certainly McNamara's take. He was "very encouraged by the excellent working relationships" between U.S. representatives and the ruling generals and was "equally encouraged by the prospects for progress in the war against the Viet Cong."[110]

Back in Washington, President Kennedy was preparing to leave on a trip to Texas, where he hoped to repair a breach in the state's Democratic Party and shore up support in a region important to his re-election campaign. Prior to his departure, he asked NSC aide Mike Forrestal to visit Cambodia to smooth over relations with its chief of state, Prince Norodom Sihanouk, who had just severed economic and military ties with the United States.[111] Kennedy shared with Forrestal his desire to talk about Southeast Asia more generally upon their return, as he was uncomfortable with the depth of strategic thought informing U.S. policy in the region—a glaring admission one thousand days into his presidency. He hoped to chug along through the 1964 election cycle, but they needed to "get prepared for whatever it was that the government under his guidance decided to do about Vietnam." As Forrestal recalled in 1969, "that's as far as he ever went. There was no suggestion that he wanted to drop it or to radically change anything, but there was certainly a suggestion that he was getting very nervous about it."[112] Two years later, Forrestal embellished his recollections, adding that Kennedy wanted "to start a complete and very profound review of how we got into this country, what we thought we were doing and what we now think we can do." The president even wanted to consider "whether or not we should be there" and how they could effect "some kind of a gradual shift" in America's presence in South Vietnam.[113] While Kennedy's discomfort is evident in both accounts, Forrestal's 1971 version, coming as Washington was exiting the war and as Kennedy aides were publicizing JFK's withdrawal plans, highlights a dynamic that would become familiar to students of the subject: the expansion of claims about Kennedy's intentions at the moment those intentions seemed most laudable and prophetic.

In November 1963, however, the president seemed very much committed to remaining in the fight. In remarks prepared for delivery at the Dallas Trade Mart on November 22 and designed to secure what remained of his foreign aid package, Kennedy planned to frame the Vietnamese conflict as part of the nation's broader responsibilities in the Cold War. American assistance, he intended to say, played a "key role in enabling those who live on the periphery of the Communist world to maintain their independence of choice." That assistance could be "painful, risky and costly, as is true in Southeast Asia today. But we dare not weary of the task."[114]

Patience and persistence—favorite themes of the president that captured his message on Vietnam, and on much of what was required on the New Frontier. His audience would have recognized the call to action, perhaps even connected it to the "ask not" commandments of his inaugural. Together, they stand as fitting bookends to his presidency and his life—complicated and unfinished, and later highly contested—which ended that fateful day in Dallas.

8

Cancellation

November 1963–March 1964

With the country in mourning and the White House in grief, President Lyndon B. Johnson mapped out his agenda for the days and weeks ahead. The business of government had to move forward—now more than ever—so even as he presided over ceremonies that laid John F. Kennedy to rest and empaneled a commission to investigate his assassination, Johnson grasped the reins of power. He asked Cabinet officials and presidential aides to stay on, hoping to provide the nation with a sense of continuity and a measure of reassurance. But LBJ turned to more familiar faces—several from his native Texas—to help run the Johnson White House. On domestic policy, he outlined efforts to enact Kennedy measures on health, the economy, education, poverty, and civil rights. In time, Johnson would tackle them all, and many others, with manic energy and legislative skill, pushing aides, the public, and Congress along a trajectory more progressive than the country had seen in a generation. The same dynamic took hold in foreign affairs as Johnson looked to sustain Kennedy initiatives on Berlin, Latin America, Soviet relations, nuclear issues, and a more fractious Western Europe. It was a full plate, especially for a caretaker president eyeing his own presidential run the following November.[1]

Near the top of that agenda lay Vietnam, a concern of Johnson's since his visit in May 1961, but a matter on which he had since played a much-diminished role. Now, as president, it was one of the first international challenges he addressed in any depth. On Sunday, November 24—two days after Kennedy's assassination—Johnson discussed Vietnam's prospects with senior national security officials, including Ambassador Henry Cabot Lodge, who had returned to Washington earlier that week, expecting to meet with JFK. According to notes from the session, Lodge was "hopeful" throughout and claimed that they were "on the road to victory." Others in attendance, including Defense Secretary Robert McNamara, Secretary of State Dean Rusk, National Security Adviser McGeorge Bundy, and DCI John McCone, were more pessimistic, with McCone the most skeptical of all. Johnson, too, was concerned, maintaining that "strong voices in the Congress felt we should get out of Vietnam."[2]

In truth, LBJ had "never been happy" with the assistance program and wanted divisions within the U.S. Country Team "cleaned up." He recognized the need for generous U.S. support but thought there had been "too much emphasis on social reforms," and far too much "bickering and quarreling of the type that has gone on in South Vietnam." His administration would pursue a win-the-war policy. "I am not going to lose Vietnam," he reportedly said. "I am not going to be the President who saw Southeast Asia go the way China went." It was vintage Johnson, full of sharp edges and bold statements. Indeed, LBJ's "tone," as McCone described it, differed markedly from that of his predecessor.[3]

Although it harkened back to Kennedy's impatience at the outset of the New Frontier, Johnson's own sense of urgency intensified over the next several weeks. South Vietnam was currently "our most critical military area," the president told JCS chair Maxwell Taylor, and wanted only the best U.S. personnel to work on it.[4] Conveying his "deep concern" to Lodge, LBJ urged that "our effort in Viet-Nam be stepped up to the highest pitch and that each day we ask ourselves what more we can do to further the struggle."[5] Johnson would preach that gospel repeatedly over the following weeks, telling Lodge he could not "overemphasize the importance which I personally attach to correcting the situation which has existed in Saigon in the past, and which I saw myself when I was out there."[6] Smacking of desperation, those comments were more insistent and categorical than the positions Kennedy had taken. While LBJ and JFK harbored doubts about the course of the struggle, Johnson assumed the more forceful and energetic stance. Kennedy was no less interested in a successful outcome, and Johnson's determination to prevail flowed, in part, from his understanding that it was Kennedy's aim as well. But LBJ's rhetoric signaled a pronounced desire to prosecute the war more vigorously.

Johnson's approach also stemmed from personal and partisan concerns. As scholars have long observed, LBJ was less sure of himself in managing the nation's foreign policy than he was in addressing domestic affairs. The shadow Kennedy cast—having prevailed in the Cuban Missile Crisis, negotiated an arms treaty, and placed superpower relations on a seemingly more stable footing—made Johnson's comparative inexperience all the more glaring. LBJ also personalized policy more readily than Kennedy, whose comparatively detached and ironic posture allowed for more measured responses to threats and slights. And though both men lived through the "loss" of China and the frustrations of Korea as members of Congress, Johnson endured those traumas while serving his party in a leadership capacity. Those experiences left him acutely conscious of what the loss of South Vietnam—on his watch—would mean for the Democrats and his own political fortunes. Johnson might also have harbored a sense of guilt over the fate of Ngo Dinh Diem. According to Press Secretary George Reedy, Johnson "felt that he had made a personal commitment to Diem" during his 1961 visit to Saigon, and that he had an obligation to keep South Vietnam free of Communist rule.[7] That sense of personal credibility, along with concerns about domestic and international credibility, was a key consideration in devising policy toward Vietnam. Although Johnson would invoke it in defense of his stature at home, it also had implications for his integrity abroad.[8]

NSAM 273

Two days after the November 24 meeting, the Johnson administration formalized its Vietnam policy in NSAM 273, guidance officials had been working toward since the Diem coup three weeks earlier. Incorporating directives that grew out of the November 20 Honolulu conference, the document was intended for President Kennedy; it now bore Johnson's signature. The United States, it declared, would continue to help South Vietnam win its war against the Communists. It would do so by maintaining the flow of economic and military aid to Saigon, helping the GVN shore up popular support, and encouraging its leaders to focus on the Mekong Delta, a Communist stronghold where the political and military situations were critical. The directive also demanded "full unity of support" from U.S. personnel, reflecting Johnson's frustration with the backbiting and disarray that marked his predecessor's policy stumbles.[9]

Curiously, the final version of NSAM 273 seemed to grant Washington more latitude for action against Hanoi than earlier drafts had allowed. Its seventh paragraph had initially called for "Government of Vietnam" resources to be used in raids on North Vietnam, but its final formulation, amended in the days following Kennedy's assassination, omitted the reference to GVN assets. According to several scholars, that change allowed Washington to assume more responsibility for cross-border activities, opening the door to greater U.S. involvement in the war. In this telling, the edit, purportedly reflecting Johnson's more hawkish approach to Vietnam, created the context for the Tonkin Gulf incident of August 1964, after which Congress granted Johnson "blank check" authority for deploying combat troops to Vietnam. For some observers, the modified language of NSAM 273—acceptable to Johnson, anathema to Kennedy—was thus of profound significance. As Oliver Stone alleged in his 1991 film *JFK*, "In that document lay the Vietnam War."[10]

But operations against North Vietnam had never generated much discomfort for JFK. In fact, Kennedy's interest in supporting covert action against Hanoi actually increased during his time in office, from his initial eagerness in January 1961, to his repeated inquiries about their impact in 1962, to his support for improving their effectiveness in 1963. None of that attention improved their efficacy, however. Evolving from intelligence collection to sabotage and harassment to psychological warfare, those efforts largely failed in their objectives. Indeed, officials were sufficiently frustrated by their inability to punish Hanoi that they looked to expand those operations in 1963. Given the challenges then facing the GVN—the Buddhist crisis, renewed hostilities in Laos, and the persistence of the Communist insurgency—"the case for bringing the war to North Vietnam," as the CIA's Thomas Ahern put it, especially to relieve pressure on the Diem regime, "became all the more compelling."[11] Attorney General Robert F. Kennedy, a mainstay on the Special Group (CI), thus urged Maj. Gen. Victor H. Krulak—the Joint Chiefs special assistant for counterinsurgency—to devise a bolder set of options against Hanoi. Those actions ultimately took shape as Operation Plan (OPLAN)

34A, a program of hit-and-run activities adopted by the Johnson administration. But the energy behind 34A emerged during the Kennedy administration and stemmed from a belief that actions against the North needed to be larger, more frequent, and more systematic, even in the face of CIA doubts about their value.[12]

Moreover, had Kennedy survived Dallas and signed an early draft of NSAM 273, it is doubtful whether the operations it sanctioned would have been much different than those postdating its final version, at least in the near term. The cross-border sabotage conducted early in the Johnson presidency could still have come under the pre-assassination Bundy draft. As Bundy himself wrote to Johnson in January, those activities involved "intensified sabotage operations in North Vietnam by Vietnamese personnel."[13] McNamara described them in comparable ways, telling Lodge they would consist of "covert operations by South Vietnamese forces, utilizing such support of US forces as necessary," the very kind of operations conducted months earlier.[14] Even after the adoption of 34A, the initial phase of that plan, according to U.S. officials, did "little more than continue the earlier CIA operations."[15] Taking the war to the north more energetically did qualify as an augmented effort, at first, but the difference was in degree, not in kind. Given Kennedy's enduring enthusiasm for those activities, he may well have authorized their continuation, regardless of whether NSAM 273 referenced a South Vietnamese or an American role in their execution; after all, actions against the North were always dependent upon U.S. support, both prior to Dallas as well as thereafter. The question is whether Kennedy would have sanctioned an increase in their frequency and intensity. The record suggests no indication to the contrary.

At any rate, senior officials expressed greater enthusiasm for going north once Johnson became president. Secretary McNamara spearheaded the effort, informing the Chiefs in early December of "an urgent need" to develop plans for increasing the pressure on Hanoi and tasking all relevant agencies working on Vietnam to contribute to it.[16] Those actions, as McNamara described them to Lodge, would assume "varying levels of pressure all designed to make clear to the North Vietnamese that the US will not accept a Communist victory in South Vietnam and that we will escalate the conflict to whatever level is required to insure their defeat."[17] Forrestal lobbied LBJ in support of that more vigorous effort, proposing an expansion of activities against the North and a more robust capacity to carry them out.[18] Johnson embraced that program, but he also made clear those actions were not to provoke a wider war. While he shared Kennedy's interest in going north, he expressed a caution about doing so, as historian Richard Shultz argues, that was absent from Kennedy's calculations.[19]

NSAM 273 also preserved the reduction in force Kennedy approved earlier that fall. Its language held that U.S. objectives regarding a troop withdrawal "remain as stated in the White House statement of October 2, 1963."[20] In fact, they figured prominently in briefing materials for Johnson's November 24 session on Vietnam. Proclaiming the outlook "hopeful," and with a better chance that the war could be won, the State Department included withdrawal in its assessment for Johnson in advance of the meeting.[21] Evidence suggests, however, that withdrawal did not arise as a topic of conversation, save for Lodge's remark that announcement of the 1965 target helped to stimulate the coup against Ngo Dinh Diem.[22] Given Johnson's disdain for the anti-Diem campaign, connections between the October 2 statement and the coup likely left LBJ even more dubious of withdrawal, a policy he had quietly opposed.

But the new president maintained the old president's policy, despite private misgivings. Media coverage of the November 24 meeting reaffirmed the continuity Johnson was desperate to project; as reported in the *New York Times,* the October 2 statement on the thousand-man troop withdrawal "remains in force."[23] True, that statement was merely aspirational, while its formulation in NSAM 263 was more concrete, directing the Pentagon to withdraw the thousand servicemen before the year was out. And that is precisely what happened. Consistent with both the October statement and NSAM 263, the initial increment of those thousand troops did indeed leave Vietnam. Speaking prior to their departure on December 3, MACV chief Paul Harkins indicated that the withdrawal of the first 300 soldiers would be followed over the next few weeks by the remaining 700. Harkins hailed their removal as a triumph—a testament to the ability of U.S. and South Vietnamese troops, to the effectiveness of the advisory relationship, and to the training of the RVNAF, which had "progressed to the point where the withdrawal of some US forces is possible."[24] Johnson was less enthusiastic. Speaking with McGeorge Bundy and John McCone, LBJ "questioned the withdrawal" of the thousand servicemen, as McCone put it. The president "could not see that this was a constructive move in view of the decision to intensify the effort." Bundy nevertheless "defended the action." The public image of troop withdrawal could sustain the appearance of progress, he argued, even if the administration had decided to escalate the war.[25]

But appearances were deceiving. Since many of those soldiers returned as part of a "normal turnover cycle," as the *Pentagon Papers* phrased it, and since additional deployments to Vietnam had been approved during the fall, the United States never did lower the absolute number of advisory troops serving in Vietnam. The thousand-man withdrawal, as implemented by the Johnson administration, became "an accounting exercise" as troops continued to move in and out of Vietnam as part of the normal sequence of force rotation.[26] In truth, it was hardly envisioned as anything more robust, as both Kennedy and McNamara anticipated it might well become an exercise in creative bookkeeping. The defense secretary did warn against the creation of military units merely for the purpose of withdrawing them, but his position stemmed from a desire to avoid charges of cynicism and opportunism, not from any ironclad interest in preserving a specific balance of logistical to advisory troops. At root, the thousand-man withdrawal was little more than a symbolic act, as all involved recognized it would be.

Fighting Neutralism

Still, the optics of withdrawal ran counter to Johnson's demand for greater energy in the war. They also merged with political and military developments in Vietnam that raised further questions about the value and persistence of the advisory effort. During the first week of December, Pentagon officials presented a "disturbing analysis" of the situation: the GVN was in a state of organizational turmoil, and insurgents were stepping up their efforts in the countryside.[27] Less than a week later, the Special Group (CI) learned that the war was "going badly," the Mekong Delta province of Long An was "rapidly deteriorating," and that earlier reports of progress "had been too optimistic." Roger Hilsman, the assistant secretary of state for Far Eastern Affairs, soon told Secretary of State Dean Rusk much the same.[28] Johnson himself heard early that month of the State Department's pessimistic evaluation in RFE-90—its October assessment of trends using Defense Department figures—which now looked even more accurate than when it first circulated. Coming just two months after the coup, which many hoped would improve the odds of victory, those reports painted a damning picture of the counterinsurgency.[29]

Saigon's faltering effort also stemmed from its perception of American intentions, which suggested a flagging commitment to a sovereign, independent, non-Communist South Vietnam. A chief concern was Washington's attitude toward neutralization, a matter that arose more forcefully after Cambodian president Norodom Sihanouk proposed an international conference to neutralize not only his own state but all of Indochina. Picking up where French president Charles de Gaulle had left off in August, Sihanouk's November 30 ploy sought to mobilize opinion in South Vietnam as well as in the United States, where key lawmakers, such as Senate Majority Leader Mike Mansfield [D-MT] and Senate Armed Services Committee chair Richard Russell [D-GA], had expressed neutralist sympathies.[30] Johnson officials recoiled at what that conference might bring and mounted even more strident efforts to counter such talk; any mention of neutralizing Southeast Asia, even by speculating about its long-term benefits, risked Saigon's near-term willingness to expend blood and treasure in fighting the Communists. A neutralized Vietnam, moreover, would likely facilitate the victory of Vietnamese Communism and ultimately Saigon's domination by the PRC. Fears therefore grew that talk of neutralism had "spread like wildfire through the Vietnamese community," according to the State Department's William Jorden, and that commentary on its virtues from columnists such as Walter Lippmann and James Reston, as well as from the *New York Times* more generally, had dealt "a body blow to morale in Saigon."[31]

Discussions about neutralism seemed so laden with peril that they altered the Johnson administration's rhetoric on Vietnam. Seeking to reassure the South Vietnamese, Lodge called for a tougher response to Sihanouk's proposal; without it, he feared there would "remain in Viet-Nam a large residue of doubt about our ultimate intentions," which itself "will inevitably have a bad effect on the determination of the new Vietnamese leadership to pursue the war effort vigorously."[32] The State Department suggested some language for Lodge to use: "Nothing is further from USG mind than 'neutral solution for Viet-Nam.' We intend to win."[33] In support of that position, Rusk proposed that Washington declare its aim "to furnish whatever assistance is required" to help Saigon defend itself.[34] Those comments signaled a portentous change in the way the United States talked about its role. No longer was the conflict merely "their war," one for the South Vietnamese to win—the phrasing frequently adopted by President Kennedy. Now, with concerns about Saigon's firmness an open question, repeated efforts to stiffen its spine, through professions of America's own resolve, sunk Washington—rhetorically, at least—deeper into the quagmire. In time, those concerns would intensify, transforming a rhetorical escalation into an operational one.

Whither Withdrawal

Compounding Saigon's worries were Washington's noises about force reduction, as well as the announced departure of those thousand servicemen in early December. According to William Jorden, both the October White House statement and the attendant troop withdrawal "were read by some, however mistakenly, as forerunners of a sharp reduction in our commitment."[35] It was an interpretation that had taken hold the previous autumn and persisted into the post-Diem era. As journalist Marguerite Higgins relayed, the South Vietnamese military thought those statements meant that "unless we got rid of Diem, you would abandon us."[36] Likewise, a late-November exchange between Roger Hilsman and GVN diplomats revealed that many South Vietnamese regarded the withdrawal announcement as a form of leverage against Diem, an interpretation Lodge believed had contributed to the coup. Hilsman maintained that the statements and withdrawals were "psychologically important in showing success," bolstering Vietnamese confidence in their capabilities and "deflating Communist propaganda about American objectives in Viet-Nam." The 1965 withdrawal date, moreover, involved "only training personnel since Vietnamese expected to be fully trained by then, and we shall keep in Viet-Nam whatever forces are needed for victory."[37] That was clearly the emerging line, even if it expanded and made more binding the commitment to South Vietnamese independence.

Voices in the United States were similarly perplexed by withdrawal statements and the troop reduction. To the director of Philadelphia's World Affairs Council, the 1963 and 1965 deadlines signaled that Washington was "getting ready to drop Vietnam," perhaps even seeking a neutral solution for it. Those sentiments seemed to represent at least a portion of public opinion. In tandem with critical editorials in the *New York Times* and the *Washington Post,* they added up to "confusion" about U.S. policy. Officials at the State Department recognized the need to dispel those misunderstandings, especially since they were becoming more widespread.[38] Indeed, the media was casting renewed doubt on the relevance of withdrawal planning. "Responsible officials no longer seriously encourage the idea that the bulk of 15,000 United States advisory and support troops might be withdrawn by 1965," wrote Seymour Topping in the *New York Times.* His colleague Hedrick Smith noted that American representatives in Saigon "already regard the 1965 target date as unrealistic." Those officials brushed off its import by reasoning that it emerged for "domestic political reasons," even if it also "stemmed from an over-optimistic military estimate of the war."[39] In fact, U.S. officials had decided during the Honolulu meeting to "increase US military advisory strength in the 13 critical provinces," a buildup that would draw initially on in-country personnel and then explore the addition of further resources.[40] Clearing up that "confusion," therefore, involved not only rethinking the troop pullout but preparing to move in the opposite direction.

The apparent about-face in U.S. policy stemmed from yet another McNamara visit to South Vietnam, this time on the direct request of President Johnson. Having already given him a tongue-lashing about Washington's inability to turn the tide, Johnson directed that McNamara travel to Southeast Asia following his attendance at a NATO meeting in Paris.[41] Arriving in mid-December, the defense secretary was deeply dismayed by what he found. PLAF incidents had almost tripled since the coup, with the area around Saigon becoming increasingly vulnerable. GVN control of the countryside, moreover, was further receding, Communist control of the Delta was solidifying, the NLF was making gains in the country's northern provinces, and the Strategic Hamlets were in shambles.[42] Conditions in South Vietnam were thus "very disturbing," and if current trends were not reversed, would lead over the next two or three months "to neutralization at best and more likely to a Communist-controlled state."[43] John McCone, who traveled with McNamara, was even more pessimistic. There simply was "no organized government in South Vietnam at this time," he said. Like McNamara, he thought Saigon's challenges were "formidable and difficult, but not impossible" to surmount. Still, he found "more reasons to doubt the future of the effort" as currently conceived than there were reasons for optimism.[44] It was a sentiment particularly evident among those on the front lines of the war. William Jorden, who had accompanied McNamara and McCone, found the South Vietnamese and U.S. communities "considerably more pessimistic" than he had expected, detecting "much skepticism about the present and much doubt about the future."[45]

As a result, more troops would likely be going to Southeast Asia than coming home. NBC's Chet Huntley, for instance, noted the "grim possibility" that instead of bringing men back from Vietnam, the United States might have to "send more to save the country." Additional reporting revealed a potential change in withdrawal policy, along with McNamara's reluctance even to comment on the October 1963 withdrawal statement.[46] By the end of his trip, the *Times* had draped its front page with the headline, "U.S. Drops Plans for 1965 Recall of Vietnam Force," noting that American troops would remain in Vietnam as long as they were "needed and wanted," a message communicated directly to the South Vietnamese leadership.[47] In fact, sources suggested the reversal was one of two key "assurances" McNamara had conveyed to the South Vietnamese generals: first, that Washington "did not envisage neutralism for Vietnam," and second, "that the plan for withdrawing U.S. forces by 1965 had in effect been dropped."[48] U.S. officials now believed "the line must be held in Vietnam to block Communist domination of Southeast Asia in spite of the heavy cost."[49]

The Johnson administration took a similar tack in discussions with Paris and London. As Joseph Mendenhall put it to Roger Duzer, a counselor at the French embassy in Washington, the 1965 withdrawal date "had never represented more than a target which we hoped to meet if the situation permitted." Moreover, the United States would "keep whatever forces are needed in Viet-Nam to do the job of winning the war."[50] But rescinding withdrawal did not amount to escalating involvement. While British officials in Saigon understood that Washington now "could see no prospect of an American withdrawal," they also sensed it had no intention "of playing a more active role in the war."[51] That was precisely the message David Ormsby-Gore, Britain's ambassador to the United States, cabled back to London. "Although it is true that the idea of pulling out all American advisers by the end of 1965 has been quietly dropped, this is a long way from implying that there is any intention to send in regular U.S. Army formations to stiffen up the Vietnamese or take over the war."[52] Even with the pessimism that ran through the McNamara and McCone memos to Johnson, U.S. officials were still bullish about their prospects for halting the Communist advance. As Lodge put it, there was reason to believe they were "getting on to the right track."[53]

Back in Washington, senior policymakers agreed that the assistance effort was moving in the right direction and sought to head off domestic opposition to their newly assertive policy. For McNamara, as well as for Rusk and Bundy, the war remained Saigon's to win, but neither could Washington "disengage U.S. prestige to any significant degree," since American assistance signaled its longstanding and deep involvement in Vietnamese affairs. Although the security situation was "serious," Mc-Namara believed "we can still win, even on present ground rules." Indeed, they simply had to win, as the contest was "both a test of U.S. firmness and specifically a test of U.S. capacity to deal with 'wars of national liberation.'" The stakes were so great, he said, that "in our judgment, we must go on bending every effort to win." Along with remarks from the formative period of November 1961 and the first weeks of October 1963, these were among the more categorical statements from the most senior officials in the national security establishment about the depth of America's commitment to Vietnam.[54]

It was an extraordinary development, particularly for the secretary of defense. Gone was the McNamara of October 2, who pleaded for "a way to get out of Vietnam." In his stead emerged a more anxious figure, fearful of abandoning the struggle. The two personas, however, were one and the same. In both cases, McNamara had sensed the general direction in which the president he served had wanted to move. For Kennedy, it was to prepare for the moment when the United States could reduce its involvement; hence, the pursuit of a framework to implement JFK's preferred course. For Johnson, it assumed a more energetic and expansive posture to avoid the loss of Vietnam; thus, the more heated rhetoric and planning to intensify the war. McNamara's conception of loyalty explains, in part, his policy positions: it was a fealty he owed the president, not the nation. It "trumped even his best judgment," writes political scientist Aurélie Basha i Novosejt. McNamara therefore would flesh out and implement policy based on the strategy his president had chosen. In time, the tension between his loyalty and his judgment would become too much to bear. But that moment was still several years and many sorrows away.[55]

For now, the friction remained between the more assertive approach and the residual effects of withdrawal, a policy that stayed on the books. Indeed, frustration intensified following McNamara's late-January remarks to lawmakers that the war in Vietnam was not going well and that the time had come for bolder steps. The fate of a non-Communist, independent South Vietnam was "so important," he said, that he "could conceive of no alternative other than to take all necessary measures within our capability to prevent a Communist victory."[56] In that environment, talk about pressuring Hanoi became even more frequent, with his most senior colleagues joining him in their enthusiasm for operations north of the 17th parallel.[57] Although McNamara said nothing to Congress about plans to withdraw troops by 1965, Pentagon officials said they still hoped to reduce those forces in two years' time, indicating that "a substantial number" would phase out of Vietnam during 1964.[58] Roger Hilsman said much the same, offering a public spin on withdrawal heard increasingly often: the goal remained the withdrawal of U.S. troops, but the United States would "continue to have a training mission" in South Vietnam and would "continue with whatever aid is necessary to win."[59] In certain respects, that was precisely what McNamara and Taylor had proposed in October 1963: the United States would hand over responsibility for discreet operations as South Vietnam became able to assume them, with the turnover presumably being completed by the close of 1965. Now, though, the commitment to victory, or at least to preventing defeat, was more vocal and consistent.

Nevertheless, pundits took McNamara and the administration to task for presenting such a muddled picture of national policy. The *Chicago Tribune*'s Walter Trohan thought the defense secretary's testimony ran "in direct opposition" to the one he and Taylor delivered in October 1963.[60] James Reston at the *New York Times* found McNamara's testimony particularly galling, telling George Ball it was not only "mystifying," but "about the worst one I have ever seen." Reston then went public with his dismay. So confounding were Pentagon pronouncements that doubt remained as to whether the administration wanted to ratchet up the pace of the war or pull out of it altogether. If the situation were as grave as McNamara described it, Reston asked, then "why are troops being withdrawn?" And if McNamara was "encouraged" by recent progress in the war, then "why is he talking about 'taking all measures within our capability?'" The time had come, Reston argued, for a clearer statement of intentions and purposes.[61] The editorial staff at the *Washington Post* agreed, characterizing McNamara's testimony as a "retreat from candor," with the administration "reluctant to tell the American people the undiluted truth" that "the outlook for clear-cut military victory is bleak."[62]

The Khanh Coup

The need for candor and clarity increased markedly over the next few days as developments in Saigon raised new questions about the war and GVN stability. On January 30, Gen. Nguyen Khanh overthrew the military junta that had governed South Vietnam since the coup against President Ngo Dinh Diem. Khanh had been a collaborator in the November putsch but subsequently found himself sidelined by Gen. Duong Van Minh and the ruling Military Revolutionary Council. Transforming his resentments into action, Khanh began to spread rumors about the fate of the U.S. assistance effort. Those claims built upon fears that Washington might support diplomacy toward neutralizing Cambodia with an eye toward neutralizing Vietnam as well. Contributing to those fears was a new alignment in international relations. French president Charles de Gaulle, who had called for neutralization back in August, now extended diplomatic recognition to the People's Republic of China. The parley put further space between Paris and the Western alliance, but it also boded ill for U.S. policy toward Saigon. Along with a lack of progress in the war, de Gaulle's courting of Mao made a neutralization scheme more likely. Capitalizing on those concerns, and inflating them as well, Khanh ousted the Minh regime in a bloodless coup and proclaimed himself leader of a new South Vietnamese government committed to taking on the PLAF and their patrons in Hanoi.[63]

Khanh's assumption of power did little to inspire greater energy in the counterinsurgency or optimism among U.S. officials.[64] Nor did his emergence quell talk about neutralizing Vietnam. Following the coup, Mansfield again lobbied President Johnson about the virtues of neutralization—first in private and then from the Senate floor.[65] Walter Lippmann said much the same, criticizing the United States for having "bolted the doors" in Southeast Asia with no fallback position.[66] Johnson was unmoved. "Nobody's going to neutralize North Vietnam," he told newspaper magnate John S. Knight, "so that's totally impractical."[67] Indeed, officials suspected Paris of actively seeking to displace the United States through the means of a negotiated settlement. Particularly troubling was a sense within the RVN that "a neutralized South Vietnam is the only way out."[68] Yet an embrace of neutralism, Bundy told Johnson, would constitute "a weakening of our support of anti-communist forces in South Vietnam" and precipitate "a wholesale collapse of anti-Communism all over Southeast Asia."[69] The CIA was saying much the same, as was Lodge, who feared its "demoralizing effect on the will to win" of South Vietnamese military and civilian officials.[70]

Such talk continued to infuse U.S. perspectives with waves of pessimism, leading policymakers to consider taking more drastic action. Since December 1963, talk about pressuring the North had moved in tandem with reports of greater trouble in the South; by January 1964, both had become more serious. Johnson thus approved the 34A operations, which were to begin on February 1, with the proviso that the actions selected were those "which promise the greatest return for the least risk."[71] By late February, the president accelerated planning for additional measures against the North. Johnson thought it "essential" to take the fight to Hanoi with operations "beyond pin-pricking," especially since charges of American passivity were growing and could lead "to a defeatist approach."[72] In fact, he had already tasked Rusk and McNamara with preparing plans to apply additional military and diplomatic pressure on Hanoi.[73] As Rusk put it, if the choice came down to losing in the South or moving on the North, he thought the current mood "would undoubtedly be for action against North Vietnam."[74]

President Johnson himself was operating according to that stark, binary framework. One option was to "run and let the dominoes start falling over," he told Knight, but the political cost of doing so would be terrific. "God Almighty," he exclaimed, reflecting upon the partisan rancor of the last fifteen years, "what they said about us leaving China would just be warming up compared to what they'd say now." Since neutralization was a nonstarter, "it really boils down to one of two decisions: getting out or getting in."[75] Getting out would likely replicate the Chinese experience. If U.S. forces withdrew from South Vietnam, Johnson predicted, "the thing would collapse like a pack of cards."[76] Senior policymakers shared Johnson's fears and spoke of the cascading effects withdrawal would have on America's credibility and strategic concerns. Rusk, for instance, believed, as did the Joint Chiefs, that "in Viet-Nam we must demonstrate to both the Communist and the non-Communist worlds that the 'wars of national liberation' formula now being pushed so actively by the Communists will not succeed." Bundy likewise thought "it would be a betrayal of trust for us to cut and run," even as he doubted the wisdom of promising an all-out defense.[77] The credibility imperative thus fastened ever more tightly around U.S. policymakers as they viewed their options in Southeast Asia. The tougher the task, the higher the perceived stakes—and the more necessary to take up the fight.

A firmer commitment was required as well, and changes in process and personnel seemed to signal a new approach to Vietnam. Although Johnson had initially retained Kennedy's senior advisers, by February 1964 he was looking to install officials more closely aligned with his own policy preferences. In Washington, that meant swapping out Paul Kattenburg as chair of the Vietnam Working Group for Joseph Mendenhall, once the former political counselor in Saigon. More significantly, the Pentagon's William P. Bundy replaced Roger Hilsman as head of the State Department's Bureau of Far Eastern Affairs. Johnson also appointed the State Department's William H. Sullivan to lead a new interdepartmental committee on Vietnam, a move designed to minimize the friction and dysfunction that marked the late-stage Kennedy approach to Vietnam. In Saigon, MACV chief Gen. Paul D. Harkins would step aside for Gen. William C. Westmoreland, while USIA director John Mecklin would rotate home, as would DCM William C. Trueheart, who was replaced by David Nes.[78]

But of all those actions targeting personnel and process, it was the president's public rhetoric that was most indicative of a coming policy shift. Speaking in Los Angeles on February 21, Johnson declared that America would "continue to honor" its ten-year commitment to South Vietnamese "freedom," even as the South Vietnamese needed to win their own struggle. That contest, however, was all the more fraught because it was "directed and supplied by outside enemies," making that form of aggression "a deeply dangerous game."[79] Reporters jumped on that locution. To the *Washington Post*'s Chalmers Roberts, it represented "a carefully prepared signal of a new American initiative in the war in South Viet-Nam." The United States would not be leaving as part of a neutralization scheme; in fact, it might change the "ground rules" and target Hanoi. Writing in the *New York Times,* Max Frankel thought it the beginning of a psychological campaign that might also include attacks on North Vietnam, as well as greater U.S. energy in South Vietnam.[80] Those two themes—the danger of neutralization and the prospect of escalation—continued to reinforce each other, sinking the Johnson administration deeper into the quagmire and distancing it further from the policy of withdrawal.

In fact, media sources thought withdrawal was either at or nearing its end. The *Los Angeles Times* told its readers that plans for withdrawal had been "quietly abandoned."[81] Indeed, with the situation in Vietnam so dire, McNamara's earlier promise to draw down troops, according to Cy Sulzberger at the *New York Times,* was "either an absurdity or a planned disaster." Sulzberger's colleague Max Frankel thought likewise; repeated "suggestions" from Johnson officials that most U.S. troops would be able to return home by December 1965, he feared, undermined a policy review on Vietnam currently underway. In the *Post,* Chalmers Roberts observed that many at the State Department thought the 1965 withdrawal announcement was "a major mistake in public relations, one that discourages the anti-Communist forces, encourages the Communists and misleads the American public." The *Post's* editors also thought it unlikely the United States could "achieve its avowed objective of enabling the regime to exert sufficient military strength to stand on its own feet by the end of 1965."[82]

With the national conversation about withdrawal back in the news, McGeorge Bundy sought to clarify the administration's position at a gathering of the Overseas Press Writers in late February. Asked how the government had settled on 1965 as the target for an American departure, Bundy characterized it as "the likely date at which the principal supporting functions, troop-using functions, of our effort there could in fact be devolved to adequately trained, managed, and operated Vietnamese force (*sic*). It has nothing to do with whether we would continue our basic commitment, or whether we would give up our purpose, or whether we think there is a date at which all of South Vietnam will be cleaned up." Rather, it spoke to "the particular business of how many Americans will be needed for certain kinds of specific undertakings" at various points in time. Washington's goal, "as President Kennedy repeatedly said," was to create "a situation in which there won't be a need for

U.S. military presence (*sic*)." The challenge was a difficult one, and something that could not "be certainly and forever confined to the particular kind of contest and particular rules of engagement which have been set by those who started the trouble in the first place." That was why, he noted, President Johnson had said the previous week that "there is danger in it."[83] Bundy thus defined the withdrawal policy in a way that opened the door to new rules of engagement and more drastic measures to support American objectives in Vietnam.

In fact, his comments actually underplayed efforts to dispense with the 1965 withdrawal date. Movement toward retiring it emerged at one of the first meetings of the newly formed Sullivan committee in mid-February. Labeling the relevant agenda item "Burial of 1965 Deadline," the group charged William Bundy, McGeorge's brother, with finding out whether McNamara wanted to do just that—"to bury quietly the 1965 deadline." To that end, he would ask U.S. personnel in Vietnam whether the timetable was compromising field operations.[84] It was one of several topics for McNamara to explore during his next trip to South Vietnam, slated for early March. Preparations for the visit further revealed the fragility of the withdrawal schedule. On February 15, CINCPAC Adm. Harry D. Felt notified the Joint Chiefs that he "considered the planning assumption that the insurgency in the northern provinces of the RVN would be under control by the end of CY 64" to be "no longer valid." Major General Krulak, who was developing McNamara's agenda for the upcoming trip, wondered whether the military situation and "organizational disarray" therefore called for thorough reappraisals of troop withdrawal, a South Vietnamese force reduction, and the dollar guidelines established for the associated Military Assistance Program. In short, Krulak was suggesting they consider drafting an entirely new Comprehensive Plan for South Vietnam.[85]

Yet official planning for withdrawal continued. Communications involving MACV and the Joint Chiefs in January and February preserved the 1965 deadline for a U.S. pullout from Vietnam. Harkins, bullish as ever, maintained that even in the face of setbacks, the GVN would be able to meet the calendar Kennedy had proposed in October 1963; given that they had lost at least "seven months," though, that timetable would have to take into account "the new starting date."[86] But he began to disentangle the military and instructional activities associated with the October directives. "Although movement toward the training goal" was "on schedule," Harkins found "little substantial progress toward completing the military campaigns in either of the two major regions" envisioned for the close of 1964.[87]

Still, talking papers for the Joint Chiefs continued to invoke the target date of two years hence, with MACV referencing the quarterly system of progress reports established back in October.[88] Even McNamara continued to aim for the removal of U.S. forces by the end of 1965. In mid-February, he told Congress that commanders had received orders "to complete their training assignments and start sending their men home," guidance that remained consistent with the removal of troops earlier in December. Some forces would remain "until the counterinsurgency operation has been successfully completed," but the United States would not bear the primary burden of winning the war. "I think it is reasonable to expect," he said, "that after four years of such training, we should be able gradually to withdraw certain of our training personnel."[89]

But Johnson himself was barely on board with that policy if he ever supported it at all. He betrayed his skepticism of withdrawal in a rambling phone conversation with McNamara near the end of February. After acknowledging the rationale behind removing those troops, Johnson decried the decision to publicize it. "I always thought it was foolish for you to make any statements about withdrawing. I thought it was bad psychologically. But you and the President [Kennedy] thought otherwise, and I just sat silent." The optics were lousy, he maintained, and the situation now parlous. With the South Vietnamese apparently unable to carry the fight, the United States needed to choose whether to assume the burden or let Saigon fall. Johnson had captured "the problem exactly," said McNamara, who feared "we're right at that point."[90]

Or maybe beyond it. Reporting in the *Times* found Washington "seriously concerned" about the state of the war and actively considering a deeper commitment, including direct strikes on North Vietnam. The *Post*, too, reported on such planning, describing the military situation as "getting worse" and the political situation as "shaky" at best.[91] McNamara, therefore, would now travel to Vietnam to evaluate the strength of the Khanh government, but also to generate consensus around a strategic approach and alleviate Saigon's fears about the depth of the American commitment. Johnson used a February 29 press conference to elaborate on those objectives and to maintain control of the broader narrative. He said little about strategy, stating falsely that the escalatory options cited in the press "are not plans that have come to my attention, or that I have approved." In fact, he had directed that contingency planning for operations against North Vietnam be devised and accelerated "to produce the maximum credible deterrent effect on Hanoi."[92] But escalating the conflict, on the one hand, or withdrawing from it, on the other, were extreme options Johnson sought to avoid—particularly in an election year, and especially since he had "inherited" the job. As he told the Joint Chiefs, he would simply "take all the steps that he could take to save this situation between now and November," asking them for military options with electoral considerations in mind.[93]

Given battlefield realities in South Vietnam and political conditions in the United States, neither escalation nor withdrawal seemed necessary options, at least not yet. The situation south of the 17th parallel continued to deteriorate, but all was not lost, and with assaults north of that line raising the specter of another Korea and a more globalized conflict, Johnson's appetite for expanding the war was limited. The administration thus settled on intensifying the existing approach—remaining firm in its commitment to defend South Vietnam, continuing to provide U.S. advice and support, and relying primarily on the South Vietnamese to carry the brunt of fighting.

But describing that mission to Congress and the American people remained a tall order. As he had done in the wake of the Mansfield speech and criticism of his UCLA address, Johnson turned to McNamara once again for remarks he might make. It was yet another occasion where Johnson tried to talk himself into supporting the policy of withdrawal. "Now, we don't say that we'll win," the president conceded in a March 2 phone call, but "we ought to have them trained" sufficiently to handle the war on their own. That was the expressed rationale behind the 1963 removal of those thousand troops and the projected withdrawal of 1965, by which time the broader training effort "ought to be in pretty good shape[.]" LBJ saw no inconsistency between those statements and actions, "except with people who know nothing about it."[94]

But as officials drafted memos for McNamara's upcoming trip to Vietnam, the withdrawal plan underwent a subtle but unmistakable change. Central to that adjustment was the more expansive commitment that had come to mark administration rhetoric. Even though the plan to reduce U.S. troop strength was "still sound . . . previous judgments that the major part of the US job could be completed by the end of 1965 should now be soft-pedaled and placed on the basis that no such date can now be set realistically until we see how the conflict works out."[95] Drafted by William Bundy—the chief author of the McNamara-Taylor Report and an early opponent of publicizing the withdrawal deadline— that directive marked the first instance of senior officials formally retiring the schedule itself. Coming three months since word of its demise had circulated unofficially among the diplomatic corps and the national press, the administration, apparently, was bowing to reality.

The timing was apt since word of McNamara's trip touched off another round of speculation about the 1965 withdrawal date. Speaking to reporters just days before his departure in early March, McNamara captured the tension of the administration's priorities, maintaining the aspirational spirit of withdrawal while pledging an ever-firmer commitment to the GVN—a commitment he described as providing aid and training "for whatever period it is required." But the American public should expect the administration "to conclude a training mission after a reasonable length of time." Disregarding the emerging guidance to bury the target date, McNamara inserted that calendar into his remarks. "During the next two years, that is by the end of 1965, additional training should be completed. As that training is completed," he said, "I think that you will agree we should bring back the Military personnel that have participated in it." Still, he noted, there were troops "we will probably retain in Viet Nam indefinitely."[96] But America's commitment to South Vietnam was unwavering. The inspection trip, therefore, would serve to improve and enhance the effectiveness of the U.S. assistance program. It was not designed to reconsider it.

Johnson elaborated on those plans days later in a press conference of his own. "I don't think that the American public has fully understood the reason for our withdrawing any advisers," he said. Those troops already recalled had been replaced by fully competent South Vietnamese forces, which was the principle upon which all withdrawals would be based. "From time to time, as our training mission is completed, other people will be withdrawn," Johnson said, without referencing the date McNamara had used. But "as additional advisers are needed, or as people to train additional Vietnamese are needed, we will send them out there."[97] As Max Frankel noted in the *Times*, Johnson's comments marked "the first official suggestion that more men would be sent as advisers to the

South Vietnamese Army if they were needed."[98] Less than a week after internal memos had sought to cashier the withdrawal policy, the administration was now embracing withdrawal without a target date, while opening the door to more troop deployments.

Those rhetorical gymnastics prompted a wave of criticism, some of which took on a partisan tone. Increasing numbers of Republicans were "hammering away" at Johnson's Vietnam policy, tarring it as "confused" and "uncertain," and deceitful to boot.[99] Presidential politics played a role, as leading GOP candidates joined the fray. In late January, Governor Nelson Rockefeller called on the administration to clarify whether it was "going to pull out troops" or send more Americans to "man the rampart for freedom." A "White Paper" he produced repeatedly wondered why the administration continued to speak about withdrawal if the war was going badly and questioned the impact of those statements on South Vietnamese morale.[100] Senator Barry Goldwater demanded that Johnson either win in Vietnam or withdraw from the fight, as the war was "drifting toward disaster." Richard Nixon regarded Johnson's approach as part of "a general Administration policy failure."[101]

Republican barbs also came from lawmakers not seeking the party's nomination. Rep. John M. Lindsay [R-NY] lamented McNamara's confusing statements about the war and the future of U.S. involvement, as did Senate Minority Leader Everett M. Dirksen [R-IL].[102] In mid-March, Rep. Melvin R. Laird [R-WI] and Sen. Kenneth Keating [R-NY] voiced similar concerns, with Keating posing a set of questions he wanted answered as part of a congressional review of administration policy.[103] "How many American troops can be withdrawn from South Vietnam by the end of 1965?," he asked, and "How many will have to remain?" Johnson officials underplayed that date in their response. Their handling of the Keating missive suggested the guidance had yet to be finalized, circulated, or both—or, if it had been issued, whether it was being effectively enforced. Thus, Keating would hear that the U.S. training program "is expected to be substantially completed by the end of 1965."[104] Democrats, too, went on the offensive. Sen. Thomas J. Dodd [D-CT] deplored the "flood of contradictory official statements and unofficial news leaks," a confusion the Pentagon exacerbated by announcing the 1965 withdrawal, despite deteriorating military and political conditions. From the opposite direction, Sen. Ernest Gruening [D-AK] added his name to a growing list of congressmen calling for a U.S. withdrawal.[105] By and large, though, senators backed the effort to steer a middle course on Vietnam.

That policy was precisely the one McNamara recommended, with significant modifications, upon his return from the war zone in mid-March.[106] The report he submitted aligned with public sentiment and with LBJ's electoral calculations. McNamara saw no need to widen the war when doing so was neither politically prudent nor militarily necessary.[107] Yet he gave the president several options for intensifying existing activities and adopting provocative new ones. For now, he maintained, the "military tools and concepts" were "generally sound and adequate"; in time, and preferably once the Khanh government had solidified its legitimacy and popularity, the effort might include covert operations into Laos, retaliatory strikes against North Vietnam, and graduated overt pressure by U.S. and South Vietnamese forces against Hanoi. The risks of such action, he believed, were offset by the magnitude of the stakes. Unless the United States could secure an "independent non-Communist Vietnam," the dominoes were likely to fall, forcing the countries of Southeast Asia, Northeast Asia, the Western Pacific, and Oceania to succumb or accommodate themselves to Communist pressure and domination.[108]

As for the disposition of U.S. troops, McNamara acknowledged the potential need for more of them. But he continued to lobby for withdrawal where possible, maintaining that the "policy of reducing existing personnel where South Vietnamese are in a position to assume the functions is still sound." Reductions in the near future were unlikely, but "adherence to this policy as such has a sound effect in portraying to the U.S. and the world that we continue to regard the war as a conflict the South Vietnamese must win and take ultimate responsibility for." Aligning himself once again with the target date his colleagues were looking to shed, McNamara maintained that "substantial reductions in the numbers of U.S. military training personnel should be possible before the end of 1965," but Washington should "continue to reiterate that it will provide all the assistance and advice required to do the job regardless of how long it takes." With the struggle in Vietnam representing a "test case" of America's capacity and resolve to confront a Communist "war of liberation," it was essential the United States "continue to make it emphatically clear that we are prepared to furnish assistance and support for as long as it takes to bring the insurgency under control."[109]

The president conveyed that message to the American public just days after McNamara's return in mid-March, and in the wake of several memos and meetings among the administration's most senior officials. Prepping Johnson for a wide-ranging interview on March 15 with the nation's television and radio networks, McGeorge Bundy crafted answers on several topics, including Vietnam. He characterized the 1965 withdrawal date as merely aspirational and not an ironclad commitment to vacate the battlefield. In fact, it "has never been anything more for us than a target for the completion of certain specific forms of technical training and assistance."[110] Although the journalists ultimately asked no questions about the withdrawal policy per se, Johnson made clear his determination to remain steadfast. The struggle in Vietnam, he told the reporters, "cannot be ignored, we must stay there and help them, and that is what we are going to do."[111]

Having delivered the message to the American people, Johnson moved to cement it as a matter of policy. Two days after his radio and TV interview, the president and his team adopted McNamara's report verbatim as NSAM 288 and then summarized it in a White House statement. Although there had "unquestionably been setbacks" since the McNamara-Taylor trip of October 1963, the Khanh government had produced a "sound central plan" for prosecuting the war. The United States, therefore, would continue to furnish economic and military assistance to Saigon in the form of aid and training, and would continue to do so "for as long as it is required to bring Communist aggression and terrorism under control." As for the matter of U.S. forces, their numbers would expand as well as contract. Although the 1965 target had now vanished, the administration held that the "policy should continue of withdrawing United States personnel where their roles can be assumed by South Vietnamese and of sending additional men if they are needed."[112] The distinction was subtle; the administration would avoid rosy predictions while conveying enduring resolve. But the change was clear.

McNamara then enshrined it in a full-dress speech in Washington later that month. After reviewing Vietnamese history and U.S. efforts to defend the South, he fixed on the current and future presence of American troops: The United States could safely withdraw only when it could expect to leave Saigon independent and stable.[113] That was indeed a higher bar than merely training the South Vietnamese to look after their own independence and stability. The media took notice and stressed the firmness of the American commitment. Washington would "accelerate" its support of the GVN, the *Times* reported, and had now "modified" plans to withdraw by 1965. The *Post* followed suit, noting approvingly that the United States would leave Vietnam "when the job is done and not before then."[114]

In fact, the day after his talk, McNamara directed Felt and Harkins to end all planning for the withdrawal of U.S. troops. As his office explained it to Pacific Command, "previous guidance re Model Plan projection for phasedown of U.S. forces and GVN forces is superseded. Policy is as announced by the White House" in its statement of March 17. The United States would continue to support Saigon "for as long as required to bring communist aggression and terrorism under control."[115]

The withdrawal of U.S. troops from Vietnam—the Kennedy withdrawal—had run its course.

EPILOGUE

The Shadow of Camelot

Although the Kennedy withdrawal had come to an end in the spring of 1964, developments afoot would grant it new life as the country came to grips with what it lost in Dallas. Indeed, the death of President Kennedy traumatized Americans as had few other events in their history. The depth of public grief, facilitated by an expanding media landscape, marked the Kennedy assassination as a "flashbulb moment," an instant in time that seared itself into the consciousness of those who lived through it. The late president's widow, Jacqueline Kennedy, shaped the texture of those events—especially his mourning and burial—and endowed them with transcendent meaning. She was not alone in doing so, but her attention to detail and evocative imagery extended and amplified her thousand-day effort to frame the Kennedy presidency as a golden era of thought and culture. One of her more notable interventions came a week after the assassination, when she spoke with author Theodore White for a *Life* magazine story on her late husband and his unfinished presidency. Characterizing his tenure as a charmed moment in time, a veritable "Camelot" of high purpose and high ideals, she willed an image of JFK into the national narrative, bequeathing a shorthand description of life at court on the New Frontier.[1]

Thereafter, numerous events would intersect to keep the Kennedy flame alive. Some involved naturally recurring dates on the calendar—ten-year anniversaries of the Cuban Missile Crisis, as well as of JFK's inaugural and assassination—along with the appearance of books and essays accompanying those commemorative moments. Other markers included the release of memoirs from Kennedy officials, family members, and confidantes, along with media commentary upon their deaths. At various turns, and particularly during the post–Cold War struggles of the twenty-first century, those moments coincided with policy challenges facing the country, prompting pundits to ask some form of "What would Jack have done?," with the ultimate "what if" hovering over them all: what might Kennedy have done about Vietnam, and what are the lessons of that virtual history?

Those questions were especially pertinent given what his successor ultimately did there. President Lyndon Johnson dramatically escalated the Vietnam war at the very moment that two major books on JFK addressed the Kennedy approach to it. Written by White House advisers Ted Sorensen and Arthur Schlesinger, each offered sympathetic accounts and established the "Camelot" school that marked early appraisals of John F. Kennedy. Schlesinger refrained from specifying what JFK would have done in Vietnam, but he left the clear impression that a war Kennedy viewed as a political conflict had, by the time of his death, become overly militarized.[2] Sorensen maintained that Kennedy's goal "was to get out of Vietnam," but he was "simply going to weather it out, a nasty, untidy mess to which there was no other acceptable solution."[3] Although both accounts appeared before majority opinion had soured on the war, Kennedy's skepticism ran through them nevertheless, as it did in works from journalists and public officials who described JFK as dubious of America's chances and willing to cap U.S. involvement.[4]

Tales of Kennedy's skepticism and restraint angered Johnson, as they invited unflattering comparisons. Given LBJ's frustrations with the Kennedy mystique and his running battles with the Kennedy crowd, Johnson sought clarity on how his handling of Vietnam stacked up with JFK's.[5] He repeatedly dispatched aides to unearth statements and records documenting their respective positions, a discovery process that yielded continuities between the two. Reviewing Kennedy statements for Johnson in September 1967, National Security Adviser Walt W. Rostow said they revealed JFK's "flat acceptance of the domino theory," his "recurrent linkage of Viet Nam to Berlin," and his belief that "the fate of our own liberty was involved in Vietnam." Regarding the great "what if," Rostow doubted whether "any objective person can read this record without knowing that President Kennedy would have seen this through whatever the cost."[6]

Regardless of Kennedy's positions and the political cover Johnson sought from them, LBJ's prosecution of the war was tearing apart his administration, his party, and his country. For the first time since he deployed combat troops in July 1965, a plurality of Americans believed that doing so had been a mistake. Even before the public reached that conclusion in October 1967, Robert McNamara was arguing that the bombing of North Vietnam was having little impact on Hanoi's calculus and calling for a total halt on those operations.[7] It was a bitter pill for Johnson and one of the last straws in their deteriorating relationship; the president announced McNamara's departure from the Pentagon the following month. More dramatic displays of policy independence—what Johnson would regard as disloyalty—were yet to come. Democrats split over the war, criticizing the president from both the right and the left. Disenchantment was so great that by the fall of 1967, Senator Eugene McCarthy [D-MN] vowed to challenge LBJ—his own party's incumbent—for the Democratic presidential nomination.

The more significant threat came from Senator Robert F. Kennedy [D-NY], who had largely refrained from speaking publicly about Vietnam following the tragedy in Dallas. Once elected to the Senate in 1964, RFK began to voice his concerns more freely. Although his first speech from the floor acknowledged a measure of continuity between LBJ's and JFK's approaches, a subsequent statement in July 1965 hinted at daylight between the two. Efforts to militarize the war, Bobby said, were distorting what was, at root, a political conflict.[8] Johnson sought to neutralize RFK by linking his own approach to that of the late president, referencing JFK's speeches and emphasizing their common course of action.

But as the war expanded, it became increasingly difficult to draw straight lines from the 16,000 military advisers JFK dispatched in an assistance effort to the hundreds of thousands of combat troops LBJ deployed in a fully Americanized war. With domestic dissent increasing and victory still a distant hope—and with Bobby more fully engaged in his own war with Johnson for the soul of the Democratic party—the senator began to associate himself with his brother's affectations and idealism, and with his own interpretation of JFK's policies. A subsequent speech in February 1966, following the combative and televised Fulbright hearings on the war, emphasized the need for negotiation and the possibility of a coalition government in Vietnam. Bobby's challenge persisted into 1967, as he encouraged Johnson privately in February to stop the bombing and negotiate a peace before doing so publicly one month later.[9]

The senator's most significant departure came that November. Amid speculation about a presidential run, Bobby emphasized his late brother's conviction that the war was South Vietnam's to win. Appearing on the CBS television program *Face the Nation,* he maintained that JFK's approach sought to provide for South Vietnamese self-determination—the primary reason, he claimed, for America's participation in the struggle. But the United States was now fighting in Vietnam to prevent the war from spreading throughout Southeast Asia and reaching America's shores. The country's moral position thus had changed, he said, and with it, the virtue of remaining in the fight.[10]

For the first time, Bobby had established a clear break between LBJ's and JFK's policies in Vietnam, even as journalists rejected his claim of an altered mission. His "distorted charge," according to the *New York Times,* had moved the debate about America's effort "into the never never land of what might have been."[11] Columnist Joseph Alsop likened Bobby's argument to outright "fraud."[12] Johnson, in turn, again asked aides to pull together presidential statements on Vietnam. The NSC's William Jorden characterized RFK's remarks as "a distortion of history." Evaluating Jorden's report, Rostow doubted "that any reasonable person could read this collection and still believe there had been any 'switch' whatsoever in our policy or our understanding of our commitment."[13] Indeed, Bobby's brief for his brother's altruism was wide of the mark.

Robert Kennedy's intervention was certainly the most significant contribution to the debate, but other voices chimed in as well. According to historian Thomas Brown, those treatments often turned on matters of personality and style. Journalists and authors noted that JFK was willing to cut his losses and learn from his mistakes—attributes allegedly not shared by Lyndon Johnson—and that he might have negotiated his way out of Vietnam; Kennedy's temperament, and notably his pragmatism, would thus have led him down a different path. Most significantly, Ted Sorensen now argued that JFK would have preserved his diplomatic and military options and sent "no combat troops to South Vietnam and no missions to bomb North Vietnam." To Sorensen, Johnson's reliance on troops and bombs "fundamentally altered John Kennedy's Vietnam policy."[14]

There the matter lay until the summer of 1970—a period of increased agitation after the invasion of Cambodia, the killing of students at Kent and Jackson State Universities, and congressional efforts to mandate a U.S. withdrawal from Vietnam. That August, *Life* magazine began to serialize *"Johnny, We Hardly Knew Ye,"* a memoir from Kennedy aides David Powers and Kenneth O'Donnell. Its assertion that the thirty-fifth president was looking to withdraw U.S. troops from Vietnam stemmed from an episode in the spring of 1963, when Kennedy, after receiving criticism from Mike Mansfield during a briefing of congressional leaders, brought the Senate majority leader into the Oval Office. As Mansfield recalled, Kennedy made his pledge to withdraw with barely any explanation. Still, there was "no doubt" that JFK "had shifted definitely and unequivocally on Vietnam," even though "he never had the chance to put the plan (1965 withdrawal) into effect."[15] According to the *Los Angeles Times,* which published the story with the front-page headline "Kennedy Plan for '65 Viet Pullout Disclosed," Mansfield was "convinced" Kennedy would have implemented it had he lived. Highlighting "Kennedy's hitherto untold turnabout on Vietnam," the story spun the notion that a Kennedy plan to withdraw U.S. troops was unknown to the American public.[16]

While the firmness of Kennedy's position was indeed news, his interest in withdrawal was not. The White House had publicly communicated that desire in its October 1963 statement and reaffirmed it in the weeks leading up to November 22. But Americans were surely unaware of the depth, duration, and seriousness of that planning. In highlighting its alleged secrecy, and therefore its knowledge by perhaps all but a few, the Mansfield revelation presumably captured Kennedy's real intentions toward Vietnam.[17] Although Robert Kennedy purportedly knew of the planning, even he kept it hidden from view, choosing not to say anything about it during his presidential run, as doing so—according to O'Donnell—would have looked "cheesy."[18]

In fact, the story might have come out three years earlier had Mansfield not convinced O'Donnell to withhold publication of his book. Mansfield sought the embargo to avoid embarrassing LBJ and hurting their relationship. But he claimed that his knowledge of Kennedy's intentions was not news. "I've been saying it for years in response to questions," he maintained, "but never in quite those terms," and so was himself surprised that the disclosure never gained traction.[19] Several versions of the story appear in Don Oberdorfer's biography of Mansfield, including the one presented in *Johnny, We Hardly Knew Ye.* While the role of the 1964 election changed in each, Kennedy's intention to withdraw remained consistent throughout.[20]

Most likely, the "secret" planning JFK shared with Mansfield was the effort McNamara kicked off in 1962, the one being refined at the time of the Mansfield-Kennedy private meeting. Since accounts of that meeting locate it in the spring of 1963, it might well have taken place prior to or just after the May 1963 SecDef conference, the interagency session that evaluated the Comprehensive Plan and its schedule to remove U.S. troops by 1965. That planning was indeed secret in the sense that it was known to a limited number of officials; when its contours became public in October 1963, the actual planning for withdrawal—beyond the aspiration to effect it—remained confined to members of the Executive Branch. Even McNamara and Taylor, in their testimony to Congress following their return from Vietnam, referenced withdrawal without revealing the extensive planning behind it. Had Kennedy truly been harboring a secret plan to disengage, he might have shared it with Mansfield during their private meeting in December 1962, when Mansfield delivered his gloomy Vietnam report. The president's failure to do so likely stemmed from the fact that the plan, such as it was, did not yet exist. By the spring of 1963, however, when JFK took Mansfield into his confidence, he could have legitimately told the senator of his intention to withdraw from Vietnam because McNamara was developing a plan to do just that.

Within a year, though, reports of a Kennedy withdrawal had moved from the stuff of hearsay to the realm of hard fact. The publication of the *Pentagon Papers* in 1971 fundamentally reshaped perceptions of withdrawal planning, indeed of the entire American approach to the war. By pulling back the curtain on Vietnam policymaking from 1945 through 1967, the *New York Times* and other papers provided access to formerly classified national security documents, as well as a narrative of events based on that evidence. Both revealed that successive administrations, and particularly the Kennedy and Johnson administrations, were routinely claiming progress in the war when internal memoranda were suggesting no such thing. Their contents contained key papers on withdrawal planning, including the McNamara-Taylor Report of October 1963. Thenceforth, scholars and commentators could marshal real-time evidence to debate the claim that Kennedy was planning to withdraw by 1965.

But first-person accounts of a Kennedy withdrawal continued to enter the public record and shape the national conversation. A December 1971 CBS News special on Vietnam featured Deputy Secretary of Defense Roswell L. Gilpatric and NSC aide Michael Forrestal relaying JFK's frustration with the war and testifying to withdrawal planning.[21] Others expanded that evidentiary base through interviews they gave to the Lyndon B. Johnson Presidential Library. Forrestal, along with journalist and Kennedy friend Charles Bartlett, conveyed Kennedy's increasing discomfort with the war. But both also doubted whether Kennedy had decided to leave Vietnam, with Forrestal referencing Kennedy's reluctance "to do anything drastic" until after the 1964 election and downplaying his commitment to any particular course of action.[22] Those recollections would not become publicly available until later that decade, meaning the most significant disclosure remained that of Kenny O'Donnell, who in 1972 alleged that JFK was "determined to pull out of Vietnam and even more determined never to send an American draftee into combat there or anywhere else overseas."[23]

As the Kennedy administration receded further into the past, and as additional records became available for use, treatments of JFK came to assume a revisionist cast, with authors approaching him more critically. Many now questioned his intention to phase out U.S. advisers, especially given the perceived hawkishness of his foreign policy. This strand of writing, which proliferated in the 1970s and 1980s, was as emblematic of Kennedy biographers and portraitists as it was for scholars of the war.[24] Although Arthur Schlesinger was now more confident that Kennedy would have withdrawn from Vietnam, his writing stood as an outlier, as many of those works rejected the argument outright.[25]

The 1991 release of Oliver Stone's film *JFK,* an incendiary exploration of the Kennedy assassination, transformed the debate into a national conversation. Positing a far-flung conspiracy to murder the president, Stone located its motive in a Kennedy effort to end the Cold War and thereby deny profits to the military-industrial complex. Kennedy's intention to withdraw from Vietnam was purportedly the final straw for those who also saw JFK failing to check the advance of communism worldwide. Touting the writings of scholars and former officials who professed knowledge of Kennedy's true intentions, Stone claimed that JFK had authorized the drawdown of U.S. forces and that LBJ reversed the policy just days after the tragedy in Dallas.[26] Over the next several years, those scholars and others, as well as Kennedy-Johnson officials, would battle over the film and its thesis.[27]

Although the discussion generated fevered debate in the nation's publications, its greater impact was yet to come. The film had sparked such interest in Kennedy's murder that Congress empaneled an Assassination Records Review Board (ARRB) to comb through government archives and declassify materials germane to Kennedy's murder. Among them was a trove of documents on Vietnam, including secret Kennedy and Johnson White House tapes. Their release, along with that of related papers, meant that the public could explore a new class of records offering intimate access to presidential decisionmaking—a process one could now experience in real-time. Once revealed and ultimately deciphered, those materials would add substantially to the understanding of key events during the era, especially the war in Vietnam.[28]

Among the first to make use of them was Robert McNamara, who did so in his 1995 memoir of policymaking on Vietnam. Although he had been largely silent on Vietnam since his departure from government, he now claimed Kennedy would have withdrawn American troops, even if it meant the loss of Southeast Asia. Numerous reviewers took issue with McNamara, some with great vehemence.[29] But key administration alumni, including Roger Hilsman and McGeorge Bundy, backed the withdrawal thesis, maintaining that Kennedy would have resisted Americanizing the war, at the very least, or pulled the country out of it altogether.[30] By the end of the decade, scholars were also gravitating toward that perspective in works on Kennedy's life and presidency, as well as in more targeted studies of the war, several of which highlighted JFK's skepticism about its prospects.[31]

Developments in the new millennium generated even further interest in the question of what Kennedy might have done in Vietnam. Following the September 11, 2001, terrorist attacks on the United States, threats to the homeland engendered a sense of fear among Americans that recalled the "hour of maximum danger" of Kennedy's Cold War. In response, President George W. Bush launched a "War on Terror" that targeted extremist groups and the governments that harbored them. Within a month of 9/11, U.S. and allied forces invaded Afghanistan, accelerating Washington's militarized and forward response to national security, with effects that would long permeate the fabric of American life.

Those efforts soon encompassed planning for a subsequent war on Iraq, suspected of conniving with terrorists and possessing weapons of mass destruction (WMD). A months-long debate about the looming assault featured a national conversation that drew on the Kennedy experience. In fact, at the very moment Congress was considering the Iraq Resolution in October 2002, which authorized the use of military force against Saddam Hussein, the country was commemorating the fortieth anniversary of the Cuban Missile Crisis. Pundits and academics cited Kennedy's search for a negotiated solution and a reluctance to go to war, at least before exhausting all other options. Those retrospectives and others were either thinly veiled or, more often, entirely explicit commentaries on current global tensions. They also proved unpersuasive. The United States attacked Iraq on March 19, 2003, toppling Saddam's regime in six weeks and ending major combat operations by May 1.[32]

Within months, though, Washington was confronting a growing insurgency in Iraq, raising more ominous parallels with the Kennedy years. Vietnam again suffused the national conversation as the United States found itself fighting adversaries who were hard to identify, defending a government of dubious legitimacy, and pacifying a country with porous borders that was descending into civil strife.[33] As the *New York Times*'s Craig Whitney observed, many of the words and phrases then swirling around Iraq—quagmire, attrition, credibility gap, Iraqification—harkened back to Vietnam; in time, they would include others, such as nation-building, counterinsurgency, "clear-and-hold," and "hearts and minds."[34] The relevance of those terms gained greater purchase through the publication of new studies of Kennedy—it was, after all, the fortieth anniversary of his murder in Dallas—as well as of Kennedy and Vietnam. Several of them made the case for a Kennedy withdrawal, claiming that Johnson reversed JFK's decision to leave Vietnam. Kennedy's perspicacity on the war, and on militarizing a political struggle, hung in the ether.[35]

Newly available documents helped to shape that scholarship and fuel the now vibrant debate linking Vietnam with current policy dilemmas. These included additional White House tapes from Kennedy and Johnson, as well as papers collections from several of their key aides.[36] McNamara himself weighed in, this time in the 2003 documentary

The Fog of War and a companion book of the same name. His contention that Kennedy was looking to wind down a war Johnson subsequently escalated was especially poignant as the war in Iraq took a decided turn for the worse. The film's director, Errol Morris, drew direct parallels between Vietnam and Iraq, arguing that LBJ, like the current president, was committed to fighting a war his aides had warned him about. Nagging questions about Iraq's weapons of mass destruction, which had yet to be found but which had been a *casus belli* for the assault on Baghdad, seemed eerily similar to the murky Tonkin Gulf incident forty years earlier.[37] Both Tonkin and WMD seemed to provide pretexts for policies already in train.

Connections between the wars in Vietnam and Iraq only deepened during the 2004 presidential campaign. The parallels became easier to draw as the United States confronted an increasingly virulent insurgency, calls for an American troop withdrawal, and a progressively energized antiwar movement. With Senator Edward M. Kennedy [D-MA] having declared that "Iraq is George Bush's Vietnam," Democrats pressed the analogy. Their standard bearer in the contest, Senator John F. Kerry [D-MA], a Vietnam veteran and subsequent antiwar activist, campaigned as a survivor who understood the ravages of war, particularly an ill-advised one.[38] Thereafter, the American experience in Vietnam became a more popular allegory for the nation's troubles—comparisons the Bush administration rejected before embracing them as arguments against precipitous withdrawal. Scholars also entered the fray, as historians highlighted similarities between the two conflicts.[39]

Beyond those targeted commentaries, further writing and reflection connected the "War on Terror" to Kennedy, Vietnam, and the use of military force. A biography of John Kenneth Galbraith made yet another case for a Kennedy withdrawal, and excerpts from the book allowed the *Nation* to draw explicit parallels between that earlier war and the current one in Iraq.[40] The release of Arthur Schlesinger's journals focused further attention on the Kennedy withdrawal, generating vigorous debate in the review literature.[41] Ted Sorensen also raised the matter, resurrecting his 1965 claim and conceding no knowledge of what JFK would have done in Vietnam.[42] McGeorge Bundy's reflections made their way into print as well, suggesting that Kennedy would have resisted deploying combat troops to Vietnam.[43] And James G. Blight—McNamara's collaborator on critical oral histories covering the Cuban Missile Crisis and

Vietnam—presented the most sustained case, in both a coauthored study and a documentary film, for a definitive Kennedy withdrawal from Vietnam.[44]

The passing of Kennedy hands—Galbraith in 2006, Schlesinger in 2007, McNamara in 2009, and Sorensen in 2010—occasioned similar commentary, particularly as the wars in South Asia and the Middle East ground on. So, too, would the death (and autobiography) in 2009 of Edward Kennedy, who had done more than anyone to keep the Kennedy flame alive.[45] The departure of those figures and the associated discussion ensured that the Kennedy aura and its evocations of presidential growth, restraint, and judgment remained alive and well. Those attributes were central to the conversation about the necessity of the Iraq War and the wisdom of prosecuting it.

They also were relevant to the emergence of Senator Barack Obama [D-IL] as a potent political force. Obama's "cool" style evoked the Kennedy brand, replete with its qualities of patience, prudence, and discernment. The family's formal endorsement of Obama as the Democratic nominee for president in 2008 further elevated the image of a more cerebral, youthful, and idealistic figure as party leader. It also spurred a new wave of Kennedy nostalgia on the cusp of celebrations marking the fiftieth anniversary of Camelot. Indeed, the outpouring of Kennedy scholarship and commentary sustained the presence of JFK in American life, weaving him more firmly into the fabric of the nation's cultural memory. The connections between the two figures became almost inescapable.

The Kennedy commemoration also informed debate about the policy choices Obama faced, particularly with respect to the wars in Iraq and Afghanistan. Obama had come into office characterizing Afghanistan as the "good" war and Iraq the "dumb" one, and he embraced the timetable Bush negotiated for leaving Iraq. But Obama elected to surge U.S. forces in Afghanistan—by then, the more troubling conflict—deploying 21,000 troops in March 2009, largely to buy time for a more sustained and strategic review later that year. In the interim, commentary linking Kennedy's Vietnam with Obama's Afghanistan filled the pages of journals and newspapers.[46] Both wars involved long-standing economic and military commitments to countries facing virulent insurgencies, run by governments of dubious legitimacy. Several pieces warned that the dangers ahead mirrored those of years ago, as writers challenged the precepts of counterinsurgency and nation-building likely to figure into Obama's plans. Others encouraged Obama to follow Kennedy's lead and resist the march toward an expanded war.[47] Indeed, Obama would make his most consequential decisions on Afghanistan in the fall of his first year, precisely matching the timing of JFK's dramatic escalation of the American commitment in Vietnam.

The parallels in policymaking between Afghanistan and Vietnam were evident not only to the chattering classes, but to government officials formulating policy. Obama himself sought insight from that earlier war, particularly from those who had written on it. But Obama heard as much about the missteps of Lyndon Johnson and the trade-offs between guns and butter as he did about the wisdom and prudence of Jack Kennedy.[48] Those lessons also came alive through the reflections of McGeorge Bundy, who had been preparing a memoir on Vietnam before his passing. Published by Gordon Goldstein, their curation became must reading for Obama aides leery of quagmires and counterinsurgencies.[49] Indeed, a series of leaked memos that summer and fall, which pushed competing strategic positions on Afghanistan, suggested stakeholders were trying to box in a young, inexperienced president, just as advisers had pressed Kennedy to employ armed force in a range of theaters. Kennedy ultimately acceded to escalation in Vietnam, but he did so on his own terms—after weeks of deliberation—rejecting the use of combat troops and opting to send military advisers instead. It was a middle course, Goldstein noted, that allowed Kennedy to apply "control and resolve mixed with realism and rigor," an approach Obama might take with respect to Afghanistan. Other voices speculated on much the same.[50]

Obama ultimately took months to devise his Afghanistan policy, a deliberative posture Frank Rich described in the *New York Times* as the president's "most significant down payment yet on being, in the most patriotic sense, Kennedyesque."[51] More than one observer regarded the troop decision, which included a surge of between 10,000 and 40,000 forces, as Obama's "Kennedy moment." They included Senate Foreign Relations chair John F. Kerry, who noted the parallels to Vietnam and advised against a major commitment of forces, and former secretary of state Colin L. Powell, who hoped Obama would mirror Kennedy's approach in the missile crisis and reject the advice of hawkish generals.[52] Others wondered whether Obama might achieve what Kennedy had only aspired to: pulling the United States out of an unwinnable war.[53]

Although Obama never framed the Afghan war as unwinnable, he pledged to withdraw the United States all the same. He would surge U.S. troops as a means toward bringing them home, a policy not unlike Kennedy's—and really, McNamara's—in Vietnam. But unlike JFK, who escalated U.S. involvement before moving to scale it down, Obama worked that full trajectory into a single policy pronouncement. On December 1, 2009, he announced the deployment of 30,000 troops to defeat al Qaeda in Pakistan and degrade the Taliban in Afghanistan, and to bring troops home after eighteen months. Commentary stressed the rigor and duration of Obama's decision-making process and his desire to avoid the blunders of earlier administrations. Yet others wondered whether Obama truly believed in "surge and withdraw," and whether, contra Kennedy and Johnson, he had effectively shielded strategy from politics.[54]

Those concerns grew over the following year. With a measure of distance from the troop decision, the parallels between Afghanistan and Vietnam became more noticeable and less complementary. The president's hybrid option of dispatching 30,000 troops—not the 10,000 floated for a counterterror operation, nor the 40,000 to 60,000 suggested for a counterinsurgency approach—conjured the compromises LBJ struck with his own generals.[55] But it was comparisons with Kennedy that seemed to leave Obama wanting. While JFK had repeatedly stressed the importance of aiding Saigon, even at the cost of rising troop and casualty figures, he largely shied away from declaring Vietnam a vital interest and mandating the need for victory. His public statements about withdrawal, moreover, were always aspirational and replete with generalities about timing. Although observers in 1963 rightly noted the tension between Kennedy's continuing commitment and his provisional 1965 withdrawal date, Obama seemed firmer on both counts. He had campaigned on the notion that Afghanistan was a war of necessity—"a war that we have to win"—but soon soured on its prospects as he looked for an exit ramp.[56] Announcements in 2010 and 2011 refined the departure date, with December 2014 marking the end, for the moment, of U.S. military involvement.[57] The contradictions in Obama's policy were thus starker than Kennedy's, and since Obama faced the consequences of his choices more fully than Kennedy ever did, JFK escaped a comparable judgment—at least during his time in office.

By then, the onset of the commemorative period ensured that all things Kennedy would mark the national conversation over the next three years. From Stephen King's time-traveling counterfactual about Dallas, to Jacqueline Kennedy's audiotaped reflections, to cable and network television broadcasts, media products on JFK proliferated from 2011 to 2013.[58] Once again, retrospectives comingled with real-time commentary, highlighting the difficulties presidents face in fighting counterinsurgencies, staring down their respective militaries, and seeking to extricate the country from its unconventional wars—or keeping out of them altogether.[59] Obama's difficulties in that realm only multiplied. The Arab Spring presented his administration with extraordinary challenges on top of those in Afghanistan and Iraq, with still others—Russian predations in Ukraine and the rise of the Islamic State in Iraq and Syria, to name just two—on the horizon. In that environment, the lessons Kennedy provided remained relevant, rooted in the realms of circumspection, empathy, and judgment, and the recognition of limits. Scholars and pundits made the most of the commemorative moment, emphasizing those insights in revisiting Vietnam and the missile crisis.[60] But their deployment fifty years hence would come in an international environment more complex and volatile than the one Kennedy faced. Still, the shadow JFK cast was long and lasting. By the end of the semicentennial, the national conversation about him had reached its apotheosis, with political scientist Larry J. Sabato arguing that those five decades amounted to a veritable Kennedy half-century.[61]

For over fifty years now, the conversation about JFK inevitably references his intentions in Vietnam. Owing to the emergence of a rich documentary base and the pioneering efforts of several scholars, we now have a better understanding of what those intentions entailed. While that knowledge cannot provide definitive proof as to what Kennedy would have done had he lived into 1964 and been elected to a second term as president, it does point to a preferred trajectory, the planning for which is unmistakable.

From the spring of 1962 through the fall of 1963, the Kennedy administration undertook a serious and systematic effort to schedule the removal of U.S. servicemen from Vietnam. The Office of the Secretary of Defense was its main proponent; though it also involved CINCPAC, MACV, and elements of the U.S. Country Team in Saigon, contributions from the State Department and the intelligence community are unclear, as are those of the White House. Although Kennedy by all accounts inspired the effort—he had expressed a desire in April 1962 to reduce troop levels when the opportunity arose—his precise role remains elusive. No paper trail connects him to that planning, and his recorded conversations betray an ignorance of its progress and a skepticism of its merits. The initiative thus emerges as the brainchild of Defense Secretary Robert McNamara, who shaped a loosely defined presidential preference into a detailed and comprehensive schedule for reducing the U.S. profile in Vietnam.[62]

The timing of that planning was significant. It began during a moment of guarded optimism about the war, with U.S. assistance ramping up and Saigon implementing new and potentially promising measures to stanch a Communist insurgency. McNamara praised those efforts and repeatedly championed their capacity, if pursued diligently, to achieve their objectives. Assuming the trajectory held, planning to pare back U.S. assistance, after first scaling it up, seemed a sensible choice. But withdrawal also stemmed from McNamara's interest in cutting costs and achieving efficiencies through systematic fiscal and project planning. Initiatives in support of those goals were coalescing at the very moment Kennedy was questioning the depth and duration of the Vietnam program. The chance to impose greater discipline on that program appealed to McNamara, reflecting his concern about long-term, open-ended commitments to the developing world, with the bottomless economic and military support of South Korea as the object lesson of what to avoid. Those dynamics seemed to be replicating in South Vietnam, as successive administrations had aided Saigon on an ad hoc, improvised basis, without integrating assistance programs into a conceptual whole.

The Comprehensive Plan for South Vietnam (CPSVN), which McNamara commissioned in July 1962, sought to change that approach by aligning inputs with outputs, and by harmonizing key programs with broader strategic objectives. Scheduled to run for five years, it sought to provide Saigon with the capacity to defeat the Communist insurgency and manage its own security thereafter. Incorporating a long-range timetable for realizing its objectives, the CPSVN took its lead from McNamara's priorities but also from efforts to impose comparable rigor on an array of federal programs. Budgeting practices now featured similar five-year calendars which encouraged agencies to plan more thoroughly and consistently. As with McNamara's efforts at the Defense Department, those initiatives aimed to rationalize administration operations and programs—efforts that were themselves indicative of a more techno-cratic, problem-solving ethos suffusing postwar management practices, and emblematic of those charting the course on the New Frontier.

That planning also moved forward with political considerations in mind. Growing discomfort with escalating levels of U.S. troops, in both South Vietnam and the United States, encouraged McNamara to accelerate plans for withdrawal—the better to head off congressional opposition to the Diem government, maintain legislative support for foreign aid, and facilitate better performance from Saigon. Indeed, McNamara's interest in speeding up American aid to Vietnam was in-fluenced by his desire to draw it back down—the more money Wash-ington devoted to the war in the near term, the less it would have to spend over the long haul.

The Kennedy withdrawal thus emerged as a highly elastic approach to a broad range of administration objectives. It was a strategic response to the Communist challenge in Southeast Asia, a bureaucratic response to economic challenges at home and abroad, and a political response to policy and administrative challenges in Washington and Saigon. It also morphed over a life span that encompassed roughly eighteen months of the Kennedy administration and the first four months of the Johnson presidency—from its conception in the spring and summer of 1962, to its development in the fall and winter of 1963, to its refinement during the spring and summer of 1963, to its completion, public articulation, and circumscribed implementation that fall.

That evolution coincided with real-time developments not only in American politics and federal policymaking, but in international poli-tics and the war itself. The Sino-Soviet split now seemed irreversible, at least to Kennedy, and the president explored a cautious détente with Moscow. Yet the rift created challenges of its own. The competition be-tween Khrushchev and Mao further internationalized the war, leading Moscow and Beijing to compete among themselves, as well as with the United States, for hearts and minds in the developing world. In that en-vironment, U.S. policymakers confronted a presumably expansionist China and the prospect of another round of hostilities between Wash-ington and Beijing.[63] A more robust, expedited, and sustained effort in Vietnam thus addressed the perceived virtues, at home and abroad, of greater vigilance against local Communists and their international brethren.

As such, the Kennedy withdrawal came to mean different things at different times to different people. For those in the military charged with its implementation, it was largely an unwelcome exercise, a distraction at best and premature at worst—diverting attention from the hard work of training the South Vietnamese to win their war against Hanoi and the NLF. For Maxwell Taylor and McGeorge Bundy, it came to serve as leverage against the GVN, as it did briefly and to a lesser degree for Robert McNamara. More importantly, for McNamara, it served departmental and programmatic objectives and enhanced his reformation of the country's approach to national security.

Its meaning for Kennedy remains obscure. On the one hand, it helped him counter political headwinds at home; on the other, it established a framework for avoiding a potential quagmire abroad. In the end, JFK likely embraced withdrawal much as he did policy toward Vietnam more generally—whatever helped to win the war he supported, whatever interfered with it he opposed. To the extent that withdrawal allowed him to sustain the assistance effort, he welcomed it. His directive to remove one thousand servicemen by the end of 1963 thus served the politics of the American commitment, even as it reflected the irrelevance of those troops to the course of the war. But since the counterinsurgency relied heavily on the training and "stiffening" functions of the 15,000 advisers who would remain thereafter, Kennedy signaled a willingness to delay their departure beyond the 1965 date projected for their removal.

Indeed, while Kennedy had become increasingly uncomfortable with the depth and implications of the U.S. commitment, his fealty to the broader dynamics that expanded it, including the many dimensions of the credibility imperative, would likely have generated cognitive dissonance were he to abandon it. This is not to say that his broader posture toward the Cold War remained static into the last months of his presidency— far from it, as he pursued a more chastened policy toward Moscow and looked to lessen the dangers of superpower conflict. He had displayed a marked capacity for growth and circumspection, dispensing with beliefs he had come to view as mistaken, and exploring—however tentatively— new departures. But as president, he never relinquished his interest in brushfire wars, nor did he dampen his rhetoric about their necessity. He continued to operate from a worldview that embraced the precepts of domino thinking, the salience of cascade dynamics, the importance of symbols, and the demonstration of resolve. While he vented in private about the commitment to Saigon—one he inherited but championed all the same—he never disowned the strategic logic on which it rested, a logic that remained operative even in an emerging era of superpower détente.

The Kennedy administration's withdrawal planning thus stands as a complicated model for adulation and emulation, one that pundits and presidents should espouse with caution. Indeed, the shadow of Camelot has obscured the history of that planning and its meaning for JFK. While Kennedy inspired the policy to reduce America's profile in Vietnam, its announcement in October 1963 served to sustain that presence into the foreseeable future. Indeed, as Kennedy himself acknowledged, that presence was bound to extend into 1964 and likely into a presumptive second administration in 1965—as even his most ardent admirers recognize. Kennedy's embrace of that policy, therefore, reveals a central irony: As much as it signaled an eagerness to wind down the U.S. assistance effort, the policy of withdrawal—the Kennedy withdrawal—allowed JFK to preserve the American commitment to Vietnam.

Notes

Acknowledgments

Index

Notes

Abbreviations

CMH   U.S. Army Center of Military History, Fort Lesley J. McNair, Washington, DC
FRUS   *Foreign Relations of the United States,* Office of the Historian, United States
           Department of State, https://history.state.gov/historicaldocuments
                FRUS, 1949, vol. 7, part 2: *The Far East and Australia,* ed. John G. Reid and
                    John G. Glennon (GPO, 1976)
                FRUS, 1952–1954, vol. 12, part 1: *East Asia and the Pacific,* ed. David W.
                    Mabon (GPO, 1984)
                FRUS, 1952–1954, vol. 13, part 1: *Indochina,* ed. Neil H. Peterson (GPO, 1982)
                FRUS, 1958–1960, vol. 1: *Vietnam,* ed. Edward C. Keefer and David W.
                    Mabon (GPO, 1986)
                FRUS, 1961–1963, vol. 1: *Vietnam, 1961,* ed. Ronald D. Landa and Charles S.
                    Sampson (GPO, 1988)
                FRUS, 1961–1963, vol. 2: *Vietnam, 1962,* ed. John P. Glennon, David M.
                    Baehler, and Charles S. Sampson (GPO, 1990)
                FRUS, 1961–1963, vol. 3: *Vietnam, January–August, 1963,* ed. Edward C. Keefer
                    and Louis J. Smith (GPO, 1991)
                FRUS, 1961–1963, vol. 4: *Vietnam, August–December, 1963,* ed. Edward C.
                    Keefer (GPO, 1991)
                FRUS, 1961–1963, vol. 8: *National Security Policy,* ed. David W. Mabon (GPO,
                    1996)
                FRUS, 1964–1968, vol. 1: *Vietnam, 1964,* ed. Edward C. Keefer and Charles S.
                    Sampson (GPO, 1992)
JFKL   John F. Kennedy Library, Boston, MA
JFK Papers Papers of President Kennedy
LBJL   Lyndon B. Johnson Library, Austin, TX

NA, UK	National Archives (UK)
NARA	National Archives and Records Administration
NYT	*New York Times*
OSDHO	Office of the Secretary of Defense Historical Office
Pentagon	
Papers	*The Pentagon Papers: The Defense Department History of United States Decision-making on Vietnam,* Gravel ed., 5 vols. (Beacon Press, 1971)
PPP:JFK	*Public Papers of the Presidents of the United States: John F. Kennedy,* 3 vols. (U.S. Government Printing Office, 1962–1964); vol. 1: 1961; vol. 2: 1962; vol. 3: 1963
PPP:LBJ	*Public Papers of the Presidents of the United States: Lyndon B. Johnson* (U.S. Government Printing Office, 1965); 1963–1964, 2 vols.
PRDE	*Presidential Recordings Digital Edition,* University of Virginia
US-VR	Department of Defense, *United States-Vietnam Relations, 1945–1967* (U.S. Government Printing Office, 1971); Books 11 and 12
WP	*Washington Post*
WSJ	*Wall Street Journal*

Introduction

1. For accounts of Kennedy and Vietnam, see Howard Jones, *Death of a Generation: How the Assassinations of Diem and JFK Prolonged the Vietnam War* (Oxford University Press, 2003); David Kaiser, *American Tragedy: Kennedy, Johnson, and the Origins of the Vietnam War* (Belknap Press of Harvard University Press, 2000); Fredrik Logevall, *Choosing War: The Lost Chance for Peace and the Escalation of War in Vietnam* (University of California Press, 1999); John M. Newman, *JFK and Vietnam: Deception, Intrigue, and the Struggle for Power* (Warner Books, 1992); William J. Rust, *Kennedy in Vietnam* (Scribner, 1985).

2. Gary R. Hess, *Vietnam: Explaining America's Lost War* (Blackwell, 2009), 57–64; Fredrik Logevall, "Vietnam and the Question of What Might Have Been," in *Kennedy: The New Frontier Revisited,* ed. Mark J. White, 19–62 (New York University Press, 1998); Marc Trachtenberg, "Kennedy, Vietnam, and Audience Costs," *H-Diplo/ISSF Forum on "Audience Costs and the Vietnam War,"* 7 November 2014, https://issforum.org/ISSF/PDF/ISSF-Forum-3.pdf; Andrew Preston, "Vietnam," in *A Companion to John F. Kennedy,* ed. Marc J. Selverstone (Wiley-Blackwell, 2014), 280–284.

3. "Rejectionist" works include George C. Herring, *America's Longest War: The United States and Vietnam, 1950–1975* (McGraw-Hill, 1979, 2018); Marilyn B. Young, *The Vietnam Wars, 1945–1990* (HarperCollins, 1991); Noam Chomsky, *Rethinking Camelot: JFK, the Vietnam War, and U.S. Political Culture* (Black Rose Books, 1993); Robert D. Schulzinger, *A Time for War: The United States and Vietnam, 1941–1975* (Oxford University Press, 1997); and John Prados, *Vietnam: The History of an Unwinnable War* (University Press of Kansas, 2009). "Exceptionalist" monographs include Rust, *Kennedy in Vietnam;* Logevall, *Choosing War;* Kaiser, *American Tragedy;* Jones, *Death of a*

Generation; and Gareth Porter, *Perils of Dominance: Imbalance of Power and the Road to War in Vietnam* (University of California Press, 2005). Preston notes that Lawrence Freedman is agnostic in *Kennedy's War: Berlin, Cuba, Laos, and Vietnam* (Oxford University Press, 2000).

4. In Preston's telling, the more presumptuous works include Arthur M. Schlesinger Jr., *Robert Kennedy and His Times* (Houghton Mifflin, 1978); and James K. Galbraith, "Exit Strategy," *Boston Review* (October / November 2003), 29–34; while the more radical include Newman, *JFK and Vietnam;* Fletcher Prouty, *JFK: The CIA, Vietnam, and the Plot to Assassinate John F. Kennedy* (Carol, 1992); and Peter Dale Scott, *Deep Politics and the Death of JFK* (University of California Press, 2003).

5. Brian VanDeMark also makes extensive use of Kennedy's White House tapes in *Road to Disaster: A New History of America's Descent into Vietnam* (HarperCollins, 2018).

6. Fredrik Logevall, *JFK: Coming of Age in the American Century* (Random House, 2020).

7. Key works on containment include John Lewis Gaddis, *Strategies of Containment: A Critical Appraisal of Postwar American National Security Policy* (Oxford University Press, 1982, rev. 2005); Melvyn P. Leffler, *A Preponderance of Power: National Security, the Truman Administration, and the Cold War* (Stanford University Press, 1992).

8. Robert J. McMahon, *The Limits of Empire: The United States and Southeast Asia since World War II* (Columbia University Press, 1999); Odd Arne Westad, *The Global Cold War: Third World Interventions and the Making of Our Times* (Cambridge University Press, 2005).

9. On the emergence of that framework, see Marc J. Selverstone, *Constructing the Monolith: The United States, Great Britain, and International Communism, 1945–1950* (Harvard University Press, 2009).

10. See Paul Thomas Chamberlin, *The Cold War's Killing Fields: Rethinking the Long Peace* (Harper, 2018), 1–19.

11. Jack Snyder, "Introduction," in *Dominoes and Bandwagons: Strategic Beliefs and Great Power Competition in the Eurasian Rimland,* ed. Robert Jervis and Jack Snyder, 3 (Oxford University Press, 1991); see also Frank Ninkovich, *Modernity and Power: A History of the Domino Theory in the Twentieth Century* (University of Chicago Press, 1994).

12. John Lewis Gaddis, *Surprise, Security, and the American Experience* (Harvard University Press, 2004).

13. Andrew Preston, "Monsters Everywhere: A Genealogy of National Security," *Diplomatic History* 38 (June 2014), 3:477–500; Andrew Preston, "John F. Kennedy and Lyndon B. Johnson," in *Mental Maps in the Early Cold War Era, 1945–68,* ed. Steven Casey and Jonathan Wright, 261–280 (Palgrave Macmillan, 2011).

14. Robert J. McMahon, "Credibility and World Power: Exploring the Psychological Dimension in Postwar American Diplomacy," *Diplomatic History* 15 (Fall 1991), 4:455, 457.

15. Christopher J. Fettweis, "Credibility and the War on Terror," *Political Science Quarterly* 122 (2007–2008), 4:622; McMahon, "Credibility," 470–471. See also Daryl G. Press, *Calculating Credibility: How Leaders Assess Military Threats* (Cornell University Press, 2005).

16. Gaddis, *Strategies of Containment*, 90.

17. Hal Brands, Eric S. Edelman, and Thomas G. Mahnken, *Credibility Matters: Strengthening American Deterrence in an Age of Geopolitical Turmoil* (Center for Strategic and Budgetary Assessments, 2018), 3–4.

18. Robert Dean, *Imperial Brotherhood: Gender and the Making of Cold War Foreign Policy* (University of Massachusetts Press, 2002).

19. Gaddis, *Strategies of Containment*, 211.

20. Gaddis, *Strategies of Containment*, 212–231; Freedman, *Kennedy's Wars*, 92–111; Marc Selverstone, "John F. Kennedy and the Lessons of First-Year Stumbles," in *Crucible: The President's First Year,* ed. Michael Nelson, Jeffrey L. Chidester, and Stefanie Georgakis Abbott, 102 (University of Virginia Press, 2018). For Kennedy's warning, see, for instance, "Special Message to the Congress on the Defense Budget, 28 March 1961, *PPP:JFK,* 1961:236, Doc. 99.

21. For Kennedy's approach to foreign policy during his Senate years, see Thomas Oliphant and Curtis Willkie, *Road to Camelot: Inside JFK's Five-Year Campaign* (Simon and Schuster, 2017), 84–99; Michael O'Brien, *John F. Kennedy: A Biography* (St. Martin's, 2005), 351–363.

22. See David Callahan, *Dangerous Capabilities: Paul Nitze and the Cold War* (Harper-Collins, 1990), 186–189.

23. "Report of Senator Kennedy's National Security Policy Committee" (hereafter "Nitze Report")," undated, JFK Papers, Pre-Presidential Papers, Transition Files, Task Force Reports 1960, Box 1077, Report of Nitze Panel, JFKL.

24. Schlesinger, *Thousand Days,* 340–342. For an overview of writing on Kennedy and counterinsurgency, see Jeff Woods, "Brushfire Wars," in Selverstone, *Companion to John F. Kennedy,* 436–457.

25. See Douglas S. Blaufarb, *The Counterinsurgency Era: U.S. Doctrine and Performance* (Free Press, 1977); William Rosenau, "The Kennedy Administration, U.S. Foreign Internal Security Assistance, and the Challenge of 'Subterranean War,' 1961–63," *Small Wars & Counterinsurgencies* 14 (2003), 3:65–99.

26. For overviews of the literature, see Daniel Immerwahr, "Modernization and Development in U.S. Foreign Relations," *Passport: The Society for Historians of American Foreign Relations Review* (September 2012), 22–25; Amada McVety, "JFK and Modernization Theory," in *The Cambridge Companion to John F. Kennedy,* ed. Andrew Hoberek, 103–117 (Cambridge University Press, 2015).

27. Michael E. Latham, *The Right Kind of Revolution: Modernization, Development, and U.S. Foreign Policy from the Cold War to the Present* (Cornell University Press, 2011),

58. See also Nick Cullather, *The Hungry World: America's Cold War Battle against Poverty in Asia* (Harvard University Press, 2010); Daniel Immerwahr, *Thinking Small: The United States and the Lure of Community Development* (Harvard University Press, 2015).

28. Walt W. Rostow, "The Liberal-Conservative Balance, the Inaugural, and the Program," undated, JFK Papers, Pre-Presidential Papers, Transition Files, Task Force Reports 1960, Box 1117, Folder Miscellaneous Reports, JFKL.

29. "Memorandum on a New Organization for the U.S. Foreign Aid Program," 15 November 1960, JFK Papers, Pre-Presidential Papers, Transition Files, Task Force Reports 1960, Box 1074, Folder Foreign Aid—Memorandum on a New Organization for the U.S. Foreign Aid Program, JFKL.

30. See Logevall, *JFK*, 327–358, 465, 475–476, 575–576.

31. Stein Tønnesson, *The Vietnamese Revolution of 1945: Roosevelt, Ho Chi Minh, and de Gaulle in a World at War* (International Peace Research Institute, 1991); David G. Marr, *Vietnam 1945: The Quest for Power* (University of California Press, 1995).

32. For an overview of this period, see Fredrik Logevall, *Embers of War: The Fall of an Empire and the Making of America's Vietnam* (Random House, 2012).

33. For background on this period, see Pierre Asselin, *Vietnam's American War: A History* (Cambridge University Press, 2018), 81–94; Jessica M. Chapman, *Cauldron of Resistance: Ngo Dinh Diem, the United States, and 1950s Southern Vietnam* (Cornell University Press, 2013).

34. See Seth Jacobs, *Cold War Mandarin: Ngo Dinh Diem and the Origins of America's War in Vietnam, 1950–1963* (Rowman and Littlefield, 2006), 18–33; Edward Miller, *Misalliance: Ngo Dinh Diem, the United States, and the Fate of South Vietnam* (Harvard University Press, 2013), 49–53.

35. James T. Fisher, "The Second Catholic President: Ngo Dinh Diem, John F. Kennedy, and the Vietnam Lobby, 1954–1963," *U.S. Catholic Historian* 15 (Summer 1997), 3:129–130.

36. For Soviet and Chinese support, see Ilya V. Gaiduk, *Confronting Vietnam: Soviet Policy toward the Indochina Conflict, 1954–1963* (Stanford University Press, 2003), 54–68; Qiang Zhai, *China and the Vietnam Wars, 1950–1975* (University of North Carolina Press, 2000), 65–91. For U.S. policy, see Chapman, *Cauldron of Resistance;* Miller, *Misalliance;* Jessica Elkind, *Aid under Fire: Nation Building and the Vietnam War* (University Press of Kentucky, 2016).

37. The Ngos characterized all critics as Communists and thus as traitors, labeling them "Viet Cong" as early as 1956; the Americans later adopted the term as referents for the NLF and PLAF. Chapman, *Cauldron of Resistance,* 175.

38. John Osborne, "The Tough Miracle Man of Vietnam," *Life,* 13 May 1957, 156.

39. Logevall, *Embers of War,* xi–xv, 286–287.

40. Robert Dallek, *An Unfinished Life: John F. Kennedy, 1917–1963* (Little Brown, 2003), 186–187.

41. See Oliphant and Wilkie, *Road to Camelot,* 90–99.

42. National Archives and Records Administration, "Vietnam War U.S. Military Fatal Casualties Statistics," https://www.archives.gov/research/military/vietnam-war/casualty-statistics.

43. William J. Rust, *Before the Quagmire: American Intervention in Laos, 1954–1961* (University Press of Kentucky, 2012); William I. Hitchcock, *The Age of Eisenhower: America and the World in the 1950s* (Simon and Schuster, 2018), 500–503.

44. See Seth Jacobs, "'No Place to Fight a War': Laos and the Evolution of U.S. Policy toward Vietnam, 1954–1963," in *Making Sense of the Vietnam Wars: Local, National, and Transnational Perspectives,* ed. Mark Philip Bradley and Marilyn B. Young, 45–66 (Oxford University Press, 2008); William J. Rust, *So Much to Lose: John F. Kennedy and American Policy in Laos* (University Press of Kentucky, 2014); and Edmund F. Wehrle, "'A Good, Bad Deal': John F. Kennedy, W. Averell Harriman, and the Neutralization of Laos, 1961–1962," *Pacific Historical Review* 67 (August 1998), 3:349–377.

45. "Vietnam Hindsight, Part 1: How It Began," NBC News White Paper, 21 December 1971.

46. Robert Rakove, *Kennedy, Johnson, and the Nonaligned World* (Cambridge University Press, 2013), 215–216.

47. See, for instance, Philip E. Tetlock and Aaron Belkin, *Counterfactual Thought Experiments in World Politics* (Princeton University Press, 1996); Niall Ferguson, *Virtual History* (Picador, 1997); James G. Blight, Janet M. Lang, and David A. Welch, *Virtual JFK: Vietnam if Kennedy Had Lived* (Rowman and Littlefield, 2009); Jeff Greenfield, *Then Everything Changed: Stunning Alternate Histories of American Politics: JFK, RFK, Carter, Ford, Reagan* (G. P. Putnam's Sons, 2011).

48. See Michael V. Forrestal Oral History, 3 November 1969, LBJL, 6–7; Ted Sorensen, *Counselor: A Life at the Edge of History* (Harper, 2009), 359.

49. Edwin O. Guthman and Jeffrey Shulman, eds., *Robert Kennedy: In His Own Words: The Unpublished Recollections of the Kennedy Years* (Bantam, 1988), 394–395.

1. Assumption

1. "Inaugural Address," 20 January 1961, *PPP:JFK,* 1961:2, Doc. 1.

2. Lansdale to Gates, "Vietnam," 17 January 1961, *US-VR,* 11:3. For background, see Max Boot, *The Road Not Taken: Edward Lansdale and the American Tragedy in Vietnam* (Liveright, 2018), 338–357.

3. Bundy to McNamara, Rusk, and Dulles, 27 January 1961, JFK Papers, NSF, Box 193, Vietnam General, 1/61–3/61, JFKL; Rostow to Bundy, 30 January 1961, *FRUS, 1961–1963,* vol. 1: *Vietnam, 1961,* 16, Doc. 4. Although Eisenhower had referenced the challenges in South Vietnam, he did so in the context of discussing Laos. Richard Reeves, *President Kennedy: Profile of Power* (Simon and Schuster, 1993), 32, 46.

4. William Taubman, *Khrushchev: The Man and His Era* (W. W. Norton, 2003), 487.

5. Rostow to Bundy, 30 January 1961, 1:16–19.

6. JFK to Rusk and McNamara, 30 January 1961, *US-VR*, 11:13.

7. NSAM 2, 3 February 1961, *US-VR*, 11:17.

8. "Annual Message to the Congress on the State of the Union," 30 January 1961, *PPP:JFK* 1961:19–28, Doc. 11.

9. See Philip Nash, "Bear *Any* Burden? John F. Kennedy and Nuclear Weapons," in *Cold War Statesmen Confront the Bomb: Nuclear Diplomacy since 1945,* ed. John Lewis Gaddis, Philip Gordon, Ernest May, and Jonathan Rosenberg, 120–140 (Oxford University Press, 1999).

10. "The Safety of Us All," *Time,* 31 March 1961, 9. See Seth Jacobs, "'No Place to Fight a War': Laos and the Evolution of U.S. Policy toward Vietnam, 1954–1963," in *Making Sense of the Vietnam Wars: Local, National, and Transnational Perspectives,* ed. Mark Philip Bradley and Marilyn B. Young, 45–66 (Oxford University Press, 2008).

11. "Asia: An Offer & a Warning," *Time,* 17 March 1961, 20.

12. Wallace Carroll, "U.S. Ready to Face All Risks to Bar Red Rule of Laos," *NYT,* 21 March 1961, 1.

13. "The President's News Conference of March 23, 1961," *PPP:JFK,* 1961:214, Doc. 92.

14. NIE 50–61, 28 March 1961, *FRUS, 1961–1963,* 1:60, Doc. 22.

15. See, for instance, PPS 51, 29 March 1949, *FRUS, 1949:* vol. 7, part 2: *The Far East and Australia,* 2:1129–1133; Paper Prepared in the Department of State, 27 March 1952, *FRUS, 1952–1954,* vol. 13, part 1: *Indochina,* 1:83–84; NCS 124/2, and Enclosure, 25 June 1952, *FRUS, 1952–1954,* vol. 12, part 1: *East Asia and the Pacific,* 1:127.

16. "The President's News Conference of April 21, 1961," *PPP:JFK,* 1961:313, Doc. 139; Howard Jones, *The Bay of Pigs* (Oxford University Press, 2010), 132.

17. Bundy to Battle, 14 March 1961, JFK Papers, NSF, Box 193, Vietnam, General, 1/61–3/61, JFKL; see also Rusk to Saigon, 1115, 1 March 1961, *FRUS, 1961–1963,* 1:40–42, Doc. 16.

18. Howard Jones, *Death of a Generation: How the Assassinations of Diem and JFK Prolonged the Vietnam War* (Oxford University Press, 2003), 40–48; Lawrence Freedman, *Kennedy's Wars: Berlin, Cuba, Laos, and Vietnam* (Oxford University Press, 2003), 310–311.

19. Bundy to Rusk, NSAM 52, 11 May 1961, *FRUS, 1961–1963,* 1:132–134, Doc. 52.

20. Gilpatric to LBJ, 6 May 1961, "Program for South Viet Nam," and attachment, "U.S. Military Forces in South Viet Nam," JFK Papers, NSF, Box 193, Vietnam, General, 4/24/61, McGarr Presentation, JFKL.

21. Editorial Note, *FRUS, 1961–1963,* 1:88, Doc. 40; see also "A Program of Action to Prevent Communist Domination of South Vietnam," 26 April 1961, *US-VR,* 11:42–57.

22. Evans to O'Donnell, 16 June 1959, *FRUS, 1958–1960,* vol. 1: *Vietnam,* 209–211, Doc. 80. See also Kathryn C. Statler, *Replacing France: The Origins of American Intervention in Vietnam* (University Press of Kentucky, 2007).

23. Durbrow to Rusk, G-320, 7 February 1961, JFK Papers, NSF, Box 193, Vietnam, General, 1/61–3/61, JFKL.

24. Memorandum of State–JCS Meeting, 14 April 1961, *FRUS, 1961–1963,* 1:70–71, Doc. 29.

25. Komer to Bundy and Rostow, 4 May 1961, *FRUS, 1961–1963,* 1:123–124, Doc. 44.

26. Memorandum for the Record, "5 May 1961 Meeting at State," *US-VR,* 11:67–68.

27. "Annexes to a Program of Action for South Vietnam," 8 May 1961, Annex 2, *US-VR,* 11:99.

28. McGarr to Felt, 6 May 1961, *FRUS, 1961–1963,* 1:89, Doc. 41.

29. Lemnitzer to JCS, 8 May 1961, *FRUS, 1961–1963,* 1:127–128, Doc. 47.

30. McGarr to Felt, 10 May 1961, *FRUS, 1961–1963,* 1:129, Doc. 50.

31. Zach Fredman, "'The Specter of an Expansionist China': Kennedy Administration Assessments of Chinese Intentions in Vietnam," *Diplomatic History* 38 (January 2014), 1:111–136; Noam Kochavi, "Opportunities Lost? Kennedy, China and Vietnam," in *Behind the Bamboo Curtain: China, Vietnam, and the World beyond Asia,* ed. Priscilla Roberts, 127–152 (Stanford University Press, 2006).

32. Komer to Rostow, 28 April 1961, *FRUS, 1961–1963,* 1:86, Doc. 38.

33. Secretary Rusk's News Conference of May 4, *Department of State Bulletin* 44 (22 May 1961), 1143:716, 763.

34. "The President's News Conference of May 5," *PPP:JFK,* 1961:359, Doc. 171.

35. Presidential Task Force Program, 22 April 1961, *FRUS, 1961–1963,* 1:77, Doc. 32.

36. Lansdale to Gilpatric, "U.S. Combat Forces for Vietnam," 18 May 1961, *US-VR,* 11:157–158; Nolting to State, 1740, 13 May 1961, *FRUS, 1961–1963,* 1:138n6, Doc. 54.

37. LBJ to JFK, "Mission to Southeast Asia, India and Pakistan," 23 May 1961, *US-VR,* 11:159–166; LBJ Paper, undated, *FRUS, 1961–1963,* 1:149–151, Doc. 59.

38. Report by the Vice President, undated, *FRUS, 1961–1963,* 1:152–157, Doc. 60.

39. "Special Message to the Congress on Urgent National Needs," 25 May 1961, *PPP:JFK,* 1961:397, Doc. 205.

40. See Michael Beschloss, *The Crisis Years: Kennedy and Khrushchev, 1960–1963* (HarperCollins, 1991), 193–231; Freedman, *Kennedy's Wars,* 51–65.

41. Stanley Karnow, *Vietnam: A History* (Penguin, 1983, 1997), 265.

42. Komer to Rostow, 20 July 1961, *FRUS, 1961–1963,* 1:234–236, Doc. 100.

43. Rostow to JFK, 21 June 1961, JFK Papers, NSF, Box 193A, Vietnam, General, 6/19/61–6/30/61, JFKL.

44. Freedman, *Kennedy's Wars,* 58–75; Beschloss, *Crisis Years,* 266–286.

45. Rusk to Saigon, 1591, 28 June 1961, *FRUS, 1961–1963,* 1:187–188, Doc. 77.

46. Nolting to State, 70, 14 July 1961, *FRUS, 1961–1963,* 1:218–219, Doc. 92.

47. See Jones, *Death of a Generation,* 71–81; NSAM 65, 11 August 1962, *US-VR,* 11:241–244.

48. Rusk to McNamara, 4 February 1961, enclosure, *FRUS, 1961–1963*, vol. 8: *National Security Policy*, 8:25–26, Doc. 10; Notes for the President, 23 February 1961, Papers of Bromley K. Smith, Box 22, NSC Meetings, 1961 [3 of 3], JFKL.

49. W. W. Rostow, "Guerrilla Warfare in the Underdeveloped Areas," in *Department of State Bulletin* 45, 7 August 1961, 233–238; Roger Hilsman, "Counter-Insurgency: Internal War: The New Communist Tactic," *Marine Corps Gazette* 47 (January 1963), 1:50–54; Douglas S. Blaufarb, *The Counterinsurgency Era: U.S. Doctrine and Performance, 1950 to the Present* (Free Press, 1977), 57–62.

50. Sharon Weinberger, *The Imagineers of War: The Untold History of DARPA, the Pentagon Agency That Changed the World* (Knopf, 2017), 68–85, 125–134; Annie Jacobson, *The Pentagon's Brain: An Uncensored History of DARPA, America's Top Secret Military Research Agency* (Little, Brown, 2015), 117–159.

51. "Special Message to the Congress on Urgent National Needs," 401.

52. "Radio and Television Report to the American People on the Berlin Crisis," 25 July 1961, *PPP:JFK*, 1961:533–540, Doc. 302.

53. Steeves to JFK, 28 July 1961, *FRUS, 1961–1963*, 1:250, Doc. 108; Memorandum of a Discussion, 28 July 1961, *FRUS, 1961–1963*, 1:252–256, Doc. 109.

54. Rostow to JFK, "Southeast Asia, 4 August 1961," Weekend Papers, President's Weekend Reading, Box 1, Weekend Reading, 8/4/61–8/6/61, JFKL.

55. Task Force on Viet-Nam, "Minutes of Meeting on June 26, 1961," JFK Papers, NSF, Box 193A, Vietnam, General, 6/19/61–6/30/61, JFKL.

56. McGarr, Aide Memoire for President Diem, 2 August 1961, *US-VR*, 11:230–231; Johnson to Rostow, 7 July 1961, JFK Papers, NSF, Box 193A, Vietnam, General, 7/5/61–7/13/61, JFKL.

57. "Night War in the Jungle," *Time*, 29 September 1961, 33.

58. Johnson, "Summary of Briefing by Brigadier General William H. Craig," 18 September 1961, Weekend Papers, President's Weekend Reading, Box 2, Weekend Reading, 9/27/61–9/29/61, JFKL.

59. Nolting to State, 421, 1 October 1961, *FRUS, 1961–1963*, 1:316–317, Doc. 142.

60. "Status Report on the Presidential Program for Viet-Nam as of September 29, 1961," JFK Papers, NSF, Box 195A, Vietnam, General, Vietnam Status Reports, JFKL.

61. Bundy to JFK, 7 October 1961, Weekend Papers, President's Weekend Reading, Box 2, Weekend Reading, 10/7/61, JFKL; Rostow to JFK, 5 October 1961, JFK Papers, NSF, Subjects, Box 194, Vietnam, General, 10/4/61–10/9/61, JFKL.

62. W. P. Bundy to McNamara, 10 October 1961, *US-VR*, 11:312.

63. Lemnitzer to McNamara, "Planning for Southeast Asia (U)," JCSM-704–61, 5 October 1961, *US-VR*, 11:295–296; Anderson Diary Entry, 9 October 1961, *FRUS, 1961–1963*, 1:328, Doc. 148.

64. "The President's News Conference of October 11, 1961," *PPP:JFK*, 1961:656, 660, Doc. 415; see also Maxwell D. Taylor, *Swords and Plowshares* (Norton, 1972), 221–223.

65. "Taylor to Saigon," *NYT*, 12 October 1961, 28; UPI, "U.S. to Increase Aid to Vietnamese Army," *NYT*, 3 October 1961, 5; Joseph Alsop, "The Hardly Noticed Crisis," *WP*, 11 October 1961, A19.

66. Nolting to Rusk, 457, 9 October 1961; see also Rusk to Saigon, 408, 10 October 1961; both in JFK Papers, NSF, Box 194, Vietnam, General, 10/4/61–10/9/61, JFKL.

67. Nolting to Rusk, 488, 13 October 1961, JFK Papers, NSF, Box 194, Vietnam, General, 10/4/61–10/9/61, JFKL.

68. Lemnitzer to Felt, 13 October 1961, *FRUS, 1961–1963*, 1:362, Doc. 163; Carroll Kilpatrick, "Gen. Taylor Is Going to South Viet-Nam," *WP*, 12 October 1961, A1; Rutherford Poats, "Kennedy Weighing Sending Troops to Viet-Nam," *WP*, 14 October 1961, A2; Jones, *Death of a Generation*, 91.

69. JFK to Taylor, 13 October 1961, *FRUS, 1961–1963*, 1:345, Doc. 157; Taylor, *Swords and Plowshares*, 225–226.

70. Felt to JCS, "Pros and Cons of Introducing U.S. Combat Forces into South Vietnam," 20 October 1961, JFK Papers, NSF, Box 194A, Vietnam, General, 10/20/61–10/26/61, JFKL.

71. Bowles to Rusk, 5 October 1961, *FRUS, 1961–1963*, 1:322–325, Doc. 145.

72. Galbraith to JFK, 9 October 1961, Weekend Papers, President's Weekend Reading, Box 2, Weekend Reading, 10/13/61, JFKL.

73. White to JFK, 11 October 1961, JFK Papers, NSF, Box 128, Vietnam General, 1960–61, JFKL.

74. Nolting to State, 495, 16 October 1961, *FRUS, 1961–1963*, 1:383–386, Doc. 171.

75. Nolting to State, 508, 18 October 1961, *FRUS, 1961–1963*, 1:391–392, Doc. 174; Lansdale to Taylor, 21 October, *FRUS, 1961–1963*, 1:411–416, Doc. 182.

76. Nolting to Rusk, A-145, 2 November 1961, JFK Papers, NSF, Box 194A, Vietnam, General, 11/1/61–11/2/61, JFKL.

77. Rostow to Taylor, 16 October 1961, *FRUS, 1961–1963*, 1:381–382, Doc. 170.

78. DOD and Other Agency Estimates, 15 October 1961, *FRUS, 1961–1963*, 1:376–377, Doc. 168.

79. Harriman to Schlesinger, 17 October 1961, JFK Papers, NSF, Box 128A, Vietnam, Security, 1961, JFKL.

80. Robert Trumbull, "500,000 Go Hungry as South Vietnam Is Hit by Floods," *NYT*, 16 October 1961, 1.

81. Nolting to Rusk, 20 October 1961, *FRUS, 1961–1963*, 1:406–407, Doc. 180.

82. McGarr to Felt, 23 October 1961, *FRUS, 1961–1963*, 1:424–425, Doc. 188; McGarr to Lemnitzer, SGN 747, 24 October 1961, JFK Papers, NSF, Box 194A, Vietnam, General, 10/20/61–10/26/61, JFKL.

83. CNO to Felt and JCS, 240253Z, 24 October 1961, JFK Papers, NSF, Box 194A, Vietnam, General, 10/20/61–10/26/61, JFKL.

84. Wood to U. A. Johnson, *FRUS, 1961–1963*, 1:437, Doc. 195.

85. Johnson to Bundy, 31 October 1961, *FRUS, 1961–1963*, 1:460, Doc. 202.

86. Johnson to Bundy, "Planning for Vietnam," 1 November 1961, JFK Papers, NSF, Box 194A, Vietnam, General, 11/1/61–11/2/61, JFKL.

87. Taylor to JFK, BAGIO 0006, 1 November 1961, *US-VR*, 11:338.

88. Taylor to Rusk and U. A. Johnson, 25 October 1961, *FRUS, 1961–1963*, 1:430, Doc. 191.

89. Taylor to U. A. Johnson, 25 October 1961, *FRUS, 1961–1963*, 1:427, Doc. 190.

90. Taylor to JFK, BAGIO 0006, 1 November 1961; Nolting to Rusk, 31 October 1961, *FRUS, 1961–1963*, 1:456–457, Doc. 201.

91. Taylor to JFK, BAGIO 0005, 1 November 1961, *US-VR*, 11:332.

92. Bundy to Taylor, 28 October 1961, *FRUS, 1961–1963*, 1:443, Doc. 198.

93. Mansfield to JFK, 2 November 1961, *FRUS, 1961–1963*, 1:467, 470, Doc. 207.

94. Rusk to State, 1 November 1961, *FRUS, 1961–1963*, 1:464, Doc. 204.

95. Cottrell to Taylor, Appendix B, 27 October 1961, *FRUS, 1961–1963*, 1:505–506, Doc. 210.

96. Galbraith to JFK, 3 November 1961, *FRUS, 1961–1963*, 1:474–476, Doc. 209; Richard Parker, *John Kenneth Galbraith: His Life, His Politics, His Economics* (Farrar, Straus and Giroux, 2005), 362–377; for Bowles, see Editorial Note, *FRUS, 1961–1963*, 1:540–541, Doc. 215.

97. Taylor to JFK, 3 November 1961, *FRUS, 1961–1963*, 1:477–479, Doc. 210.

98. Taylor Paper, Attachment 1, *FRUS, 1961–1963*, 1:479–481.

99. Taylor Paper, Attachment 2, *FRUS, 1961–1963*, 1:491, 502.

100. McNamara Notes, 6 November 1961, *FRUS, 1961–1963*, 1:543–544, Doc. 217.

101. McNamara Draft Memorandum, 5 November 1961, *FRUS, 1961–1963*, 1:539, Doc. 214; Rusk Draft Memorandum, 7 November 1961, *FRUS, 1961–1963*, 1:551, Doc. 222.

102. George W. Ball, *The Past Has Another Pattern: Memoirs* (Norton, 1982), 366–367.

103. Memcon, 6 November 1961, *FRUS, 1961–1963*, 1:532–534, Doc. 211; Arthur M. Schlesinger Jr., *A Thousand Days: John F. Kennedy in the White House* (Houghton Mifflin, 1965), 547.

104. McNamara Draft Memorandum, 5 November 1961, *FRUS, 1961–1963*, 1:538–540, Doc. 214.

105. Memorandum for the President, 11 November 1961, *US-VR*, 11:359–367.

106. Meeting Notes, 11 November 1961, *FRUS, 1961–1963*, 1:577, Doc. 236.

107. Meeting Notes, 11 November 1961, *FRUS, 1961–1963*, 1:577–578, Doc. 236; Memorandum for the President, *US-VR*, 11:362–363.

108. Fredrik Logevall, *Choosing War: The Lost Chance for Peace and the Escalation of War in Vietnam* (University of California Press, 1999), 25–29.

109. Memcon, 13 November 1961, *FRUS, 1961–1963*, 1:584, Doc. 241; Memcon, 13 November 1961, *FRUS, 1961–1963*, 1:587, Doc. 243.

110. Logevall, *Choosing War,* 12–20.

111. Rusk to Nolting, 6989, 14 November 1961, Sorensen Papers, 5/9/61–10/1/63, Box 55, JFKL.

112. McNamara to Lemnitzer, 13 November 1961, *FRUS, 1961–1963,* 1:590, Doc. 246. See also Parker, *Galbraith,* 371.

113. Parker, *Galbraith,* 369–372.

114. See Rusk-U. A. Johnson Telcon, 13 November 1961, *FRUS, 1961–1963,* 1:586, Doc. 242. See also Parker, *Galbraith,* 374.

115. See Rusk-Taylor Telcon, 13 November 1961, *FRUS, 1961–1963,* 1:588, Doc. 244.

116. Rostow to JFK, "Comments on JKG's Attached Memorandum," 13 November 1961, JFK Papers, NSF, Box 195, Vietnam, General, 11/11/61–11/13/61, JFKL; Johnson to Rostow, 14 November 1961, *FRUS, 1961–1963,* 1: 598–599, Doc. 250.

117. See Rusk to Nolting, 6990, 14 November 1961, Sorensen Papers, 5/9/61–10/1/63, Box 55, JFKL.

118. Rostow to JFK, 14 November 1961, *FRUS, 1961–1963,* 1:602–603, Doc. 251.

119. Bundy to JFK, 15 November 1961, *FRUS, 1961–1963,* 1:605, Doc. 253.

120. NSC Notes, 15 November 1961, *FRUS, 1961–1963,* 1:607–610, Doc. 254.

121. Bundy to JFK, 15 November 1961, *FRUS, 1961–1963,* 1:612–614, Doc. 256.

122. Galbraith to JFK, 20 November 1961, *US-VR,* 11:406.

123. Galbraith to JFK, 21 November 1961, *US-VR,* 11:417.

124. Rusk to Galbraith, 28 November 1961, *FRUS, 1961–1963,* 1:680–681, Doc. 290. Rusk did suggest that Indian foreign minister Manilal Jagdish Desai convey Washington's views to Hanoi's representative. Rostow to JFK, 24 November 1961, *FRUS, 1961–1963,* 1:662, Doc. 274.

125. Bundy to JFK, "Miscellaneous Papers for Weekend Reading," 22 November 1961, Weekend Papers, President's Weekend Reading, Box 3, Weekend Reading, 11/22/61–11/26/61, JFKL; NSAM 111, 22 November 1961, *FRUS, 1961–1963,* 1:656–657, Doc. 272.

126. Bundy to JFK, 15 November 1961, *FRUS, 1961–1963,* 1:612–614, Doc. 256. Kennedy approved the changes Bundy proposed except for replacing Nolting in Saigon with George McGhee. For accounts of those changes, see Schlesinger, *Thousand Days,* 437–447; and Sorensen, *Kennedy,* 287–290.

127. Chayes to Rusk, and Tab A, 16 November 1961, *FRUS, 1961–1963,* 1:629–631, Doc. 261.

128. NSAM 104, 13 October 1961, *US-VR,* 11:328.

129. "Status Report on the Presidential Program for Viet-Nam as of October 27, 1961," JFK Papers, NSF, Box 195A, Vietnam, General, Vietnam Status Reports, JFKL.

130. "Status Report on the Instructions to Ambassador Nolting (Deptel 619 of November 15)," 20 November 1961, JFK Papers, NSF, Box 195, Vietnam, General, 11/1/61–11/16/61, Memos and Reports, JFKL.

131. Nolting to Rusk, 720, 28 November 1961, JFK Papers, NSF, Box 195, Vietnam, General, 11/26/61–11/28/61, JFKL.

132. Rusk Circular, 1981, 7 December 1961, JFK Papers, NSF, Box 195A, Vietnam, General, 12/6/61–12/7/61, JFKL; William C. Gibbons, *The U.S. Government and the Vietnam War: Executive and Legislative Roles and Relationships*, part 2: *1961–1964* (Princeton University Press, 1986), 103; "Editorial Note," *FRUS, 1961–1963,* 1:725, Doc. 315.

133. Parker to Lemnitzer, 18 December 1961, *FRUS, 1961–1963,* 1:740, Doc. 325.

134. Martin to Cottrell, 18 December 1961, *FRUS, 1961–1963,* 1:742, Doc. 326.

135. Record of Secretary of Defense Conference, 16, December 1961, Box 235, OSDHO.

136. See CIA Information Report, 29 November 1961, *FRUS, 1961–1963,* 1:692–693, Doc. 295.

137. Trueheart to Rusk, 822, 19 December 1961, JFK Papers, NSF, Box 195A, Vietnam, General, 12/19/61–12/23/61, JFKL.

138. Trueheart to Rusk, 813, 16 December 1961, JFK Papers, NSF, Box 195A, Vietnam, General, 12/14/61–12/18/61, JFKL.

139. Sorensen to JFK, 24 November 1961, Sorensen Papers, Vietnam, 5/9/61–10/1/63, Box 55, JFKL; "Address in Seattle at the University of Washington's 100th Anniversary Program," 16 November 1961, *PPP:JFK,* 1961:726, Doc. 473.

140. "The President's News Conference of November 29, 1961," *PPP:JFK,* 1961:756–757, Doc. 488.

141. See Exchange of Messages with the President of the Republic of Viet-Nam," 15 December 1961, *PPP:JFK,* 1961:801–802, Doc. 505. For the Kennedy-Diem Memorandum of Understanding, see Nolting to Diem, 5 December 1961, with Enclosure, 4 December 1961, *FRUS, 1961–1963,* 1:713–716, Doc. 307.

2. Escalation

1. "Inaugural Address," 20 January 1961, *PPP:JFK,* 1961:2, Doc. 1; "Annual Message to Congress on the State of the Union," 30 January 1961, *PPP:JFK,* 1961:19–28, Doc. 11; Richard Reeves, *President Kennedy: Profile of Power* (Simon and Schuster, 1993), 274.

2. "Annual Message to the Congress on the State of the Union," 11 January 1962, *PPP:JFK,* 1962:5, 13, Doc. 7.

3. Subcommittee on Far Eastern Affairs, 12 January 1962, and Committee on Foreign Relations, 20 February 1962, *Executive Sessions of the Senate Foreign Relations Committee: Together with Joint Sessions with the Senate Armed Services Committee* (Historical Series), vol. 14, 87th Cong., 2nd sess., 1962 (GPO, 1986), 38–39, 48, 199 (hereafter *Executive Sessions*); Robert Mann, *A Grand Delusion: America's Descent into Vietnam* (Basic Books, 2001), 255–256.

4. Burrows to Warner, 24 January 1962, FO 371/166717, DV103145/20, NA, UK.

5. McGarr to Felt, 6 January 1962, RG 218, Lemnitzer Files, Box 8, 091 Vietnam, NARA.

6. Martin to Cottrell, 19 January 1962, *FRUS, 1961–1963*, vol. 2: *Vietnam, 1962*, 52, Doc. 29.

7. Burrows to Warner, 24 January 1962.

8. For background, see Peter Busch, *All the Way with JFK?: Britain, the US, and the Vietnam War* (Oxford University Press, 2003).

9. Trueheart to Cottrell, 12 February 1962, *FRUS, 1961–1963*, 2:120, Doc. 57.

10. See "Joint Statement Following Discussions with the Vice President of the Republic of China," 2 August 1961, *PPP:JFK*, 1961:545, Doc. 309; "Letter to President Ngo Dinh Diem on the Sixth Anniversary of the Republic of Viet-Nam," 26 October 1961, *PPP:JFK*, 1961:680–681, Doc. 435.

11. See Yuen Foong Khong, *Analogies at War: Korea, Munich, Dien Bien Phu, and the Vietnam Decisions of 1965* (Princeton University Press, 1992), 177.

12. Hohler to Home, "South Viet Nam: Annual Report for 1961," 2 January 1961 (*sic*), FO 371 166697, DV1011/1, NA, UK.

13. Lemnitzer to McNamara, JCSM-33–62, 13 January 1962, *US-VR*, 12:452–453.

14. E. W. Kenworthy, "Pentagon Sets Up Vietnam Command under a General," *NYT*, 9 February 1962, 1. Harkins's immediate prior appointment was as deputy commander in chief, U.S. Army, Pacific.

15. Nolting to State, 963, 24 January 1962, *FRUS, 1961–1963*, 2:58, Doc. 33. The MAAG would remain operative into 1964, when its functions were folded into MACV.

16. Lemnitzer to Felt, 6 January 1962, *FRUS, 1961–1963*, 2:15, Doc. 9.

17. Kenworthy, "Pentagon Sets Up Vietnam Command under a General"; The *Washington Post* recounted the remark as "one war the West cannot afford to lose." John G. Norris, "U.S. Sets Up S. Viet-Nam Command," *WP*, 9 February 1962, A1.

18. Gilpatric Memorandum, 3 January 1962, *FRUS, 1961–1963*, 2:4, Doc. 2.

19. Kenworthy, "Pentagon Sets Up Vietnam Command under a General"; Homer Bigart, "U.S. Is Expanding Role in Vietnam," *NYT*, 10 February 1962, 3.

20. Jack Raymond, "Fears on Vietnam Rising in Capital," *NYT*, 12 February 1962, 1.

21. *Executive Sessions*, 39–40, 160.

22. "The President's News Conference of January 15, 1962, *PPP:JFK*, 1962:17, Doc. 8; see also Kennedy's news conferences for January 31, 1962: *PPP:JFK*, 1962:93, Doc. 27; and February 7, 1962, *PPP:JFK*, 1962:122, 125, Doc. 40.

23. "The President's News Conference of February 7, 1962," *PPP:JFK*, 1962:121–122, Doc. 40.

24. Fredrik Logevall, *JFK: Coming of Age in the American Century, 1917–1956* (Random House, 2020), 576–577.

25. "The Battle of Southeast Asia: Guerrilla Warfare," *Newsweek*, 12 February 1962, 11, 29.

26. James Reston, "The Undeclared War in South Vietnam," *NYT,* 14 February 1962, 34.

27. "The Truth about Vietnam," *NYT,* 14 February 1962, 34.

28. "The President's News Conference of February 14, 1962," *PPP:JFK,* 1962:136–137, Doc. 50.

29. Cottrell to Harriman, 17 February 1962, *FRUS, 1961–1963,* 2:142, Doc. 67.

30. Rowan to Johnson, 15 February 1962, *FRUS, 1961–1963,* 2:129–131, Doc. 62.

31. Rusk to Saigon, 1006, 21 February 1962, *FRUS, 1961–1963,* 2:159, Doc. 75; see also William Conrad Gibbons, *The U.S. Government and the Vietnam War: Executive and Legislative Roles and Relationships,* part 2: *1961–1964* (Princeton University Press, 1986), 111–112.

32. "Where War Is Hot and Getting Hotter," *U.S. News & World Report,* 19 February 1962; Jack Raymond, "Fears on Vietnam Rising in Capital," *NYT,* 12 February 1962, 1.

33. *Executive Sessions,* 196–213.

34. "Memorandum of Conference with the President," 21 February 1962, NSF, Box 345, Conferences with the President: Congressional Leaders, 1961–1962, JFKL.

35. Sylvester Memo, DEF 911763, "Public Affairs Policy Guidance for Personnel Returning from South Viet-Nam," 23 March 1962, NSF, Box 196, Vietnam, General, 3/29/62–3/31/62, JFKL.

36. 15 February 1962, *Congressional Record,* 2325–2326.

37. 21 February and 1 March 1962, *Congressional Record,* 2751, 3264.

38. "Robert Kennedy Assures Vietnam," *NYT,* 19 February 1962, 1.

39. Ball-Dutton Telcon, 1 March 1962, Ball Papers, Box 3, Congress, 6/23/61–10/8/62, JFKL.

40. See Gibbons, *U.S. Government and the Vietnam War,* 126–127.

41. Terry Dietz, *Republicans and Vietnam, 1961–1968* (Greenwood, 1986), 38; Gibbons, *U.S. Government and the Vietnam War,* 127–128.

42. Julian E. Zelizer, "When Liberals Were Hawks: Liberal Internationalism, the Republican Right, and the Cold War," unpublished manuscript, 38–39.

43. Dietz, *Republicans and Vietnam,* 42–43.

44. Jack Raymond, "G.O.P. Asks Candor on Vietnam War," *NYT,* 14 February 1962, 1; Reston, "The Undeclared War in South Vietnam," *NYT,* 14 February 1962, 34.

45. For Keating and Fulbright references, see "G.O.P. in New Attack on Vietnam Secrecy," *NYT,* 18 February 1962, 26. For additional color on these attacks, see Andrew L. Johns, *Vietnam's Second Front: Domestic Politics, the Republican Party, and the War* (University Press of Kentucky, 2010), 26–27.

46. George H. Gallup, *The Gallup Poll: Public Opinion 1935–1971,* vol. 3: *1959–1971* (Random House, 1972), 1751, 1756–1757, 1759.

47. Poll taken April 6–11, 1962, and published on April 29, 1962, *Gallup Poll,* 1764.

48. McNamara to Lemnitzer, 13 November 1961, *FRUS, 1961–1963,* vol. 1: *Vietnam, 1961,* 1:589n3, Doc. 245.

49. McNamara to Stahr and Decker, "Requirements for Advisory Personnel in Vietnam," 21 December 1961, JFK Papers, NSF, Box 195A, Vietnam, General, 1/6/62–1/12/62, JFKL.

50. Clifton Memorandum, December 4, 1961, 14 December 1961, NSF, Box 345, Conferences with the President, Joint Chiefs of Staff, 10/61–11/62, JFKL. See also Sharon Weinberger, *The Imagineers of War: The Untold History of DARPA, the Pentagon Agency That Changed the World* (Knopf, 2017), 68–85, 125–134; Annie Jacobson, *The Pentagon's Brain: An Uncensored History of DARPA, America's Top Secret Military Research Agency* (Little, Brown, 2015), 117–159.

51. Rusk to Saigon, 1171, 4 April 1962, *FRUS, 1961–1963,* 2:305, Doc. 144.

52. Krulak to Gilpatric, SACSA-M 63–62, 26 March 1962, *FRUS, 1961–1963,* 2:278, Doc. 132.

53. NSAM 124, 18 January 1962, *FRUS, 1961–1963,* 2:48–50, Doc. 26; NSAM 132, 19 February 1962, *US-VR,* 12:455–456; NSAM 131, 13 March 1962, *US-VR,* 12:457–459; NSAM 162, 19 June 1962, *US-VR,* 12:481–484; NSAM 182, 24 August 1962, *US-VR,* 12:485–486.

54. Roger Hilsman, *To Move a Nation: The Politics of Foreign Policy in the Administration of John F. Kennedy* (Dell, 1967), 52–53, 427.

55. RFE-27, 18 June 1962, *US-VR,* 12:469.

56. Hilsman Memorandum, 2 February 1962, *FRUS, 1961–1963,* 2:73–90, Doc. 42; Bagley to Taylor, 12 March 1962, *FRUS, 1961–1963,* 2:218, Doc. 105.

57. Philip E. Catton, *Diem's Final Failure: Prelude to America's War in Vietnam* (University Press of Kansas, 2003), 142–143.

58. Catton, *Diem's Final Failure,* 129–153; see also David Kaiser, *American Tragedy: Kennedy, Johnson, and the Origins of the Vietnam War* (Belknap Press of Harvard University Press, 2000), 168–176; Edward Miller, *Misalliance: Ngo Dinh Diem, the United States, and the Fate of South Vietnam* (Harvard University Press, 2013), 231–244.

59. Howard Jones, *Death of a Generation: How the Assassinations of Diem and JFK Prolonged the War in Vietnam* (Oxford University Press, 2004), 163–164; William M. Hammond, *The United States Army in Vietnam: Public Affairs: The Military and the Media, 1962–1968* (Center of Military History, 1988), 24–25.

60. Memorandum of Conference with the President, 1 March 1962, [dated 7 March 1962], NSF, Box 345, Conferences with the President, Joint Chiefs of staff, 10/61–11/62, JFKL. Underline in original.

61. Clifton to Bundy and Smith, 29 March 1962, NSF, Box 320, Staff Memoranda, Chester Clifton, 3/61–6/62, JFKL; for those earlier concerns, see Bowles to Nolting, 1423, 20 May 1961, *FRUS, 1961–1963,* 1:141, Doc. 56.

62. John Kenneth Galbraith, *A Life in Our Times: Memoirs* (Houghton Mifflin, 1981), 467–477; Richard Parker, *John Kenneth Galbraith: His Life, His Politics, His Economics* (Farrar, Straus and Giroux, 2005), 362–377.

63. Galbraith, *Ambassador's Journal: A Personal Account of the Kennedy Years* (Houghton Mifflin, 1969), 338–341; Galbraith to JFK, 4 April 1962, *FRUS, 1961–1963,* 2:297–298, Doc. 141; Parker, *Galbraith,* 389–391.

64. See Galbraith to Kennedy, 5 April 1962, NSF, Box 196 Vietnam General, 4/1/62–1/10/62, JFKL; "Following from Ambassador Galbraith, re attached," 5 April 1962, Harriman Papers, Box 463, Galbraith (1), Library of Congress.

65. Memorandum of Conversation, 6 April 1962, *FRUS, 1961–1963,* 2:309, Doc 148.

66. According to Richard Parker, Harriman never forwarded to Galbraith the president's directive that the ambassador open Indian channels to Hanoi. Parker, *Galbraith,* 389–391.

67. Lemnitzer to McNamara, "US Policy toward Vietnam," JCSM-282-62, 13 April 1962, *US-VR,* 12:464–465.

68. Williams to McNamara, 14 April 1962, and Attachment, *FRUS, 1961–1963,* 2:324–327, Doc. 156.

69. McNamara chose to discuss the matter privately with Galbraith. Forrestal to McNamara, 7 April 1962, RG 330, OASD/ISA, Secret and Below, General Files 1962, Box 108, Vietnam 092 Jan–June 1962, NARA. See also Williams to McNamara, *FRUS, 1961–1963,* 2:324n1, Doc. 156.

70. Bagley to Taylor, 9 April 1962, *FRUS, 1961–1963,* 2:317n1, Doc. 151.

71. Williams to McNamara, 14 April 1962, *FRUS, 1961–1963,* 2:325, Doc. 156.

72. Draft Memorandum of a Conversation, 1 May 1962, *FRUS, 1961–1963,* 2:367, Doc. 176. For talks with Indian officials, see Galbraith to Harriman, 10 May 1962; and Harriman to Galbraith, 11 May 1962, both in Harriman Papers, Box 463, Galbraith (1), Library of Congress; Kaiser, *American Tragedy,* 133.

73. "Vietnam: General Maxwell Taylor's Report," 29 March 1962, FO 371 166721, DV103145/93, NA, UK.

74. Bagley to Taylor, 5 April 1962, *FRUS, 1961–1963,* 2:307–308, Doc. 147; Cottrell to Harriman, 6 April 1962, *FRUS, 1961–1963,* 2:313, Doc. 149.

75. See Ormsby-Gore to Home, 17 April 1962; Warner to Ledward, 1 June 1962; and Ledward to Warner, 7 June 1962, all in FO 371/166722, DV 103145/110, NA, UK. American documentation is generally silent on Thompson's recommendation for a troop withdrawal.

76. Ball-Reston Telcon, 23 March 1962, 11:50, Ball Papers, Box 9, Vietnam, 1/15/62–10/4/62, JFKL; State Department to Saigon, 4 April 1962, *FRUS, 1961–1963,* 2:305–306, Doc. 145.

77. Circular 1730, 11 April 1962, *FRUS, 1961–1963,* 2:323–324, Doc. 155.

78. "South Viet Nam: Cutting the Arc," *Time,* 6 April 1962, 26.

79. Transcript of Harriman interview on ABC's "Issues and Answers," 8 April 1962, FO 371/166355, DV103145/10, NA, UK.

80. Tillman Durdin, "U.S. Role in Vietnam Holds Many Risks," *NYT,* 22 April 1962, E4.

81. *Life* nevertheless referenced Kennedy's "determination to make sure that Vietnam will save itself." "For a Year's Foreign Policy: 'A' for J.F.K.," *Life,* 13 April 1962, 4; "Far Off War We Have Decided to Win," *Life,* 16 March 1962, 36–39, 42–43; Scot Leavitt, "Dilemma for U.S.: Clever Adversary, a Difficult Friend," *Life,* 16 March 1962, 40–41.

82. Ball-Bundy Telcon, 26 April 1962, Ball Papers, Box 9, Vietnam, 1/15/62–10/4/63, JFKL. Ball cleared the idea of a speech with the president two days later. Ball-Johnson Telcon, 28 April 1962, ibid.

83. Ball to Bundy, 1 May 1962, NSF, Box 196, Vietnam General, 5/1/62–5/14/62, JFKL. Although Harriman and Alex Johnson had cleared the speech, Kennedy did not see it prior to its delivery, even though he had requested a look. Ball-Bundy Telcon, 1 May 62, 11:20, Ball Papers, Box 9, Vietnam, 1/15/62–10/4/63, JFKL

84. "Vietnam—Free World Challenge in Southeast Asia," NSF, Box 288, Department of State, Under Secretary Ball's Speeches, Etc. [1 of 2], JFKL.

85. Ball-Bundy Telcon, 1 May 1962, 11:20 a.m., Ball Papers, Box 9, Vietnam, 1/15/62–10/4/63, JFKL.

86. See Forrestal to Bundy, 5 May 1962, NSF, Box 196, Vietnam, General, 5/5/62–5/10/62, JFKL; Ball-Harriman Telcon, 6 May 1962, 11:15 a.m.; Ball Papers, Box 5, Laos, 1/20/61–7/1/63, JFKL.

87. Harriman to Bundy, Attachment, 7 May 1962, NSF, Box 228, Department of State, Under Secretary Ball's Speeches, etc. [1 of 2], JFKL, with cover note from Forrestal stating, "This O.K. with the White House."

88. Jones, *Death of a Generation,* 179. More persuasively, Kaiser notes that it signified Kennedy's fear of "overcommitment" to the conflict. Kaiser, *American Tragedy,* 133.

89. See also James A. Bill, *George Ball: Behind the Scenes in U.S. Foreign Policy* (Yale University Press, 1997), 153–154.

90. See Forrestal Memorandum for Bundy, 5 May 1962, NSF, Box 196, Vietnam General, 5/5/62–5/10/62, JFKL; Roger Hilsman, INR Memorandum, undated, *FRUS, 1961–1963,* 2:391, Doc. 189.

91. McGarr to Lemnitzer, 12 October 1961, *FRUS, 1961–1963,* 1:353, Doc. 159.

92. Warren Unna, "McNamara to Inspect Warfare in Viet-Nam," *WP,* 1 May 1962, A6.

93. Deborah Shapley, *Promise and Power: The Life and Times of Robert McNamara* (Little, Brown, 1993), 146–152.

94. George W. Allen, *None So Blind: A Personal Account of the Intelligence Failure in Vietnam* (Ivan R. Dee, 2001), 149–150. The *Pentagon Papers* makes no mention of this episode, and McNamara writes that he first raised the matter with Harkins during the July SecDef meeting at Honolulu. Robert S. McNamara, *In Retrospect: The Tragedy and Lessons of Vietnam* (Vintage, 1996, 1995), 48–49.

95. *Pentagon Papers,* 2:175. See, for instance, Fredrik Logevall, *Choosing War: The Lost Chance for Peace and the Escalation of the War in Vietnam* (University of California Press, 1999), 34; Howard Jones, *Death of a Generation: How the Assassinations of Diem*

and JFK Prolonged the Vietnam War (Oxford University Press, 2003), 189. Although the *Pentagon Papers* assert that Kennedy directed McNamara to initiate that process, no such evidence exists in textual form. Leslie H. Gelb, interview by author, 11 July 2007.

96. DoD Paper, undated, *FRUS, 1961–1963,* 2:387, Doc. 187; "—And in South Vietnam," *NYT,* 12 May 1962, 22.

97. See McNamara Interview on *Today,* 26 February 1962; News Release, 21 March 1962; McNamara Press Briefing Summary Regarding His Trip to South Vietnam, 11 May 1962; McNamara Interview with Howard K. Smith on a News and Comment ABC Television Program Devoted to "Guerilla (sic) Warfare: The Challenge in Southeast Asia," 23 May 1962 (taped on 19 May 1962), all in McNamara Papers, Part II, Speeches & Writings, Box 89, Folder 4C, Library of Congress.

98. Memorandum for the Record, "Visit of RAIM L.C. Heinz, USN to Vietnam," 22 May 1962, RG 330, OASD/ISA, Assistant for (CI) Files, 1962–1965, Vietnam-Special Group (CI) 1962, Box 4, NARA.

99. Warner to Ledward, 6 June 1962, FO 371/166722, DV 103145/117G, NA, UK.

100. Bagley to Taylor, "Viet-Nam Task Force Meeting," 9 May 1962, *FRUS, 1961–1963,* 2:377–378, Doc. 184.

101. "Minutes of Meeting of Special Group (CI), 3 May 1962," *FRUS, 1961–1963,* 2:373, Doc. 180.

102. Bagley to Taylor, "Viet-Nam Task Force Meeting," 9 May 1962.

103. F. H. Jackson to McGhie, 17 May 1962, FO 371 166723, DV103145/123, NA, UK.

104. Aurelie Basha i Novosejt, *"I Made Mistakes": Robert McNamara's Vietnam War Policy, 1960–1968* (Cambridge University Press, 2019), 123–125.

105. Cottrell to Harriman, 27 April 1962, *FRUS, 1961–1963,* 2:351, Doc. 172.

106. Homer Bigart, "M'Namara Backs U.S. Role in Vietnam," *NYT,* 10 May 1962, 7.

107. McNamara Press Briefing Summary Regarding His Trip to South Vietnam, 11 May 1962, McNamara Papers, Part II, Speeches & Writings, Box 89, Folder 4C, Library of Congress; Homer Bigart, "M'Namara Terms Saigon Aid Ample," *NYT,* 12 May 1962, 1; "McNamara Returns to U.S.," *NYT,* 12 May 1962, 2.

108. McNamara Interview with Howard K. Smith.

109. Homer Bigart, "M'Namara Terms Saigon Aid Ample," *NYT,* 12 May 1962, 1; "McNamara Returns to U.S.," *NYT,* 12 May 1962, 2.

110. Cottrell Briefing Paper for the Special Group (CI), 22 March 1962, *FRUS, 1961–1963,* 2:258–260n1, Doc. 123. See also McNamara and Harriman comments reported in Denson to McGhie, 23 February 1962; and McGhie Note, 27 February 1962, both in FO 371/166719, DV103145/59, NA, UK.

111. "The President's News Conference of April 11, 1962," *PPP:JFK,* 1962:322, Doc. 139; "The President's News Conference of June 14, 1962," *PPP:JFK,* 1962:493, Doc. 245.

112. For Laos and its impact on U.S. policy toward Vietnam, see Lawrence Freedman, *Kennedy's Wars: Berlin, Cuba, Laos, and Vietnam* (Oxford University Press, 2003), 340–355.

113. UPI, "Goldwater Assails State Department," *NYT,* 30 May 1962, 40; John A. Goldsmith, "U.S. Policy Is 'Very Positive,' Ball Tells Senate Probers," *WP,* 5 June 1962, A2.

114. Ball-Bundy Telcon, 30 May 1962, 11:05; see also Ball's telephone conversations with Robert Manning and McGeorge Bundy, both in Ball Papers, Box 3, Congress, 6/23/61–10/8/62, JFKL.

115. "Remarks at West Point to the Graduating Class of the U.S. Military Academy," 6 June 1962, *PPP:JFK,* 1962:453–454, Doc. 226.

116. Edmund F. Wehrle, "'A Good, Bad Deal': John F. Kennedy, Averell Harriman, and the Neutralization of Laos, 1961–1962," *Pacific Historical Review* 67 (August 1998), 3:351n3.

3. Formulation

1. Michael V. Forrestal Oral History, 28 July 1964, JFKL. For events that spring in Laos, see William J. Rust, *So Much to Lose: John F. Kennedy and American Policy in Laos* (University Press of Kentucky, 2014), 111–150.

2. Mendenhall Memorandum, 26 June 1962, *FRUS, 1961–1963,* vol. 2: *Vietnam, 1962,* 473–475, Doc. 228; Mendenhall Memorandum, 26 June 1962, *FRUS, 1961–1963,* 2:475–478, Doc. 229.

3. Mendenhall to Rice, 16 August 1962, *FRUS, 1961–1963,* 2:597, Doc. 268.

4. Memorandum of a Conversation, 22 July 1962, *FRUS, 1961–1963,* 2:541–543, Doc. 246; see also Memorandum of a Conversation, 22 July 1962, *FRUS, 1961–1963,* 2:543–546, Doc. 247.

5. Rusk to Saigon, 9 July 1962, *FRUS, 1961–1963,* 2:512, Doc. 238.

6. "Record of the Sixth Secretary of Defense Conference" (hereafter "Sixth SecDef"), 23 July 23, 1962, *FRUS, 1961–1963,* 2:548, Doc. 248.

7. Robert S. McNamara, with Brian VanDeMark, *In Retrospect: The Tragedy and Lessons of Vietnam* (Vintage, 1995), 48.

8. *Pentagon Papers,* 2:160–162.

9. Hilsman to Harriman, RFE-27, 18 June 1962, *US-VR,* 12:479.

10. "Status Report on Southeast Asia," 27 June 1962, *FRUS, 1961–1963,* 2:478, Doc. 230.

11. David Kaiser, *American Tragedy: Kennedy, Johnson, and the Origins of the Vietnam War* (Belknap Press of Harvard University Press, 2000), 128.

12. Burris to LBJ, 17 August 1962, *FRUS, 1961–1963,* 2:602, Doc. 269; Bem Price, "S. Viet-Nam Is Fouled Up, Officers Say," *WP,* 8 July 1962, A1.

13. "Sixth SecDef," *FRUS, 1961–1963,* 2:546, 548, Doc. 248.

14. William B. Rosson, "Four Periods of American Involvement in Vietnam: Development and Implementation of Policy, Strategy, and Programs" (Ph.D. diss., New College, University of Oxford, 1979), 155.

15. *Pentagon Papers,* 2:174.

16. UPI, "Mansfield Urges New Asian Policy," *NYT,* 11 June 1962, 2.

17. "The President's News Conference of June 14, 1962," *PPP:JFK,* 1962:492, Doc. 245.

18. ORC Poll, "What Voters Say about Kennedy Programs," Question 22, USORC.62465R.Q07C, Opinion Research Corporation (Roper Center, 1962), Roper iPoll.

19. George Gallup, "Democrat Popularity Drops in Far West," *Los Angeles Times,* 20 July 1962, 7; George Gallup, "Sharp Republican Gains Seen in Midwest States," *WP,* 22 July 1962, A2; Chalmers M. Roberts, "Beleaguered JFK Bothered but Not Bewildered," *WP,* 22 July 1962, E1.

20. For those earlier efforts, see *Pentagon Papers,* 2:23–29, 137–138.

21. "Sixth SecDef," *FRUS, 1961–1963,* 2:549–550, Doc. 248; James Lawton Collins Jr., *The Development and Training of the South Vietnamese Army, 1950–1972* (Center of Military History, 1991), 28–29.

22. Deborah Shapley, *Promise and Power: The Life and Times of Robert McNamara* (Little, Brown, 1993), 99–103.

23. Marc J. Selverstone, "It's a Date: Kennedy and the Timetable for a Vietnam Troop Withdrawal," *Diplomatic History* 34 (June 2010), 3:489.

24. Lawrence S. Kaplan, Ronald D. Landa, and Edward J. Drea, *The McNamara Ascendancy, 1961–1965* (Office of the Secretary of Defense Historical Office, 2006), 72–78; Alain C. Enthoven and K. Wayne Smith, *How Much Is Enough? Shaping the Defense Program, 1961–1969* (Harper and Row, 1971), 32–53; William W. Kaufman, *The McNamara Strategy* (Harper and Row, 1964), 173–178.

25. Kaplan, Landa, and Drea, *McNamara Ascendancy,* 453–462; Selverstone, "It's a Date," 488.

26. U.S. Department of Labor, Bureau of Labor Statistics, data.bls.gov. The unemployment rate in 1957 was 4.3 percent.

27. "Statement by the President to Cabinet Officers and Agency Heads on the 1962 and 1963 Budget Outlook," 26 October 1961, Taylor Papers, Box 17, T-138-69A, National Defense University.

28. Francis J. Gavin, *Gold, Dollars, and Power: The Politics of International Monetary Relations* (University of North Carolina Press, 2004), 59–88; Diane B. Kunz, "Cold War Dollar Diplomacy: The Other Side of Containment," in Kunz, ed., *The Diplomacy of the Crucial Decade: American Foreign Relations in the 1960s,* 81–85 (Columbia University Press, 1994).

29. The Military Assistance Program, along with the Agency for International Development, was a component of the Foreign Assistance Act of 1961, which Congress passed that October. MAP subsumed operations authorized by the Mutual Security Act of 1951 and the Mutual Security Act of 1954.

30. Committee on Appropriations, *Foreign Operations Appropriations for 1963,* 16 March 1962, 87th Cong, 2nd sess., part 1:340–341.

31. Committee on Appropriations, *Foreign Operations Appropriations for 1962,* 29 June 1961, 87th Cong., 1st sess., part 1:76.

32. Draft NSC Record of Action, "Guidelines for the Military Aid Program," 13 January 1962, Vice President's Security File, Box 5, Supporting Data on NSC Discussion of Military Aid Program, LBJL.

33. Kaplan, Landa, and Drea, *McNamara Ascendancy,* 277. Douglas C. Dacy cites figures of $71M in FY 1961 and $275.9M in FY 1963. Dacy, *Foreign Aid, War, and Economic Development: South Vietnam, 1955–1975* (Cambridge University Press, 1986), 200.

34. "Military Assistance Program Comparison of NOA Request with Actual Funding, FY 1961–FY 1965," Table 8, Kaplan, Landa, and Drea, *McNamara Ascendancy,* 446.

35. McNamara to Felt and McGarr, 28 November 1961, *FRUS, 1961–1963,* vol. 1: *Vietnam, 1961,* 679–680, Doc. 289.

36. 8 February 1962, *Executive Sessions of the Senate Foreign Relations Committee: Together with Joint Sessions with the Senate Armed Services Committee* (Historical Series vol. 14, 87th Cong., 2nd sess., 1962 (GPO, 1986), 156 (hereafter *Executive Sessions*); Wood to Felt, DEF 919386, 21 September 1962, RG 330, OASD/ISA, Outgoing Message Files, January 1962 to September 1963, Box 1, September 1962, NARA.

37. Kaplan, Landa, and Drea, *McNamara Ascendancy,* 421–431; *Foreign Operations Appropriations for 1963,* 358. By comparison, those figures stood at 38 percent for FY 1960.

38. Lawrence S. Kaplan, "McNamara, Vietnam, and the Defense of Europe," in *War Plans and Alliances in the Cold War: Threat Perceptions in the East and West,* ed. Vojtech Mastny, Sven S. Holtsmark, and Andreas Wenger, 287–288 (Routledge, 2006).

39. Aurelie Basha i Novosejt, *"I Made Mistakes": Robert McNamara's Vietnam War Policy, 1960–1968* (Cambridge University Press, 2019), 100.

40. *Executive Sessions,* 156.

41. Forrestal to Bundy, 8 August 1962, NSF, Box 320, Staff Memoranda, Michael Forrestal, 8/62–10/62, JFKL. On the DoD review, see DEF 918027, 13 August 1962, OASD/ISA, Outgoing Message Files, January 1962 to September 1963, Box 1, NARA. For Kennedy's support of that review, see Forrestal to Bundy, 4 October 1962, NSF, Box 320, Staff Memoranda, Michael Forrestal, 6/62–10/62, JFKL.

42. Basha i Novosejt, *"I Made Mistakes,"* 98–99.

43. "Meeting with Maxwell Taylor on His Far Eastern Trip on 25 September 1962," *The Great Crises,* vol. 2, ed. Timothy Naftali and Philip Zelikow, *PRDE* (University of Virginia Press, 2014–).

44. Enthoven and Smith, *How Much Is Enough?* 49–50.

45. "Sixth SecDef," *FRUS, 1961–1963,* 2:548, Doc. 248.

46. Press Release, 23 July 1962, McNamara Papers, Part II, Speeches & Writings, Box 89, Folder 4C, Library of Congress.

47. See, for instance, "Action Program for Vietnam," 14 August 1962, *Declassified Documents Reference System,* 1978, 113A.

48. Burris to LBJ, 17 August 1962, *FRUS, 1961–1963,* 2:603, Doc. 269.

49. Forrestal to Bundy, 8 August 1962, NSF, Box 320, Staff Memoranda, Michael Forrestal, 8/62–10/62, JFKL.

50. Nolting to State, 3 August 1962, *FRUS, 1961–1963,* 2:576, Doc. 258.

51. Pierre Asselin, *Hanoi's Road to the Vietnam War, 1954–1965* (University of California Press, 2013), 109–110; Peter Busch, *All the Way with JFK? Britain, the US, and the Vietnam War* (Oxford University Press, 2003), 126–127; Mark Moyar, *Triumph Forsaken: The Vietnam War, 1954–1965* (Cambridge University Press, 2006), 183–184. Lien-Hang T. Nguyen maintains that the balance of power in the countryside nevertheless remained the same as in 1961. Nguyen, *Hanoi's War: An International History of the War for Peace in Vietnam* (University of North Carolina Press, 2012), 61.

52. Thompson, "Record of Meeting with General Taylor," 13 September 1962, FO 371/166723, DV 103145/140, NA, UK.

53. Thompson, "Record of Meeting with General Taylor," 13 September 1962.

54. "Meeting with Maxwell Taylor on His Far Eastern Trip on 25 September 1962," *PRDE.*

55. ORC Poll: What Voters Say about Kennedy Programs, Question 21, USORC. 62465R.Q07B, Opinion Research Corporation (Roper Center, 1962), Roper iPoll.

56. ORC Poll: What Voters Say about Kennedy Programs, Question 19, USORC. 62465R.Q06N, Opinion Research Corporation (Roper Center, 1962), Roper iPoll.

57. See Nick Bryant, *The Bystander: John F. Kennedy and the Struggle for Black Equality* (Basic Books, 2006), 329–356.

58. The story itself is titled "JFK and His Critics," *Newsweek,* 16 July 1962, 15. See also Richard Reeves, *President Kennedy: Profile of Power* (Simon and Schuster, 1993), 294–337.

59. Gallup Organization, Gallup Poll # 656, Question 1, USGALLUP.62-656. R001, Gallup Organization, (Roper Center, 1962), Roper iPoll; Gallup Organization, Gallup Poll # 1962-0664: Cigarettes/Safety Belts in Automobiles/Peace Corps, Question 1, USGALLUP.62-664.R001.

60. Harris to JFK, 4 October 1962, POF, Box 105, Polls, General, JFKL. An August Opinion Research Corporation poll found that 42 percent thought Kennedy's Cuba policy "good" or "fairly good," 36 percent thought it "poor," and 22 percent offered "no opinion." ORC Poll: What Voters Say about Kennedy Programs, Question 20, USORC.62465R. Q07A, Opinion Research Corporation, (Roper Center, 1962), Roper iPoll.

61. "Vietnam: The Unpleasant Truth," *Newsweek,* 20 August 1962, 40.

62. "South Viet Nam: Situation: Better," *Time,* 20 July 1962, 26.

63. ORC Poll: What Voters Say about Kennedy Programs, Question 22, USORC.62465R.Q07C, Opinion Research Corporation (Roper, 1962), Roper iPoll.

64. Wood to U. A. Johnson, 11 October 1962, *FRUS, 1961–1963*, 2:690, Doc. 298.

65. Memorandum for the Record, 10 September 1962, *FRUS, 1961–1963*, 2:626–627, Doc. 277.

66. U. A. Johnson Notes, 10 December 1962, *FRUS, 1961–1963*, 2:761, Doc. 327.

67. Nolting to Harriman, 19 November 1962, *FRUS, 1961–1963*, 2:739, Doc. 320.

68. Wood to U. A. Johnson, 11 October 1962, *FRUS, 1961–1963*, 2:689, Doc. 298. Those pilots eventually deployed to Vietnam on Kennedy's approval. See Gilpatric to JFK, attachment, 20 December 1962, *FRUS, 1961–1963*, 2:794–797, Doc. 333.

69. CINCPAC to OSD/ISA, undated, RG 59, National Security Action Memoranda Files, 1961–1968, Box 6, October 1962, NARA; Wood to U. A. Johnson, 11 October 1962, *FRUS, 1961–1963*, 2:690, Doc. 298.

70. Memorandum for Director, Policy Planning Staff, 11 October 1962, RG 330, OASD/ISA, Assistant for (CI) Files, 1962–1965, Military Assistance Program, Box 1, NARA.

71. Clark Clifford, with Richard Holbrooke, *Counsel to the President: A Memoir* (Random House, 1991), 460.

72. Planeside—Andrews Air Force Base, 9 October 1962, RG 200, McNamara Records, Box 179, NARA.

73. Forrestal to JFK, 18 September 1962, *FRUS, 1961–1963*, 2:649–650, Doc. 283.

74. Minutes of the Eighth Meeting of the Southeast Asia Task Force, 19 September 1962, *FRUS, 1961–1963*, 2:655–656, Doc. 286.

75. Paper Prepared in the Department of State, undated, *FRUS, 1961–1963*, 2:679, Doc. 297.

76. RFE-59, 3 December 1962, *US-VR*, 12:505, 519.

77. Heavner Report, 11 December 1962, *FRUS, 1961–1963*, 2:771, Doc. 328.

78. Memorandum for the Record, 20 October 1962, *FRUS, 1961–1963*, 2:705–716, Doc. 305.

79. Johnson Notes, 10 December 1962, *FRUS, 1961–1963*, 2: 761, Doc. 327.

80. R. H. Johnson to Rostow, 16 October 1962, *FRUS, 1961–1963*, 2:703–704, Doc. 303.

81. Harriman to Nolting, 12 October 1962, *FRUS, 1961–1963*, 2:693–695, Doc. 300.

82. Forrestal to RFK, 7 November 1962, Special Group (CI) Vietnam (Folder 2 of 2), RFK Papers, Box 211, JFKL.

83. Bagley to Taylor, 12 November 1962, *FRUS, 1961–1963*, 2:727–728, Doc. 314.

84. Paper Prepared in Department of State, undated, *FRUS, 1961–1963*, 2:687, Doc. 297.

85. See Aleksandr Fursenko and Timothy Naftali, *One Hell of a Gamble: Khrushchev, Castro, and Kennedy, 1958–1964: The Secret History of the Cuban Missile Crisis* (Norton, 1997); Michael Dobbs, *One Minute to Midnight: Kennedy, Khrushchev, and Castro on the Brink of Nuclear War* (Vintage, 2009).

86. Mansfield Report, "Southeast Asia—Vietnam," 18 December 1962, *FRUS, 1961–1963*, 2:779–787, Doc. 330.

87. Robert Dallek, *An Unfinished Life: John F. Kennedy, 1917–1963* (Little, Brown, 2003), 666.

88. "Television and Radio Interview: 'After Two Years—a Conversation with the President,'" 17 December 1962, *PPP:JFK*, 1962:889, Doc. 551.

4. Modification

1. David M. Toczek, *The Battle of Ap Bac: They Did Everything but Learn from It* (Naval Institute Press, 2001); Neil Sheehan, *A Bright Shining Lie: John Paul Vann and America in Vietnam* (Random House, 1988), 203–265.

2. "U.S. Military Support for Vietnam," 13 December 1962, Box 235, OSDHO; State to All Posts, 8 February 1963, Special Group (CI) Vietnam (folder 1 of 2), RFK Papers, Box 211, JFKL.

3. J. P. Harris, "The Early Military History of the Second Indochina War and the Moyar Thesis," *Journal of Military History* 85 (July 2021), 3:748–752; Edward Miller, *Misalliance: Ngo Dinh Diem, the United States, and the Fate of South Vietnam* (Harvard University Press, 2013), 250–251.

4. "Setback in Vietnam," *NYT*, 5 January 1963, 6; "What's Wrong in Vietnam?" *NYT*, 15 January 1963, 6; Arthur Krock, "Kennedy's Foresight of the Events at Ap Bac," *NYT*, 8 January 1963, 6.

5. "War without Will," *WSJ*, 10 January 1963, 16; "Kennedy's Priorities and Our Own," *Chicago Tribune*, 4 January 1963, 10.

6. Neil Sheehan, "Role of U.S. in Viet-Nam to Increase," *WP*, 2 January 1963, A17; "Richard Hughes, "U.S. Combat Command over Vietnamese Urged," *WP*, 13 January 1963, A27.

7. "Year of the Man," *Newsweek*, 21 January 1963, 46; *Time*, "The Helicopter War Runs into Trouble," 11 January 1963, 29.

8. "A Bloody Nose," *Newsweek*, 14 January 1963, 34. A subsequent *Newsweek* story pegged the official count at sixty-three Americans killed over the previous twelve months. "Year of the Man," *Newsweek*, 21 January 1963, 46. The National Archives and Records Administration stipulates that fifty-three Americans died during 1962. https://www.archives.gov/research/military/vietnam-war/casualty-statistics.

9. Kenneth Crawford, "News from Vietnam," *Newsweek*, 28 January 1963, 32; "The Helicopter War Runs into Trouble," *Time*, 11 January 1963, 29; Milton Orshefsky, "Despite Battlefield Setbacks, There Is Hope—With Caution," *Life*, 28 January 1963, 31.

10. Gallup Poll # 1962–0664: Cigarettes / Safety Belts in Automobiles / Peace Corps, Question 1, USGALLUP.62-664.R001; Gallup Poll # 1963-0667: Kennedy / Federal Spending / Labor Unions / Taxes / 1964 Presidential Election, Question 1,

USGALLUP.63-667.R001, both in Gallup Organization (Roper Center, 1962), Roper iPoll.

11. "Annual Message to the Congress on the State of the Union," 14 January 1963, *PPP:JFK,* 1963:11–19, Doc. 12; "Annual Budget Message to the Congress, Fiscal Year 1964," 17 January 1963, *PPP:JFK,* 1963:34, Doc. 21; "Magazine Article 'Where We Stand,'" 15 January 1963, *PPP:JFK,* 1963:20, Doc. 14.

12. Minutes of a Meeting of the Special Group for Counterinsurgency, 17 January 1963, *FRUS, 1961–1963,* vol. 3: *Vietnam, January–August, 1963,* 28, Doc. 14.

13. "Foreign Policy Briefing for Legislative Leaders on 8 January 1963," *The Winds of Change,* vol. 6, ed. David Coleman, *PRDE* (University of Virginia Press, 2014–).

14. Memorandum for the Chairman, "Helicopter Incident—South Vietnam," 7 January 1963, RG 218, Taylor Records, Box 11, 091—Vietnam, NARA.

15. Hohler to FO, 1011/2/63, 8 January 1963, FO 371/170131, DV1201/4, NA, UK.

16. Burrows to FO, No. 9, 6 February 1963, FO 371/170132, DV1201/24, NA, UK.

17. Rusk-McNamara Telcon, 8 January 1963, 09:16, RG 59, Records of Secretary of State Dean Rusk, Transcripts of Telephone Calls, Box 47, NARA.

18. RFE-59, 3 December 1962, *US-VR,* 12:488.

19. Wheeler to JCS, January 1963, *FRUS, 1961–1963,* 3:73–74, 84, 91, 94, Doc. 26.

20. "Meeting on Vietnam on 1 February 1963," *PRDE.*

21. Forrestal to JFK, 4 February 1963, *FRUS, 1961–1963,* 3:97, Doc. 29; Hilsman and Forrestal to JFK, 25 January 1963, *FRUS, 1961–1963,* 3:49–59, Doc. 19.

22. Hilsman Memorandum, January 1963, *FRUS, 1961–1963,* 3:16, Doc. 8.

23. Felt to JCS, "Comprehensive Plan for South Vietnam" (hereafter CPSVN), 25 January 1963, *FRUS, 1961–1963,* 3:35–49, Doc. 18. A slightly different conception pointed toward victory emerging when the insurgency "would be brought within acceptable limits" during Fiscal 1967. Memorandum for Director, Policy Planning Staff, 11 October 1962, RG 330, OASD/ISA, Assistant for (CI) Files, 1962–1965, Military Assistance Program, Box 1, NARA.

24. See Manfull to Wood, 23 January 1963, *FRUS, 1961–1963,* 3:32–34, Doc. 16.

25. CPSVN, *FRUS, 1961–1963,* 3:36–49.

26. *Pentagon Papers,* 2:177–179.

27. CPSVN, *FRUS, 1961–1963,* 3:38.

28. CPSVN, *FRUS, 1961–1963,* 3:36; Wheeler Report, January 1963, *FRUS, 1961–1963,* 3:93, Doc. 26.

29. Heinz to Bundy, "Comprehensive Plan South Vietnam," I-20804/63, 1 February 1963, Box 236, OSDHO.

30. William B. Rosson, "Four Periods of American Involvement in Vietnam: Development and Implementation of Policy, Strategy, and Programs" (Ph.D. diss., New College, University of Oxford, 1979), 163–166.

31. Rusk to Saigon, 24 January 1963, *FRUS, 1961–1963,* 3:34, Doc. 17.

32. Wilson to Murrow, 30 January 1963, *FRUS, 1961–1963*, 3:65, Doc. 23.

33. Nolting to State, 5 February 1963, *FRUS, 1961–1963*, 3:100, Doc 30.

34. JCS Team Report on South Vietnam, January 1963, *FRUS, 1961–1963*, 3:89, Doc. 26.

35. Wilson to Murrow, 30 January 1963, *FRUS, 1961–1963*, 3:66, Doc. 23.

36. Department of Defense Press Briefing, The Pentagon, Admiral H. D. Felt, Wednesday, January 30, 1963, Box 236, OSDHO; AP, "Victory Predicted in Viet Nam," *Lincoln* (NB) *Star*, 31 January 1963, 16.

37. "Press Briefing by General Earle G. Wheeler, Chief of Staff, U.S. Army, The Pentagon, Monday, February 4, 1963," Box 236, OSDHO.

38. AP, "Wheeler Sees 'Long Effort' in Viet-Nam," *WP*, 27 January 1963, A14.

39. Harriman to Nolting, 30 January 1963, *FRUS, 1961–1963*, 3:68, Doc. 24.

40. McNamara Press Conference, 28 February 1963, McNamara Papers, Part II, Speeches & Writings, Box 89, Folder 4C, Library of Congress.

41. Hannah to Harriman, Mansfield Report, 7 February 1963, RG 59, FEA, Assistant Secretary for Far Eastern Affairs, Subject, Personal Name and Country Files—1960–1963, 1963 Subject Files, Box 21, NARA.

42. Felix Belair Jr., "Senators Warn of Growing Risks in Vietnam War," *NYT*, 25 February 1963, 1; Hanson Baldwin, "Mansfield and U.S. Role in Vietnam," *NYT*, 28 February 1963, 6.

43. "Southeast Asia Burden," *NYT*, 12 March 1963, 6.

44. "Southeast Asia," *NYT*, 1 April 1963, 26.

45. "The President's News Conference of March 6, 1963," *PPP:JFK*, 1963:243, Doc. 89.

46. Kenneth P. O'Donnell and David F. Powers, with Joe McCarthy, *"Johnny, We Hardly Knew Ye": Memories of John Fitzgerald Kennedy* (Little, Brown, 1972), 16.

47. R. C. Forbes, "South Vietnam," 4 March 1963, Vietnam Center and Sam Johnson Vietnam Archive, https://vva.vietnam.ttu.edu/images.php?img=/images/132/1320101005.pdf.

48. CINCPAC to JCS, DTG 202310Z Mar 63, 20 March 1963, RG 218, Central File, 1963 Security Classified, Box 10, JCS Official File, 9155.3/3360 (25 Jan 63) Sec. 2, NARA.

49. Nitze Notes, 6 March 1963, Nitze Papers, Box 82, 1963, Folder 4, Library of Congress.

50. CPSVN, *FRUS, 1961–1963*, 3:36.

51. Taylor to McNamara, JCSM-180-63, "Comprehensive Plan, South Vietnam," *FRUS, 1961–1963*, 3:134–135, Doc. 51.

52. Taylor to McNamara, JCSM-152–63, 21 February 1963, Box 236, OSDHO; McNamara to Taylor, Reference JCSM-152–63, 8 March 1963, Box 236, OSDHO.

53. State to Embassy Saigon, 857, 12 March 1963, RG 59, Subject-Numeric, Box 3740, DEF 19 2/1/63, S. Viet Folder, NARA; *Pentagon Papers*, 2:177–180.

54. JCS to COMUSMACV, JCS 9438, 11 April 1963, RG 218, JCS, Central File, 1963 Security Classified, Box 10, JCS Official File, 9155.3/3360 (1 Feb 63) Sec. 2, NARA.

55. William Bundy to McNamara, "Comprehensive Plan for South Vietnam," 20 April 1963, Box 236, OSDHO.

56. Richard Reeves, *President Kennedy: Profile of Power* (Simon and Schuster, 1993), 454; JFK to the NSC, 22 January 1963, *FRUS, 1961–1963,* vol. 8: *National Security Policy,* 8:461, Doc. 125.

57. "Annual Budget Message to the Congress, Fiscal Year 1964," 17 January 1963, *PPP:JFK,* 1963:27, Doc. 21; "Remarks and Question and Answer Period at the American Bankers Association Symposium on Economic Growth," 25 February 1963, *PPP:JFK,* 1963:214, Doc. 77.

58. "Memorandum of Conference with President Kennedy," 27 December 1962, *FRUS, 1961–1963,* 8:446–453, Doc. 121.

59. See Francis J. Gavin, *Gold, Dollars, and Power: The Politics of International Monetary Relations, 1958–1971* (University of North Carolina Press, 2004), 89–104.

60. JFK to the NSC, 22 January 1963, *FRUS, 1961–1963,* 8:460, Doc. 125.

61. See Andrew David and Michael Holm, "The Kennedy Administration and the Battle over Foreign Aid: The Untold Story of the Clay Committee," *Diplomacy & Statecraft* 27 (2016) 1:65–92.

62. "Report on Aid," *Time,* 29 March 1963, 14–16.

63. "Special Message to the Congress on Free World Defense and Assistance Programs," 2 April 1963, *PPP:JFK,* 1963:302, Doc. 118.

64. "A Cutting Report on Foreign Aid," *Newsweek,* 1 April 1963, 17; "A Quest for Concepts," *Time,* 12 April 1963, 22.

65. David and Holm, "The Kennedy Administration and the Battle over Foreign Aid," 74.

66. "Foreign Aid Is a Good Long-Term Policy Tool," *Life,* 12 April 1963, 4.

67. Wood to Trueheart, 27 February 1963; and Thompson schedule, 29 March 1963, both in RG 59, FEA, VWG Subject Files, 1963–1966, Box 2, R. G. K. Thompson Visit to U.S.—April 1963, NARA.

68. Although British ambassador to South Vietnam Harry Hohler found Thompson's report "a heartening document," he was less optimistic about the war's prospects. Hohler to Peck, 1016063, 20 March 1963, FO 371/170100, NA, UK; Hohler to FO, No. 158, 28 March 1963, FO 371/17011, DV1017/17, NA, UK.

69. Thompson, "The Situation in South Vietnam," March 1963, FO 371/17011, DV1017/17, NA, UK.

70. Hohler to Peck, 20 March 1963.

71. Thompson, "The Situation in South Vietnam," March 1963.

72. CINCPAC to JCS, Thompson Visit, 26 March 63, CMH; "Plan to Withdraw 1,000 U.S. Military by 31 Dec 63," Item 2-A-2, CINCPAC Booklet for SECDEF, 6 May 1963, CMH.

73. McNamara writes that his instruction to "prepare a plan" for withdrawing one thousand servicemen was informed by a 29 March 1963 conversation with Thompson, and that he himself raised the subject. Robert S. McNamara, with Brian VanDeMark, *In Retrospect: The Tragedy and Lessons of Vietnam* (Vintage, 1995), 49.

74. Memorandum of a Conversation, 1 April 1963, *FRUS, 1961–1963*, 3:193, Doc. 73.

75. Ledward to Home, 6 April 1963, FO 371/170111, DV103145/22/G, NA, UK; Memorandum of a Conversation, 4 April 1963, *FRUS, 1961–1963*, 3:198–200, Doc. 77.

76. Wood to Nolting, 4 April 1963, *FRUS, 1961–1963*, 3:205, Doc. 79.

77. "Minutes of a Meeting of the Special Group for Counterinsurgency," 4 April 1963, *FRUS, 1961–1963*, 3:202, Doc. 78.

78. Peck Minute, 10 April 1963, FO 371/170111, DV103145/22/G, NA, UK.

79. Wood to Nolting, 4 April 1963, *FRUS, 1961–1963*, 3:204–205, Doc. 79.

80. Wood to Hilsman, 18 April 1963, *FRUS, 1961–1963*, 3:244–245, Doc. 97.

81. "Plan to Withdraw 1,000 U.S. Military by 31 Dec 63," Item 2-A-2, CINCPAC Booklet for SECDEF, 6 May 1963, CMH; AP, "'Own Medicine' Favored for Viet Cong by Wheeler," *WP*, 5 February 1963, A4.

82. Rusk to Nolting, 18 April 1963, *FRUS, 1961–1963*, 3:235, Doc. 95. Rusk's admonition against discussing withdrawal planning with Diem stemmed from a cable in which Nolting proposed to brief Diem on the planning then underway. See Nolting to Rusk, 7 April 1963, *FRUS, 1961–1963*, 3:213–214, Doc. 82.

83. JCS-Sec Def Discussions, 29 April 1963, U.S. Joint Chiefs of Staff, Proceedings of Eighth Secretary of Defense Conference on Vietnam, Vietnam Center and Sam Johnson Archive, https://vva.vietnam.ttu.edu/images.php?img=/images/132/1320101002E.pdf, 218.

84. Nitze Notes, S/D, JCS Mtg., 29 April 1963, Nitze Papers, Box 81, Folder 2, Library of Congress. The relevant passage reads, "Plan to take out, with plan for SV to take over. Pres. wld like."

85. See Nolting to Thuan, 18 March 1963, *FRUS, 1961–1963*, 3:156–61, Doc. 61; Nolting to State, 852, 28 March 1963, *FRUS, 1961–1963*, 3:184, Doc. 68.

86. Hohler to Home (11210G/63), Despatch No. 17, 12 March 1963, FO 371/170110, DV103145/19/G, NA, UK.

87. Hohler to Warner (1015/63), 3 April 1963, FO 371/170111, DV103145/23, NA, UK.

88. Nolting to State, 5 April 1963, *FRUS, 1961–1963*, 3:207–213, Doc. 81.

89. Wood to Harriman and Rice, 9 April 1963, RG 59, Bureau of Far Eastern Affairs, Vietnam Working Group Subject Files, 1963–1966, Box 1, NARA. For insight into that dilemma, see Douglas S. Blaufarb, *The Counterinsurgency Era: U.S. Doctrine and Performance* (Free Press, 1977), 73.

90. Wood to Harriman and Rice, "Viet-Nam: Funding and U.S. Personnel," 9 April 1963, RG 59, FEA, VWG Subject Files, 1963–1966, Box 1, NARA. A handwritten note in the text reads, "Also, excess numbers could be withdrawn from Saigon now."

91. Nolting to State, 7 April 1963, *FRUS, 1961–1963*, 3:213–214, Doc. 82.

5. Acceleration

1. For accounts of these events, see Edward Miller, *Misalliance: Ngo Dinh Diem, the United States, and the Fate of South Vietnam* (Harvard University Press, 2013), 260–268; Miller, "Religious Revival and the Politics of Nation Building: Reinterpreting the 1963 'Buddhist Crisis' in South Vietnam," *Modern Asian Studies* 49 (2015) 6:1903–1962; A. J. Langguth, *Our Vietnam: The War, 1954–1975* (Simon and Schuster, 2000), 210–216.

2. Nick Bryant, *The Bystander: John F. Kennedy and the Struggle for Black Equality* (Basic Books, 2006), 387.

3. National Opinion Research Center, Amalgam Study #160, Question 50, US-NORC.16OSRS.R33 (Roper Center, 1963), Roper iPoll; Louis Harris & Associates, June 1963, Question 2, USHARRIS.070163.R2 (Roper Center, 1963), Roper iPoll.

4. Warren Weaver, "Rockefeller Scores U.S. Cuban Policy," *NYT*, 11 April 1963, 1. For commentary on Rockefeller's prospects, see James Reston, "The 'New Rockefeller' Comes to Town," *NYT*, 12 April 1963, 21.

5. James Reston, "Foes Put Kennedy on the Defensive," *NYT*, 1 April 1963, 1; Richard Wilson, "An Air of Indecision Runs through Present Phase of Kennedy Policies," *Los Angeles Times*, 2 April 1963, A5.

6. Gallup Poll #1963-0667 and Gallup Poll #1963-0673, both in Gallup Organization (Roper Center), Roper iPoll.

7. Hilsman and Forrestal to JFK, 25 January 1963, *FRUS, 1961–1963*, vol. 3: *Vietnam, January–August, 1963*, 49–62, Doc. 19; Wheeler to JCS, January 1963, *FRUS, 1961–1963*, 3:73–94, Doc. 26.

8. NIE 53–63, 17 April 1963, *FRUS, 1961–1963*, 3:233–234, Doc. 94. See also Harold P. Ford, *CIA and the Vietnam Policymakers: Three Episodes, 1962–1968* (Center for the Study of Intelligence, 1998), 1–28, for the problematic nature of that assessment.

9. George C. Herring, *America's Longest War: The United States in Vietnam* (McGraw-Hill, 2002), 111; see also David Kaiser, *American Tragedy: Kennedy, Johnson, and the Origins of the Vietnam War* (Belknap Press of Harvard University Press, 2000), 186–202.

10. Lawrence Freedman, *Kennedy's Wars: Berlin, Cuba, Laos, and Vietnam* (Oxford University Press, 2000), 352–355; William J. Rust, *So Much to Lose: John F. Kennedy and American Policy in Laos* (University Press of Kentucky, 2014), 197–216.

11. Wood Memorandum, "The Secretary of Defense's Honolulu Conference on Viet-Nam 6 May 1963," 7 May 1963, RG 330, OASD/ISA, Assistant for (CI) Files, 1962–1965, Vietnam (CI) 1963, Box 4, NARA.

12. Wood Memorandum, 7 May 1963. See also U.S. Joint Chiefs of Staff, Proceedings of Eighth Secretary of Defense Conference on Vietnam, 6 May 1963 (hereafter Eighth SecDef), Vietnam Center and Sam Johnson Vietnam Archive, https://vva.vietnam.ttu.edu/images.php?img=/images/132/1320101002A.pdf, 39–41; Douglas C. Dacy, *Foreign Aid, War, and Economic Development: South Vietnam, 1955–1975* (Cambridge University Press, 1986), 200.

13. Eighth SecDef, 39.

14. Eighth SecDef, 42.

15. Agenda items included the general situation in South Vietnam, the CPSVN, the role of attack aircraft, and U.S.-GVN relations.

16. Eighth SecDef, 26–27.

17. Eighth SecDef, 158.

18. Eighth SecDef, 25, 47.

19. Eighth SecDef, 115.

20. "Plan to Withdraw 1,000 U.S. Military by 31 Dec 63," Item 2-A-2, CINCPAC Booklet for SECDEF, 6 May 1963, CMH.

21. Heinz Memorandum, 6 May 1963, 8 May 1963, *FRUS, 1961–1963*, 3:270, Doc. 107.

22. Eighth SecDef, 115, 47.

23. Eighth SecDef, 48.

24. "Plan to Withdraw 1,000 U.S. Military by 31 Dec 63," Item 2-A-2, CINCPAC Booklet for SecDef, 6 May 1963, CMH.

25. Eighth SecDef, 48.

26. "Plan to Withdraw 1,000 U.S. Military by 31 Dec 63," Item 2-A-2, CINCPAC Booklet for SECDEF, 6 May 1963, CMH.

27. Meeting Tape 85, 7 May 1963, JFK Papers, POF, Presidential Recordings, JFKL. Draft Transcript, Presidential Recordings Program, Miller Center of Public Affairs, University of Virginia.

28. *Pentagon Papers*, 2:181. McNamara to Nitze, 8 May 1963, *FRUS, 1961–1963*, 3:276n4, Doc. 111.

29. McNamara to Nitze, 8 May 1963, *FRUS, 1961–1963*, 3:276, Doc. 111.

30. Taylor to McNamara, CM-601-63, 28 May 1963, RG 218, Central File, 1963, Security Classified, Box 3, NARA.

31. Felt to JCS, 11 May 1963, *FRUS, 1961–1963*, 3:293, Doc. 121.

32. William B. Rosson, "Four Periods of American Involvement in Vietnam: Development and Implementation of Policy, Strategy, and Programs" (Ph.D. diss., New College, University of Oxford, 1979), 178–180.

33. AP, "G.I. Killed by Fire of Vietnam Sniper," *NYT*, 8 May 1963, 10.

34. Warren Unna, "Viet-Nam Wants 50% of GIs Out," *WP*, 12 May 1963, A1.

35. See, for example, Nicholas Turner, "U.S., Vietnam Quarrel over Military Advisers," *WP*, 27 April 1963, A12; see also Miller, *Misalliance*, 256–260.

36. "U.S. and South Viet-Nam," *WP*, 14 May 1963, A18. In the wake of the article, several figures, including Nhu, questioned Unna's reporting, denying that Nhu called for a 50 percent cut in the advisory presence. See also D. F. Murray to A. J. Williams, 23 May 1963, FO 371/170111, DV103145/30, NA, UK.

37. Unna, "Nhu Explains Anti-U.S. Views," *WP*, 13 May 1963, A5; David Halberstam, "Vietnamese Dispute U.S. Advisers on Strategy," *NYT*, 14 May 1963, 10.

38. Unna, "Viet-Nam Wants 50% of GIs Out."

39. Editorial Note, *FRUS, 1961–1963,* 3:307–308, Doc 127. "U.S. and Saigon Want No Cut in G.I. Force," *NYT,* 18 May 1963, 5.

40. Hearings before a Subcommittee of the Committee on Appropriations, 88th Congress, 1st session, 15 May 1963, *Foreign Operations Appropriations for 1964* (GPO, 1963), 90, 94.

41. "The President's News Conference of May 22, 1963," *PPP:JFK,* 1963:421, Doc. 202.

42. On the U.S.-South Korean relationship, see Gregg Brazinsky, *Nation Building in South Korea: Koreans, Americans, and the Making of a Democracy* (University of North Carolina Press, 2007).

43. Mansfield to JFK, 2 November 1961, *FRUS, 1961–1963,* vol. 1: *Vietnam, 1961,* 470, Doc. 207; Galbraith to JFK, 4 April 1962, *FRUS,1961–1963,* vol. 2: *Vietnam, 1962,* 297, Doc. 141.

44. AP, "Mansfield Condemns Proposals to Bomb Viet-Nam," *WP,* 1 May 1963, A9. See also Mansfield to JFK, 19 August 1963, *FRUS, 1961–1963,* 3:585, Doc. 258.

45. Bowles to JFK, 7 March 1963, *FRUS, 1961–1963,* 3:138, Doc. 52. Mansfield also warned that taking the war to Hanoi could result in a Korean-type conflict. "7 Americans Hurt in Vietnam Attacks," *NYT,* 1 May 1963, 4.

46. "10 Years since Stalin," *NYT,* 11 March 1963, 13.

47. Jack Anderson, "Viet-Nam War Enters New Stage," *WP,* 5 May 1963, E7.

48. See C. L. Sulzberger, "A Time for Surgery in Laos," *NYT,* 24 April 1963, 26; Burris to Johnson, 16 March 1962, *FRUS, 1961–1963,* 2:237, Doc. 112.

49. David Halberstam, "Complexities Cloud Battle in Vietnam," *NYT,* 5 May 1963, 195.

50. Noam Kochavi, "Opportunities Lost? Kennedy, China, and Vietnam," in *Behind the Bamboo Curtain: China, Vietnam, and the World Beyond Asia,* ed. Priscilla Roberts (Woodrow Wilson Center Press, 2006), 127–151; Zach Fredman, "'The Specter of an Expansionist China': Kennedy Administration Assessments of Chinese Intentions in Vietnam," *Diplomatic History* 38 (January 2014), 111–136.

51. Max Frankel, "World Events—A Survey of the Past Four Months," *NYT,* 7 April 1963, E5.

52. "Seoul Syndrome in Saigon," *NYT,* 19 July 1963, 24.

53. "Free Elections, Korean Style," *NYT,* 7 September 1963, 18.

54. Eighth SecDef, 39.

55. Wood Memorandum, "The Secretary of Defense's Honolulu Conference on Viet-Nam 6 May 1963."

56. Meeting Tape 85, Draft Transcript. For broader concerns about supporting Seoul, see Komer to Kennedy, 31 May 1963, and Forrestal to Legere, 11 June 1963, both in NSF, Box 431, Korea—1961–1963, JFKL.

57. Gordon to the Heads of Executive Departments and Establishments, Bulletin No. 63-13, "Office and Missions Abroad," 10 May 1963, RG 218, Central File 1963, Security Classified, Box 3, NARA.

58. McNamara News Conference, 11 July 1963, Box 236, Vietnam, Jan–Aug 1963, Box 236, OSDHO. For the Cost Reduction Program, see Lawrence S. Kaplan, Ronald D. Landa, and Edward J. Drea, *The McNamara Ascendancy, 1961–1965* (OSDHO, 2006), 453–462.

59. WPB to Taylor, "Review of MAAG's, Missions, Attaches—BoB Bulletin 63-13," 24 May 1963, RG 218, Central File 1963, Security Classified, Box 3, NARA.

60. Gordon to McNamara, 18 May 1963; and WPB to Taylor, "Review of MAAG's, Missions, Attaches—BoB Bulletin 63-13," 24 May 1963, both in RG 218, Central File 1963, Security Classified, Box 3, NARA.

61. See "Review of MAAGs, Missions, Attaches—Bureau of the Budget Bulletin 63-13 (U)," 3 June 1963, RG 218, Central File 1963, Security Classified, Box 3, NARA.

62. OASD to USCINCEUR, CINCPAC, CINCARIB, 13 May 1963, RG 330, OASD/ISA, Outgoing Message File, July 1962–September 1963, Box 1, May 1963, NARA.

63. Meyer to Taylor, "Interview with the Secretary of Defense (U)," J4DM-165-63, 3 July 1963, RG 218, Central File 1963, Security Classified, Box 3, NARA.

64. John Prados, *Vietnam: The History of an Unwinnable War, 1945–1975* (University Press of Kansas, 2009), 76. Miller, *Misalliance*, 268–275.

65. See Neil Sheehan, *A Bright Shining Lie: John Paul Vann and America in Vietnam* (Random House, 1988), 337–339.

66. Krulak Report, undated, *FRUS, 1961–1963,* 3:455–456, 464–465, Doc. 207.

67. SNIE 53-2-63, "Situation in South Vietnam," 1 July 1963, CIA Records Search Tool.

68. R. G. K. Thompson, "Report on Visits to Provinces," June 1963, FO 371/170101, DV1017/29, NA, UK.

69. J. P. Harris, "The Early Military History of the Second Indochina War and the Moyar Thesis," *Journal of Military History* 85 (July 2021), 3:755–756. Krulak, on the other hand, reported that 97 percent of those living in Ninh Thuan province resided in strategic hamlets, and that it "will probably soon be declared officially 'white.'" Krulak Report, *FRUS, 1961–1963,* 3:458, Doc. 207.

70. Krulak Report, *FRUS, 1961–1963,* 3:465, Doc. 207; Appendix, Visit to Vietnam, 25 June–1 July 1963, Questions Presented to the Assistance Command, F-2, RG 200, McNamara Records, Visit to Vietnam, June 25–July 1, 1963, Box 63, NARA.

71. Krulak Report, *FRUS, 1961–1963,* 3:465, Doc. 207.

72. Appendix, Visit to Vietnam, F-1, G-2.

73. Appendix, Visit to Vietnam, F-2.

74. Appendix, Visit to Vietnam, F-2.

75. CINCPAC Conference, 12 Jul 63, Tab E, RG 472, MACV HQ, Secretary of the Joint Staff (MACJ03), Box 1, CINCPAC Conference, NARA. The document indicates that Harkins "was requested" to plan for the 1,000-man reduction "prior" to the 6 May SecDef Conference.

76. CINCPAC to JCS, "Withdrawal 1000 U.S. Military from Vietnam," 212210Z Jul, 21 July 1963, NSF, Box 200A, Vietnam, General, 10/6/63–10/14/63, Defense Cables, JFKL.

77. "An Angry Buddhist Burns Himself Alive," *Life,* 21 June 1963, 24–25; "Time for Diem to Mend His Ways," *Life,* 26 July 1963, 4; "The Battle of Time and the River," *Newsweek,* 15 July 1963, 36; "South Vietnam: Suicide in Many Forms," *Time,* 19 July 1963, 32.

78. American Opinion Survey, "U.S. Policy on South Vietnam," 11 July 1963, Thomson Papers, Box 23, Vietnam: American Opinion Survey, July 1963 and October 1963, JFKL.

79. "Commencement Address at American University in Washington," 10 June 1963, *PPP:JFK,* 1963:459–464, Doc. 232.

80. "The President's News Conference of July 17, 1963," *PPP:JFK,* 1963:569, Doc. 305.

81. For an overview of the domino theory and the Kennedy administration, see Frank Ninkovich, *Modernity and Power: A History of the Domino Theory in the Twentieth Century* (University of Chicago Press, 1994), 241–275; for a critical approach to its use by Kennedy and Johnson officials, see Gareth Porter, *Perils of Dominance: Imbalance of Power and the Road to War in Vietnam* (University of California Press, 2005), 229–258.

82. McNamara News Conference, Pentagon, 19 July 1963, McNamara Papers, Part II, Speeches & Writings, Box 89, Folder 4C, Library of Congress.

83. American Opinion Survey, "South Viet-Nam," 24 July 1963, Thomson Papers, Box 23, Vietnam: American Opinion Survey, July 1963 and October 1963, JFKL.

84. Meeting Tape 96, 4 July 1963, JFK Papers, POF, Presidential Recordings, JFKL. Draft Transcript, Presidential Recordings Program, Miller Center of Public Affairs, University of Virginia. The published memcon of the meeting includes no mention of Kennedy's comment. See Memorandum of a Conversation, 4 July 1963, *FRUS, 1961–1963,* 3:451–453, Doc. 205.

85. See particularly his comments regarding Ap Bac and his remarks to Lodge. Meeting Tape 104/A40, 15 August 1963, JFK Papers, POF, Presidential Recordings, JFKL. Draft Transcript, Presidential Recordings Program, Miller Center of Public Affairs, University of Virginia.

86. For a narrative of those developments, see Richard Reeves, *President Kennedy: Profile of Power* (Simon and Schuster, 1993), 507–585.

87. Rowen (for W. P. Bundy), to McNamara, 30 August 1963, Box 236, OSDHO; Covering Brief from Nitze (ISA) to the McNamara, I-26004/63, 30 August 1963, Box 236, OSDHO.

88. Taylor to McNamara, JCSM-629–63, 20 August 1963, RG 218, Central File, 1963 Security Classified, Box 11, JCS Official File, 9155.3/3440 (26 May 63), NARA.

89. Mecklin to Trueheart, "U.S. Military Strength in Vietnam," 8 July 1963, RG 472, MACV HQ, Secretary to the Joint Staff (MACJO3), Box 1, CINCPAC Conference, 12 July 163, Tab E, NARA.

90. Saigon to FO, No. 386, 7 August 1963, FO 371/170111, DV103145/36, NA, UK. See also Saigon to FO, No. 381, 3 August 1963, and Washington to FO, No. 2446, 5 August 1963, FO 371/170111, DV103145/36, NA, UK.

91. Cover Notes, "American Presence in Saigon," 12 August 1963, FO 371/170111, DV103145/36, NA, UK.

92. Burrows to Warner, 10310/63, 8 August 1963, FO 371/170111, DV103145/38/G, NA, UK.

93. For background on Lodge's appointment, see Rusk-Reston Telcon, 11 March 1964, 12:30, RG 59, Records of Secretary of State Dean Rusk, Transcripts of Telephone Calls, Box 50, NARA; Forrestal Oral History, 8 April 1964, 46–51, and 14 August 1964, 142–146, JFKL; Harriman Oral History, 6 June 1965, 111–112, JFKL; Roger Hilsman, *To Move a Nation: The Politics of Foreign Policy in the Administration of John F. Kennedy* (Doubleday, 1967), 478.

94. Brian VanDeMark, *Road to Disaster: A New History of America's Descent into Vietnam* (HarperCollins, 2018), 163–165.

95. CIA Information Report, 17 July 1963, JFK Papers, NSF, Box 198, Vietnam, General 7/1/63–7/20/63, JFKL.

96. Meeting Tape 104/A40, 15 August 1963, JFK Papers, POF, Presidential Recordings, JFKL. Draft Transcript.

97. Ball to Lodge, 243, *FRUS, 1961–1963,* 3:628–629, Doc. 281; Maxwell D. Taylor, *Swords and Plowshares* (Norton, 1972), 292.

98. As Rusk told Lodge, "highest levels in Washington are giving this problem almost full-time attention." Rusk to Lodge, 284, 30 August 1963, *FRUS, 1961–1963,* vol. 4: *Vietnam, August–December, 1963,* 63, Doc. 31.

99. Hilsman memcon, 26 August 1963, 12:00, Hilsman Papers, Box 4, Vietnam, White House Meetings, 8/26/63–10/29/63, State Memoranda, JFKL. See also Krulak memcon, 26 August 1963, *FRUS, 1961–1963,* 3:638–641, Doc. 289.

100. CIA Station Saigon to Agency, 28 August 1963, *FRUS, 1961–1963,* 3:671, Doc. 207; Smith memcon, 28 August 1963, *FRUS, 1961–1963,* 4:2, 5, Doc. 1.

101. Lodge to State, 375, 29 August 1963, *FRUS, 1961–1963,* 4:20–21, Doc. 12.

102. Smith memcon, 27 August 1963, *FRUS, 1961–1963,* 3:663–664, Doc. 303.

103. Smith memcon, 28 August 1963, *FRUS, 1961–1963,* 4:5, Doc. 1.

104. JFK to Lodge, 29 August 1963, *FRUS, 1961–1963,* 4:35, Doc. 18.

105. CIA Station Saigon to Agency, 31 August 1963, *FRUS, 1961–1963,* 4:64, Doc. 32.

106. Miller, *Misalliance,* 295–298.

107. Hilsman memcon, 31 August 1963, *FRUS, 1961–1963,* 4:70–74, Doc. 37.

108. Krulak memcon, 31 August 1963, Taylor Papers, Box 50-F, 10-71B, National Defense University. The Krulak memcon cites McNamara agreeing with Rusk's position, while the Hilsman memcon does not.

109. These quotations draw on both the Hilsman and Krulak memcons of the meeting. Meeting memcon, "Vietnam," 31 August 1963, *FRUS, 1961–1963,* 4:74, Doc. 37; Meeting memcon, 31 August 1963, *US-VR,* 12:543.

110. Meeting memcon, 31 August 1963, *FRUS, 1961–1963,* 4:72, Doc. 37; Rusk to Lodge, 272, 29 August 1963, *FRUS, 1961–1963,* 4:32–33, Doc. 16; Lodge to Rusk, 391, 31 August 1963, *FRUS, 1961–1963,* 4:68, Doc. 34; Rusk to Lodge, 294, 31 August 1963, *FRUS, 1961–1963,* 4:76, Doc. 39.

6. Declaration

1. Peter Grose, "De Gaulle Offers to Help Vietnam End Foreign Role," *NYT,* 30 August 1963, 1; Fredrik Logevall, *Choosing War: The Lost Chance for Peace and the Escalation of War in Vietnam* (University of California Press, 1999), 1–42; Sean J. McLaughlin, *JFK and de Gaulle: How America and France Failed in Vietnam, 1961–1963* (University Press of Kentucky, 2019).

2. Memorandum of a Conversation, 30 August 1963, Department of State, *FRUS, 1961–1963,* vol. 4: *Vietnam, August–December, 1963,* 60, Doc. 28.

3. See Saigon to State, 31 August 1963, *FRUS, 1961–1963,* 4:67, Doc. 34; Memorandum of a Conversation, 31 August 1963, *FRUS, 1961–1963,* 4:72, Doc. 37.

4. "Transcript of Broadcast with Walter Cronkite Inaugurating CBS Television News Program," September 2, 1963, *PPP:JFK,* 1963:652, Doc. 340.

5. "Transcript of Broadcast on NBC's 'Huntley-Brinkley Report,'" 9 September 1963, *PPP:JFK,* 1963:659–660, Doc. 349.

6. "The President's News Conference of September 12, 1963," *PPP:JFK,* 1963:673, Doc. 356.

7. "Transcript of Broadcast on NBC's 'Huntley-Brinkley Report,'" *PPP:JFK,* 1963:659.

8. Fredrik Logevall, *JFK: Coming of Age in the American Century, 1917–1956* (Random House, 2020), 575.

9. "The President's News Conference of April 24, 1963," *PPP:JFK,* 1963:349, Doc. 144.

10. Forrestal to JFK, 4 September 1963, JFK Papers, NSF, Box 199, Vietnam, General, 9/1/63–9/10/63, Memos and Misc., JFKL; Rusk to Lodge, 324, 4 September 1963, *FRUS, 1961–1963,* 4:108–109, Doc. 59.

11. Walter Lippmann, "Mr. Kennedy on Viet-Nam," *WP,* 5 September 1963, A17; Arthur Krock, "The Value of Continuity in Interviewing," *NYT,* 5 September 1963, 30.

12. "Foreign Relations: Diplomacy by Television," *Time,* 13 September 1963, 23; "Getting to Know the Nhus," *Newsweek,* 9 September 1963, 33; Emmet John Hughes, "A Lesson from Vietnam," *Newsweek,* 9 September 1963, 17.

13. "What to Do about Vietnam," *Newsweek,* 23 September 1963, 23; see also "Embarrassment or Defeat?" *Newsweek,* 16 September 1963, 13.

14. "Confusion on Vietnam," *NYT,* 22 September 1963, 176.

15. American Opinion Survey, "Viet-Nam," 18 September 1963, copies sent from Read to Bundy, 23 September 1963, NSF, Box 200, Vietnam, General, 9/22/63–10/5/63, JFKL.

16. Arthur Krock, "U.S. Policy in Asia," *NYT,* 22 September 1963, 177; Chalmers M. Roberts, "Impatient American: Peril to Win-War Policy," *WP,* 14 September 1963, A9; Walter Lippmann, "Whither Viet-Nam?" *WP,* 17 September 1963, A13.

17. Louis Harris & Associates Poll: September 1963, Question 5, USHARRIS .093063.R1, Louis Harris & Associates (Roper Center, 1963), Roper iPoll. For the ambiguities of opinion in 1964 and 1965, see Logevall, *Choosing War.*

18. Lodge to Rusk, 4 September 1963, *FRUS, 1961–1963,* 4:108, Doc. 58.

19. State to Saigon, 5 September 1963, *FRUS, 1961–1963,* 4:113, Doc. 63.

20. Chalmers M. Roberts, "Viet-Nam Aid Cutoff Threatened on 'Hill,'" *WP,* 7 September 1963, A1.

21. Smith Memcon, 6 September 1963, *FRUS, 1961–1963,* 4:118, 117, Doc. 66.

22. Rusk to Lodge, 6 September 1963, *FRUS, 1961–1963,* 4:131–132, Doc. 72.

23. *Congressional Record,* 9 September 1963, 88th Cong. 1st sess., 109, pt. 12:16522. For Hilsman's collaboration with Church, see Thomson Papers, Box 23, 1963, General, 4/63–9/63, JFKL.

24. For Goldwater, see *Congressional Record,* 17 September 1963, 88th Cong., 1st sess., 109, pt. 13:17321–17323; for Jackson, see *Congressional Record,* 16 September 1963, 17028–17029; for Symington, see *Congressional Record,* 6 September 1963, pt. 12: 16451–16452.

25. See, for instance, James Reston, "On Suppressing the News Instead of the Nhus," *NYT,* 11 September 1963, 42; David Halberstam, "Setback in Vietnam," *NYT,* 8 September 1963, E4; Tad Szulc, "U.S. Considering Cut in Saigon Aid to Force Reform," *NYT,* 9 September 1963, 1.

26. Tom Wicker, "Kennedy Says Red Threat Bars Saigon Aid Cut Now," *NYT,* 10 September 1963, 1.

27. Robert Mann, *A Grand Delusion: America's Descent into Vietnam* (Basic Books, 2001), 289–290.

28. "The President's News Conference of September 12, 1963," *PPP:JFK,* 1963:676, Doc. 356.

29. Note to Hilsman, 12 September 1963, Thomson Papers, Box 23, 1963 General, 4/63–9/63, JFKL; see also Memcon, 11 September 1963, "Vietnam," *FRUS, 1961–1963,* 4:190–193, Doc. 94.

30. Saigon to State, 7 September 1963, *FRUS, 1961–1963,* 4:131, Doc. 72; Saigon to State, 14 September 1963, *FRUS, 1961–1963,* 4:208, Doc. 106. For more on the Church resolution, see LeRoy Ashby and Rod Gramer, *Fighting the Odds: The Life of Senator Frank Church* (Washington State University Press, 1994), 168–171.

31. Taylor to McNamara, "Summary Report on Eighth Secretary of Defense Conference Honolulu, 7 May (Withdrawal of 1,000 US Military from Vietnam," JCSM-629–63, 20 August 1963; and McNamara to Taylor, "Withdrawal of 1,000 US Military from Vietnam," 3 September 1963, both in RG 218, JCS, Central File, 1963 Security Classified, Box 11, JCS Official File, 9155.3/3440 (26 May 63), NARA.

32. Taylor to JFK, CM-882–63, 9 September 1963, RG 218, Taylor Records, Box 12, NARA; CIA, "The Situation in South Vietnam," 16 September 1963, NSF, Box 317, Meetings on Vietnam, 9/16/63 (B), JFKL.

33. McNamara-Taylor Report, 2 October 1963, *US-VR,* 12:559.

34. Sarris memo, 30 September 1963, Hilsman Papers, Box 4, Vietnam, 9/21/63–9/26/63, Folder 10, JFKL.

35. Thompson, Report on Visits to Delta Provinces, June–August 1963, RG 200, McNamara Records, Box 63, NARA.

36. Taylor to McNamara, "Projection of US Military Strength in the Republic of Vietnam (RVN)," CM-874-63, 11 September 1963, RG 218, Taylor Records, Box 12, NARA.

37. CINCPAC to JCS, 032250Z, "Withdrawal 1000 U.S. Military Personnel from Vietnam," 3 September 1963, RG 218, Central File, 1963 Security Classified, Box 11, JCS Official File, 9155.3/3440 (26 May 63), NARA; Taylor to McNamara, CM-874-63, 11 September 1963, RG 218, Taylor Records, Box 12, NARA.

38. JCS to CINCPAC, JCS 2388, "Withdrawal of 1000 US Military from Vietnam," 6 September 1963, RG 218, Central File, 1963 Security Classified, Box 11, JCS Official File, 9155.3/3440 (26 May 63), NARA.

39. McNamara to Taylor, "Approval of 'Model Plan' for Vietnam," 6 September 1963, RG 218, JCS, Central File, 1963 Security Classified, Box 10, JCS Official File, 9155.3/3360 (25 Jan 63) Sec. 4, NARA.

40. CINCPAC to JCS, "Transmittal of FY65–69 Alternate MA Plans for Republic of Vietnam," 18 July 1963, RG 218, JCS, Central File, 1963 Security Classified, Box 10, JCS Official File, 9155.3/3360 (25 Jan 63) Sec. 4, NARA.

41. Smith memcon, 6 September 1963, *FRUS, 1961–1963,* 4:117–120, Doc. 66; see also Editorial Note, *FRUS, 1961–1963,* 4:121, Doc. 67.

42. Meeting Tape 109, 10 September 1963, JFK Papers, POF, Presidential Recordings, JFKL. Draft Transcript, Presidential Recordings Program, Miller Center of Public Affairs, University of Virginia.

43. Meeting Tape 109, 10 September 1963. Draft Transcript. See also Memcon, 10 September 1963, *FRUS, 1961–1963,* 4:161–167, Doc. 83.

44. Krulak Memorandum, 1745, 10 September 1963, RG 218, Taylor Records, Box 12, NARA. Several of those references are absent from the Smith memcon, 10 September 1963, *FRUS, 1961–1963,* 4:169–171, Doc. 85.

45. Lodge to State, 11 September 1963, *FRUS, 1961–1963,* 4:173–174, Doc. 86; Rusk-McG. Bundy Telcon, 11 September 1963, *FRUS, 1961–1963,* 4:176, Doc. 88.

46. Smith Memcon, 11 September 1963, *FRUS, 1961–1963,* 4:174–175, Doc. 87.

47. Hilsman, "U.S. Objectives in Current Viet-Nam Situation," 11 September 1963, *FRUS, 1961–1963,* 4:177–180, Doc. 89; see also Hilsman, "Possible Political Pressure Weapons for Use against Diem and Nhu," 11 September 1963, *FRUS, 1961–1963,* 4:180–181, Doc. 90.

48. Forrestal memorandum, 11 September 1963, *FRUS, 1961–1963,* 4:182, Doc. 91.

49. Krulak Memcon, 11 September 1963, "Vietnam," Taylor Papers, Trip to Vietnam, September 7–10, National Defense University; Smith Memcon, 11 September 1963, "Vietnam," *FRUS, 1961–1963,* 4:185–190, Doc. 93; Rusk to Lodge, 12 September 1963, *FRUS, 1961–1963,* 4:196–198, Doc. 98; Rusk to Lodge, 12 September 1963, *FRUS, 1961–1963,* 4:195, Doc. 97.

50. Lodge to Rusk, 13 September 1963, *FRUS, 1961–1963,* 4:203, Doc. 102.

51. Hilsman memorandum, 16 September 1963, Attachment 1, *FRUS, 1961–1963,* 4:221–230, Doc. 114.

52. "CIA Station in Saigon to the Agency," 0698, 6 September 1963, *FRUS, 1961–1963,* 4:125, 127, Doc. 69.

53. "CIA Station in Saigon to the Agency," 2 September 1963, *FRUS, 1961–1963,* 4:89, Doc. 47. Numerous sources address Nhu's gambit; for instance, see also "CIA Station in Saigon to the Agency," 0940, 17 September 1963, *FRUS, 1961–1963,* 4:239–240, Doc. 119; McCone-Harriman Telcon, 13 September 1963, *FRUS, 1961–1963,* 4:204, Doc. 103; CIA Memorandum, "The Situation in South Vietnam," 17 September 1963, JFK Papers, NSF, Box 200, Vietnam, General, Memos & Misc., 9/16/63–9/18/63, JFKL. For a review of this episode, see Miller, *Misalliance,* 302–311.

54. McCone Memorandum, 13 September 1963, *FRUS, 1961–1963,* 4:206–207, Doc. 105; Hughes Memorandum, 15 September 1963, *FRUS, 1961–1963,* 4:213–214, Doc. 110.

55. Hughes to Rusk, "The Problem of Nhu," 15 September 1963, NSF, Box 317, 9/16/63 (B), JFKL; Kattenburg to Lodge, 7 September 1963, Hilsman Papers, Box 4, Vietnam, 9/1/63–9/10/63, Folder 1, JFKL.

56. Attachment 2, Draft telegram from State to Lodge, 16 September 1963, *FRUS, 1961–1963,* 4:225, Doc. 114.

57. Forrestal to Bundy, 16 September 1963, *FRUS, 1961–1963,* 4:236, Doc. 116.

58. "Saigon Arresting Leading Civilians," *NYT,* 15 September 1963, 1.

59. Meeting Tape 111, 17 September 1963, JFK Papers, POF, Presidential Recordings, JFKL. Draft Transcript, Presidential Recordings Program, Miller Center of Public Affairs, University of Virginia.

60. JFK to Lodge, 17 September 1963, *FRUS, 1961–1963,* 4:252–54, Doc. 125. See also Harriman-Forrestal Telcon, 17 September 1963, *FRUS, 1961–1963,* 4:251, Doc. 124.

61. This narrative comes from Meeting Tape 111, 19 September 1963, JFK Papers, POF, Presidential Recordings, JFKL. Draft Transcript.

62. Memorandum for the Record, "SVN Trip," 19 September 1963, RG 218, Taylor Records, Box 12, NARA.

63. JFK to McNamara, 21 September 1963, *FRUS, 1961–1963,* 4:278–279, Doc. 142.

64. Meeting Tape 112, 23 September 1963, JFK Papers, POF, Presidential Recordings, JFKL. Draft Transcript, Presidential Recordings Program, Miller Center of Public Affairs, University of Virginia.

65. Meeting Tape 112, 23 September 1963. Draft Transcript.

66. Meeting Tape 112, 23 September 1963. Draft Transcript.

67. Andrew L. Johns, *Vietnam's Second Front: Domestic Politics, the Republican Party, and the War* (University Press of Kentucky, 2010), 36–37.

68. Taylor to Harkins, 21 September 1963, RG 218, Taylor Records, Box 12, NARA. See JFK to Lodge, 21 September 1963, NSF, Box 404, Chron File, September 1963 (1 of 2), JFKL, which indicated Kennedy's desire for the trip to happen promptly so that it might have "desired Congressional impact here."

69. Lodge to State, 19 September 1963, *FRUS, 1961–1963,* 4:258–259, Doc. 129.

70. "Time of Decision Fast Ebbing for Diem," *Salt Lake City Tribune,* cited in *Congressional Record,* 23 September 1963, pt. 13:17794.

71. *Congressional Record,* 26 September 1963, pt. 13:18205; Mann, *Grand Delusion,* 294. Morse had called for a US withdrawal on September 9.

72. Ball-Hilsman Telcon, 6:30 p.m., 23 September 1963, Ball Papers, Box 9, Vietnam, 1/15/63–10/4/63, JFKL.

73. See Ball-Bundy Telcon, 12:00 p.m., 24 September 1963, Ball Papers, Box 9, Vietnam, 1/15/63–10/4/63, JFKL.

74. Robert David Johnson, *Congress and the Cold War* (Cambridge University Press, 2006), 93–101.

75. For a snapshot of their itinerary, see Taylor appointment calendar in Taylor Papers, Box 21, Diary 1963, National Defense University. For accounts of the McNamara-Taylor mission, see Howard Jones, *Death of a Generation: How the Assassinations of Diem and JFK Prolonged the Vietnam War* (Oxford University Press, 2003), 369–376; John M. Newman, *JFK and Vietnam: Deception, Intrigue, and the Struggle for Power* (Warner Books, 1992), 388–397.

76. Report of McNamara's 27 September 63 Interview with Richardson, *FRUS, 1961–1963,* 4:301–303, Doc. 154.

77. Report of McNamara 26 September 63 Interview with Professor Smith, *FRUS, 1961–1963,* 4:293–295, Doc. 150, which identified Honey by a pseudonym, "Professor Smith."

78. "Release of U.S. Forces," Submission to the SECDEF Party, September 1963, RG 472, MACV HQ, Secretary to the Joint Staff (MACJ03), Box 15, Submission to the SECDEF Party, Sep 63, NARA.

79. "Mission of U.S. Personnel in Vietnam," Submission to the SECDEF Party, September 1963, RG 472, MACV HQ, Secretary to the Joint Staff (MACJ03), Box 15, Submission to the SECDEF Party, Sep 63, NARA.

80. "Mission of U.S. Personnel in Vietnam," September 1963.

81. Maxwell D. Taylor, *Swords and Plowshares: A Memoir* (Norton, 1972), 298. Mc-Namara and Taylor had two meetings with Diem, the first during the afternoon of 29 September and the second after dinner with Diem that evening. An account of the afternoon meeting, which is devoid of talk about a 1965 target date, is available in "Memorandum of a Conversation," 29 September 1963, *FRUS, 1961–1963*, 4:310–321, Doc. 158.

82. Taylor to Diem, 1 October 1963, *FRUS, 1961–1963*, 4:328–330, Doc. 163.

83. Taylor's appointment book indicates that he worked on it at MACV headquarters on 29 and 30 September. Taylor Papers, Box 21, Diary, 1963, National Defense University. William Bundy also notes that it was "largely written in Saigon but re-worked and revised" on the plane home. William P. Bundy Oral History, 12 November 1964, JFKL.

84. William P. Bundy, unpublished manuscript, 9–23, WPB Papers, Box 1, LBJL.

85. McNamara-Taylor Report, 2 October 1963, *US-VR*, 12:557. This passage in the report, part of its section on "Military Situation and Trends," is absent from the *FRUS* version, as are the sections titled "Economic Situation and Trends," "Political Situation and Trends," and "Effect of Political Tension."

86. McNamara-Taylor Report, 2 October 1963, *FRUS, 1961–1963*, 4:339, Doc. 167.

87. McNamara-Taylor Report, 2 October 1963, 4:346, 340–343.

88. McNamara-Taylor Report, 2 October 1963, 4:337–338.

89. William H. Sullivan Oral History, 16 June 1970, 47, JFKL.

90. According to Taylor's calendar, the conversation addressed a "change in draft trip report for the President," and continued until McNamara and Taylor motored to the White House to brief Kennedy at 11:00 a.m. Taylor Papers, Box 21 Diary, 1963, NDU.

91. McNamara-Taylor Report, *FRUS, 1961–1963*, 4:338.

92. McNamara-Taylor Report, *US-VR*, 12:560.

93. McNamara-Taylor Report, *FRUS, 1961–1963*, 4:339. In this context, suppressing the insurgency meant reducing it "to proportions manageable by the national security forces of the GVN" without the help of US troops. McNamara-Taylor Report, *FRUS, 1961–1963*, 4:339.

94. McNamara-Taylor Report, *FRUS, 1961–1963*, 4:339.

95. McNamara-Taylor Report, *US-VR*, 12:560. These passages are absent from the *FRUS* version of the report.

96. See Bundy, unpublished manuscript, 9–26.

97. Kennedy's Daily Appointment Book excludes McGeorge Bundy from the attendance list, though he was clearly present. No memorandum of the conversation exists, but Kennedy taped roughly fifty-seven minutes of the meeting that his diary lists as running from 11:00 to 11:55 a.m. For Johnson's schedule, see Vice-President's Daily Diary entry, 10/2/1963, Pre-Presidential Daily Diary Collection, LBJ Presidential Library, https://www.discoverlbj.org/item/vpdd-19631002. Dean Rusk was attending United Nations functions in New York.

98. This narrative rests on Meeting Tape 114/A49, 2 October 1963, JFK Papers, POF, Presidential Recordings, JFKL. Draft Transcript, Presidential Recordings Program, Miller Center of Public Affairs, University of Virginia.

99. "M'Namara Agrees to Call It His War," *NYT,* 25 April 1964, 2.

100. Meeting Tape 114/A49, 2 October 1963. Draft Transcript.

101. Krulak to Smith, "Vietnam," SACSA-M 500–63, 6 September 1963, JFK Papers, NSF, Box 199, Vietnam, General, 9/1/63–9/10/63, Memos and Misc., JFKL; Taylor to JFK, CM-882-63, 9 September 1963, JFK Papers, NSF, Box 128A, Vietnam, Security, 1963, JFKL.

102. Hilsman, "Viet-Nam," 23 September 1963, Hilsman Papers, Box 4, Vietnam, 9/21/63–9/26/63, Folder 10, JFKL.

103. JFK to McNamara, 21 September 1963, *FRUS, 1961–1963,* 4:279, Doc. 142.

104. Thompson, "Report on Visits to Delta Provinces, June–August 1963," 14.

7. Implementation

1. Meeting Tape 114/A49, 2 October 1963, JFK Papers, POF, Presidential Recordings, JFKL. Draft Transcript, Presidential Recordings Program, Miller Center of Public Affairs, University of Virginia.

2. "Draft statement to be issued following NSC meeting," 2 October 1963, JFK Papers, NSF, Box 404A, Chron File, Oct 1963, [2 of 2], JFKL; Draft Statements, 2 October 1963, Sorensen Papers, Box 55, Vietnam, 10/2/63–1/19/64, JFKL.

3. "Remarks at the Yellowstone County Fairgrounds, Billings, Montana," 25 September 1963, *PPP:JFK,* 1963:724, Doc. 382.

4. Sullivan and Schlesinger reference that Oval Office meeting, though the McNamara and Taylor memoirs are silent on its existence. William H. Sullivan Oral History, 16 June 1970, 47, JFKL; Arthur M. Schlesinger, Jr., *Robert Kennedy and His Times* (Houghton Mifflin, 1978), 716.

5. At one point during the morning session, Bundy suggested that he, McNamara, and Taylor "go down" to work on the statement after the meeting's conclusion. Meeting Tape 114/A49, 2 October 1963, POF, Presidential Recordings, JFKL. Draft Transcript. See also versions of the statement at JFK Papers, NSF, Box 404A, Chron File, October 1963 [2 of 2], JFKL.

6. Draft, JFK Papers, NSF, Box 200, Vietnam-General 9/22/63–10/5/63, JFKL. Bracketed passage in original.

7. Accounts describe the day's meetings as heated, though they differ on when those contentious exchanges occurred. See Schlesinger, *Robert Kennedy,* 716; John M. Newman, *JFK and Vietnam: Deception, Intrigue, and the Struggle for Power* (Warner Books, 1992), 403; McNamara, *In Retrospect,* 79; Gareth Porter, *Perils of Dominance: Imbalance of Power and the Road to War in Vietnam* (University of California Press, 2005), 175. William P. Bundy, unpublished manuscript, 9–26, William Bundy Papers, Box 1, LBJL.

8. Cooper to McCone, "Comments on McNamara-Taylor Report," 2 October 1963, JFK Papers, NSF, Box 200, Vietnam-General 9/22/63–10/5/63, JFKL. Single and double underlining in original.

9. Chester L. Cooper, *The Lost Crusade: The Full Story of U.S. Involvement in Vietnam from Roosevelt to Nixon* (MacGibbon and Kee, 1970), 215–216. See also Cooper Oral History, 9 June 1966, 49–50, JFKL.

10. Bundy manuscript, 9–23.

11. Handwritten notes, undated, RG 200, McNamara Records, Box 63, NARA.

12. Kai Bird, *The Color of Truth: McGeorge Bundy and William Bundy: Brothers in Arms* (Simon and Schuster, 1998), 257.

13. Etherington-Smith to FO, No. 557, 3 October 1963, FO 371/170112, DV103145/50, NA, UK. See also Etherington-Smith to Earl of Home, 10510/63, Despatch No. 54, 8 October 1963, FO 371/170112, DV103145/54, NA, UK; Roger Hilsman, *To Move a Nation: The Politics of Foreign Policy in the Administration of John F. Kennedy* (Doubleday, 1967), 509–510; Deborah Shapley, *Promise and Power: The Life and Times of Robert McNamara* (Little, Brown, 1993), 260–261.

14. Unless otherwise noted, quotations from the evening NSC session are from Meeting Tape 114/A49, 2 October 1963, JFK Papers, POF, Presidential Recordings, JFKL. Draft Transcript, Presidential Recordings Program, Miller Center of Public Affairs, University of Virginia.

15. For McNamara's later claims that he insisted on withdrawal even in the face of defeat, see McNamara Oral History, 24 July 1986, McNamara Papers, Speeches & Writings, Interviews, OSDHO, Transcripts 1986, Library of Congress; "Notes re JFK and Vietnam," McNamara Papers, Box II:101, Folder 2, Speeches & Writings, "In Retrospect," Drafts & Notes, Miscellaneous 1964, Library of Congress.

16. Meeting Tape 114/A49, 2 October 1963. Draft Transcript.

17. "Summary Record of the 519th Meeting of the NSC," 2 October 1963, U.S. Department of State, *FRUS, 1961–1963,* vol. 4: *Vietnam, August–December, 1963,* 351–352.

18. "White House Statement Following the Return of a Special Mission to South Viet-Nam," 2 October 1963, *PPP:JFK,* 1963:759–760, Doc. 399; "News Conference at the White House with Pierre Salinger," 2 October 1963, McNamara Papers, Part II, Speeches & Writings, Box 89, Folder 5, Library of Congress.

19. American Opinion Survey, "Vietnam," 9 October 1963, Thomson Papers, Box 23, American Opinion Survey, July 1963 and October 1963, JFKL.

20. "Candor Needed on Vietnam," *NYT,* 4 October 1963, 32; "The Mismanaged War," *WSJ,* 4 October 1963, 16.

21. Harriman-Agronsky Telcon, 3 October 1963, Box 581, Telcons October 1963, Harriman Papers, Library of Congress; "Clouded Crystal Ball," *WP,* 4 October 1963, A20.

22. American Opinion Survey, "Vietnam," 9 October 1963.

23. American Opinion Survey, "Vietnam," 9 October 1963.

24. Ball to Lodge, 524, 4 October 1963, RG 59, Subject-Numeric 1963, Box 4050, Political & Rel., 2/1/63, S. Viet, NARA.

25. Etherington-Smith to FO, No. 557, 3 October 1963, FO 371/170112, DV103145/50, NA, UK. See also Etherington-Smith to Earl of Home, 10510/63, Despatch No. 54, 8 October 1963, FO 371/170112, DV103145/54/NA, UK.

26. Ormsby-Gore to FO, No. 3091, 5 October 1963, FO 371/170112, DV103145/50, NA, UK; Historical Division, Joint Secretariat, Joint Chiefs of Staff, *The History of the Joint Chiefs of Staff: The Joint Chiefs of Staff and the War in Vietnam, 1960–1968,* pt. 1, 7–14.

27. Annex to the Draft Report Prepared for the Executive Committee of the National Security Council, 4 October 1963, *FRUS, 1961–1963,* 4:360–364, Doc. 175; Memcon, 4 October 1963, *FRUS, 1961–1963,* 4:358–359, Doc. 174.

28. Memcon, 3 October 1963, *FRUS, 1961–1963,* 4:356–357, Doc. 172.

29. Meeting Tape 114/A50, 5 October 1963, JFK Papers, POF, Presidential Recordings, JFKL. Draft Transcript, Presidential Recordings Program, Miller Center of Public Affairs, University of Virginia.

30. Memcon, 4 October 1963, *FRUS, 1961–1963,* 4:359, Doc. 174.

31. Meeting Tape 114/A50, 5 October 1963. Draft Transcript.

32. Forrestal memcon, 5 October 1963, *FRUS, 1961–1963,* 4:370, Doc. 179.

33. Rusk to Lodge, 5 October 1963, *FRUS, 1961–1963,* 4:371, Doc. 180.

34. Rusk to Lodge, 5 October 1963, *FRUS, 1961–1963,* 4:371–379, Doc. 181.

35. CJCS to CINCPAC, "Approved Actions for South Vietnam," JCS 2792, 5 October 1963, RG 218, Taylor Records, Box 12, NARA.

36. CJCS to CINCPAC, "Approved Actions for South Vietnam."

37. Dutton to Rusk, 8 October 1963, *FRUS, 1961–1963,* 4:390–392, Doc. 190.

38. U.S. Senate, *Executive Sessions of the Committee on Foreign Relations,* "Situation in Vietnam," 8 October 1963, 700–702.

39. "Situation in Vietnam," 8 October 1963, 743–745.

40. "Situation in Vietnam," 8 October 1963, 743–745.

41. See Dutton to Rusk, 8 October 1963, *FRUS, 1961–1963,* 4:390–392, Doc. 190.

42. "The President's News Conference of October 9, 1963," *PPP:JFK,* 1963:769–770, 773–774.

43. Joseph Kraft, "Our Viet Nam Policy Over-Subtle," *Washington Star,* 11 October 1963, Kaplan Box 236, OSDHO. American Opinion Survey, "Viet-Nam," 17 October 1963, JFK Papers, NSF, Box 201, Vietnam-General, 10/15/63–10/28/63, Memos & Miscellaneous, JFKL.

44. State to Lodge, 598, 18 October 1963; and State to Saigon, 644, 25 October 1963, both in RG 84, Vietnam, U.S. Embassy, Saigon, General Records, 1936–1963, Box 82 (old Box 7), 350 Internal Political Affairs, GVN Folder, NARA.

45. Transcript, "Today," NBC-TV, 18 October 1963, Thomson Papers, Box 8, NBC Interview on Vietnam, 10/18/63, JFKL.

46. Bowles to Thomson, 15 October 1963, Thomson Papers, Box 8, 8/63–10/63, JFKL.

47. Lee to WO, MA/17/1A, 17 October 1963, FO 371/170136, DV1201/112, NA, UK.

48. See Memcon, 7 October 1963, *FRUS, 1961–1963,* 4:387, Doc. 187.

49. NSAM 263, 11 October 1963, *FRUS, 1961–1963,* 4:395–396, Doc. 194.

50. Felt to JCS, 17675, 8 October 1963, JFK Papers, Box 200A, Vietnam, General, 10/6/63–10/14/63, Defense Cables, JFKL.

51. Felt to JCS, "Withdrawal of 1000 U.S. Military from Vietnam," DTG 212109Z, 21 October 1963, JFK Papers, Box 201, Vietnam, General, 10/15/63–10/28/63, Defense Cables, JFKL.

52. Felt to JCS, 17675, 8 October 1963, JFK Papers, Box 200A, Vietnam, General, 10/6/63–10/14/63, Defense Cables, JFKL.

53. CJCS to CINCPAC, "Approved Actions for South Vietnam," 24 October 1963, RG 218, Taylor Records, Box 12, NARA.

54. AP, "Saigon's Need of U.S. Eased, Harkins Says," *NYT,* 31 October 1963, 10.

55. Kattenburg to Hilsman, 18 October 1963, *FRUS, 1961–1963,* 4:408, Doc. 201.

56. State to Saigon, 607, 19 October 1963, JFK Papers, NSF, Box 204, Vietnam, Top Secret Cables, Tabs A-B, 10/63, JFKL.

57. Felt to JCS, "Withdrawal of 1000 U.S. Military from Vietnam," 19 October 1963, DTG 190640Z OCT 63, RG 218, Central File, 1963 Security Classified, Box 11, JCS Official File, 9155.3/3440 (26 May 63), NARA.

58. Riley to Taylor, "1,000 U.S. Military Withdrawal from Vietnam," DJSM-1788-63, 28 October 1963; and Rogers to Riley, "1,000 U.S. Military Withdrawal from Vietnam," CM-985-63, 31 October 1963, both in RG 218, Taylor Records, Box 12, NARA.

59. SACSA-T 10–63, 2 November 1963, RG 218, JCS, Central File, 1963 Security Classified, Box 11, JCS Official File, 9155.3/3440 (26 May 63), NARA.

60. Rogers to Riley, "1,000 U.S. Military Withdrawal from Vietnam," CM-985-63, 31 October 1963.

61. JCS to Felt, JCS 4302, 5 November 1963, RG 218, JCS, Central File, 1963 Security Classified, Box 11, 9155.3/3440 (26 May 63), NARA.

62. Newman, *JFK,* 432–434.

63. McNamara-Taylor Report, 2 October 1963, *FRUS, 1961–1963,* 4:338, Doc. 167.

64. CINCPAC Agenda Items, MACV COC, 311400H Oct 63, "U.S. Military Personnel Ceiling in RVN and Problems Associated Therewith," RG 472, MACV HQ, MACJ03, Box 15, CINCPAC Agenda Items, NARA.

65. Jack Anderson, "Foreign Aid Worries Committee," *WP,* 14 October 1963, B23.

66. Felix Belair Jr., "Aid Bill Attacked in Senate Debate," *NYT,* 29 October 1963, 1; Robert C. Albright, "Foreign Aid Bill Runs into a Fight," *WP,* 29 October 1962, A1.

67. Bell to JFK, 25 October 1963, JFK Papers, NSF, Box 297, Foreign Aid, 10/25/63–11/22/63 and Miscellaneous Undated Items, JFKL.

68. Lodge to JFK, 16 October 1963, *FRUS, 1961–1963,* 4:403, Doc. 197.

69. Neubert to Hilsman, 18 October 1963, *FRUS, 1961–1963,* 4:406–407, Doc. 200; Lodge to State, 23 October 1963, *FRUS, 1961–1963,* 4:421–424, Doc. 207.

70. CIA memorandum, "The Current Situation in South Vietnam," 30 October 1963, JFK Papers, NSF, Box 201, Vietnam, General, 10/29/63–10/31/63, CIA Reports, JFKL.

71. RFE-90, 22 October 1963, *US-VR,* 12:582. The Joint Chiefs contested that analysis after it circulated throughout the upper reaches of government. See Hughes to Rusk, "JCS Comments on Department of State Research Memorandum RFE-90," 8 November 1963, Tab A, *FRUS, 1961–1963,* 4:584–586, Doc. 306.

72. CIA memorandum, "The Current Situation in South Vietnam," 30 October 1963; Harold P. Ford, *CIA and the Vietnam Policymakers: Three Episodes, 1962–1968* (Center for the Study of Intelligence, 1998), 21.

73. Newman, *JFK,* 419–425.

74. Lodge to JFK, 23 October 1963, *FRUS, 1961–1963,* 4:422, Doc. 207.

75. David Kaiser, *American Tragedy: Kennedy, Johnson, and the Origins of the Vietnam War* (Belknap Press of Harvard University Press, 2002), 4, 277.

76. See "Report on Visits to Delta Provinces," June–August 1963, along with cover memo from E. E. Anderson, to Distribution List, 21 September 1963, RG 200, McNamara Records, Box 63, NARA. For commentary on this episode, see Peter Busch, *All the Way with JFK? Britain, the US, and the Vietnam War* (Oxford University Press, 2003), 157–168.

77. John M. Newman, "The Kennedy-Johnson Transition: The Case for Policy Reversal," in *Vietnam: The Early Decisions,* ed. Lloyd C. Gardner and Ted Gittinger (University of Texas Press, 1997), 163; James K. Galbraith, "Exit Strategy," *Boston Review,* 1 September 2003; Howard Jones, *Death of a Generation: How the Assassinations of Diem and JFK Prolonged the Vietnam War* (Oxford University Press, 2003), 377; Porter, *Perils of Dominance,* 169–170.

78. CAS to CIA, 3 October 1963, *FRUS, 1961–1963,* 4:354–355, Doc. 171.

79. Jones, *Death of a Generation,* 400.

80. State to Saigon, 753, 7 November 1963, RG 84, Vietnam, U.S. Embassy, Saigon, General Records, 1936–1963, Box 82 (old Box 7), Agreements, 320.1: U.S.-GVN, NARA.

81. State to Saigon, 783, 13 November 1963, RG 84, Vietnam, U.S. Embassy, Saigon, General Records, 1936–1963, Box 82 (old Box 7), 350 Internal Political Affairs, GVN Folder, NARA.

82. Department of State, "Secretary Rusk's News Conference of November 8," *Department of State Bulletin,* 49 (25 November 1963), 1274:811.

83. Forrestal to McG. Bundy, 7 November 1963, *FRUS, 1961–1963,* 4:581–582, Doc. 305; Mendenhall to Hilsman, 12 November 1963, *FRUS, 1961–1963,* 4:592–593, Doc. 311.

84. "The President's News Conference of October 31, 1963," *PPP:JFK,* 1963:828, Doc. 448; "The President's News Conference of November 14, 1963," *PPP:JFK,* 1963:846, 852, Doc. 459.

85. W. P. Bundy to Hilsman, 2 November 1963, Hilsman Papers, Box 4, Vietnam, White House Meetings, 8/26/63–10/29/63, State Memoranda, JFKL.

86. "The President's News Conference of November 14, 1963," *PPP:JFK,* 1963:847–848, Doc. 459.

87. "Outline for Discussion at Inter-Agency Review of Economic Aid Program for FY 1965 for Vietnam," undated, JFK Papers, NSF, Box 204, Vietnam, Honolulu Briefing Book, 11/20/63, Part II, JFKL.

88. Allan R. Scholin, "Big Lift: Boon, Boondoggle, or Bust?" *Air Force Magazine,* December 1963, 33–37.

89. UPI, "U.S. to Trim Forces and Spending Abroad," *WP,* 20 October 1963, A1; "The President's News Conference," 31 October 1963, *PPP:JFK,* 1963:826–828, Doc. 448.

90. "Mr. Solbert's Meeting with Country Team, Taipei, 23 October 1963," 18 November 1963, RG 330, OASD/ISA, Assistant for (CI) Files, 1962–1965, Far East Trip Report (Mr. Solbert)–Dec 63, Box 2, NARA.

91. "Country Team Meeting, Bangkok, 30 October," RG 330, OASD/ISA, Assistant for (CI) Files, 1962–1965, Far East Trip Report (Mr. Solbert)–Dec 63, Box 2, NARA.

92. "Meeting with Ambassador Berger and Country Team, Korea, 26 October 1963"; and "MND Briefing and Comments of Korean Minister Kim, Seoul, 26 October 1963," both in RG 330, OASD/ISA, Assistant for (CI) Files, 1962–1965, Far East Trip Report (Mr. Solbert)–Dec 63, Box 2, NARA.

93. Aurelie Basha i Novosejt, *"I Made Mistakes": Robert McNamara's Vietnam War Policy, 1960–1968* (Cambridge University Press, 2019), 110–115.

94. State to Saigon, 830, 19 November 1963, RG 59, Subject-Numeric 1963, Box 4050, Political Affairs & Rel., 2/1/63, S. Viet, NARA.

95. For an overview of conference proceedings, see Memcon, November 20, 1963, *FRUS, 1961–1963,* 4:608–624, Doc. 321.

96. "Measures for Improved Prosecution of the war under the New Regime (1) Overall Progress of the Counter-Insurgency Effort," 15 November 1965, JFK Papers, NSF, Box 204, Vietnam, Honolulu Briefing Book, 11/20/63, Part I, JFKL.

97. SACSA, "Highlights of the Military Situation," 15 November 1965, JFK Papers, NSF, Box 204, Vietnam, Honolulu Briefing Book, 11/20/63, Part I, JFKL.

98. "McNamara Press Conference upon Arrival in Hawaii for Pacific Conference, 19 November 1963," McNamara Papers, Part II, Speeches & Writings, Box 89, Folder 5, Library of Congress.

99. Neil Sheehan, "U.S. to Start Pullout from Viet-Nam December 3," *WP*, 16 November 1963, A9; see also "U.S. Leaders to Discuss Vietnam Troop Cutback," *Los Angeles Times*, 20 November 1963, 2; Jack Raymond, "G.I. Return Waits on Vietnam Talk," *NYT*, 15 November 1963, 13.

100. UPI, "U.S. Drops Plans for Big Viet Cut," *Stars & Stripes*, 16 November 1963, 1.

101. AP, "1,000 U.S. Troops to Leave Vietnam," *NYT*, 16 November 1963, 1. Newman argues that Kennedy lifted the secrecy requirement on the 1,000-man withdrawal, allowing Timmes to make it official, though he provides no documentation for the claim. Newman, *JFK*, 426.

102. "U.S. Aides Report Gains: 1,000 Troops to Return," *NYT*, 21 November 1963, 8.

103. "1000-Man Withdrawal," 15 November 1963, JFK Papers, NSF, Box 204, Vietnam, Honolulu Briefing Book, 11/20/63, Pt. 2, JFKL. The totals for "Unit/Source of Personnel" fail to generate the figures of either 496 or 507.

104. SACSA, "The Transfer of US Military Functions to Vietnamese Forces," 15 November 1963, JFK Papers, NSF, Box 204, Vietnam, Honolulu Briefing Book, 11/20/63, Pt. 2, JFKL.

105. SACSA, "U.S. Comprehensive Plan—Vietnam"; "Record of Special meeting on RVN," 20 November 1963, C-1-4, RG 472, MACV HQ, Secretary to the Joint Staff (MACJ03), Box 15, CINCPAC Conf—20 Nov 63, NARA.

106. For Cooper's remarks, see Memorandum for the Director, "Proposal for a U.S. Policy in South Vietnam," 30 September 1963, JFK Papers, NSF, Box 200, Vietnam—General, 9/22/63–10/5/63, Memos & Misc., JFKL.

107. Memcon, 20 November 1963, *FRUS, 1961–1963*, 4:610, Doc. 321.

108. "U.S. Aides Report Gain: 1,000 Troops to Return," *NYT*, 21 November 1963, 8.

109. Jerry Kluttz, "Fall of Diem Revives Optimism of Yanks," *WP*, 22 November 1963, A1.

110. "McNamara Statement upon Returning to the United States from a Pacific Conference in Hawaii," 21 November 1963, McNamara Papers, Part II, Speeches & Writings, Box 89, Folder 5, Library of Congress.

111. AP, "Cambodia Breaks U.S. Military Ties," *NYT*, 20 November 1963, 1.

112. Michael Forrestal Oral History, 3 November 1969, 6–7, LBJL, deeded 22 November 1978.

113. Forrestal in "Vietnam Hindsight, Part II: The Death of Diem," NBC News White Paper, 22 December 1971, Act XI, 20–21. In his 1964 oral history for the Kennedy Library, Forrestal is silent on whether Kennedy wanted to review or revise Vietnam policy. Michael Forrestal Oral History, 8 April 1964, JFKL.

114. "Remarks Prepared for Delivery at the Trade Mart in Dallas," 22 November 1963, *PPP:JFK,* 1963:892, Doc. 477. See also "Remarks at the High School Memorial Stadium, Great Falls, Montana," 26 September 1963, *PPP:JFK,* 1963:728, Doc. 383.

8. Cancellation

1. For overviews of this period, see Robert Dallek, *Flawed Giant: Lyndon Johnson and His Times, 1961–1973* (Oxford University Press, 1998), 54–71; Randall B. Woods, *LBJ: Architect of American Ambition* (Free Press, 2006), 415–466; Robert A. Caro, *The Years of Lyndon Johnson: The Passage of Power* (Knopf, 2012), 319–436.

2. Memorandum for the Record, "South Vietnam Situation," 24 November 1963, *FRUS, 1961–1963,* vol. 4: *Vietnam, August–December, 1963,* 635–637, Doc. 330.

3. "South Vietnam Situation," 24 November 1963. For Johnson's remark about not losing Vietnam, see Tom Wicker, *JFK and LBJ: The Influence of Personality upon Politics* (Penguin, 1968), 205.

4. LBJ to Taylor, 2 December 1963, *FRUS, 1961–1963,* 4:651, Doc. 337.

5. State to Lodge, 908, 6 December 1963, *FRUS, 1961–1963,* 4:685–687, Doc. 351.

6. LBJ to Lodge, 7 December 1963, NSF, Files of McGeorge Bundy, Box 1, Chron File, December 1963 [2 of 3], LBJL; see also "Remarks to Employees of the Department of State," 5 December 1963, *PPP:LBJ,* 1963–1964, 1:28, Doc. 26.

7. George E. Reedy Oral History, Interview XIX, 13 June 1985, LBJL, 38.

8. Fredrik Logevall, *Choosing War: The Lost Chance for Peace and the Escalation of the War in Vietnam* (University of California Press, 1999), 388–389.

9. NSAM 273, 26 November 1963, *FRUS, 1961–1963,* 4:637–640, Doc. 331.

10. Oliver Stone and Zachary Sklar, *JFK: The Book of the Film* (Applause, 1992), 112. For commentary on the change, see Peter Dale Scott, *Deep Politics and the Death of JFK* (University of California Press, 1993), 24–28; James K. Galbraith, "Exit Strategy," *Boston Review,* 1 September 2003; John M. Newman, "The Kennedy-Johnson Transition: The Case for Policy Reversal," in *Vietnam: The Early Decisions,* ed. Lloyd C. Gardner and Ted Gittinger, 158–176 (University of Texas Press, 1997). For contrary arguments, see Larry Berman, "NSAM 263 and NSAM 273: Manipulating History," in *Vietnam: The Early Decisions,* 177–203; William Conrad Gibbons, "Lyndon Johnson and the Legacy of Vietnam," in *Vietnam: The Early Decisions,* 119–157.

11. Thomas L. Ahern, *The Way We Do Things: Black Entry Operations into North Vietnam, 1961–1964* (Center for the Study of Intelligence, 2005), 42; see also Richard H. Shultz, *The Secret War against Hanoi: Kennedy's and Johnson's Use of Spies, Saboteurs, and Covert Warriors in North Vietnam* (HarperCollins, 1999), 35–36.

12. Evan Thomas, *Robert Kennedy: His Life* (Simon and Schuster, 2000), 269; Ahern, *The Way We Do Things,* 49–50. Edwin E. Moïse, *Tonkin Gulf and the Escalation of the Vietnam War* (University of North Carolina Press, 1996), 4–25.

13. Bundy to LBJ, 7 January 1964, *FRUS, 1964–1968,* vol. 1: *Vietnam, 1964,* 4, Doc. 4.

14. McNamara to Lodge, 12 December 1963, *FRUS, 1961–1963,* 4:702, Doc. 362.

15. Colby, "Presidential Meeting on Vietnam," 20 February 1964, McCone Memoranda, Meetings with the President, 23 November–27 December 1963, Box 1, LBJL.

16. "Situation in South Vietnam and Recent Military Operations in that Country," 2 December 1963, 5411 (CY 1963) JCS Meetings + Agenda (Jul–Dec) 1963 + Notes to Control, RG 218, Central File 1963, Security Classified, Box 3, NARA.

17. McNamara to Lodge, 12 December 1963, 702.

18. Forrestal to LBJ, 11 December 1963, *FRUS, 1961–1963,* 4:699–700, Doc. 360.

19. Shultz, *Secret War,* 310–321.

20. NSAM 273, 638.

21. State to LBJ, 23 November 1963, *FRUS, 1961–1963,* 4:629–630, Doc. 325.

22. McCone memcon, 24 November 1963, *FRUS, 1961–1963,* 4:635–637, Doc. 330.

23. Richard L. Lyons, "President Sees Lodge, Renews Viet-Nam Pledge," *WP,* 25 November 1963, A1; E. W. Kenworthy, "Johnson Affirms Aims in Vietnam," *NYT,* 25 November 1963, 1.

24. "Editorial Note," *FRUS, 1961–1963,* 4:652–653, Doc. 339.

25. McCone Memorandum, 3 December 1963, John McCone Memoranda, Meetings with the President, Box 1, 23 November–27 December 1963, LBJL.

26. *Pentagon Papers,* 2:191–192.

27. Rusk to Lodge, 6 December 1963, *FRUS, 1961–1963,* 4:685, Doc. 351.

28. "Minutes of a Meeting of the Special Group for Counterinsurgency," 12 December 1963, *FRUS, 1961–1963,* 4:704–705, Doc. 364; Hilsman to Rusk, 20 December 1963, *FRUS, 1961–1963,* 4:719–720, Doc. 371.

29. Lyndon Baines Johnson, *The Vantage Point: Perspectives of the Presidency, 1963–1969* (Holt, Rinehart and Winston, 1971), 62.

30. George McT. Kahin, *Intervention: How America Became Involved in Vietnam* (Knopf, 1996), 190–194; Fredrik Logevall, "De Gaulle, Neutralization, and American Involvement in Vietnam, 1963–1964," *Pacific Historical Review* 61 (February 1992), 1:82.

31. Jorden to Harriman, 31 December 1963, *FRUS, 1961–1963,* 4:753–758, Doc. 383; see also Lodge to State, 4 December 1963, *FRUS, 1961–1963,* 4:661–663, Doc. 344.

32. Lodge to Rusk, 13 December 1963, cited in Lodge to Rusk, 931, 12 December 1963, *FRUS, 1961–1963,* 4:706–707, Doc. 365n4.

33. Ball to Lodge, 16 December 1963, *FRUS, 1961–1963,* 4:710, Doc. 367; see also Rusk to Lodge, 10 December 1963, *FRUS, 1961–1963,* 4:695–696, Doc. 358.

34. Rusk to Lodge, 12 December 1963, *FRUS, 1961–1963,* 4:706, Doc. 365.

35. Jorden to Harriman, 31 December 1963, *FRUS, 1961–1963,* 4:754, Doc. 383.

36. Marguerite Higgins, "Saigon Summary: Our Country Played an Inglorious Role in the Final Days of the Diem Regime," *America,* 4 January 1964, cited by Sen. Thomas J. Dodd, 14 January 1964, *Congressional Record,* 88th Congress, 2nd Session,

356–357. Higgins later quoted Gen. Tran Thien Khiem as stating that "We took it as a sign that unless we got rid of Diem, the United States would wash its hands of the war no later than 1965." Higgins, *Our Vietnam Nightmare* (Harper and Row, 1965), 209.

37. State to Lodge, 27 November 1963, *FRUS, 1961–1963,* 4:640, Doc. 332.

38. Breckon to Mendenhall, "Public Posture of Post-Coup Viet-Nam and U.S. Commitment There," 18 December 1963; and Mendenhall to Hilsman, "Public Posture of Post-Coup Viet-Nam and U.S. Commitment There," 18 December 1963, both in Thomson Papers, Box 23, 1963 General, 10/63–12/63, JFKL.

39. Seymour Topping, "U.S. Seeks to Spur War," *NYT,* 15 December 1963, 24; Hedrick Smith, "McNamara Opens Inquiry in Vietnam on War Crisis," *NYT,* 20 December 1963, 1.

40. OSD to CINCPAC, 949322, 21 December 1963, LBJ Papers, Box 1, Country File—Vietnam, Vietnam Cables (1 of 2), Vol. II, 12/63–1/64, LBJL.

41. Rusk-McNamara Telcon, 7 December 1963, *FRUS, 1961–1963,* 4:690, Doc. 354. "The President's First News Conference," 7 December 1963, *PPP:LBJ,* 1:34, Doc. 28.

42. Logevall, *Choosing War,* 80, 89.

43. McNamara to LBJ, 21 December 1963, *FRUS, 1961–1963,* 4:732, Doc. 374.

44. McCone to LBJ, 23 December 1963, attachment, "Highlights of Discussions in Saigon, 18–20 December 1963," *FRUS, 1961–1963,* 4:736–738, Doc. 375.

45. Jorden to Harriman, 31 December 1963, *FRUS, 1961–1963,* 4:753, Doc. 383.

46. Radio TV Dialog, "McNamara on Another 'Mission' to Viet Nam," 19 December 1963, Kaplan Box 236, OSDHO.

47. Hedrick Smith, "U.S. Drops Plans for 1965 Recall of Vietnam Force," *NYT,* 21 December 1963, 1.

48. "Saigon Survey," *NYT,* 22 December 1963, E2. Murrey Marder noted McNamara's reluctance to discuss the earlier withdrawal statements, adding that observers thought them "militarily unwise and intended mainly for the American audience." Marder, "LBJ Defers Departure for Texas," *WP,* 22 December 1963, A1.

49. Seymour Topping, "U.S. Seeks to Spur War," *NYT,* 15 December 1963, 24.

50. Memorandum of Conversation, "Situation in Vietnam," 24 December 1963, RG 59, Subject-Numeric 1963, Box 4046, Political Affairs & Rel., S. Viet, NARA.

51. Forster to Wakefield, 8 January 1964, 10298/64, FO 371/175493, DV103145/2, NA, UK.

52. Ormsby-Gore to Caccia, 24 January 1964, FO 371/175482, DV1017/3, NA, UK.

53. Lodge to State, 1 January 1964, *FRUS, 1964–1968,* 1:1, Doc. 1.

54. McNamara to LBJ, 7 January 1964, Tab B, in Bundy to LBJ, 9 January 1964, *FRUS, 1964–1968,* 1:12–13, Doc. 8; see also Rusk to LBJ, Tab A and Attachment to Tab A, in *FRUS, 1964–1968,* 1:9–11, Doc 8.

55. Paul Hendrickson, *The Living and the Dead: Robert McNamara and Five Lives of a Lost War* (Vintage, 1996), 323. Aurélie Basha i Novosejt, *"I Made Mistakes": Robert McNamara's Vietnam War Policy, 1960–1968* (Cambridge University Press, 2019), 5, 10, 46.

56. Paul Grimes, "Downhill Story for U.S. in Saigon," *NYT,* 31 January 1964, 9; Sam Fogg, "McNamara Pessimistic on Viet-Nam," *WP,* 28 January 1964, A9. Lawmakers queried McNamara about his statement, but his reply was deleted from the transcript. House Armed Services Committee, "Hearings on Military Posture and H.R. 9637," 27 January 1964, 88th Congress, 2nd Session (GPO: 1964), 6979.

57. Bundy to LBJ, 7 January 1964, *FRUS, 1964–1968,* 1:4–5, Doc. 4.

58. Jack Raymond, "McNamara Eases View on Conflict in Vietnam," *NYT,* 29 January 1964, 3.

59. Spencer Davis, "Hilsman Sees Slash in Aid Adding to Danger from Reds," *Washington Star,* 12 January 1964.

60. Walter Trohan, "Report from Washington," *Chicago Tribune,* 29 January 1964, 2.

61. Ball-Reston Telcon, 28 January 1964, 17:30, Ball Papers, Box 7, Vietnam I (1/15/62–10/11/63), LBJL; James Reston, "A Mystifying Clarification from McNamara," *NYT,* 29 January 1964, 32.

62. "Retreat from Candor," *WP,* 29 January 1964, A14.

63. See Reston, "U.S. Aides Laud Leader but Deny a Role in Coup," *NYT,* 30 January 1964, 1. For background on the relationship between neutralist fears and the coup, see Logevall, "De Gaulle, Neutralization, and American Involvement in Vietnam," 83–87.

64. See, for instance, SNIE 50–64, 12 February 1964, *FRUS, 1964–1968,* 1:71–72, Doc. 42; Helms to Rusk, 18 February 1964, *FRUS, 1964–1968,* 1:84–86, Doc. 50.

65. Mansfield to LBJ, 1 February 1964, NSF, Memos to the President, Box 1, McGeorge Bundy, Vol. 1 [1 of 2], 11/63–2/64, LBJL; Mansfield, 19 February 1964, *Congressional Record,* Senate, 88th Congress, 2nd Session, 3114.

66. Walter Lippmann, "The French-American Argument," *WP,* 4 February 1964, 13.

67. "Lyndon Johnson and John Knight on 3 February 1964," Tape WH6402.03, Citation #1839, *PRDE* (Virginia, 2014–), http://prde.upress.virginia.edu/conversations /9040021.

68. Rostow to Rusk, 10 January 1964, *FRUS, 1964–1968,* 1:15, Doc. 9.

69. Bundy to LBJ, 10 February 1964, *FRUS, 1964–1968,* 1:67, Doc. 39.

70. Lodge to LBJ, 22 February 1964, *FRUS, 1964–1968,* 1:102–103, Doc. 59; SNIE 50–64, "Short-Term Prospects in Southeast Asia," 12 February 1964, Gibbons Papers, Box 3, Jan.–Aug. 1964 [1 of 8], LBJL. For an assessment of how this "bandwagon" argument differed from the "domino" argument in both form and reception, see Gareth Porter, *Perils of Dominance: Imbalance of Power and the Road to War in Vietnam* (University of California Press, 2005), 243–258.

71. CIA to State and Defense, 21 December 1963, NSF, Country File-Vietnam, Box 52, Vietnam: Special Category Messages, Vol. 1, 11/63–7/64, LBJL; Joint State-DOD-CAS Message, 23 January 1964, NSF, Messages to the President, Box 1, McGeorge Bundy, Vol. 2, 3/1–31/64 [1 of 2], LBJL; Lodge to Rusk, 21 January 1964, *FRUS, 1964–1968,* 1:29, Doc. 14.

72. Colby memcon, "Presidential Meeting on Vietnam, 20 February 1964," 21 February 1964, McCone Memoranda, Meetings with the President, 23 November–27 December 1963, Box 1, LBJL; an abridged version is available as Forrestal memcon, 20 February 1964, *FRUS, 1964–1968*, 1:93–94, Doc. 54.

73. LBJ to Lodge, 21 February 1964, *FRUS, 1964–1968*, 1:96, Doc. 56.

74. Caccia to Greenhill, 17 February 1964, FO 371/17544493, CV103145/11/G, NA, UK. Rusk made those comments to Britain's Permanent Under-Secretary of State for Foreign Affairs Harold Caccia.

75. "Lyndon Johnson and John Knight on 3 February 1964."

76. "Lyndon Johnson and McGeorge Bundy on 6 February 1964,"Tape WH6402.07, Citation #1911, *PRDE*, http://prde.upress.virginia.edu/conversations/9040073.

77. Rusk to McNamara, 5 February 1964, *FRUS, 1964–1968*, 1:63, Doc. 36; Bundy to Sorensen, 12 February 1964, NSF, Files of McGeorge Bundy, Chron File, January 1964 [3 of 3], LBJL.

78. Johnson wanted to remove Ambassador Lodge as well, owing to longstanding displeasure with Lodge's administrative approach and his support for dumping Diem. Political concerns, however, stayed Johnson's hand. See, for instance, Robert David Johnson, *All the Way with LBJ: The 1964 Presidential Election* (Cambridge University Press, 2009), 66–112.

79. Lyndon B. Johnson: "Remarks at the 96th Charter Day Observance of the University of California at Los Angeles," 21 February 1964, *PPP:LBJ*, 1:304, Doc. 192.

80. Chalmers M. Roberts, "Hint of a New Initiative Voiced by President," *WP*, 22 February 1964, A1; Max Frankel, "Washington Hints at Saigon Raids on North Vietnam," *NYT*, 23 February 1964, 1.

81. "A New Policy in Vietnam?" *Los Angeles Times*, 26 February 1964, A4.

82. C. L. Sulzberger, "The Need for Another Showdown," *NYT*, 26 February 1964, 34; Max Frankel, "Washington Hints at Saigon Raids on North Vietnam," *NYT*, 23 February 1964, 1; Chalmers M. Roberts, "U.S. Divided on Viet-Nam Crisis Move," *WP*, 20 February 1964, A13; "Choices in South Viet-Nam," *WP*, 27 February 1964, A18.

83. "Talk by McGeorge Bundy to Overseas Press Writers at the Sheraton Carlton Hotel, February 26, 1964," NSF, Messages to the President, Box 1, McGeorge Bundy, Vol. 2, 3/1–31/64 [1 of 2], LBJL.

84. Sullivan to Members of Viet Nam Coordinating Committee, "Action Summary of February 18 Meeting," 19 February 1964, NSF, Country File-Vietnam, Box 2 [1 of 2], Vietnam Cables, Vol. IV, 2/64–3/64 [2 of 2], LBJL.

85. SACSA, Agenda Item Number C 7, "Planning for the Reduction of US and GVN Forces," 27 February 1964, Papers of Paul C. Warnke, John McNaughton Files, Box 3, McNT VI-Briefing Book-29 Feb. 1964 (2), LBJL.

86. Harkins to Taylor, 16 January 1964, MAC 0144, RG 218, Taylor Records Box 12, NARA.

87. "Commander's Personal Military Assessment of the 4th Quarter CY 63," in Nes to State, A-455, 3 February 1964, NSF, Country File-Vietnam, Box 2, Vietnam Cables, vol. III [2 of 2], LBJL.

88. Supplemental Talking Paper, JCS, 17 January 1964, RG 200, McNamara Records, Box 63, NARA; Harkins to JCS and CINCPAC, MAC J3 0902, 6 February 1964, NSF, Country File-Vietnam, Box 2, Vietnam Cables, vol. III [2 of 2], LBJL.

89. Jack Raymond, "U.S. Will Resume Vietnam Pullout," *NYT,* 19 February 1964, 1.

90. "Lyndon Johnson and Robert McNamara on 25 February 1964," Tape WH6402. 21, Citation #2191, *PRDE,* http://prde.upress.virginia.edu/conversations/9040237.

91. Max Frankel, "U.S. Moves to Spur Action in Vietnam," *NYT,* 25 February 1964, 1; Chalmers M. Roberts, "U.S. Divided on Viet-Nam Crisis Move," *WP,* 20 February 1964, A13.

92. "The President's News Conference of February 29, 1964," *PPP:LBJ,* 1:324, Doc. 201; Forrestal memcon, 20 February 1964, *FRUS, 1964–1968,* 1:94, Doc. 54.

93. Clifton memcon, undated (4 March 1964), NSF, Files of C. V. Clifton, Box 2, Joint Chiefs of Staff, Vol. 1, LBJL. See also Taylor Memcon, 4 March 1964, *FRUS, 1964–1968,* 1:129–130, Doc. 70. For the Chiefs critique of Johnson's approach, see H. R. McMaster, *Dereliction of Duty: Lyndon Johnson, Robert McNamara, the Joint Chiefs of Staff, and the Lies that Led to Vietnam* (HarperCollins, 1997).

94. "Lyndon Johnson and Robert McNamara on 2 March 1964," Tape WH6403.01, Citations #2301 and #2302, *PRDE,* http://prde.upress.virginia.edu/conversations /9040273.

95. "South Vietnam and Southeast Asia," 1 March 1964, NSF, Country File-Vietnam, Box 2 [1 of 2], Vietnam Cables, Vol. IV, 2/64–3/64 [2 of 2], LBJL.

96. McNamara News Conference, 5 March 1964, RG 200, McNamara Records, Records Relating to Vietnam and Southeast Asia, 1961–1966, Box 179, NARA.

97. "The President's News Conference of March 7, 1964," *PPP:LBJ,* 1:345, Doc. 211.

98. Max Frankel, "Johnson Pledges Greater U.S. Help If Saigon Needs It," *NYT,* 8 March 1964, 1.

99. "The President's News Conference of March 7, 1964," *PPP:LBJ,* 1:343, Doc. 211.

100. Carl Greenberg, "Rockefeller Leaves, Hits Johnson and Goldwater," *Los Angeles Times,* 31 January 1964, 3; *Congressional Record,* House, 7 February 1964, 88th Congress, 2nd Session, vol. 110, 2:2527–2559; *Congressional Record,* House, 4 March 1964, 88th Congress, 2nd Session, 4:4326.

101. UPI, "Johnson Is 'Fiddling,' Goldwater Charges," *WP,* 4 February 1964, 2; Joseph A. Loftus, "Nixon Says Lodge May Be 'Fall Guy,'" *NYT,* 27 February 1964, 17.

102. *Congressional Record,* House, 28 January 1964, 88th Congress, 2nd Session, vol. 110, 1:1555; *Congressional Record,* Senate, 27 February 1964, 88th Congress, 2nd Session, 3:3805.

103. AP, "McNamara is Criticized on Viet-Nam by Laird," *WP,* 10 March 1964, A9.

104. *Congressional Record,* 9 March 1964, 88th Congress, 2nd Session, 4780–4782. "Answers to Senator Keating's Questions of March 9, 1964 on Viet Nam," Thomson Papers, Box 24, Diem Coup, Background & Congressional Inquiries, JFKL.

105. *Congressional Record,* 11 March 1964, 4814, 4986; *Congressional Record,* 10 March 1964, 4850.

106. John D. Morris, "Policy in Vietnam Divides Senators," *NYT,* 21 March 1964, 1.

107. A March 1964 Harris survey asking whether Washington should apply greater military pressure on Hanoi found that 45 percent opposed, 26 percent favored, and 29 percent were not sure. Louis Harris & Associates Poll: March 1964, Question 2, USHARRIS.033064.R2 (Roper Center, 1964), Roper iPoll.

108. McNamara to LBJ, 16 March 1964, *FRUS, 1964–1968,* 1:153–167, Doc. 84.

109. McNamara to LBJ, 16 March 1964.

110. Bundy to LBJ, 14 March 1964, *FRUS, 1964–1968,* 1:149, Doc. 81.

111. "Transcript of Television and Radio Interview Conducted by Representatives of Major Broadcast Services," 15 March 1964, *PPP:LBJ,* 1:370, Doc. 218.

112. NSAM 288, 17 March 1964, *FRUS, 1964–1968,* 1:172–173, Doc. 87; "White House Statement on the Situation in South Vietnam," 17 March 1964, *PPP:LBJ,* 1:387–388, Doc. 223.

113. McNamara Address, 26 March 1964, Thomson Papers, Box 24, McNamara Vietnam Speech, 3/26/64, JFKL.

114. Jack Raymond, "M'Namara Bars Vietnam Pullout," *NYT,* 27 March 1965, 1; "McNamara on Viet-Nam," *WP,* 27 March 1964, A16.

115. *Pentagon Papers,* 2:198.

Epilogue

1. Barbara A. Perry, *Jacqueline Kennedy: First Lady of the New Frontier* (University Press of Kansas, 2004); Michael J. Hogan, *The Afterlife of John F. Kennedy: A Biography* (Cambridge University Press, 2017).

2. Arthur M. Schlesinger Jr., *A Thousand Days: John F. Kennedy in the White House* (Houghton Mifflin, 1965, 2002), 538, 997–998, 1019; see also transcript of "Meet the Press," 28 November 1965, vol. 9, no. 42, Schlesinger Papers, Box 435, 5/15/65 Vietnam Teach-In, New York Public Library.

3. Theodore C. Sorensen, *Kennedy* (Harper and Row, 1965, 651, 660–661.

4. See John Mecklin, *Mission in Torment: An Intimate Account of the U.S. Role in Vietnam* (Doubleday, 1965), 217; David Halberstam, *The Making of a Quagmire* (Random House, 1964), 258; Arthur Krock, *In the Nation: 1932–1966* (McGraw-Hill, 1966), 324–325; Roger Hilsman, *To Move a Nation: The Politics of Foreign Policy in the Administration of John F. Kennedy* (Dell, 1967), 536.

5. On Johnson and the New Frontiersmen, see Robert Dallek, *Flawed Giant: Lyndon Johnson and His Times, 1961–1973* (Oxford University Press, 1998), 3–53; Robert A.

Caro, *The Years of Lyndon Johnson: The Passage of Power* (Knopf, 2012); Jeff Shesol, *Mutual Contempt: Lyndon Johnson, Robert Kennedy, and the Feud that Defined a Decade* (Norton, 1997); Paul R. Henggeler, *In His Steps: Lyndon Johnson and the Kennedy Mystique* (Ivan R. Dee, 1991).

6. Rostow to LBJ, 15 September 1967; see also Peabody to LBJ, "John McCloy on Vietnam and the Presidency," 6 November 1967; and, for a 1964 review of Kennedy statements, see Smith to LBJ, 22 February 1963 (*sic*), with attachment, all in NSF, Country File-Vietnam, Box 97, Vietnam: 7 C (1) 1953–12/67, Past Presidential Statements on USG Commitment in SE Asia [1 of 2], LBJL.

7. Lydia Saad, "Gallup Vault: Hawks vs. Doves on Vietnam," https://news.gallup.com/vault/191828/gallup-vault-hawks-doves-vietnam.aspx; George C. Herring, *America's Longest War: The United States and Vietnam*, 5th ed. (McGraw-Hill, 2014), 223–226.

8. Henggeler, *In His Steps*, 173–178; Edwin O. Guthman and C. Richard Allen, eds., *RFK: Collected Speeches* (Viking, 1993), 270–280.

9. John R. Bohrer, "No Vietnam Secrets between RFK, LBJ," *Politico*, 20 October 2009; Henggeler, *In His Steps*, 187–231; Shesol, *Mutual Contempt*, 363–376, 385–389.

10. Peter Grose, "Kennedy Asserts Johnson Shifted U.S. Aim in Vietnam," *NYT*, 27 November 1967, 1; John Herbers, "President Kennedy's Vietnam Aim Debated Again," *NYT*, 28 November 1967, 4. One month earlier, Bobby had told Daniel Ellsberg of JFK's reluctance to send ground troops to Vietnam and the likely shape of his withdrawal plan. Daniel Ellsberg, *Secrets: A Memoir of Vietnam and the Pentagon Papers* (Viking, 2002), 195.

11. "Kennedy v. Kennedy," *NYT*, 28 November 1967, 46.

12. Joseph Alsop, "JFK Backed the Hard-Boiled, Not the Soft-Boiled Advisers," *WP*, 27 November 1967, A19.

13. Rostow to LBJ, "U.S. Goals in Viet-Nam," 28 November 1967, and attachment, "U.S. Goals in Viet-Nam and Southeast Asia," NSF, Country File-Vietnam, Box 97, Vietnam: 7 C (1) 1953–12/67, Past Presidential Statements on USG Commitment in SE Asia [1 of 2], LBJL.

14. Thomas Brown, *JFK: History of an Image* (Indiana University Press, 1988), 38–41; Theodore C. Sorensen, *The Kennedy Legacy* (Macmillan, 1969), 204, 214.

15. Richard Harwood, "JFK Decided in '63 to Order Viet Pullout after Election," *WP*, 3 August 1970, A1.

16. John H. Averill, "Kennedy Plan for '65 Viet Pullout Disclosed," *Los Angeles Times*, 3 August 1970, 1.

17. "President Kennedy and Vietnam," *WSJ*, 10 August 1970, 6.

18. Kenneth D. Campbell, "O'Donnell Withheld Book on JFK at Mansfield's Request," *WP*, 4 August 1970, A2.

19. Campbell, "O'Donnell Withheld Book."

20. Don Oberdorfer, *Senator Mansfield: The Extraordinary Life of a Great American Statesman and Diplomat* (Smithsonian, 2003), 194–197.

21. "Vietnam Hindsight, Part II: The Death of Diem," NBC News White Paper, 22 December 1971, Act IX, 9, and Act XI, 20–21.

22. Michael V. Forrestal Oral History, 3 November 1969, LBJL, 6–7, deeded 22 November 1978; Charles L. Bartlett Oral History, 6 May 1969, 30, deeded 15 November 1978, LBJL.

23. Kenneth P. O'Donnell and David F. Powers with Joe McCarthy, *"Johnny, We Hardly Knew Ye": Memories of John Fitzgerald Kennedy* (Little, Brown, 1972), 413; see also 13–18.

24. See, for instance, Herbert S. Parmet, *JFK: The Presidency of John F. Kennedy* (Dial, 1983), 329, 336; Garry Wills, *The Kennedy Imprisonment: A Meditation on Power* (Little, Brown, 1982), 280–285; Brown, *JFK,* 34–41; Thomas C. Reeves, *A Question of Character: A Life of John F. Kennedy* (Free Press, 1991), 409–412; Herring, *America's Longest War,* 2nd ed. (Wiley, 1986), 94–95, 106; George McT. Kahin, *Intervention: How America Became Involved in Vietnam* (Knopf, 1986), 147; Lawrence J. Bassett and Stephen E. Pelz, "The Failed Search for Victory: Vietnam and the Politics of War," in *Kennedy's Quest for Victory: American Foreign Policy, 1961–1963,* ed. Thomas G. Paterson, 223–252 (Oxford University Press, 1989).

25. Arthur Schlesinger Jr., *Robert Kennedy and His Times* (Houghton Mifflin, 1978), 715–722. William Rust also maintains Kennedy would have resisted bombing the North and deploying combat troops. Rust, *Kennedy in Vietnam* (Charles Scribners' Sons, 1985), 181.

26. Oliver Stone, "Who Is Rewriting History?" *NYT,* 20 December 1991, 35.

27. Walt W. Rostow, "Kennedy Would Have Stood by Vietnam in '65," *NYT,* Letters, 15 February 1992; Joseph A. Califano Jr., "A Concoction of Lies and Distortions," Letters, *WSJ,* 28 January 1992, A15; George Lardner Jr., "The Way It Wasn't: In 'JFK,' Stone Assassinates the Truth," *WP,* 20 December 1991, D02; Leslie H. Gelb, "Kennedy and Vietnam," *NYT,* 6 January 1992, 17; Roger Hilsman, "How Kennedy Viewed the Vietnam Conflict," *NYT,* 20 January 1992, 20; Arthur M. Schlesinger Jr., "What Would He Have Done?" *NYT,* 29 March 1992; John Newman, "The 'Gimmick' in JFK's Vietnam Withdrawal Plan," *Boston Globe,* 14 January 1992.

28. Key volumes on these materials include Michael R. Beschloss, *Taking Charge: The Johnson White House Tapes, 1963–1964* (Simon and Schuster, 1997); Beschloss, *Reaching for Glory: Lyndon Johnson's Secret White House Tapes, 1964–1965* (Simon and Schuster, 2001); Ernest May and Philip Zelikow, *Inside the White House during the Cuban Missile Crisis,* conc. ed. (Norton, 2002); John Prados, *The White House Tapes: Eavesdropping on the President* (New Press, 2003); Marc J. Selverstone, gen. ed., *Presidential Recordings Digital Edition* (Virginia, 2014–).

29. McNamara, *In Retrospect,* 96; Robert S. McNamara, "We Were Wrong, Terribly Wrong," *Newsweek,* 17 April 1995. For criticism, see Max Frankel, "McNamara's Retreat," *NYT Book Review,* 16 April 1995, 1; Richard Reeves, "War Stories," *Washington*

Monthly, April 1995; Ronald Steel, "Blind Contrition," *New Republic,* 5 June 1995, 34–38.

30. Roger Hilsman, "McNamara's War—Against the Truth: A Review Essay," *Political Science Quarterly* 111 (1996), 1:151–163; Hilsman, *Foreign Affairs* (July/August 1995), 74:164–166; McGeorge Bundy, 23 February 1993, Stimson Lectures, McGeorge Bundy Papers, Box 232, JFKL; Bundy, 9 May 1994, John F. Kennedy Library, McGeorge Bundy Papers, Box 189, JFKL. According to Hilsman, Kennedy installed him as assistant secretary for Far Eastern Affairs to prevent the Vietnam war from being Americanized. Edwin E. Moise, "JFK and the Myth of Withdrawal," in *A Companion to the Vietnam War,* ed. Marilyn B. Young and Robert Buzzanco (Wiley-Blackwell, 2006), 169. Dean Rusk maintained that Kennedy had made no decision to withdraw from Vietnam, though he declined to speculate on what Kennedy might have done in a second term. Dean Rusk, as told to Richard Rusk, *As I Saw It* (Penguin, 1990), 441–442.

31. Lawrence Freedman, *Kennedy's Wars: Berlin, Cuba, Laos, and Vietnam* (Oxford University Press, 2000); Fredrik Logevall, "Vietnam and the Question of What Might Have Been," in *Kennedy: The New Frontier Revisited,* ed. Mark J. White, 19–62 (NYU, 1998); Fredrik Logevall, *Choosing War: The Lost Chance for Peace and the Escalation of the War in Vietnam* (University of California Press, 1999); David Kaiser, *American Tragedy: Kennedy, Johnson, and the Origins of the Vietnam War* (Belknap Press of Harvard University Press, 2000).

32. Lawrence Freedman, "Kennedy, Bush, and Crisis Management," *Cold War History* 2 (April 2002), 3:1–14; Jefferson Morley, "A Precedent That Proves Neither Side's Point," *WP,* 13 October 2002, B4; Todd Purdum, "The Missiles of 1962 Haunt the Iraq Debate," *NYT,* 13 October 1962, 1; Frankel, "Learning from the Missile Crisis," *Smithsonian* 33 (October 2002), 7:53–64.

33. Robert G. Kaiser, "Iraq Isn't Vietnam, but They Rhyme," *WP,* 28 December 2003, B1.

34. Craig R. Whitney, "Watching Iraq, Seeing Vietnam," *NYT,* 9 November 2003, Week in Review, 1.

35. See, for instance, Robert Dallek, *An Unfinished Life: John F. Kennedy, 1917–1963* (Little, Brown, 2003); Fred Kaplan, "The War Room: What Robert Dallek's New Biography Doesn't Tell You about JFK and Vietnam," *Slate,* 19 May 2003; Howard Jones, *Death of a Generation: How the Assassinations of Diem and JFK Prolonged the Vietnam War* (Oxford University Press, 2003); James K. Galbraith, "Exit Strategy," *Boston Review,* Oct/Nov 2003; Gareth Porter, *Perils of Dominance: Imbalance of Power and the Road to War in Vietnam* (University of California Press, 2005).

36. See, for instance, Brian Bender, "Papers Reveal JFK Efforts on Vietnam," *Boston Globe,* 6 June 2005.

37. *The Fog of War,* dir. Errol Morris (2003); James G. Blight and janet M. Lang, *The Fog of War: Lessons from the Life of Robert S. McNamara* (Rowman and Littlefield, 2005);

Errol Morris, "'Fog of War' vs. 'Stop the Presses,'" *The Nation*, 26 January 2004, 2. See also Letters to the Editor, 29 March 2004, *Nation*, 2.

38. David Stout, "Bush Firm on Iraq Policy, as Kennedy Assails Him for Deceit," *NYT*, 5 April 2004; Michael Dobbs, "After Decades, Renewed War on Old Conflict," *WP*, 28 August 2004, 1.

39. See, for example, Robert K. Brigham, *Is Vietnam Another Iraq* (Public Affairs, 2006); Lloyd C. Gardner and Marilyn B. Young, eds., *Iraq and the Lessons of Vietnam, or How Not to Learn from the Past* (New Press, 2007); John Dumbrell and David Ryan, eds., *Vietnam in Iraq: Tactics, Lessons, Legacies, and Ghosts* (Routledge, 2007).

40. Richard Parker, *John Kenneth Galbraith: His Life, His Politics, His Economics* (Farrar, Straus and Giroux, 2005); Parker, "Galbraith and Vietnam: Kennedy, Unlike Bush, Had One Adviser Who Told Him What He Needed to Hear," *Nation*, 14 March 2005, 16–20.

41. Joseph Lelyveld, "The Adventures of Arthur," *New York Review of Books*, 8 November 2007; James K. Galbraith, "JFK's Plans to Withdraw," *New York Review of Books*, 6 December 2007; Francis M. Bator, "Vietnam Withdrawal?" *New York Review of Books*, 17 January 2008.

42. Ted Sorensen, *Counselor: A Life at the Edge of History* (Harper, 2009), 359.

43. Gordon Goldstein, *Lessons in Disaster: McGeorge Bundy and the Path to War in Vietnam* (Times Books, 2008), 230–235. See also William Pfaff, "Mac Bundy Said He Was 'All Wrong,'" *New York Review of Books*, 10 June 2010; Kai Bird, reply by William Pfaff, "Would JFK Have Left Vietnam? An Exchange," *New York Review of Books*, 30 September 2010.

44. James G. Blight, janet M. Lang, and David A. Welch, *Virtual JFK: Vietnam if Kennedy Had Lived* (Rowman and Littlefield, 2009); *Virtual JFK*, dir. Koji Masutani (2008).

45. Edward M. Kennedy, *True Compass: A Memoir* (Twelve, 2009).

46. See, for instance, John Barry et al., "Obama's Vietnam," *Newsweek*, 9 February 2009, 28–35; Walter Rodgers, "A Reality Check for Obama in Afghanistan," *Christian Science Monitor*, 17 February 2009, 9; Burt Solomon, "Judging a War," *National Journal*, 13 June 2009, 14.

47. William Rosenau, "Counterinsurgency: Lessons from Iraq and Afghanistan," *Harvard International Review* (Spring 2009), 52–56; James Kitfield, "Can the National Security Bureaucracy Carry Out an Ambitious Afghanistan Strategy," *National Journal*, 2 May 2009, 13; James G. Blight, "Is Afghanistan Obama's Vietnam?" *Chronicle of Higher Education*, 27 February 2009, 11–13.

48. Kenneth T. Walsh, "Obama's History-Making Dinner," *U.S. News Digital Weekly*, 10 July 2009, 9.

49. Goldstein, *Lessons in Disaster;* see also Peter Spiegel and Jonathan Weisman, "Behind Afghan War Debate, A Battle of Two Books Rages," *WSJ*, 7 October 2009;

Jonathan Alter, "Bundy's Blunders," *Newsweek*, 12 October 2009; Jonathan Alter, *The Promise: President Obama, Year One* (Simon and Schuster, 2010), 370.

50. Gordon M. Goldstein, "From Defeat, Lessons in Victory," *NYT*, 17 October 2009. See also Gordon Lubold, "More Troops in Afghanistan? Naysayers Gain Clout with Obama," *Christian Science Monitor*, 11 October 2009; Evan Thomas and John Barry, "The Surprising Lessons of Vietnam," *Newsweek*, 16 November 2009; Jonathan Schell, "The Fifty-Year War," *Nation*, 20 November 2009, 18–22; Jackson Diehl, "It's Vietnam, Again," *WP*, 25 October 2009.

51. Frank Rich, "Obama at the Precipice," *NYT*, 26 September 2009.

52. Simon Tisdall, "Obama's Kennedy Moment on Afghanistan," *The Guardian*, 4 October 2009; Robert Dreyfuss, "The Generals' Revolt," *Rolling Stone*, 29 October 2009, 41–44; John F. Kerry, "Beware the Revisionists," *Newsweek*, 16 November 2009, 40–41.

53. Matt Bai, "Escalations: How Afghanistan Might Be Vietnam—and Obama the Real Kennedy," *NYT Magazine*, 1 November 2009; see also Robert Dallek, "U.S. History Is Littered with War Blunders," *USA Today*, 9 December 2009.

54. See Peter Baker, "Inside the Situation Room," *NYT*, 6 December 2009, 1; Mehdi Hasan, "Obama Is Wrong: This Is His Vietnam," *New Statesman*, 17 December 2009.

55. See Alter, *The Promise*, 369; Simon Serfaty, "The Limits of Audacity," *Washington Quarterly* 33, January 2010, 1:99–100; David Kaiser, "Absurd or Worse: Are We Fooling Ourselves in Afghanistan," *Commonweal*, 12 March 2010, 12–14; Paul Glastris, "36 and 44," *Washington Monthly* 42 (May / June 2010), 5 / 6:3; Bob Hebert, "No 'Graceful Exit,'" *NYT*, 17 August 2010.

56. "Obama's Remarks on Iraq and Afghanistan," *NYT*, 15 July 2008; Tom Bowman and Mara Liasson, "Obama's Afghan War Decision: A Team of Rivals," *NPR*, 3 December 2009; Paul D. Miller, "Withdrawal Deadlines in War: Vietnam, Iraq, and Afghanistan," report, Atlantic Council, 6 February 2020, 20; Rufus Phillips, "Déjà vu All Over Again: Are We Repeating Vietnam?" *World Affairs*, September / October 2010, 15–24.

57. Peter Baker and Rod Nordlund, "U.S. Envisions Plan to Ending Afghan Combat," *NYT*, 14 November 2010.

58. Stephen King, *11 / 22 / 63: A Novel* (Scribner, 2011); *Jacqueline Kennedy: Historic Conversations on Life with John F. Kennedy* (Hyperion, 2011). Among other works published during this period, see Chris Matthews, *Jack Kennedy: Elusive Hero* (Thorndike, 2011); Thurston Clarke, *JFK's Last Hundred Days: The Transformation of a Man and the Emergence of a Great President* (Penguin, 2013); Robert Dallek, *Camelot's Court: Inside the Kennedy White House* (HarperCollins, 2013).

59. See, for instance, Chris Matthews, "Five Things JFK Could Teach Obama," *Time*, 7 November 2011; Robert Dallek, "The Untold Story of the Bay of Pigs," *Newsweek*, 22 August 2011; Ross Douthat, "The Enduring Cult of Kennedy," *NYT*, 27 November 2011.

60. On Vietnam, see, for instance, Robert Dallek, "Power and the Presidency," *Smithsonian* (January 2011), 36–43; David Barrett, "The Truth about JFK and Vietnam," *Salon*, 22 November 2013; Rick Perlstein, "Kennedy Week: JFK's Uncertain Path in Vietnam," *The Nation*, 21 November 2013; James K. Galbraith, "JFK's Withdrawal Plan Is a Fact, Not Speculation," *The Nation*, 22 November 2013; Robert Kennedy Jr., "John F. Kennedy's Vison of Peace," *Rolling Stone*, 20 November 2013. Regarding the missile crisis, see the list of events at https://www.wilsoncenter.org/50th-anniversary-the-cuban-missile-crisis.

61. Larry Sabato, *The Kennedy Half-Century: The Presidency, Assassination, and Lasting Legacy of John F. Kennedy* (Bloomsbury, 2013).

62. Kennedy officials differ on how loosely defined it was. According to Thomas Hughes, McNamara's persistence in the matter suggests that he was relying on more than just offhand comments from the president. Interview with author, 1 November 2007. Roger Hilsman claims that McNamara was "peripheral" and that withdrawal was indeed "Kennedy's plan." Interview with author, 23 January 2009. Louis Sarris also believes withdrawal had been "a hot item at the White House" since early 1963. Interview with author 7 May 2009.

63. Noam Kochavi, "The Sino-Soviet Split," in *A Companion to John F. Kennedy*, ed. Marc J. Selverstone (Wiley-Blackwell, 2014), 375–377.

Acknowledgments

This book emerged out of my work at the University of Virginia's Miller Center of Public Affairs, where for over twenty years I have had the good fortune to be transcribing and analyzing the secret White House tapes of American presidents from Franklin D. Roosevelt through Richard M. Nixon. In 2005, as a member of the Miller Center's Presidential Recordings Program, I participated in a conference on Vietnam and the transition between the John F. Kennedy and Lyndon B. Johnson presidential administrations. I had hoped that the Kennedy tapes then publicly available would shed light on JFK's intentions in Vietnam, especially on planning to withdraw the United States from Vietnam. While those tapes indeed referenced that planning, they failed to fully resolve what JFK thought of it. In time, the release of additional tapes and documents would provide a firmer basis for drawing conclusions. I therefore set out to gain greater clarity on these matters through a research agenda that evolved from minor musings into a blog post, an article, and finally a full-blown manuscript. Chapter 3, in fact, builds on ideas first presented in "It's a Date: Kennedy and the Timetable for a Vietnam Troop Withdrawal," *Diplomatic History* 34, no. 3 (June 2010): 485–495.

Along the way, I have been aided by historians and archivists at several repositories, all of whom were generous with their time and expertise. I would like to thank the many specialists at the National Archives and Records Administration, especially Stephanie Coon and Stanley Fanares; Allen Fisher, Jenna de Graffenried, Brian McNerny, and John Wilson at the Lyndon B. Johnson Library; Maryrose Grossman, Sharon

Kelly, Abigail Malangone, and Stephen Plotkin at the John F. Kennedy Library; Andrew Birtle, David Keough, and Erik Villard at the U.S. Army Center of Military History; Sarah Barksdale and Erin Mahan at the Office of the Secretary of Defense Historical Office; Scott Gower at the National Defense University; Dan Linke at Princeton University's Seeley G. Mudd Manuscript Library; Brian Cuthrell at the University of South Carolina's South Caroliniana Library; Tal Nadan and Susan Waide at the New York Public Library; and Tracy Potter at the Massachusetts Historical Society. I also would like to thank the staffs at the Library of Congress and the National Archives (U.K.) for their assistance during multiple visits to both sites.

I also benefited from grants and fellowships that facilitated my research, and my thanks go to the John F. Kennedy Library Foundation for an Arthur M. Schlesinger Jr. Research Fellowship, the Lyndon B. Johnson Foundation for a Moody Research Grant, and the Massachusetts Historical Society for a short-term Research Fellowship.

I also had the chance to speak with several individuals who were close to the events I address as either participants or observers. All of them were patient with my questions and generous with their time. I therefore would like to thank George Allen, Francis Bator, George Carrington, James Furlich, Leslie Gelb, Paul Gorman, Roger Hilsman, Thomas Hughes, Anthony Lake, John Negroponte, Bittie Nolting, Rufus Phillips, and Louis Sarris for their willingness to be interviewed for this book.

Friends, colleagues, and fellow scholars also aided my efforts by answering the random question, supplying the stray document, refining a line of argument, and providing a forum for conversation. Thanks to Pierre Asselin, Jim Blight, Bob Brigham, Phil Catton, Greg Daddis, Jamie Galbraith, Patricia Gibbons, Gordon Goldstein, Ray Haberski, George Herring, Jim Hershberg, Andrew Johns, janet Lang, Mitch Lerner, Steve Maxner, Lien-Hang Nguyen, Chester Pach, John Prados, Andrew Preston, Robert Schulzinger, Jeremi Suri, Charlie Trueheart, Larry Tye, Jeff Woods, Randall Woods, and Julian Zelizer for their help. A special thanks goes out to Aurélie Basha i Novosejt, whose study of Robert McNamara has informed my own thinking.

Several scholars gave the manuscript a particularly close read, and their observations were enormously helpful as I polished it for publication. I am indebted to Jim Giglio, Mel Leffler, Fred Logevall, Ed Miller, and Brian VanDeMark for highlighting overstatements, understatements, faulty statements, and missing elements, and for pushing me to rethink the overall presentation. Their deep knowledge of the era was indispensable as I sought to balance the work's tone, texture, and narrative. I am particularly grateful for the help Mel provided and for his ongoing friendship and support.

Scholars at the University of Virginia, including those presently or previously associated with the Miller Center, also provided valuable guidance and direction. Brian Balogh, Doug Blackmon, Dale Copeland, Will Hitchcock, David Leblang, Sid Milkis, Jeffrey Olick, Russell Riley, and Brantly Womack pushed me to think harder about key matters during formal presentations, lunch talks, office chats, or hallway banter. I am particularly indebted to Barbara Perry for sharing her expertise in all things Kennedy, and to current and former colleagues in the Presidential Recordings Program, including David Coleman, Taylor Fain, Kent Germany, Nicole Hemmer, Ken Hughes, Keri Matthews, Guian McKee, Tim Naftali, and David Shreve; our collective work is very much at the center of this book. The staff at the Miller Center has also provided valuable administrative, communications, research, and technology support, and my thanks go out to Stefanie Georgakis Abbott, Sheila Blackford, Andrew Chancey, Sean Gallagher, Mike Greco, Meghan Murray, Alfred Reaves IV, Cristina Lopez-Gottardi Chao, Tom van de Voort, Natalie Russell, and Howard Witt for their help. The Center's leadership has also aided my efforts through a sabbatical leave and research assistance, as well as through their interest and encouragement. I greatly appreciate the generosity and support of directors Philip Zelikow, Gerald Baliles, and William Antholis.

I would like to extend a special note of thanks to Kathleen McDermott, my editor at Harvard University Press, who has been involved in this project since I first proposed it. I deeply appreciate her help in tightening its presentation and her patience in guiding it to completion. It also has been a pleasure to work with Kathi Drummy, Stephanie Vyce, and Kate Brick at the Press, and with Mary Ribesky at Westchester Publishing Services. I thank them all for helping to shepherd the project through its final phases.

It is family, though, that ultimately pulled me through and deserves my most heartfelt thanks. My sister Amy was always sympathetic, checking on my progress and sounding welcome notes of encouragement. Jake and Alison, who were mere tykes when the project began, have grown up listening to me talk about Vietnam—again and again—and were perpetually understanding of my absence during research trips and extended stretches of writing; I relish their wit and wisdom, and my own good fortune in being their dad. My wife, Bonnie, was, as always, at the center of it all. She continues to inspire me with her integrity, guide me with her insight, lighten me with her humor, and sustain me with her love, keeping us focused on what matters. I am grateful every day for the life we've made together.

Without the love and support of my parents, Harriet and Robert Selverstone, none of this would have been possible. I am so fortunate to have grown up in their care and to have learned from their example. They remain the most selfless and compassionate people I know—the wisest, too—committed to family and to making the world a better place. It is to them that I dedicate this book.

Index